Masculinities - Maskulinitäten

Therese Steffen (Hrsg.)

Masculinities - Maskulinitäten

Mythos - Realität -
Repräsentation - Rollendruck

Verlag J. B. Metzler
Stuttgart · Weimar

Mit grosszügiger Unterstützung
der Freiwilligen Akademischen Gesellschaft, Basel (Symposium)
und der Schweizerischen Akademie
der Geistes- und Sozialwissenschaften (Druckkostenzuschuss)

Anglistische Beiträge bleiben in diesem transdisziplinären Rahmen
unübersetzt.

Die Deutsche Bibliothek - CIP-Einheitsaufnahme

Masculinities - Maskulinitäten:
Mythos - Realität - Repräsentation - Rollendruck/Therese Steffen (Hrsg.)
- Stuttgart ; Weimar : Metzler, 2002
(M-&-P-Schriftenreihe für Wissenschaft und Forschung)
ISBN 3-476-45293-X

Gedruckt auf säure- und chlorfreiem, alterungsbeständigem Papier.

M & P Schriftenreihe für Wissenschaft und Forschung

© 2002 J.B.Metzlersche Verlagsbuchhandlung
und Carl Ernst Poeschel Verlag GmbH in Stuttgart
Einbandgestaltung: Willy Löffelhardt unter Verwendung
eines Cartoons von Magi Wechsler, Zürich
© Magi Wechsler, Zürich
Druck und Bindung: Franz Spiegel Buch GmbH, Ulm
Printed in Germany
April / 2002

INHALT

v

4. MASCULINITIES/MASKULINITÄTEN: LITERARISCHE REPRÄSENTATION

5. MASCULINITIES/MASKULINITÄTEN: ROLLENDRUCK

6. MASCULINITIES/MASKULINITÄTEN: FORSCHUNGSGEGENSTAND

1. EINLEITUNG

Therese Frey STEFFEN, Alexander MARZAHN

MASCULINITIES/MASKULINITÄTEN
Mythos — Realität — Repräsentation — Rollendruck

Der ältere Mann posiert in seinem protzigen Cabriolet, den linken Arm lässig über das offene Chassis gelegt, das Haar zurückgekämmt, als stünde das Fahrzeug nicht im Hinterhof, sondern befände sich in voller Fahrt. Die Bildunterschrift: "Küntschner war ein Liebhaber von schnellen Autos. Seinen BMW fuhr er grundsätzlich bei jedem Wetter ohne Verdeck." Der Fundort: Die 12. Auflage eines medizinischen Handbuchs, das zum 25. Todestag den Mitautor Küntschner mit dieser Fotografie zu würdigen wusste.

Denn Gerhard Küntschner ist nicht nur ein sportlicher Automobilist. Er ist auch ein erfolgreicher Chirurg, genauer gesagt ein Spezialist für Unfallverletzungen, hat also jeden Tag mit den Opfern genau jener Risikobereitschaft zu tun, die er selbst mit Stolz verkörpert. Funktion und Freizeitverhalten stehen in einem beinahe schon grotesken Widerspruch, der sich allenfalls darin auflösen lässt, dass zum Berufsethos des Chirurgen auch der entschlossene, mutige Eingriff gehört. Ansonsten ist Küntschner ein Mann, dessen Vorstellungen vom Leben im Wind der Überholspur nicht eben aussergewöhnlich sind. Und nichts könnte die maskuline Entschiedenheit besser symbolisieren als der schnelle Flitzer: "Bei jedem Wetter ohne Verdeck". In diesem Bild findet sich alles vereint, was zum Thema *Masculinities/Maskulinitäten* in den folgenden Beiträgen interessiert: *Mythos, Realität, Repräsentation, Rollendruck*.

Derart zur Schau gestellte Männlichkeit mag aufgeklärten Köpfen längst suspekt geworden sein; schon wähnten wir uns klug und sensibilisiert genug, um nicht gleich jedem maskulinen Muskelzucken zu erliegen. Doch die Realität stereotyper "hegemonialer" Maskulinität inmitten vielfältiger Maskulinitäten entbindet uns auch heute nicht von der Pflicht, scheinbar Selbstverständliches zu diskutieren.

Subtil kaschiert, strukturell verankert, selbstbewusst manifestiert, ironisch gebrochen, postmodern verspielt, psychoanalytisch verschoben, narzisstisch gespiegelt oder sprachlich verdeckt: Wo Männer sind, und das ist bekanntlich fast überall, sind auch Vorstellungen von Männlichkeit präsent, die sich mit einiger Beharrlichkeit nicht nur dem Fahrtwind, sondern auch dem aufklärerischen Mythos zunehmender Gleichstellung widersetzen.

Heute ist man davon abgerückt, Mann und Mensch als Synonyme, und Männlichkeit als in sich geschlossenes Phänomen zu verstehen. Trotz Vorbehalten, so wird deutlich, wird Männlichkeit zumindest implizit als sozialpsychologisch begründete "Deformation" verhandelt, deren symptomhaft aufscheinende "Bewältigungsprinzipien" von der anglo-amerikanischen Forschung längst aufgezeigt wurden: Orientierung nach aussen, Neigung zur Gewalt, Funktionalisierung und Kontrolle der Umwelt, Vereinsamung im Sinne eines übertriebenen Autonomie- und Differenzierungszwangs, Stummheit durch mangelnden reflexiven Selbstbezug, Körperferne, Überbetonung der Rationalität. Der Mann, ein ewig Mängelwesen?

So einfach ist es natürlich nicht. Nicht grundlos tritt Männlichkeit in der modernen Forschung nur noch im Plural auf: Makulinitäten, statt eindimensionaler Maskulinität. Männlichkeit ist demnach nichts Gottgegebenes, vielmehr ein komplexes Konstrukt der jeweiligen Gesellschaft. Die biologische Differenz allerdings lässt sich weder negieren noch wegdiskutieren. Der Mann ist zwar anders, aber nicht länger die absolute Norm. Er findet sich tatsächlich zunehmend diskutiert und kritisiert als Mängelwesen, als die einem typischen Geschlechtsrollendruck ausgesetzte und verunsicherte Krisenfigur Mann. (Judith Butler, 1993, *Körper von Gewicht*, 79). So liegt die männliche Lebenserwartung sechs Jahre hinter der weiblichen zurück. Erreicht jedoch der Mann ein hohes Alter, bleibt er eher von körperlichen Beschwerden verschont als die Frau. Neuen medizinischen und psychologischen Erkenntnissen, die durchaus einen Wandel in der Wahrnehmung und Darstellung von Weiblichkeit und Männlichkeit anzeigten, stehen aber Jahrhunderte alter Vorurteile entgegen, die sich unentwegt tradieren: zum Nachteil der Gesellschaft und beider Geschlechter.

Der Blick auf den Mythos Maskulinität hat sich, wie Judith Butler in *Gender Trouble* —und in diesem Band Elisabeth BRONFEN anhand von Kinofilmen wie *Boys Don't Cry* aufzeigen—, erweitert, vervielfacht, differenziert. Er nutzt die ganze Bandbreite methodischer Zugangsweisen moderner Geistes-, Kultur- und Sozialwissenschaften, geht bisweilen auch über diese hinaus. Martin LENGWLERS Beitrag über "Männer und Autos in den 1960er Jahren" ist zugleich ein Plädoyer, Technik und Naturwissenschaft als Vermittlung von Symbol- und Handlungsebene mit institutiuonellen und strukturellen Bedingungen zu verknüpfen. Das Risikoverhalten aus psychologischer Sicht untersucht Andreas THIELE in "Männlicher Geschlechtsrollenstress über die Lebensspanne". Ausgehend von der niedrigeren Lebenserwartung der Männer zeigt er den Einfluss des Rollenstresses auf, der besonders bei älteren Männern im Spannungsfeld von viriler Jugendlichkeit und tatsächlicher (körperlicher) Verfassung auftreten kann.

Ebenfalls einen programmatisch präzisen Blick in die Alltagswelt, genauer in das schillernde Reich der Popkultur, werfen Britta HERRMANN und Walter ERHART: Die spielerische und zitathafte Inszenierung bei Prince und Madonna ("XY ungelöst: Männlichkeit als Performance") habe eine ambivalente Wirkung: Rollenmuster würden durch die Verschiebung ins "Uneigentliche" zwischen Parodie, Mimikri und Travestie zwar aufgebrochen und subversiv hintergangen, gleichzeitig aber gegen aussen auch erneut zementiert: Ein Macho kann, muss aber nicht ironisch betrachtet werden. Ausserhalb der Showbühne sind Geschlechtermasken weit weniger frei wählbar.

Klaus THEWELEIT, im deutschsprachigen Raum so etwas wie ein Gender-Forscher 'avant la lettre,' hat in *Männerphantasien* schon 1977 die faschistische Gewaltbereitschaft auf Gender-Bedingungen zurückgeführt. Er betont, dass die Maskerade keine Erfindung der Performance-Künstler sei: Sein psychoanalytisch begründetes Konzept vom stets von Fragmentierung bedrohten Körper, auf den der Mann mit der Ausbildung eines "Körperpanzers" reagiere, wehre sich zugleich gegen den traditionellen Identitätsbegriff. Wie auch Dominique ZIMMERMANN ("Männliche Schwangerschaftsphantasien") stellt Theweleit den "Gebärneid" als wesentliche Ursache für ein männliches Kompensationsbedürfnis vor, das durch das Erleben der gesellschaftlichen Machtlosigkeit der Mutter weiter gestärkt würde. "Wo Frauen Lebendiges zur Welt bringen, setzen Männer Institutionen in die Welt; das Gesetz ist männlich." Im hierarchischen Handlungsrahmen würde die Gewalt geboren: Anhand von Schilderungen aus dem Vietnam- und Bosnienkrieg sowie Fotos der Wehrmachtausstellung zeigt Theweleit die symbolische Transformation von Gewalt und Zerstörung zum ritualisierten, männlichen Schöpfungsakt.

Geschlechtermythen in Literatur, Film und im Alltag; Risiko-verhalten, Gewalt und Schwangerschaftsphantasien: Das trans-disziplinäre internationale Symposium zum Thema "Maskulinitäten" am Englischen Seminar der Universität Basel (24.-25. Juli 2000) vereinigt Beiträge aus verschiedenen Fachdisziplinen: Aus dem Blickwinkel der Sprach- und Kulturwissenschaften, der Anglistik und Germanistik, sowie der Philosophie, Geschichte und Psychologie werden aktuelle Vorstellungen von " Männlichkeit" in Literatur, Film und Theorie in ihrer je eigenen medialen und genretypischen Repräsentation diskutiert.

Nach der grundsätzlichen Studie von Britta Herrmann und Walter Erhart zu "XY ungelöst: Männlichkeit als Performance" — sie widmet sich Videoclips,— umfasst das Kapitel "Visuelle Repräsentationen" ausschliesslich filmisch vermittelte Männlichkeitsbilder. In Alfred Hitchcocks *North by Northwest* (1959) verfolgt Barbara STRAUMANN ("The Masculine Space of *North by Northwest*, or: Mapping the Vicissitudes of Masculinity as Performance") unterschiedliche Stränge: eine in den 50er (Nachkriegs)-Jahren zunehmend verunsicherte Form von Männlichkeit, die jedoch ihre kompensatorische Anlehnung an die Technik sucht. Dabei gerät sie in die geistige Nähe einer postmodernen Risikogesellschaft. Die Studie kombiniert gekonnt kulturelle mit technologischen Ansätzen.

In "Feminized Men or Non-Hegemonic Masculinity" überprüft Klaus RIESER den Begriff Feminisierung auf seine ambivalent aufbrechende wie neopatriarchalische Wirkung: einerseits bezeichnet "feminization" eine anti-hegemoniale Form von Männlichkeit, anderseits geht mit dem Begriff eine Abwertung, d.h. "Verweiblichung" einher. Rieser erhellt, wie Medien und Film, beispielsweise Jackie Chan und Chris Tuckers *Rush Hour*, nicht nur gegenläufige Männlichkeitsentwürfe via Feminisierung unterlaufen und bannen, sondern dabei vor allem die Norm des weissen heterosexuellen Helden in Hollywood reetablieren. Stefan BRANDT widmet sich in "'Acting Heroes': Heroic Masculinity and Performative Action in Recent Hollywood Fiction" der Konstruktion heroischer Maskulinität in Quentin Tarantinos *Pulp Fiction* (1994) und Luc Bessons Film *The Fifth Element* (1997). Brandt bestätigt mit seiner These eines vielschichtig kontradiktorischen Männlichkeitsbildes Klaus Riesers

Wahrnehmung: die wahren Helden der 90er Jahre bewegen sich, in der Nachfolge eines RudolphValentino oder Gary Cooper, zwischen harter dominierender Männlichkeit (Sylvester Stallone, Bruce Willis, Jean Claude Van Damme) und einer seltsam koketten, sogar narzisstischen "Femininität" (Arnold Schwarzenegger, Wesley Snipes, Dustin Hoffman, John Travolta oder Patrick Swayzee). Der Hollywood-Held der 90er Jahre kämpft zugleich für, mit und gegen den Mythos "unangefochtene Maskulinität;" er bewegt sich zwischen den Polen eines triumphierenden und krisenanfälligen Körperideals. Er scheint über seinen Körper zu verfügen.

Veronika GROB ("Fear of Falling: White Middle Class Masculinity in Joel Schumacher's *Falling Down*") und Elisabeth SCHÄFER-WÜNSCHE ("Rolling into History: Time and Community in Spike Lee's *Get on the Bus*") befassen sich in ihren Studien mit klassen- und rassenspezifischen Maskulinitäten der US-amerikanischen Gesellschaft: dem weissen Mittelklassemann D-FENS und dem Afro-Amerikaner des "Million Man March." Obschon durch seinen Arbeitsverlust traumatisiert, leitet den weissen D-FENS im bezeichnenden Filmtitel *Falling Down* noch immer der amerikanische Aufstiegstraum. D-FENS scheitert aber gerade daran, dass er noch nie jenseits davon, ausgegrenzt, leben musste, eine Realität, die dem Afro-Amerikaner mehr als vertraut ist. Erprobt in den Kämpfen der Bürgerrechtsbewegung und mit einem ganz andern Bewusstsein ausgestattet, reisen die schwarzen, grossenteils ebenfalls arbeitslosen Männer in Spike Lees Film Richtung Washington. Auf den historischen Spuren Martin Luther Kings fordert der von Louis Farrakhan 1995 initiierte "Million Man March" eine politische und wirtschaftliche Gleichberechtigung für Schwarze ein, die weissen "Verlierern" garantiert schien. Allerdings bestimmt eine reine Männeragenda den Marsch; immerhin soll auf Gewaltanwendung gegen Frauen und Kinder verzichtet werden.

Elisabeth BRONFENS brillante Analyse zum Geschlechterwandel der Figur Brandon Teena in *Boys Don't Cry* beschliesst das Kapitel visuelle Repräsentationen.

Literarische Darstellungen von Männlichkeiten werden im folgenden an Texten der Antike, des Altenglischen, der Renaissance, der Klassik, Romantik und Postmoderne vorgestellt. Die Thematik einer von Weiblichkeit bedrohten, gar feminisierten und instabilen, im besten Fall spielerisch wandelbaren Maskulinität —kennzeichnend für die meisten der vorgehend behandelten visuellen Texte— bestimmt auch das postmoderne Werk von Philip Roth. Ingrid THALERS Studie, "Masculinity and Culture at War: Sexualized culture and culturalized sexuality in Philip Roth's *Portnoy's Complaint*," gilt der männlichen Identitätsuche in dem oft als pornographisch bezeichneten Adoleszenz-Roman. In *Portnoy's Complaint* interessiert einerseits, wie sich jüdische Männlichkeit in den U.S.A. einerseits mit und gegen Weiblichkeit, anderseits gegen gesellschaftliche Mainstream-Strukturen durchsetzt. Stets gilt es auch, über patriarchale homosoziale Muster das "Andere, Bedrohliche, Weibliche" von der Kernfamilie fernzuhalten. Zwar dominieren Roths männliche Figuren den Geschlechterkampf, vermögen sich aber nicht von der Frau zu lösen: ein frustrierendes Dilemma.

Eine ganz andere, vorab auf Männerfreundschaft und Männerliebe ausgerichtete Maskulinität findet sich in den nachfolgenden Studien: Sven LIMBECK ("Geschlechter in Beziehung: Die 'heterosexuelle' Konstruktion gleichgeschlechtlicher Beziehungen im Mittelalter") und Philipp SCHWEIGHAUSER ("Concepts of Masculinities in the *Wife's Lament* and its Critical Literature") deuten die Klage von Frauen neu im Spannungsfeld spiritueller Freundschaft und profaner Liebe. Ein männlich gedachtes Du kann darin durchaus weibliche Züge annehmen, eine bislang als männlich gedeutete Stimme darf durchaus einer Frau gehören.

Ladina BEZZOLA LAMBERT ("The Consumed Image: Male Friendship in Montaigne and Bacon") und Joachim PFEIFFER ("'... in Eurem Bunde der Dritte.' Männerfreundschaften in der Literatur des 18. Jahrhunderts") widmen sich den Ausprägungen des männlichen Freundschaftskultes in der englischen Renaissance und in der deutschen Klassik. Doch während Montaigne Feundschaft als etwas radikal Schenkendes versteht, ist sie für Bacon ein Zweckbündnis. Anhand von Literaturbeispielen des 18. Jahrhunderts analysiert Joachim Pfeiffer die Normen und Grenzen des männlichen Freundschafts-diskurses. Er betont, wie sehr sich diese affektiven, schwärmerischen, auch künstlerischen und gelegentlich frauenausschliessenden Beziehungen vom Ungeist der faschistischen Männerbünde unterscheiden. Julia RICHERS Untersuchung zu "John Keats's Odes and Masculinitiy" schlägt geschlechter-versöhnlichere Töne an, denn das lyrische Ich bei Keats verbindet sich in dessen früher Dichtung nicht nur mit einer Frau, sondern sscheint in einem utopischen Raum weiblicher Schönheit aufzugehen. In den grossen späteren Oden allerdings distanziert sich das männliche Subjekt klar von einer idealisierten Weiblichkeit.

2. MASCULINITIES/MASKULINITÄTEN: MYTHOS-REALITÄT

Klaus THEWELEIT
Männliche Geburtsweisen

Dominique ZIMMERMANN
Männliche Schwangerschaftphantasien

Britta HERRMANN / Walter ERHART
XY ungelöst: Männlichkeit als Performance

Klaus THEWELEIT

Männliche Geburtsweisen
Der männliche Körper als Institutionenkörper

Es ist nicht so, daß Männer in ihren Produktionen bloßer *Gebärneid* je getrieben hätte; wo Frauen Kinder auf die Welt bringen, "Lebendiges", *erzeugen* Männer, und das ihrer Selbstgewißheit nach schon seit ewigen Zeiten, große Teile dieser "Welt" überhaupt erst, auf die die von Frauen Geborenen ihren Fuß dann setzen können: Denkwelten, wissenschaftliche Welten, Kunstwelten, politische Welten, Gefängniswelten, militärische Welten, Fabrikationswelten, juristische Welten, jeweils gebündelt in Macht-Organen, die "Institutionen" heißen.

"Denken und Fühlen sind etwas für Individuen. Aber kann auch eine soziale Gruppe denken oder fühlen?" fragt Mary Douglas in ihrem Buch *Wie Institutionen denken* und beantwortet diese Frage, wie man dem Titel schon entnehmen kann, mit "ja".[1] Es gibt *Denkkollektive, Denkstile,* institutionell in Gesellschaften veran kert oder auch informell, kaum bewußt wahrgenommen. Der Denkstil eines jeden sozialen Gebildes, sagt Mary Douglas, "setzt den Rahmen für jede Erkenntnis, und er bestimmt, was als vernünftige Frage und was als wahre oder falsche Antwort gelten kann. Der Denkstil setzt den Kontext und die Grenzen für jedes Urteil über die objektive Wirklichkeit. Zu seinen wesentlichen Merkmalen gehört die Tatsache, daß er den Mitgliedern des betreffenden Denkkollektivs verborgen bleibt."'

Von einem solchen Verborgenbleiben ("Verborgenbleiben des Offenkundigsten") will ich reden am Beispiel einer der zentralsten institutionellen Produktionen unserer (und jeder anderen männer-dominierten) Gesellschaft, von der *institutionellen Herstellung des Männerkörpers* — einem *der* (offenen) Kerngeheimnisse der jüdisch-christlich-islamischen und anderer mannregierter Kulturen.

Seltsamerweise erwähnt Mary Douglas in ihrem Buch nicht, daß so gut wie alle Institutionen, die wir kennen, männliche sind: überwiegend männlich besetzt, nach männlichen Gesetzen aufgebaut, männlich geführt; das ist vielleicht ihr Tribut an *ihre* Institution: Auch die Universitäten, der Wissensbetrieb, sind, trotz aller weiblicher Beteiligten, *institutionell* männlich. Nicht einmal *Quoten* ändern etwas daran; erst gesetzliche Verankerung spezieller weiblicher Rechte für die einzelnen Institutionen würde etwas daran ändern.

ˇMännliche Geburtsweisen " aus: Klaus Theweleit, *Das Land, das Ausland heisst. Essays, Reden, Interviews zu Politik und Kunst,* München, 1995. Veränderte Fassung eines Vortrags, zuerst gehalten auf dem Symposium "Die Macht der Männerbünde einst und jetzt", Graz, 13. Juni 1992. Der abschliessende Paragraph, *Dein Feind—das Bild,* ist Teil des neuen Nachwortes zur Neuausgabe der *Männerphantasien,* München, Zürich: Piper, 2000, 491 ff.. Abdruck beider Texte mit freundlicher Genehmigung des Autors.

[1]Mary Douglas, *Wie Institutionen denken,* Frankfurt 1991, S. 31.

Wir haben in unserer Gesellschaft nur eine einzige partiell weibliche Institution: Das ist die Mutterschaft (die aber wiederum männlich dominierter Gesetzgebung unterliegt). Die Diskussion um das Abtreibungsrecht in den letzten Jahren und die dazugehörigen Gerichts-entscheidungen zeigen in aller Deutlichkeit, wie wenig männliche Institutionen gewillt sind, auch nur Schnipselchen ihrer Macht (freiwillig) herzugeben, und wie *bewußt* herrschaftsausübende Männer sich ihrer institutionellen Funktionen in jeder entscheidenden Frage sind.

Für das öffentliche Leben gilt, sagt Mary Douglas, generell: "Der einzelne überläßt eher die wichtigen Entscheidungen den Institutionen, während er sich selbst mit Kleinigkeiten und taktischen Fragen abgibt."[2] Institutionen schaffen derart Verbindlichkeit, nehmen das Denken ab, stecken Handlungsrahmen, sie strafen, sie vergessen, sie treffen Entscheidungen über Leben und Tod, sie verlangen, gegebenenfalls, die Tötung anderer.

Der "falsche Weg" der Geburt und seine Korrekturen

Und sie geben Leben: *Selbstzeugung* ist der Begriff, der hierher gehört. Nicht nur "selbst ist der Mann", wie es so unschön heißt, nicht nur businessmäßig *seifmade*, sondern *selbstgeboren*. Von einer Mutter geboren zu sein ist der falsche Weg, ruft es durch die abendländische Geschichte von Plato bis Goebbels. "Mann" will die Verbindung zu ihrem Leib loswerden, nicht einmal aus ihm gekommen will er sein; und entsprechend organisiert hat er seine Gesellschaften: Zwar wird "das Kind" von einer Mutter geboren (und auch bei ihr gelassen für eine gewisse Weile), aber dann schreitet das männlich-staatliche Prinzip ein zur Korrektur dieses biologischen Unsinns und nachbehandelt die Körper auf seine spezifische Weise. Faktisch werden die Kinder nach ein paar Jahren ihren Müttern "weggenommen" und anderen Institutionen überantwortet, die einen weiblichen Touch (wie Kindergärten und manchmal Schulen) zwar noch haben können, aber durchaus nicht müssen; und die ihn meistens überhaupt nicht haben, wie all die bekannten Körperumbildungsinstitute von der Fabrik zum Militär, vom Jugendbund zum Sportverein und anderen zivilen Männerkorporationen. Zwar werden auch Mädchen ihren Müttern prinzipiell weggenommen und einer körperlichen Nachgeburtsbehandlung durch die Gesellschaft, Kirchen, Verbände unterworfen. Aber das Resultat ist nicht ein in gleicher Weise "positiv verfügbarer" institutioneller Körper wie bei männlichen Kindern. Um den geht es hier.

Nehmen wir den Körper des Kindes, wie er aus der Verbindung mit der Mutter kommt: Auch dieser Körper ist schon in sich gespalten, mehrpolig gespannt. Er ist mütterlich (möglicherweise auch väterlich) belebt in Hautkontakten, Zuwendungen, Fütterungen, im Spiel, er ist aber auch unbelebt, "totgestellt" durch Strafen, Grobheit,

---

[2] Ebenda, S. 179.

angsterregende Eingriffe verschiedenster Art, durch Hungerphasen, Verlassenheiten etc.: Diese Spaltung in einen belebten und in einen unbelebten, in einen fühlenden und in einen *anästhesierten* Teil ist jedem Körper in verschiedenen Graden und Abstufungen zu eigen. Der *institutionelle* Zugriff auf den Körper setzt meistens an an dessen anästhesierten Teilen; dort ist nicht nur der geringste Widerstand zu erwarten; dort ist sogar eine gewisse Bündniskraft am Werke: Unbelebte Teile oder Gebiete des Körpers, in denen angsterregende Eingriffe gespeichert sind, lassen sich gern transformieren in muskuläre Reaktionsgebilde ohne Gefühle; eine strenge Umpolung aufs muskulärmotorische kann als Errettung erlebt werden vor unintegrierbaren, angstmachenden Gefühlen, die aus eigener dunkler Geschichte stammen. Ohne Gewalt und Gewaltinstitutionen geht dieser Umbau nicht; der umzugebärende Körper muß sich in einer genau festgelegten *Abhängigkeit* befinden, in einer klar definierten Materialposition. Auch wo das Militär aus seiner Funktion des Haupt-Nachgebärers entlassen ist, spielen direkte oder indirekte körperlich-muskuläre Eingriffe eine große Rolle bei der Herstellung des Männerkörpers als "handelndem Gesellschaftswesen"; hochentwickelte technologische Gesellschaften wie unsere kommen aber inzwischen mit einem Minimum direkter muskulärer Eingriffe aus.

Ich will an einigen prägnanten Beispielen zunächst die Selbstbenennung männlicher Gewalt-Tätigkeiten als *Geburten* beschreiben, die den entsprechend kundigen Institutionenmännern keineswegs verborgen ist, im Gegenteil, die sie immer und immer wieder herausstellen, wenn man ihnen bei der Schilderung ihrer menschen wie weltenzeugenden Tätigkeiten zuhört. Geburten jeweils durch Gewalt.

So hat General Westmoreland im Vietnamkrieg die Bombardierung Hanois und Nordvietnams mit den Sätzen verteidigt, all diese fernöstlichen *Orientalen* seien noch, menschheitsgeschichtlich betrachtet, im Zustande von *toddlers* — so heißen in Amerika die Kleinkinder, die gerade aus dem Krabbelalter heraus sind, und, hin- und herschwankend, das Laufen lernen. Die Bombardements sah Westmoreland als die Art Hilfe an, die *er* zu geben in der Lage war, die im weithistorischen Kleinkindstadium herum-stolpernden Vietnamesen "ins Erwachsenenalter zu bomben". (Westmoreland vor der Kamera in Peter Davis Vietnam-Film *Hearts and Minds).* Dies Modell des "Erwachsenmachens" der "dritten" wie "vierten" Welten scheinen eine ganze Menge Welterzeugungsmänner in ihren Köpfen herumzutragen (sieht man sich die aktuellen Wege der Waffenlieferungs-ströme daraufhin an).

Etwas Ähnliches schwebte offenkundig auch den Vätern der ersten Atombombe vor, und zwar mit dem ganzen Erdball. Die erste erfolgreich gezündete Atombombe wurde von ihnen begrüßt als eine neue, entwicklungs-fähige Form von *Leben,* und gefeiert, in Ermangelung wirklich angemessener Namensgebung, als neugeborener *Junge.* (Edward Teller als die Mutter, die den Jungen ausgetragen hatte.)

In den Protokollen von den ersten erfolgreichen Tests finden sich die Lebensäußerungen der Bombe festgehalten als *Schreie des Neugeborenen.* Winston Churchill bekommt die Nachricht vom erfolgreichen Test während der Potsdamer Konferenz in einem verschlüsselten Telegramm überreicht, das lautet: " *Babies satisfactorily born."* "Geburt der Zwillinge verlief ohne Komplikationen.")

4

Die Amerikanerin Carol Cohn, die ein paar Jahre lang mit den Defense Intellectuals des Weißen Hauses zusammengearbeitet hat, resümierte erstaunt: "Die gesamte Geschichte des Bombenprojekts ist durchsetzt mit Bildern, die die grenzenlose technologische Kraft der Männer, die Welt zu zerstören, mit der Kraft zu gebären verwechselt oder gleichsetzt."[3] *Gleichsetzt! Zufall? Bildersprache?*

William L. Laurence, Augenzeuge des "Trinity-Tests" (= erste Atombombe) notiert: "Der große Knall kam ungefähr hundert Sekunden nach dem großen Blitz — der erste Schrei einer neugeborenen Welt. (...) Wir alle sprangen hoch und klatschten in die Hände — erdgebundene Männer als Symbole einer neugeborenen Kraft. "

Im Angesicht des überwältigenden milchig, wolkig, dynamischen Gebrodels des Bombenpilzes hat Laurence die *Wahrnehmung*, die Bombe verwandle sich in ein lebendes Wesen. Es ist *keine* Metaphorik, sondern der ziemlich bewußte Versuch einer Parallelisierung der Explosion mit dem menschlich-mütterlichen Geburtsprozeß.

Was passiert bei der alten, der traditionellen, Geburt: Das Kind wird (nach langer Vorarbeit) aus der Mutter herausgepreßt ... ein Blitz von Licht zuckt in die Augen ... die Explosivgeräusche des Geburtszimmers detonieren in Babys Ohr ... der Klatsch auf den Hintern durch den Arzt, der das Baby an den Beinen hält, liefert den *Big Bang* ... "der große Knall kam ungefähr hundert Sekunden nach dem großen Blitz" ... und die "neugeborene Welt" beginnt zu schreien ... draußen vor der Tür stehen die Angehörigen, der Vater etc. ... sie hören den Schrei, springen hoch und klatschen in die Hände ... die Tür geht auf und die Schwester flüstert: *es ist ein Junge* ... ... und die Welt ist erlöst.

Die Parallelisierung ist in der Tat umwerfend. Aber was da neu *lebt*, ist die Kraft, die Erde zu *töten*. And it was done by *birth*. Die Wissenschaftsmänner des "Manhattan Project" bauten also nicht die Atombombe, nein, sie schufen eine neue Welt, der "Natur" ein und für alle Mal *überlegen*. Deren erster Existenz- und Siegbeweis war dann der Niedergang des "Fat Boy" (Name der Bombe —kräftig gewachsen der Junge!) auf Hiroshima. Wir haben seitdem tatsächlich eine *neue Erde* (diejenige, die der Regierungs- oder Militärmann kaputtmachen kann).

Die Rede von der "Geburt einer Nation", ein Topos des 19. und 20. Jahrhunderts, war uns durch unsere Nachkriegsgeschichte schon ein bißchen fremd geworden, fast vergessen, bis sie uns in Erinnerung gerufen wurde durch die Ereignisse des November 1989. Antje Vollmer notierte dazu, nach ihren Mauervisitationen im März 1990: "Männer, wohin ich seh, ein unübersehbares Heer dunkelblauer Anzüge, Männer in permanenter Männerpaarbildung. (...) "Macht das Tor auf!" An allen Mauer- und Stacheldraht-Durchbrüchen waren es Herren, die sich als erste Wort und Hand nehmen. Das Recht der ersten Nacht war ihrs — und dann durfte auch das einfache Volk: fließen, strömen (...). Das ist die Blütezeit der eingeschlechtlichen Schöpferkraft. Der Nationalismus,

---

[3] Carol Cohn, "Sex and Death in the Rational World of Defense Intellectuals. " In: *Signs. Journal of Women in Culture and Society*, 12. 4 (1987), S. 687-718.

der Staat und die Partei sind die männlichen Produktionen künstlicher Wirklichkeiten schlechthin."[4]

Man mußte nicht die nachfolgenden Einschränkungen von Frauenrechten und die verstärkte Offensive gegen den Feminismus abwarten, um zu *wissen*, daß sie kommen würden. "Nation" ist immer eine Mann-Mann-Geburt, und "die Frau" ist in ihr ausgeschaltet oder unten. "Geburt der Nationen". Warum nicht gleich "Geburt der Menschheit"? In einem Beitrag zu James Camerons Film *Terminator II* in der *Zeit* vom 30. April 1993 macht uns Peter Sloterdijk mit dem "ältesten Aktionsmuster der Menschheit" bekannt. Das ist für ihn der historische Moment, in dem ein flüchtendes (Affen-) Wesen in seinem Lauf einhält, sich umdreht, sich zum Gegenangreifer transformiert und einen Gegenstand, Ast oder Stein, auf seinen Verfolger wirft. Sloterdijk: "Man könnte geradezu von der Geburt des Menschen aus dem Geist des Gegenangriffs sprechen. Am Anfang war die Gegengewalt — das heißt die Gewaltflucht, die durch Würfe Grenzen in den Raum zieht."

Wirklich? Er hätte doch auch sagen können, der Kreis der Werfer schützt das Paar, das, in seiner Mitte, abgeschirmt, für den Nachwuchs sorgt ... und daraus dann die Menschwerdung, die *Hominisation*, mit der sie es dauernd haben, die Philosophen: Wo *entsprang* "der Mensch", eine ihrer Haupt- und Lieblingsfragen, mit der sie nie zu Ende kommen, weil sie die zutreffende Antwort partout nicht geben wollen: aus einer Mutter. Vor jedem werfenden Werfer muß es eine Mutter geben, der daran liegt, ihr Kind lebendig zu machen und zu schützen, sonst kommt es erst gar nicht zum Wurf, weder zum Steinwurf noch zum philosophischen.

Selbst ein feministisch nicht ungewitzter Mensch wie Sloterdijk liefert uns ein Modell von der "Geburt des Menschen", ein Weltgeburtsmodell, das ganz ohne Frauen auskommt. Er begnügt sich damit, die Philosophen von Hegel bis Heidegger zu übermuttern, die "den Menschen" als Sich-selbst-Entwerfenden sehen (was auch Brecht gern so tat), wogegen Sloterdijk, "dekonstruktionistisch" reduziert: nein, er ist ein Werfer, nicht ein Geworfener; der Werfer, dessen Stein ins Ziel trifft. Aus diesem Wurf leitet sich her, sagt P. S., "der Wachheitsüberschuß, der dem Aufmerksamkeitstier Homo sapiens die Augen freigibt für luxurierende Blicke in das stille Feld"; damit soll die Arbeit des Philosophen beschrieben sein, seine eigene: luxurierende Blicke ... Starten von Denkstreifzügen ins stille Feld ... um sich dann wiederzufinden als potentieller Cheftheoretiker der Bonner Hardthöhe ...

Es ist nicht ganz leicht zu sehen, was da vor sich geht: Ich habe lange gebraucht zu begreifen, daß dieser Ausschluß der Frauen aus der Weltgeburtsarbeit auch in der Philosophie tatsächlich eine ihrer entscheidenden Grundvoraussetzungen ist, ihr Basisopfer sozusagen ... und noch länger gebraucht, daß Philosophen oder Menschen, die sich für solche halten, in der Regel nicht in der Lage sind, diesen Grundmangel überhaupt als Mangel zu erkennen ... sie denken tatsächlich, sie *denken* (wo sie doch bloß die Frauen weglassen) ... sie machen das nicht mit Absicht ... es ist ein echter

---

[4] Antje Vollmer, "Lange nichts mehr von Bärbel Bohley gehört. " In: *Constructiv*, Berlin, März 1990.

blinder Fleck. Spricht man einen der Denk- oder Wissenschaftsherren auf diesen Mangel an, stellt man fest: Sie verstehen einen meist überhaupt nicht, sie wissen gar nicht, was gemeint ist, und wenn sie es doch zu verstehen meinen, halten sie es für einen Witz ... ja gut, die Frauen, die Mütter ... richtig ... aber keine philosophische Kategorie ... keine Kategorie
der Erkenntnis ... die gehören doch nicht hierher.

Und bleibt man etwa dabei, daß sie doch hierher gehören und zwar *gerade* hierher, wird man in ihren Augen zu einem denkunfähigen Wesen ... man kann geradezu sehen, wie man sich in ihrem Gesichtsausdruck, einer institutionellen Maske, zu einem Flachkopf verwandelt ... zu einer Art Frau, die keine Ahnung hat von den Geheimnissen des männlichen/ philosophischen Diskurses ... sie denken tatsächlich, da ist ein *Geheimnis*, hinter das sie kommen müssen mit ihren Gedanken. Die meisten philosophischen (wie auch religiösen) Gedanken dieser Art bestehen aber ganz schlicht aus der Tatsache, die Mutter gestrichen zu haben aus der Geburt. Sie einzubeziehen ergäbe in der Tat völlig andere Probleme, solche, die nur *zwischen* Männern und Frauen lösbar wären, nicht denkerisch. Das aber will der Institutskopf nicht; er will sein mit andern Männern geteiltes
institutionelles Denkgebäude ... er ist ein großer Architekt, Weltenbauer ... Frauen können *Teil* seines institutionellen Apparates werden (aber keine Blutspuren in den Papieren ... jedenfalls nicht *"dies"* Blut, bitte).

Die zwei Seiten der Folter

Den Kern männlich-selbstgemachter Geburtsarbeit begreift man allerdings erst, wenn man das männliche Agieren in direkten Gewaltsituationen untersucht, zugespitzt in der Folter. Der Vorgang des Sich-Gebärens bedarf einer physischen Energie, über die der Mannkörper in seiner institutionellen Einbindung von sich aus nicht verfügt. Er muß sie woanders hernehmen; er nimmt sie aus anderen Körpern. Im Kern besteht seine Geburt in der Tötung anderer.

In Tim O'Briens Vietnam-Roman *The Things They Carried* (Die Dinge, die sie trugen) gibt es dazu eine Szene, die den Vorgang (in "teuflischer Unschuld") modellhaft festhält. Held der Szene ist ein Soldat namens Rat Kiley, der mit seinem Freund Curt Lemon in einer Kampfpause mit Handgranaten herumgespielt hat, wie die Jungs zu tun pflegen, und diesmal ging es schief, eine Granate ging los und nahm Curt Lemon mit rauf in das Geäst eines Baums, aus dem sie ihn dann herunterkratzen mußten, um die Reste beerdigen zu können, und nun hat Rat Kiley keinen guten Freund mehr, und er nimmt, als die Truppe weitermarschiert, ein kleines Wasserbüffelbaby mit, das am Wegrand steht, und führt es mit sich an einem Seil, bis das Platoon am Abend Rast macht und seine Essensration zu sich nimmt. Tim O'Brien:

"Nach dem Essen ging Rat Kiley rüber und streichelte das Büffelbaby am Kopf. Er öffnete eine Dose mit der C-Ration, Schweinefleisch mit Bohnen, aber das Büffelbaby war nicht interessiert. Rat zuckte die Achseln. Er ging einen Schritt zurück und schoß es ins rechte Vorderknie. Das Tier gab keinen Ton von sich. Es brach hart nieder, stand dann wieder auf, und Rat zielte sehr sorgfältig, bevor er ihm ein Ohr abschoß. Er schoß ihm in die Hinterbacken und in den kleinen Buckel auf seinem Rücken. Er schoß es zweimal in die Flanken; es war nicht umzubringen; aber weh tun konnte man ihm. Rat drückte die Mündung seiner Rifle gegen das Maul und schoß das Maul weg. Niemand sagte groß was. Das ganze Platoon stand da und schaute zu, fühlte alle Sorten Dinge, aber viel Mitleid für das Wasserbüffelbaby war nicht dabei. Gurt Lemon war tot. Rat Kiley hatte seinen besten Freund auf der Welt verloren. Später in der Woche würde er einen langen persönlichen Brief an die Schwester des Typs schreiben, die nicht antworten würde, aber im Moment war es eine Frage des Schmerzes. Er schoß ihm den Schwanz weg. Er schoß ihm Stücke Fleisch aus den Rippen. Überall um uns herum war der Geruch von Rauch und Moder und von tiefem Grün, und der Abend war feucht und nicht sehr heiß. Rat ging zur Automatic über. Er schoß beiläufig, beinah zufällig, schnelle kleine Garben in den Bauch und die Hinterkeulen. Dann lud er nach, kniete nieder und schoß es durchs linke Vorderknie. Wieder brach das Tier hart zusammen und versuchte wieder aufzustehn, aber es schaffte es nicht mehr diesmal. Es zitterte und brach seitwärts nieder. Rat schoß ihm in die Nase. Er beugte sich vor und flüsterte ihm etwas zu, wie einem Kuscheltier, dann schoß er es durch die Kehle. Die ganze Zeit war das Büffelbaby" *(das Baby, das Baby, das Baby)* "still, oder beinahe still, nur ein leichter blubbernder Ton kam von da, wo die Nase gewesen war. Es lag sehr still. Nichts bewegte sich, außer den Augen, Augen von enormer Größe, die Pupillen glänzend schwarz aber nun stumpf. Rat Kiley weinte. Er versuchte, etwas zu sagen, aber dann wiegte er nur sein Gewehr im Arm und verließ, allein, den Platz."[5]

Wahrscheinlich ist es nicht nötig, etwas über den versierten Haß auf die Intimität zwischen Mutter und Baby in dieser Erzählung zu sagen. O'Brien ist zu clever, seine Truppe *offen* ein Kind oder eine Frau töten zu lassen (wie es in entsprechender Nazi-Literatur der Fall wäre). Er begnügt sich damit, es einer "Schwester" zu geben, die nicht "zurückschreibt", und einem Tierbaby, einem Kuscheltier ("pet", sagt der amerikanische Text) ... und läßt den Killer sein Gewehr umarmen und es "in seine Wiege" legen ("he cradled his rifle"). Das ist klar und häßlich genug in seiner perfekten Distorsion (zusätzlich im Büffel die Tötung *des* indianischen Totemtiers ... auch dieser Krieg wird nochmal mitgewonnen. No end of the re-wins and the replays).

Was noch fehlt, ist der Anschluß an den Komplex "Geburt". Die Zuschauer des Zeugungsdramas haben bisher dagestanden und zugesehen... (zugesehen im Sonnenuntergang)...: Eine ganze Weile sprach niemand. Wir waren Zeuge von etwas Essentiellem geworden, einer Sache, ganz brandneu und profund, ein Stück einer Welt, so neu und aufregend, daß es noch keinen Namen gab dafür.

Jemand kickte in den Körper des Büffelbabys.

---

[5] Tim O'Brien, *The Things They Carried. A Work of Fiction*, Boston 1990.

Es lebte noch, wenn auch kaum noch, grad noch in den Augen.
"Erstaunlich", sagte Dave Jensen. "Mein ganzes Leben hab ich sowas noch nicht gesehen, noch nie."
"Echt niemals?"
"Noch nie. Überhaupt nicht."
(...)
"Amazing," murmelte Dave Jensen unaufhörlich.
"Ein völlig neuer Blickwinkel. Niemals gesehen sowas vorher."
Mitchell Sanders holte sein Yo Yo Spiel raus. "Ja, — das ist Vietnam", sagte er.
"Garten des Bösen. hier drüben, Mann, ist jede Sünde völlig frisch und wie beim ersten Mal." (Im Original: "Well, that's Nam", he said. "Garden of Evil. Over here, man, every sin's real fresh and original.")

Sie sind Männer *vor dem Sündenfall:* Dies ist eine moderne Version der Schöpfungsgeschichte, sollen wir verstehen ... die "wirklich wahre" diesmal...im Männerbuch wird der "Garden of Evil" zum "Garden of Eden".

Diese Schöpfungsgeschichte sagt: das "Coming Out" und das "Getting Clear" geschieht durch Bedeinung des Gewehrabzugs in einer absoluten Übertretungssituation. Die *neugeborene* Welt erscheint in einem See von Blut ... in röchelndem Atem, in dem etwas Schönes stirbt.

Atem und Blut der gebärenden Mütter sind dabei ersetzt vom Röcheln eines verendenden *Babys* und vom Blut, das jemand aus einem lebenden Körper schießt, um selbst zu werden, was er und seine Mitmänner nicht sind bis dahin: lebendige Wesen.

So die Wieder-und-Wieder-Neugeburt des erfahrungslosen jungen "soldatischen Manns" aus einer rituellen Folterung. So etwas "schweißt zusammen," natürlich, zu einem neuen, institutionellen Leib, aus dem der Korpus solcher "wahrer Kriegsromane" springen kann.

Rigoberta Menchú, Quiché-Indianerin aus Guatemala, hat in ihrem Bericht von der Folter in Guatemala (aufgeschrieben von Elisabeth Burgos),[6] den *Schaucharakter* der Folter genau beschrieben, die bewußte öffentliche Inszenierung der Folter, die deutlich macht, daß die Arbeit des Folterers immer zwei Seiten hat: Sie vernichtet die Gefolterten und belebt die Folterer.

Schauplatz ist eine Indianersiedlung in Guatemala Anfang der achtziger Jahre. Das Militär ist da. Das ganze Dorf ist zum Antreten befohlen, damit es eine Ansprache "des Offiziers" entgegennehme. Der Hauptmann hat vor, eine Lehrstunde abzuhalten über gefangene "Guerilleros" und eine Demonstration, was mit denen geschieht, die sich mit der Guerilla einlassen. Rigoberta Menchú:

"Der Offizier eröffnete die Versammlung und sagte, sie hätten eine Gruppe von Guerilleros in ihre Gewalt gebracht und sie erwarte jetzt eine kleine Strafe. "Es ist nur eine kleine Strafe", sagte er "denn es gibt noch größere Strafen, und ihr werdet jetzt sehen, welche Strafe sie bekommen." (...) Minuten später trafen drei Armeelastwagen

---

[6] Elisabeth Burgos, *Rigoberta Menchú. Leben in Guatemala*, Göttingen 1989.

ein. Einer vorneweg, auf dem in der Mitte waren die Gefolterten, und einer fuhr hinterdrein. Sie holten einen nach dem anderen herunter, alle trugen Armeeuniformen. Wir sahen die entstellten Gesichter, die nicht zu erkennen waren. Meine Mutter näherte sich dem Lastwagen, um zu sehen, ob sie ihren Sohn erkennen könne. Jeder der Mißhandelten sah anders aus, keiner hatte dieselben Mißhandlungen. Und meine Mutter erkannte meinen kleinen Bruder, ihren Sohn, zwischen all den anderen. (...)

Allen Gefolterten gemeinsam war, daß sie keine Fingernägel mehr hatten und daß man ihnen Teile der Fußsohlen abgeschnitten hatte. Sie waren barfuß. Der Offizier fing wieder mit seiner Rede an und sagte, daß wir uns mit dem zufrieden geben müßten, was wir hätten, uns damit begnügen müßten, unsere Tortillas mit Chili zu essen, und uns nicht von kommunistischen Ideen fortreißen lassen dürften. (...)

In der Mitte seiner Ansprache — eineinhalb oder zwei Stunden waren wohl vergangen — befahl der Hauptmann seinen Soldaten, den Gefolterten die Kleider auszuziehen, damit alle die Wunden sehen konnten, denn wenn wir uns mit dem Kommunismus, mit dem Terrorismus einließen, würde uns das gleiche erwarten. Sie konnten ihnen die Kleider nicht ausziehen. Da kamen die Soldaten und schnitten sie ihnen mit Scheren von den Füßen bis zu den Schultern auf und rissen ihnen die Sachen von den mißhandelten Leibern. Jeder hatte andere Folterspuren.

Der Hauptmann erklärte eingehend die verschiedenen Folterungen: "Dies sind Nadelstiche", sagte er. "Dies Verbrennungen von elektrischen Drähten." Und so erklärte er jede Wunde der Mißhandelten. Es gab drei, die sahen aus wie aufgeblasen, aber man sah keine Wunden. Aber sie waren ganz dick aufgeblasen. Und der Hauptmann sagte: "Wir stecken ihnen was in den Körper, und das tut weh. Worauf es ankommt, ist, daß sie wissen, daß das weh tut und daß das Volk sich vorstellen kann, wie es sein muß, mit so einem Körper herumzulaufen." "

Die Mischung aus Vorlesung, Theater und Verbrechen für die "auf dem Schulhof" angetretenen Dorfbewohner verfehlt ihre "Wirkung" nicht:

"Ich konnte das nicht mehr mitansehen. Wenn man dachte, was diese Körper, die doch Menschen waren, für Schmerzen ertragen hatten, bis sie so unkenntlich gemacht worden waren. Das ganze Volk weinte. Sogar die Kinder weinten und klammerten sich an ihre Mütter." Nach mehr als drei Stunden (drei Stunden im Zustand *absoluter Machtausübung*) schreitet "der Offizier", der Regisseur dieses gnadenlosen Erziehungstheaters, zum Anlauf auf die Klimax. "Dann befahl der Offizier, die nackten, geschwollenen Mißhandelten an eine Stelle zu bringen, von der aus das ganze Volk sie sehen konnte. Sie wurden hingeschleift, weil sie nicht mehr gehen konnten. Dann rief er die schlimmsten aller Verbrecher, die Kaibiles. Sie tragen eine andere Uniform als die normalen Soldaten. Sie sind besonders ausgebildet und werden zur Guerilla-Bekämpfung eingesetzt. Er rief also die Kaibiles, und sie fingen an, die Gefolterten mit Benzin zu übergießen. (...) Dann zündeten sie jeden einzelnen an. Viele riefen um Hilfe. Als sie so da standen, schienen sie mehr tot als lebendig, aber als die Körper Feuer fingen, riefen sie um Hilfe. Einige schrien, andere sprangen und hatten keine Stimmen mehr. Das Feuer nahm ihnen sofort den Atem. Das Volk kochte vor Zorn. Es war unglaublich; einige hatten zwar ihre Macheten dabei, die meisten aber waren völlig unbewaffnet, und doch wollten alle losschlagen, als sie sahen, daß die Soldaten Feuer legten. Sie wollten ihr Leben einsetzen, trotz all der Waffen. Die Armee merkte, daß die Leute wütend waren, und der Hauptmann gab Befehl zum Rückzug. Die Soldaten zogen sich mit den Waffen in der Hand zurück und brüllten Parolen wie auf einer Fiesta. Ihnen machte es Spaß. Sie lachten und riefen: "Viva la Patria! Viva Guatemala! Es lebe der Präsident! Es lebe die Armee! Es lebe Lucas!"

In ihrem Buch *Entmenschlicht. Versuch über die Folter*[7] schreibt Kate Millett: "Die vielen Formen des Staatsterrorismus sind heute ein globales Phänomen, dem sich diese und auch die nächste Generation stellen muß, um es möglicherweise, mit Stärke und Entschlossenheit, zu demontieren und aus der Welt zu schaffen." So weit sind wir lange nicht: "Die Folter wird heute in einem Maße praktiziert, das die Welt bisher noch nie gekannt hat und das selbst die Jahrhunderte der Inquisition in den Schatten stellt", fährt sie fort; und das, obwohl die Folter in allen Verfassungen aller Länder offiziell verboten ist. Ein merkwürdiger Widerspruch. Was hat es auf sich mit diesem "Verbot"? Ich glaube, der Bericht von Rigoberta Menchü gibt eine Antwort auf diese Frage: Warum *schießen* die Soldaten nicht in die aufgebrachte Menge, die sich anschickt, sie anzugreifen? Es wäre ein leichtes ... sie tun es auch sonst ohne Umstände. Aber nicht in diesem *Moment* ... es würde ihn *zerstören* ... sie genießen das Produkt ihres Mordtheaters: sich selbst als Teil einer übergeordneten Macht, die dies alles *erlaubt* sie handeln aus dem Zentrum des Gesetzes heraus. Der Kern der Aktion ist die *erlaubte Übertretung ins Verbrecherische* ... eine *Befreiung* ... und diese feiern sie mit ihrem Gelächter ... es ist *Fiesta* ...

"Es lebe dies! .. ." ... "lang lebe jener! .. ." schreien sie, während sie dabei sind zu schlachten, während vor ihren Augen durch ihre Schuld gestorben wird. Es ist ihr *Belebungsmoment,* ihr Fest, ihr Sieg, ihre Geburt als körperliche Teile dieser staatlich-männlichen Institution Armee, die sie "ganz und heil" werden läßt. Unser Impuls, das mit Begriffen wie "Satanismus" oder "Sadismus" zu belegen, ist so richtig (an der Oberfläche unserer Empörung) wie falsch zur Bezeichnung dessen, was tatsächlich geschieht: Dies schreckliche "Lachen" ist mir aufgefallen in so vielen Berichten von Folterungen. Berichten, die die Folterer selbst gegeben haben oder Berichten von Augenzeugen von Folterungen. Nur in den Berichten von Überlebenden der Folter fehlt es. Sie haben diesen Moment des "Freudenausbruchs" des Folterers nicht erlebt; sie waren schon bewußtlos, von Schmerz überwältigt, ausgelöscht in der Wahrnehmung, wenn das "erlösende Lachen" eintrat bei ihrem Quäler, und die meisten, die davon hätten berichten können, sind tot. Der Gequälte kann den psychophysischen Vorgang beim Folterer nicht bis zu "seinem Ende" sehen. Auf ganz andere Weise erlebt aber auch der Folterer die Qual und das Sterben der Opfer nicht.

---

[7] Kate Millett, *Entmenschlicht. Versuch über die Folter*, Hamburg 1993.

Er ist mit seinem hocherregten Körper und mit seiner Wahrnehmung ganz woanders, er ist *absorbiert* von seinem eigenen Wachstum, vom Durchbruch in den neuen riesigen Körper, den er hier erhält: Körper einer männlichen Gewaltinstitution, die all dies absegnet, gutheißt, die ihn erhebt für das, was er tut, ihn bezahlt, belohnt. Kate Millett betont in ihrem Buch immer wieder, daß die Folter nicht im "Illegalen" passiert, sondern streng staatlich geregelt ist. Die Folter kommt aus dem Zentrum der offiziellen staatlichen Macht, bezeichnet aber einen Umschlagspunkt dieser Macht, den Umschlag ins Kriminelle: "Das Vorbild ist nicht die Ethik des Kriegers oder des Offiziers, sondern die Mafia, die Kriminalität. Aber es ist eine hochtechnisierte und hochentwickelte kriminelle Gewalt, die alle Vorteile der Verbindung mit der Regierungsmacht auf ihrer Seite hat: Ihr technisches Kernstück ist das große Kommunikationszentrum im National-palast, wo alle Geheimdienstinformationen koordiniert und die Befehle für die Todesschwadronen ausgegeben werden."[8]

.... denn das Wesen der Folter ist ihre bewußte Grausamkeit, ihre gewollte Unmoral, ihre willentliche Ungerechtigkeit. Ein höhnisches Lachen."[9] Dies Lachen, dies Fest, ist der Geburtsschrei des "in machtvoller Freiheit" erstehenden Institutionenleibs.

Elaine Scarry in ihrem Buch *Der Körper im Schmerz*[10] hat ebenfalls den Prozeß beschrieben, in dem in dem Maße, wie der Gefolterte sein Leben verliert, Leben in den Folterer einströmt. Der Gefolterte verliert seine Sprache, der Folterer gewinnt eine Sprache, sagt sie. Schmerz ist nicht "sprechbar". Der Körper des Gefolterten, auch wenn er die Folter überlebt, wird ausgelöscht in den Zustand eines "plötzlichen Todes" hinein. Dieser entzieht sich jeder Sprache. Sogar die *Geschichte* der eigenen Folter wird den Gefolterten damit genommen. Die Folterer *nehmen* sie und *verwenden* sie für sich ... (Sie können mit einem Mal *reden* und *schreiben*, und sie schreiben ihre Taten, sehr oft, dann auch auf. Es findet etwas so Furchtbares wie ein *Lebendigkeitsaustausch* statt; im Moment, in dem das Opfer ganz Schmerz ist, ist der folternde Mann dem Schmerz ganz *entkommen,* im Moment des Todes des einen ist der andere im *High.)*

Entsprechend waren die KZs in Deutschland nicht nur als Vernichtungsfabriken angelegt, sondern als Großlabore für die *Geburt* des nordischen Übermenschen. Dieser sollte erstehen aus dem Tod der Juden; deren (überlegene) *Energie* sollte eingehen in den deutschen Über-Leib. Noch einmal Kate Millett: "Entscheidend ist die Erlaubnis: Seinen Phantasien auf diese Art und Weise *ohne* Erlaubnis nachzugehen ist kriminell und strafwürdig, ein rein individueller Akt ohne Bedeutung, der nur der eigenen Befriedigung dient, abnorm, verboten. Aber mit staatlicher Erlaubnis ist es Patriotismus, Dienstpflicht, lobenswertes, bezahltes, professionelles Handeln. "[11]

---

[8] Ebenda, S. 255.

[9] Ebenda, S. 290.

[10] Elaine Scarry, *Der Körper im Schmerz. Die Chiffren der Verletzlichkeit und die Erfindung der Kultur,* Frankfurt 1992.

[11] Kate Millett (Anm. 7), S. 29.

Dies ist der entscheidende Punkt für alle Männerbünde wie für alle männlichen Institutionen. Sie alle haben als Kern den Moment der *erlaubten Übertretung*, sei es gegen andere ("Fremde"), sei es gegen die eigenen Leute in den verschiedenen Formen der sogenannten Initiationsriten (quälende Körpereingriffe an den neu Beitretenden mit einer potentiellen Todesdrohung im Hintergrund). Die "erlaubte Übertretung": Die Bombenmänner treten ein ins potentielle "Recht" der Weltzerstörung, so wie im alten Institut "Ehe" der Mann die Frau "zu recht" schlug, sowie die "Lynchjustiz" der erlaubt/verbotene Justiz-Exekutiv aller männerbeherrschten Gesellschaften ist.

Die Todesdrohung ("erlaubtes Töten") richtet sich aber auch nach innen, gegen das einzelne Mitglied jeder männlichen Institution im Fall seiner Nichtanpassung, auch in allen zivilen Institutionen. Jeder weiß (mehr oder weniger dunkel), daß er fallengelassen werden kann von seiner Institution bei Abweichen von deren Vorschriften und Regeln. Dem einfachen zivilen Satz "Ich arbeite aber nicht" entspricht die Antwort "dann verhungerst du eben". Und wenn du nicht spurst ... in einer Schule, in einer Universität, in einer Klinik ... dann wird dir der Boden entzogen ... und du *fliegst*.

Diese Todesdrohung auf der einen *und* die Gratifikation des Versprechens der *erlaubten Übertretung* auf der anderen Seite bilden den Kern, den Kitt jeder männlichen Institution, auch der zivilen. Jeder Männerkörper, der hier heranwächst, *weiß* etwas davon, hat etwas davon *in den Knochen*, ist Teil dieser Gewalt, hat Anteil an dieser gewalttätigen Alchemie der "Selbstverlebendigung durch Lebennehmen" und Vergrößerung der eigenen Macht durch Zusammenschluß mit dem Körper der Institution ... ("Rostock" ... die Stunde der erlaubten Übertretung). Das Prinzip Folter ist das *offene Organisationsgeheimnis* am Grund männerstaatlicher Institutionen, die Realverbindung jedes einzelnen Männerkörpers mit dem Prinzip "göttlicher Kriminalität".

Dies unterscheidet ihn vom weiblichen Körper wahrscheinlich stärker als der bloße Geschlechtsunterschied. Die in letzter Zeit so beliebte Rede emanzipierter Frauen, die die eigenen "bösen Potenzen" spüren und sie nicht einfach unterdrücken möchten: "Frauen sind auch nicht besser als Männer", sieht nicht diese Differenz. Natürlich gibt es böse und sogar folternde Frauen; aber auf das vergleichbare Gerüst einer institutionellen Gewalt gezogen wie der männliche ist ihr Körper *nicht*. Auch gibt es keine weibliche Folterkultur im Sinne der (hochentwickelten) männlichen irgendwo auf der Welt. "Wozu Frauen in der Lage wären, *wenn* .. .", ist eine andere Frage. Zu allem möglichen, womöglich. Aber der halb in der *kriminellen* Übertretung, halb in der *gesetzlichen* Gewalt wurzelnde Männerkörper ist eine *Tatsache*. Ihr entspricht bei den Frauen höchstens die Verfügungsgewalt über die kleinen Kinder. Die ist aber in sich selber zumindest ambivalent, aus fördernden wie vernichtenden Teilen zusammengesetzt und hat strukturell ein völlig anderes Gerüst: das Leben, das Mütter dem Kind möglicherweise nähmen, war Teil von ihnen selber. Eine Mutter, die ihr Kind "folterte", träte nicht ein in die Gratifikation eines "freieren", "mächtigeren" Körpers, eher gefährdete sie, potentiell, auch den eigenen.

13

Der männlich-institutionelle Körper erscheint im Alltag in eher "harmlosen Zügen" als eingefahrenes Gestenrepertoire. Gewisse Handbewegungen ... der Neigungswinkel des Kopfes ... der dynamisch ausladende Arm ... die wichtigen Finger ... das Ausfahren des Schritts ... das Schulterzucken ... die kurzen Blicke zwischen Männern "über Frauen" in Diskussionen, Arbeitsbesprechungen und "privat": "... was *die* da wieder *sagt!*" ... die Expressivität der Mundwinkel ... der Nasenflügel (meist ist es der linke, der etwas angehoben wird) ... und schon folgen die Brauen, wie von alleine, nach ... ein lustiges Wölkchen huscht über die Stirne (die eisenharte) ... ein Gestenrepertoire, jeder Frau bekannt in seiner Ausschlußsetzung (und den Männern, nur anders, auch).

Dann dies charakteristische An- und Abschalten von Haltungen, Wahrnehmungsweisen, Anteilnahmen. Institutionenkörper schalten ein, sie schalten aus. Switch. Der eine (Körper) kommt, der andere geht. Zum nicht enden wollenden Erstaunen der Frauen: .... ist das noch derselbe Typ?" "Eben war er doch *der!*" Nein, es ist nicht derselbe Typ. Der individuelle Körper, der teilanästhesierte Körper, der institutionelle Körper leben im Männerleib unintegriert nebeneinander, übergangslos, umschaltbar eben. Und wenn die reine Institution aus ihm spricht — "das Gesetz" —, spricht gar keine Person (beziehungsweise eine irre, das heißt eine verdeckt gewalttätige).

Ob im Sport, bei den Rotariern, im Wissenschaftsclub, im Versicherungsbüro, beim Unternehmer, im Journalisten, im Lehrer ... der andauernde "Macho" ist ein institutionelles Gestenrepertoire mit Umschaltvorrichtung; deren mehr oder weniger raffinierte Auslegung bestimmt den Grad seiner "Professionalität".

Das für die Organisation eines Staates entscheidende an diesen Körpern ist ihr äußerst direktes, ihr unmittelbares Verhältnis zur politischen, militärischen, technologischen Macht. Zwar gibt es "höhere Männer" der direkten Umgebung, deren Anordnungsund Strafmacht gefolgt werden muß, aber deren Macht ist eine sichtbarlich geliehene oder abgeleitete. Als psychische Vater-Instanzen oder Helfer-Instanzen sind sie, speziell im Sohn, nicht verankert. Dieser setzt sich direkt mit dem Führer in Verbindung, mit dem Prinzip "Führung", mit dem Land, mit "der Kultur", mit Körperschaften wie dem Militär, der Kirche, oder, wenn er tatsächlich religiös ist, direkt mit dem Körper Gottes oder eines anderen Paten einer anderen Großmacht, deren Überkörper er sich einfügen kann, um selber in den Genuß von Ganzheitsgefühlen zu kommen, die zu erreichen ihm auf uninstitutionelle Weise nicht möglich ist.

Dazwischen geistert, irgendwo, eine Restperson, ein armes, meist dann auch ängstliches Stück Fleisch, das seinen Stempel noch nicht trägt, das ein Mensch vielleicht werden möchte. (Irgendwer sei ihm gnädig.)

Und die Mütter ... die doch all das *geboren* haben? Sicher haben sie. Und sie haben auch meist, zumindest in den ersten Jahren, eine starke Verbindung zu den Körpern der Kleinen und umgekehrt ebenso. Nicht nur eine Emotion, sondern eine Arbeitsweise. Sara Ruddick hat in ihrem Buch *Mütterliches Denken*[12] den Versuch unternommen, die Tätigkeiten der Mütter in unseren Gesellschaften in einem speziellen Arbeitsbegriff zu fassen, zu dem ein ganz spezifisches mütterliches *Denken* gehört. Zuerst einmal ist die meiste Arbeit der Mütter nicht privat, im Haus, geheim, "mütterlich", sondern öffentlich, verbunden mit der andauernden Notwendigkeit von Entscheidungen, die ein spezifisches Denken erfordern, sagt sie. Mütter befinden sich ständig unter den beobachtenden, kritischen Augen von Ärzten, Lehrern, Kindergärtnerinnen — die sie selber wiederum kritisch betrachten —, in Berührungen mit Kaufhauspersonal, den Leuten in der Straßenbahn, vor den Augen der Nachbarn, in Auseinandersetzungen mit Sozialbehörden, städtischen Behörden, bei der Krankenkasse etc. Sie sind dabei mit der (halbinstitutionellen) Aufgabe bedacht, irgendwie das Leben, das in ihren Kindern steckt, zu entfalten, zumindest es zu schützen und es zu erhalten. Diese Arbeit, die der männlichen, die so oft durch *Zerstörungen* Neues schafft, diametral entgegengesetzt ist, hat Sara Ruddick mit dem Begriff "Caring Labor" zu bezeichnen versucht. "Sorgende Arbeit" wäre zu wenig gesagt; eine lebenerzeugende Arbeit ist gemeint, nicht einfach bloß "Mutterarbeit", und auch nicht eine Arbeit, die nur von Frauen getan werden könnte, im Gegenteil: Das Feld für männliche Sorten von "Garing Labor" wäre riesig, nicht nur den Kindern gegenüber. Der Begriff zielt auf eine insgesamt andere *Ökonomie* als die herrschende Kosten/Nutzen-Okonomie, nach der wir funktionieren. Ruddicks Begriff von "Caring Labor" umschließt das Ökologische, geht aber über dieses hinaus, weil es diese Arbeit nicht etwa als "natürliche" faßt, sondern als artifizielle; die sogenannte Natur der sogenannten Menschen ist überwiegend eine barbarische. Man kann ihr mit Künsten und Techniken entkommen, je entwickelter diese sind, desto besser. Eine entwickelte Frau/Mann/Kinder-Politik gegen das Männer-bündlerische, gegen das Kriegerische als Mittel der Politik, gegen die Isolierung der Frauen von der gesellschaftlichen Macht, wäre eine Zivilisationstechnik, nichts Naturhaftes; eine Belebungsarbeit, die durchaus auch im Sinne einer Geldökonomie "rentabel" sein kann, wenn man entsprechend ökonomisch umdächte.

Warum ist der Boden für "Caring Labor" so karg bei uns. Warum scheren so wenige Männer aus aus ihren institutionellen Leibern (die sie am Grunde doch mit nichts weniger als Tod bedrohen). Ich glaube, dies wird bei uns verhindert an erster Stelle durch einen künstlich erzeugten Haß auf "die Mutter", "das Mütterliche".
" ... in Gesellschaften, deren Kinder beinah ausschließlich von Frauen großgezogen werden, während öffentliche Macht und Autorität fast ausschließlich bei Männern

---

[12] Sara Ruddick, *Mütterliches Denken*, Frankfurt 1993.

liegen und in denen die sogenannte "Unabhängigkeit" höher bewertet wird als die Fähigkeit zu gegenseitiger Abhängigkeit und Unterstützung, assoziieren kleine Kinder den Komplex "Abhängigkeit" und Fürsorge, den sie zugleich fürchten und ersehnen, ausschließlich mit Frauen/dem Weiblichen, und das Erreichen von Freiheit und Unabhängigkeit ausschließlich mit dem Männlichen", schreibt Sara Ruddick.

Jeder *normale Junge* schon wird mehr oder weniger in eine Verachtung der Mutter/des Mütterlichen hineingezwungen, wenn er realisiert, daß jene mütterlichen Züge, die ihn nährten, die ihn gehalten haben, die ihn angeregt und entwickelt haben, einfach ausgelöscht werden können und ausgelöscht werden durch die Ansprüche männlich dominierter gesellschaftlicher Institutionen und Gegebenheiten wie den Sport, industrielle Arbeit, Militär, aber auch Schulen und Universitäten. Die Attraktionen der Mutter sind zu schwach — lernt der Junge, zu schwach, um woanders damit zu überleben. Wer an ihnen festhält, wird ausgelacht.

Mütter *bemerken* das in aller Regel. Sie wissen und kennen das. Aber was bleibt ihnen zu tun? Sie nehmen in der Regel die männlichen Gesetze als gegeben hin und bekämpfen sie (aus dem Gefühl der Machtlosigkeit heraus) meist nicht. Der Junge, der die männlichen Regeln und Gesetze vielleicht gar nicht annehmen will (und sehr viele *wollen* diesen Terror nicht freiwillig annehmen), findet sich in der Falle, wenn er sich von der mütterlichen Macht jetzt verlassen sieht: tief enttäuscht, wenn er bemerkt, daß *sie nicht in der Lage ist*, den Forderungen eines Vaters, Lehrers, Trainers oder Chefs etwas entgegenzusetzen. Er wendet sich von ihr ab; von ihr, deren äußerst mächtige und wirksame Lehren ausgelöscht werden können von irgendeiner beliebigen Art Mann. Mutters Macht dauert nicht ... lernt der Junge.

Eines späteren Tages wird er sich rächen. Rache nehmen an der mütterlichen Verheißung von Stärke und Selbständigkeit. Männer haben ihn gelehrt, wo die Mutter sich in den Gebäuden der männlichen Hierarchien befindet: ganz unten. Und er wird sie treten für ihre Schwäche, für den Mangel durchgehender Macht in ihr und ihrer Arbeit. Müttern gelingt es nicht, ihre Söhne zu schützen vor den grausamen Ansprüchen und Zugriffen der Väter und anderer Männer: Das ist der springende Punkt, der Punkt, der nicht vergeben wird — wie alle Angriffe von schwachen Söhnen/Männern gegen schwächere Mütter/Frauen zeigen.

Wenn "normale" Jungs derart lernen, die Weiblichkeit zu fürchten als etwas, das sie personlicher Stärke und Bewegungsfreiheit beraubt, dann werden diejenigen, die zusätzlich Soldaten werden, nicht nur die Abhängigkeit von einer Mütterfürsorge zurückweisen; sie werden zusätzlich einen besonderen Haß auf jene Körper entwickeln, die die Fähigkeit hatten und auch weiter haben, sich als Bedrohung des eigenen "Freigewordenseins" darzustellen. Nehmen wir an, der jugendliche Mann ist der mütterlichen Arbeit und Zuneigung noch verbunden, er ist vielleicht auch verliebt, mag Frauen. Diese Neigung wird zuerst ausgetrieben in der brutalen Körperumkehrungszeremonie des militärischen Drills. Schlimmer: Was er selbst erfährt, ist eine Art *Folter*. Sie drehen sein Inneres nach außen ... er hat sich dafür zu bedanken ... Dank für jeden Schlag und Tritt ... Dank dafür, selber Schmerz zu werden, neugeboren zu werden vom Schmerzprinzip und vom Prinzip der

Selbstverleugnung ... aber bitte, SIR, bitte, Herr Offizier, wenn ich dies hinter mir habe, nenne mich nicht mehr Waschlappen, Weib, Lady oder Girl, sondern nenne mich Mann. Mann, Mann, Supermann. Mika Haritos-Fatouros hat in einem Aufsatz über "Die Ausbildung des Folterers. Trainingsprogramme der Obristendiktatur in Griechenland" gezeigt, wie all das, was Folterern ihren Opfern später antun, zuerst an ihnen selber vollzogen wird; mit dem einen Unterschied, daß sie am Leben gelassen und am Leben *gehalten* werden von der Aussicht, selber all dies, und dann ungestraft, ausüben zu dürfen. "Der interviewte Militärpolizist M. Petrou gab in einem einzigen Satz eine treffende Charakterisierung der gesamten Ausbildung.
>Wir mußten lernen, den Schmerz zu lieben.< Die Mißhandlung Untergebener bereitete den Kadetten in modellhaften Abläufen auf seine Tätigkeit als Folterer vor. Menschen Schmerz zuzufügen, wurde auf diese Weise zur alltäglichen Handlung, zur Routine, zu einem Akt der Macht, zu einem >Wettkampf< zwischen Opfer und Peiniger. "[13]

Auf den damit verbundenen Umbau der gesamten Sexualität vom Lustprinzip auf ein "Schmerz- und Gewaltprinzip", den ich in den *Männerphantasien* beschrieben habe (er wird von Haritos-Fatouros an gleicher Stelle eindrucksvoll belegt), komme ich gleich noch einmal zurück. Im gequälten Jungmannkörper wächst die dunkle Rede: "Gib mir eine Waffe und zeig mir das Böse ... zeig mir SIE ... ich werde ihr zeigen, was es heißt, mich nicht beschützt zu haben vor dem männlichen Teufelsprinzip: Schmerzzufügung und Gewalt." Auf diesem Hintergrund liest sich die Hinrichtung des Wasserbüffelbabys bei O'Brien mit ihrer Betonung der *Sorgfalt* des Zielens, der Sorgfalt des ganzen Tötungsvorgangs, wie eine sorgfältig gedrechselte Pervertierung des Prinzips von "Caring Labor".

Wozu zum Teufel (geht die stumme Rede weiter) sind Frauen, wozu sind Mütter gut, wenn sie ihre Kinder nicht vor den Qualen schützen können, die eine männliche Gesellschaft für sie auf Lager hat? Wozu sind ihre schönen Seiten gut, ihre womögliche Weichheit, ihr nachgiebigerer Körper, ihre Lieder, ihre Haarwolken, ihre Plätze mit den weichen Kissen (die selbst ein härterer Haushalt mit einer härteren Mutter in der Regel irgendwo hat) ... wozu all das, wenn ein gewalttätiger Vater und seine Truppe von Scheißjungs ausreichen, schlichtweg *nichts* daraus zu machen.

Das könnte man "tragisch" nennen, wäre es nicht in unseren Gesellschaften präzise so hergestellt und kalkuliert. Mütter müssen in männerbeherrschten Gesellschaften in der Rolle der Körper erscheinen, die so etwas wie die Möglichkeit eines leichten Lebens versprechen. Glücks- und Paradiesversprechen sind verbunden dem weiblichen Leib.

Männer sind gesellschaftlich dazu angestellt, später (mit einem institutionalisierten Lächeln) klarzustellen, daß diese Glücksversprechen bestenfalls eines waren: ein frommer Betrug. Jeden Tag müssen Myriaden von Frauen vor den Augen ihrer Kinder

---

[13] Mika Haritos-Fatouros, "Die Ausbildung des Folterers. Trainingsprogramme der Obristendiktatur in Griechenland." In: *Folter. Zur Analyse eines Herrschaftsmittels*, hrsg. von Jan Philipp Reemtsma. Hamburg 1991, S. 8i.

vor irgendeinem (selber relativ machtlosen) Typ von Mann in die Knie gehen und öffentlich einräumen, daß sie nichts zu sagen haben, daß sie hiervon nichts verstehen, daß sie dort nicht hinreichen mit ihrer Kraft etc. etc.

Jeder Fünfzehnjährige ist schon weitgehend überzeugt, daß es den Frauen "irgendwo nicht reicht", daß sie diejenigen sind, die es bei Gelegenheit abkriegen, daß man beizeiten auf eine Distanz gehen muß, um nicht mit in den Strudel zu geraten, wenn er (von einer Männerbande) angestellt wird.

Die *Götter* sind zwar verrückt; aber sie haben Macht. "Die Mütter?" ... "Vergiß sie" ... "Sie werden dir nicht helfen, letztendlich."

So lebt der Körper von Institutionen von der Verwerfung des Körpers der Mutter. Wenn Männer durch Institutionen "lebendig" werden, "geboren werden", so leben sie vom Tod, den der Körper der Mutter dabei nimmt.

Ein Sonderfall ist die institutionelle Psychoanalyse als Körperumbau- und Neugeburtsinstanz. Ich habe sie in *Objektwahl* als "Töchterstaat unter männlicher Führung" bezeichnet, als eine mann/weibliche Mischinstitution. Sie ist, soweit ich sehe, die einzige Institution, die regelmäßig (in der "Technikdiskussion" und in der Supervision) den eigenen Gewaltanteil reflektiert, der in der Arbeit am Patienten wirksam wird. Aber noch vor wenigen Jahren (und vielleicht immer noch) äußer(te)n Ausbildungsanalytiker weiblichen Kandidaten gegenüber, daß Kinder die Ausbildung stören würden. Sie sollten besser nicht "Mütter" sein, nur dann sei die rechte Hingabe möglich an die Verwandlungsarbeit des Vereins .... "Wird die mütterliche Hingabe gerade deshalb nicht als Beitrag für die Gesellschaft erkannt und anerkannt, weil er so ungeheuer groß ist?" fragte Donald W. Winnicott 1957, und weiter, was denn passieren würde, *würde* er einmal anerkannt: Nicht "Dankbarkeit oder gar Lobeshymnen" wären die Folge; "die Anerkennung wird vielmehr zur Verminderung einer tief in uns sitzenden Angst führen."[14] Diese Angst kursiert in öffentlich sohnlicher Begrifflichkeit vornehmlich als Angst vor dem "mütterlichen Beherrscht-werden".

"Tatsächlich definieren Männer ihre Geschlechtsidentität im Gegensatz zu den Frauen negativ: männlich ist, was nicht weiblich ist", schreibt Walter Hollstein.[15] Der darauffolgende Schritt heißt: männlich ist, was gesellschaftliche Institutionen dafür ausgeben.

Je mehr ich auf die Methoden und Stile der Gewalt und der Folter sehe in verschiedenen Teilen der Welt, je mehr finde ich, daß der besondere Haß gegen den weiblichen Körper, der in so vielen Aktionen durchschlägt, möglicherweise mit der Tatsache verbunden ist, Rache nehmen zu wollen: Rache nehmen zu wollen für den Umstand, von einer Mutter geboren zu sein, aber später von dieser Mutter nicht "genügend" geschützt und gehalten zu werden. Die regelmäßig berichtete Wut und

---

[14]Donald W. Winnicott, "Der Beitrag der Mutter zur Gesellschaft." In: D. W. Winnicott, *Der Anfang ist unsere Heimat*, Stuttgart 1990.

[15]Walter Hollstein, *Der Kampf der Geschlechter. Frauen und Männer im Streit um Liebe und Macht*, München 1993.

Aggression von Soldaten gegen die Körper von schwangeren Frauen ist dann kein so großes Rätsel mehr. Diese Aggression hat etwas Gesetzhaftes für junge Männer, deren Obere zielstrebig daran arbeiten, Frauenmacht in den von ihnen geführten Gesellschaften nicht entstehen zu lassen (außer einer imaginären Macht, der angeblich *verschlingenden* Kraft der Frauen).

So ist die allerschlimmste unter den Folterungen, von denen Rigoberta Menchú berichtet, diejenige, die ihrer Mutter durch die Soldaten widerfährt. Ihre Mutter ist tatsächlich das gewesen, was das Militar sonst immer bloß blind von allen Gequälten behauptet: Eine politische Aktivistin. Als solche und als Mutter widerständlerischer Kinder wird sie von den Soldaten behandelt, ausradiert. Sie wird öffentlich angebunden unter Verbreitung der Nachricht, daß sie freigelassen würde, wenn ihre Kinder sich stellen. Jeder weiß, laß dann alle sterben würden. Niemand stellt sich.

"Am dritten Tag der Folter schnitten sie ihr die Ohren ab. Sie schnitten ihr nach und nach alle Körperteile ab. Sie mußte all die Schmerzen erleiden, die ihr Sohn auch erlitten hatte. Sie gaben ihr viele Tage lang nichts zu essen. Ihr Körper war von der Folter ganz entstellt, und als sie nichts mehr zu essen bekam, verlor sie das Bewußtsein. Sie kämpfte mit dem Tod. Da holten sie die Armeeärzte, die ihr Injektionen gaben und sie an einen Tropf legten, damit sie wieder zu sich komme. Sie gaben ihr Medikamente und pflegten sie und ließen sie ausruhen. Als es ihr etwas besser ging, verlangte sie zu essen. Sie gaben ihr zu essen. Danach wurde sie aufs neue vergewaltigt. Sie mußte viel erdulden, aber sie starb nicht. "[16]

Die "Söhne" (ihre höhnischen *Adoptivsöhne* — es sind tatsächlich sehr viele Waisen unter den Angehörigen der Death Squads) päppeln sie auf, bringen wieder etwas Leben in sie, um das Ganze noch einmal haben zu können. Sie wollen sie nicht sterben lassen so schnell. Sie wird gepflegt, wieder vergewaltigt, wieder ausgestellt, angebunden im Freien.

"Sie ließen sie da vier oder fünf Tage liegen, in der Hitze der brennenden Sonne, im Regen und in der Kälte der Nacht. Im Urwald gibt es eine Mücke, die sich in die offenen Wunden setzt, und wenn man die Wunden nicht gleich versorgt, kommen schon nach zwei Tagen Würmer aus den Wunden gekrochen, die die Mücke berührt hat. Und da meine Mutter am ganzen Körper offene Wunden hatte, war sie voller Würmer, und sie lebte noch. Dann, nach langem Todeskampf, starb meine Mutter.

Als sie tot war, stellten sich die Soldaten noch über sie und urinierten meiner Mutter in den Mund, als sie schon tot war. Sie ließen Soldaten als Wachen zurück, damit niemand die Leiche weghole, auch nicht die Reste von ihr. (...)

Meine Mutter wurde von den Tieren gefressen, von Hunden und Geiern und anderen Tieren, die sich beteiligten. Erst nach vier Monaten, als sie sahen, daß von meiner Mutter nichts mehr — nicht einmal die Knochen — übrig geblieben war, verschwanden die Wachen."[17] Wie zum Beweis, daß alles, was "Mutter" heißt,

---

[16] Elisabeth Burgos (Anm. 6), S. 195.

[17] Ebenda, S. 196.

geheißen hat, möglicherweise heißen könnte, zum Verschwinden gebracht werden kann, absolut total und wirklich ein für alle Mal. "Fiesta".

Sexualität als Gewalt

In den vielen Berichten über die Massenvergewaltigungen in Bosnien hat es erstaunlich selten die Frage gegeben, wie es kommt, daß Tausende von Männern zu Vergewaltigungen auch ihnen bekannter Frauen, Nachbarinnen, Arbeitskolleginnen überhaupt imstande waren und sind. Haben die meisten von ihnen nicht zuvor ein ganz "normales" Leben geführt?

Das Nichtstellen dieser Frage schließt ein Wissen ein: das verbreitete Wissen, daß Gewalt ein institutioneller Bestandteil des bürgerlichen Normallebens in männerdominierten Gesellschaften ist. Nur eine Männersexualität, die von Kindesbeinen an (seitens der Eltern, der Geschwister, der Kirchen, Schulen, Vereine, Jugendbünde und Parteien) mit Formen der Gewalt legiert ist, ist im Angesicht einer zu vergewaltigenden Frau überhaupt erektionsfähig. Eine Sexualität, die in freundlichen Beziehungen zwischen Menschenkörpern entstanden wäre, würde ihren Dienst verweigern, wenn sie als Frauenzerstörung funktionieren soll. Das wird auch bei vielen serbischen, kroatischen, bosnischen Männern der Fall sein. Der durchschnittliche "soldatische Mann" aber bezieht seine Erektionsfähigkeit, wie Männer in Männerbünden immer, nicht aus der individuellen Beziehung zu einem anderen Körper, sondern aus der (Zerstörungs-)Macht des Bundes selber; weshalb die militärischen Vergewaltigungen meist im Verband geschehen, und nach der Vergewaltigung kollektiv in die Lobpreisung des "Führers" ausgebrochen wird: Er ist es, der garantiert, daß ihnen (institutionell) einer stand im verlangten Moment (einem Tötungsmoment).

Die Legierung der männlichen Sexualität mit Gewalt erfolgt nicht nur beim Militär; dort allerdings oft als eine totale, irreversible Koppelung der Sexualität mit Gewalt, wie Mika Haritos-Fatouros es für die Foltererausbildung in den Lagern der griechischen Obristen beschreibt. Es gibt "unfreiwillige Samenergüsse" bei Durchführung von Strafmaßnahmen und eine permanente Verkehrung des Penis zu einer Waffe, deren Anwendung unter den Männern dann zwar mit dem Stichwort "homosexuell" behaftbar ist; aber *ist* denn das überhaupt *irgendeine* Sexualität: "Bei der Armee herrschte generell ein homosexuelles Klima. Beim Duschen hatte man Angst, sich zu bücken. Später bei der EAT gingen die Militärpolizisten mit homosexuellen Männern vor das Lager, wenn sie knapp bei Kasse waren. Man vermittelte uns das Gefühl, wir seien solche Übermenschen, daß wir auch Männer ficken könnten. "Niemand wird sich gegen euch erheben; ihr könnt jeden schlagen und ficken", sagten sie zu uns. Die

Soldaten machten sich einen Jux daraus, ihre Knüppel wie Penisse vor sich her zu tragen."[18]

So "ficken" die jungen Kerle der Wachmannschaften im Bericht von Rigoberta Menchú sogar noch einen Körper, dem sie schon einige Glieder abgeschnitten, dem sie schon die Haut abgezogen haben. Ihre "Sexualität" ist soweit umgepolt, daß ihr Glied nur in Gewaltaktionen oder Gewaltphantasien überhaupt erregbar erscheint. "Arbeit", "Geburt", "Sexualität", sie alle leben in schrecklichen Umkehrungsformen in den institutionell geformten Gebieten des Männerleibs.

Erziehung zum Männertum rächt sich. Man kann nicht auf der einen Seite im täglichen Leben Mütter rechtlos halten, Frauen öffentlich entmachten, kleinen heranwachsenden männlichen Scheißern Macht über ihre Schwestern und teilweise ihre Mütter einräumen und gleichzeitig erwarten, daß sie diese, die gesellschaftlich unter ihnen stehen (=Dreck sind), später mit Vorsicht berühren und wie Menschen behandeln. Man kann auch nicht erwarten, daß ein Typ, der tagsüber seine Gefühle beim Töten an ein Gewehr gekoppelt hat oder eine andere Waffe, abends in die Stube tritt und sich benimmt wie ein Gentleman (was heißt: ein sanfter Mann). Die wenigen, die das können, sind Ausnahmen.

Man kann denen, denen die zivilisatorische Hemmschwelle vor dem körperlichen Eingriff in einen anderen Menschen mehr oder weniger systematisch genommen worden ist, nicht sagen, hier darfst du (eindringen, töten, schlachten, ein Blutbad anrichten), und hier mußt du nett und schonend sein: Der soldatische Mann kann zwar "umschalten", er hat aber nur in den selteneren Fällen zwei physische Körper, die er feierabends oder wenn er eine Frau sieht gegeneinander auswechseln kann. Er kann das bis zu einem gewissen Grad in der Kaserne oder bei der Arbeit, wo alle daran arbeiten, das zivilisatorische Korsett zusammenzuhalten, aber wenn das Schlachten freigegeben ist, kann er es nicht.

Wer prinzipiell für die Möglichkeit von Kriegen spricht, nimmt die Vergewaltigung jedenfalls in Kauf; Kampfgewalt ist immer auch als Mordgewalt und als Vergewaltigungsgewalt abrufbar. Wie tabuisiert der ganze Komplex aber ist, zeigt sich deutlich an der erst *jetzt* begonnenen Aufarbeitung dieser Seite der Kriegs-und Nachkriegsgeschichte. Die vielen Vergewaltigungen von DDR-Frauen durch russische Soldaten und deren Folgen (uneheliche Kinder, die 1990 fünfundvierzig Jahre alt waren und die Russen offiziell immer lieben mußten) kamen kurz in den Blick, der sich aber schnell wieder trübte; zu viel steht auf dem Spiel: Die deutsche Normal-Armee des Weltkriegs hat sich in der Öffentlichkeit als überwiegend "sauber geblieben" darstellen können (trotz aller offenkundigen Mithilfe an der Durchführung der KZ-Transporte in den jeweiligen besetzten Gebieten; von den zivilen Morden zu schweigen); wer will solch saubere Institute schon beschmutzen bloß um ein paar womöglich wahrer Wort~ ("für Frauen") willen.

---

[18] Mika Haritos-Fatouros (Anm. 13), S. 87.

Gewalt im Körper eines Volkes abzubauen ist ein langer und schwieriger Prozeß. Der deutsche "Volkskörper" war voll von Gewalt durchs Hitlerreich. Die Nichtauseinandersetzung der BRD mit dieser Gewalt nach 1945 und der Beschluß der DDR, man(n) sei jetzt antifaschistisch, hat die Gewalt in den Körpern völlig unberührt gelassen: das heißt, weiter den Händen von Müttern und Vätern überantwortet, die, auch wo nicht institutionalisierte Faschisten, mit der Abarbeitung dieser fürchterlichen Hypothek völlig überfordert waren. Die eigene Gewalt mit aller Macht zu verdrängen wurde das übliche Verfahren, daß heißt aber, die latent in den Körpern vorhandene Gewalt wurde blind, in institutionell nur geringfügig abgemilderter Form an die Körper der Kinder weitergegeben. So "vererbt" sich ein Sozialcharakter und nicht anders: durch Berührungen und institutionalisierte Weitergabe. Diese können Gewalt weitergeben, sie können "blinde Flecken" weitergeben, Erstarrungen, aber auch Belebungen, es könnte auch Respekt vorm Menschenkörper sein.

In Deutschland West wie Ost sind sehr viel blinde Flecken weitergegeben worden; diese erscheinen jetzt im täglichen Verkehr als Empfindungslosigkeiten. Kälte ist die zivile Vorstufe, die Einfrierstufe der Gewalt. Davon gibt es hier (in der dritten Generation nach den Lagern, die sich nicht mehr "verantwortlich" fühlen will) reichlich.

Re-Maskulinisierungen

Vermutlich ist der Pegel der latenten Gewalt hier nach zwanzig Jahren Frauenbewegung und anderen Zivilisationsversuchen an der bundesdeutschen Gesellschaft geringer als vor fünfzig Jahren; den tatsachlichen Stand kann man nur erahnen. Er steigt allerdings, je "männlicher" eine Gesellschaft sich definiert.

Die Amerikanerin Susan Jeffords hat in ihrem Buch *Die Wiedervermännlichung Amerikas*[19] beschrieben, wie das öffentliche Amerika in den achtziger Jahren seine antiweiblichen Kampagnen durchgeführt hat auf dem Hintergrund einer Neuschreibung der Geschichte des Vietnamkrieges: "To re-win Vietnam", Vietnam nachträglich gewinnen, war die Parole, siegreich durchgeführt im Golfkrieg, der psychisch in der Tat ein nachträglich gewonnenes Vietnam für die amerikanische Öffentlichkeit geliefert hat. Der Preis: die Zurückdrängung zivilerer, "weiblicherer" Verhaltensweisen im öffentlichen Leben, im Fernsehen, im Kino, in den Büros, an Arbeitsplätzen, und (in einem geringeren Maß) sogar in den Universitäten. Überall wurde ausgestellt der kämpferische Mann, bewaffnet mit schickem Outfit, Autos, Flugzeug, Pistolen, Sprechfunk an der Jacke, unterstützt von der ebenso schicken Frau als seiner *Assistentin*, zugespitzt das Ganze in der Re-Maskulinisierung der Abtreibungsfrage. Mit den Clintons schien es eine Gegenbewegung zu geben.

---

[19] Susan Jeffords, *The Remasculinization of America. Gender and the Vietnam War*, Bloomington 1989.

Etwas Vergleichbares geschah in Deutschland. Der Zusammenbruch der DDR und dann der Sowjetunion wurde als nachträglich gewonnener Zweiter Weltkrieg erlebt, mit der gleichen Folge einer Vermännlichung der deutschen Öffentlichkeit: Herausdrängen der Frauen aus Berufen, Abbau von Kindergärten, öffentliche Demontage von Parteifrauen, Lächerlichmachen des Feminismus, um nur einige zu nennen, auch hier zugespitzt zu einer männlichen Radikalisierung der Abtreibungsfrage. Niemand, außer ein paar Frauen, hat das groß aufgeregt.

So kommt es, daß zum Beispiel die Frage nach militärischen Einsätzen der Bundeswehr *heute* nicht als ein Problem, das die Beziehungen zwischen Männern und Frauen und das Verhältnis zu ihren Kindern entscheidend berührt, öffentlich behandelt wird, sondern als rein männlich-politische Angelegenheit unter dem Stichwort einer angeblichen deutschen "Verantwortung" für die Belange anderer Nationen. All das wirft uns Jahrzehnte zurück (wenn man sich für einige kurze Traummomente die theoretische Möglichkeit eines geschichtlichen Fortschritts gewisser Bevölkerungen nicht grundsätzlich versagen will).

Was die Frauen gebären, wird in männerdominierten Gesellschaften umstandslos als Rohmaterial für den männlichen Weltbau betrachtet. Wer fragt die Frauen nach ihrer Ansicht, ob das von ihnen geborene und "anbehandelte" Material dort "angemessen", "vernünftig" weiterentwickelt wird? Kein Mensch/das heißt: kein Mann; die gesetzgebenden Mächte geben sich hier komplett ungerührt von weiblichen Ansprüchen/ Einsprüchen/ Einsichten, wenn sie sie nicht geradezu als feindliches, störendes, irrelevantes Gewäsch, lästig wie Fliegen, beiseite tun.

De-Maskulinisierungen

Institutionen sind überall; das Militär ist nur eine, wenn auch immer noch eine heimlich maßgebende. Helfen würde nur eine allmähliche, aber tatsächliche Feminisierung der Gesellschaft, oder, für diejenigen, denen das Wort Angst macht, eine "Verringerung ihrer männlichen Dominanzen". Die Wurzeln der männlichen Gewalt werden nicht verschwinden (nicht verschwinden können) ohne eine vorbehaltlose, gesetzlich durchgeführte wie psychisch wirklich akzeptierte Gleichstellung der Frauen auf allen gesellschaftlichen Ebenen, bei der Arbeit, im Haus.

Der Kleinkindkörper ist, zunächst, kein tötendes Wesen. Man übersieht immer, daß auch kleine heranwachsende Jungen von der gesellschaftlichen Männergewalt erst einmal vergewaltigt werden müssen, bis sie als die Vergewaltigermänner funktionieren, die sie später, meistens, sind. Sie bräuchten mächtige Frauen zum Schutz gegen den Zugriff der männlichen Instanzen und Institutionen. Weibliche Institutionen mit Gesetzgebungskraft, einzelne Frauen allein können das (fürs Ganze) nicht schaffen. Man traut sich nicht einmal, die Forderungen *auszusprechen,* so "utopisch" scheinen sie: Weibliche Belange wie die Abtreibungsfrage gehören völlig in Frauenhand; ein Frauenparlament, gewählt nur von Frauen. Ob dieses sich dann (in

Ausschüssen oder sonstwie) einer Männermitarbeit bedienen will, wäre der Frauen Sache. Ein Friedensnobelpreis für Rigoberta Menchú ist gut, aber reicht nicht. Vernünftige Frauen, die tatsächliche Entscheidungsmacht haben, ziehen die Geschlechtergrenzen ohnehin nicht so rassistisch, wie die männlichen Instanzen (insbesondere die Gerichte) das tun.

Auflösung der Männerbundstrukturen geht nicht im Männerbund oder im Männerclub. Sie geht nur mit und durch Frauen und durch die Verbindung von Männern mit Kindern. Die Männer müßten, als Väter ihrer meist nur auf dem Papier existierenden "Familien", selbst hinunter auf die Ebene des Materials des Prozesses, wo alle Material sind: Material der Veränderung und nicht des Krieges. Herstellung von Gleichheitsebenen.

"In den vergangenen fünfzig Jahren ist das Bewußtsein für den Wert und die Bedeutung des Elternhauses stark gewachsen. (Es ist nun einmal nicht zu ändern, daß dieses Bewußtsein zunächst aus der Erkenntnis erwuchs, welche Auswirkungen das schlechte Elternhaus hat.) Wir wissen einiges über die Gründe, weshalb dieses langwährende und mühevolle Geschäft, die Aufgabe der Eltern nämlich, ihre Kinder durch alle Entwicklungs-schwierigkeiten hindurch zu geleiten, eine lohnende Aufgabe ist; und wir glauben, daß gerade die Erfüllung dieser Aufgabe der Gesellschaft die einzige solide Grundlage bietet und nur durch sie die demokratischen Tendenzen im sozialen Gefüge eines Landes sich entwickeln können."[20]

Vielleicht ein bißchen viel verlangt von der Elternarbeit, *ganz allein* für eine vernünftige gesellschaftliche Entwicklung verantwortlich zu sein: "Nur durch sie", sagt Winnicott. Aber "ohne sie" wird es ganz gewiß nichts mit "Demokratisierung", das heißt männlicher Ent-Institutionalisierung; soviel ist "sicher".

Die Frau gebiert das Kind (auch noch in weiterer Zukunft; ungeachtet der verschiedenen Retorten); der Mann kann dabei helfen, er kann dabei stören, er kann konkurrieren, wie bisher etc. Eine Differenz bleibt immer: Auch wenn er emotional beteiligt ist, auch wenn er mithilft, so gut es geht, das Austragen des Kindes und der Geburtsschmerz bleiben ihm fremd, sind nicht Teil seines körperlichen Erlebens. Das "Ins-Leben-Pressen" eines neuen Menschen bleibt seiner Erfahrung unzugänglich, er erlebt nicht die physische und psychische Metamorphose, die der Frauenkörper bei der Geburt durchläuft; dies merkwürdige "Wunder der Geburt" ist, ganz nüchtern betrachtet, für ihn tatsächlich eins. Diese Methode der Selbstvervielfältigung unter höchstem Einsatz der eigenen Leiblichkeit ist eine Frauensache, weder nachvollziehbar noch "erreichbar". Aber in den Körpern der sich ständig verwandelnden Kinder ist zumindest die Möglichkeit gegeben, sich abzusetzen vom Prinzip der *Übertrumpfung* des Weiblichen durch Entfesselung ("Geburt") ungeheurer (destruktiver) Energien: dem Lieblingsspiel der Bekämpfer des "falschen Wegs" der Geburt, Geburt durch die Frau.

---

[20] D. W. Winnicott (Anm. in), S. 136.

Heute ist der Männerkörper nach militärischen Maßstäben überwiegend entdrillt, nach dem Zweiten Weltkrieg entmilitarisiert. Der Zugriff auf den männlichen Körper erfolgt nicht mehr direkt muskulär (vom Staat aus), sondern auf Umwegen: Sport, Arbeit, Disziplinierung untereinander, allgemeine Abweichungskontrolle, Klamotten, Haarschnitt, Design, dann Ordnung des Familien- wie des öffentlichen Lebens: Wo alles ohne viel Abweichung in vorgeschriebenen Bahnen läuft, bekommt der Körper auch davon eine Form. Am besten ist die zu erhaltende Form in Waren sichtbar: Die ganze Glätte, Schönheit, Oberflächenverliebtheit der Waren gibt die Körpervorbilder ab. Warenaussehen/Design ist an die Stelle des militärischen Drills getreten.

Die Jugendlichen *stylen* ihren Körper nach dem Outfit von Stereomaschinen, Motorrädern, nach Benetton, Levi, Nike, Reebok und was "der Schirm" sonst so hergibt. Die Baseballcap auf jedem Schadel now. Warenpolitik ist Körperpolitik. Der Osten lief in den Westen über, weil die Ostleute den Westkörper haben wollten, den sie im Fernsehen und in den Westwaren gesehen haben. Ihn sich zu kaufen kostet ein Höllengeld. Bisher wird das dadurch balanciert, daß man die Schufterei immer mit grad so viel Gratifikationen bedenkt, daß der Körper, den man jeweils haben will, grade eben noch bezahlbar ist: Man kriegt im Laden ein Stück von dem, was man sein *will*, zu kaufen. Das scheint gut zu funktionieren (solange die Gehälter nicht unter ein bestimmtes Level sinken). Tun sie es, kommen *andere* Sorten Gewalt hervor, dann soll man sich nicht wundern. Kleider machen *nicht* Leute ... ; sie machen nur (das sah man auch im "alten Jugoslawien") ein, wenn's hoch kommt, schöneres Bild.

Dein Feind— das Bild

Und was zeigen die Fotos der Wehrmachtausstellung? Sie zeigen (an erster Stelle) den *Blick* der Soldaten auf das Ereignis. Dieser Blick muss beschrieben werden, wenn man das "Dokumentarische" der Bilder würdigen will. Worin besteht dieser Blick? Er besteht aus dem Auge des Fotografen am Sucher und den Einstellungen, die er vornimmt an seinem Apparat, zweitens aus der Situation, in der er fotografiert, drittens aus dem, was er anblickt beim Schuss, und viertens aus dem, was er dabei "denkt." Von all diesem wird etwas auf dem Bild zu sehen sein.

Zum Auge: das Auge des Soldaten in Russland 1941 ff. verfügt über einen Fotoapparat. Erstaunlich viele dieser deutschen Soldaten in Russland trugen so ein Fotogerät mit sich herum. Das unterscheidet sie von allen Soldaten aller früheren Kriege und ist sehr erstaunlich in mehrfacher Hinsicht. Man braucht zum Beispiel Filme. Die gab es nciht zu kaufen in russischen Läden und auch nicht zun rauben von der Zivilbevölkerung. Sie mussten entweder die langen Nachschubwege gehen aus der sogenannten Heimat, dann waren sie offiziell verteilte, oder aber mitgebracht werden von Heimat-Urlauben. Offensichtlich wurden sie *hergestellt*—damit sind sie ausgewiesen als "kriegswichtiges Material", denn sonst wären sie nicht hergestellt worden. Und der Soldat, der nicht eben wenig zu schleppen hat, schleppt sie (begeistert: *das* zeigen die Fotos) überall mit.

Zweitens: es ist nicht Urlaub, sondern Krieg. Die Fotos sind alle in Situationen entstanden, die mit militärischen Aktionen im Zusammenhang stehen. Wenn auch nicht immer ein Kommandierender in der Nähe gewesen sein muss, so findet doch jeder dieser Foto-Schüsse innerhalb des Gesamtkomplexes von Militärrecht statt, d.h. im Universum von Befehl unhd Gehorsam. Nun weiss jeder, der mit Militärdingen auch nur marginal zu tun hat(te), dass eines der obersten Gestze im Zusammenhangmit Militäranlagen oder militärischen Aktionen lautet: "Fotografieren strengstens verboten." Nähern Sie sich heute irgendeiner harmlosen Bundeswehranlage, und sei es nur einem Sendemasts; da finden Sie das Schild mit genau dieser Aufschrift am Maschendrahtzaun.

Allgemein geht die Mediengeschichtsschreibung davon aus, dass Vietnam der erste Krieg war, in dem das Fotografieren sozusagen freigegeben war. Dies muss korrigiert werden: die deutschen Soldaten im Russland-feldzug sind ganz offensichtlich diejenigen, denen dies erstmals eingeräumt wurde. Vor allem anderen, was sie sonst noch zeigen, zeigen die Fotos: die Soldaten *durften* das. Sie durften hier —ganz entgegen aller sonst geltenden Geheimhaltung im militärischen Komplex—ihre Linsen auf alles richten, was da an östlichem (=minderwertigem) Leben vor ihren Kameras durch ihr Blickfeld kreuchte.

Nun ist, drittens, interessant, was sie aufnahmen. Sie nahmen nicht die malerischen oder auch elenden Gehöfte auf und den Blick in die exotischen *Erthnien*, wie das sonst Toursiten tun. Sie nahmen überwiegend, *Morde auf. Sie fotografierten genau das*, was sonst zu fotografieren absolut verboten war. Sie posieren sogar für die richtige fotografische Erfassung ihres Tuns durch ihren Mit-Menschen; durch ihren Mit-Herrenmenschen, muss man sagen. Das zeigen *zweifelsfrei* viele der ausgestellten Bilder. Sie zeigen, dass die Täter wie die Fotografen mit offizieller *Erlaubnis* handeln, und sie zeigen ebenso, dass sie gerade das sonst absolut *Verbotene* aufnehmen.

Die Soldaten handeln damit genau in dem Zusatnd, den ich als den *Zentralkitt*, im Innern aller Männerbünde beschrieben habe: in der offenen, erlaubten Übertretung ins Kriminelle, die nur deshalb nicht als "kriminell" erscheint im Moment der Übertretung, weil sie von den offiziellen Autoritäten gedeckt oder sogar gewünscht ist. Der Mord wird nicht als "Mord" wahrgenommen, weil er genehmigt ist, er kann als Urlaubsfoto nach Hause gehen oder neben die Familienbilder ins Portemonnaie geraten, weil er das eigenen Leben im Zustand krimineller paradiesischer Freiheit zeigt, das sich dabei gefällt, die Erde von *Ungeziefer* zu befreien. "Strafe?" keine zu erwarten. Wir werden gesiegt haben.

Dieses Bewusstsein, diesen *Blick* zeigen Fotos der fotografierenden Soladten in Russland, in Polen oder auf dem "Balkan" in aller Klarheit; in aller *unschuldigen* Klarheit. Die ganze Rede von der behaupteten *Schuldlosigkeit* des deutschen Soldaten im Osten, wie sie nach dem Ende des Krieges in den westdeutschen Rechtfertigungsreden zur Wehrmacht auftauchte, ist auf diesen Fotos vor- und abgebildet. Dies ist der Schock, den die Fotos bei den Gegnern der *Wehrmachtausstellung* auslöste; deshalb blieben sie der Ausstellung ja auch meist fern, weil der *Evidenz* dieses *Blicks* in der Ausstellung selber nicht zu entkommen war und ist. (...) Die Diskussion um den "Wahrheitsgehalt" der Bilder der Wehrmachtausstellung ist also eine Diskussion um den Zustand der deutschen Filmkritik, ein Beleg mehr, auf welch elendem Stand die Zivilationstechnik des Sehens sich in Deutschland immer noch befindet. (...)

Bilder

Nicht von ungefähr war *Männerphantasien* das erste Buch in Deutschland, das *Bilder* vom Faschismus (aber nicht *nur* vom Faschismus) so in den Text zu montieren suchte, dass sie nicht bloss als Illustrationen zu laufenden Textteilen "lesbar" würden, sondern als Bilder, auf denen *Blicke* gespeichert sind; historische Blicke, aktuelle Blicke, Blicke von Malern, von Fotografen, von Plakatmachern, von Propagandisten, von Kinomachern, von Nazis, von Nicht-Nazis. Die Bilder bilden damit einen eigenen "Text."

Dominique ZIMMERMANN

Männliche Schwangerschaftsphantasien

Die anerzogene, geschlechtsspezifische Prägung beeinflusst den Umgang mit männlichen Schwangerschaftsphantasien massgebend. Damit auch Männer Schwangerschaftsphantasien hegen können, ist nicht zwingend eine Identifikation mit dem Frausein notwendig, zumal unsere Phantasien und die geschlechtliche Identität nicht biologisch begründet sein müssen. Männliche Schwangerschaftsphantasien können als interessanten Hinweis darauf interpretiert werden, dass sich die herkömmlichen Geschlechterrollen nicht zuletzt im Rahmen von geschlechterübergreifenden Phantasien auflösen können, indem sie sich auch unseren Körperzonen einschreiben und wesentlich zu einer in diesem Sinne multisexuellen Identitätskonstruktion beitragen.

Die Thematik der männlichen Schwangerschaftsphantasien bestimmte bereits meine Magisterarbeit, welche die Zusammenhänge und Parallelen der Kind- und Kopfgeburt in verschiedenen Philosophiekonzepten analysierte. Wiederholt stiess ich auf die Schwierigkeit, die beiden Termini „männlich" und „weiblich" reflektiert zu verwenden. Letztlich bestand die Hauptsache meiner Untersuchung in der Dekonstruktion der herkömmlichen Annahmen, was die differenten Konstruktionen der beiden Geschlechter aufgrund biologischer Unterschiede betrifft.

Herkömmlicherweise war die Frau auf ihre Körperlichkeit reduziert, während man dem Mann in erster Linie rationale Fähigkeiten zusprach. Die Schwangerschaft wurde ebenso wie das Phantasieren mit Körperlichkeit in Verbindung gebracht und als das Geschäft der Frauen und Kinder von den meist männlichen Denkern nur am Rande erwähnt. Die Frau wurde in der Reduktion auf ihren Körper generell als etwas Unheimliches abgewertet und die vom Uterus verursachten Leiden als hysterische ebenfalls weiblich spezifiziert. So entsteht beispielsweise bei Platons *Timaios* die Frau aus Menschen, die für ein feiges und unrechtes Leben in der nächsten Inkarnation strafweise mit dem Uterus versehen wurden, Lebewesen, mit der innewohnenden Begierde, Kinder zu gebären. Weiter galt bei Aristoteles nur der Mann als zeugungsfähig, da die Frau infolge eines Wärmemangels die Nahrung nicht zur Vollendung des Samens verarbeiten konnte: die Frau war quasi ein impotenter Mann. Im christlichen Kontext hatte das Gebären wiederum Sühnecharakter, was sich in verschiedenen Diskursen bis heute zeigt: sobald der Geburtsschmerz mit Hilfe von Chloroform gelindert werden konnte, leisteten kirchliche Kreise Widerstand, da es als sündig galt, diesen gottgewollten Schmerz zu unterdrücken. (Fischer-Homberger: 1977, 163). Und doch ist es offensichtlich, dass sich durch die gesamte Mythologie und Philosophiegeschichte die Verknüpfung von Männlichkeit und Geburt zieht. Athene soll dem Haupt von Zeus entsprungen sein, Adam gebiert Eva aus seiner Rippe und die philosophisch konstruierten Gottheiten von Spinoza, Augustinus und Plotin gleichen sich selbst gebärenden, omnipotenten Helden. (Pieper: 1996, 6-7). Das sind geistige Erzeugnisse, die nur im Lichte eines patriarchalen Machtanspruchs nachvollzogen werden können. Auch im Bereich der konkreten Schwangerschaft und Geburt versuchten Männer wiederholt, die medizinische Kontrolle zu behalten. Auf den Aspekt einer männlichen Aneignung und Transzendenz der Gebärfähigkeit, geht Luce Irigaray in *Speculum. Spiegel des andern Geschlechts* ein. (Irigaray: 1980, 303 ff.) Ihre Analyse verdeutlicht, dass der klassischen Philosophie ein Verdrängungsprozess eingeschrieben ist, um dem weiblichen Körper und somit der eigenen Geburtlichkeit zu entgehen. Diese Verschränkung von Machtansprüchen, Aneignung und Verdrängung mag zur Distanzierung der Männer von einer reflexiven Identifikation mit der Schwangerschaft beigetragen haben. Seit dem Aufkommen der Psychoanalyse und einem bewussteren Umgang mit den Geschlechterkonstruktionen wird allmählich anerkannt, dass alle Menschen, auch männliche Philosophen, sexuelle Wesen mit Phantasien und einem Körper sind. Doch auch hier schreiben sich die herkömmlichen Geschlechtsstereotypen erneut ein, was ich an Freuds Studien näher erläutern werde, während das dekonstruktive Vorgehen von Luce Irigaray auf eine weitere Entzifferung dieser Einschreibungen abzielt. Wilhelm Schmid macht in seinem Buch *Die Geburt der Philosophie im Garten der Lüste* in diesem Kontext einen interessanten Hinweis, wenn er sagt: Es reicht nicht aus, zu einer 'Haltung' zu kommen: Man muss sie auch verlieren können. Es genügt nicht, wegzukommen vom Trugbild einer 'Sexualität', die sich erschöpft in fleischloser Leidenschaft - man muss zurückkommen zu jener Sexualität, die grundlegend 'ein ins Spielbringen der eigenen Identität ist und ein Versuch, sie zu verlieren (bis hin zur Tatsache, Kinder zu machen).' (Schmid: 1987, 109) Dieses Zitat lese ich so, dass wir eben mit allem, das wir tun und auch unterlassen, unsere Identität konstruieren. Ob und wie wir Kinder haben, ist eine Frage, die sich jedes zeugungsfähige Subjekt stellen muss. Wenn also auch denkende, männliche Subjekte zulassen dürfen, dass sie nicht völlig abgenabelt sind von konkreten reproduktiven Tatsachen, können auch sie eine Identität bilden, deren Basis sich auf der herkömmlich als „männlich" *und* „weiblich" bezeichneten Identifikation gründet. Mein Anliegen besteht nun nicht darin, die biologischen Differenzen zu nivellieren oder hormonelle Einflüsse während der Schwangerschaft auf die beiden Geschlechter hin zu untersuchen. Interessanter scheint mir die Tatsache, dass ein Mann auch ohne biologische Fähigkeit, schwanger zu werden, durchaus mental und auch körperlich an einer realen oder bloss vorgestellten Schwangerschaft partizipieren kann. Dies möchte ich als Stütze meiner These benutzen, nämlich, dass mit Hilfe der Phantasie die angeblichen Grenzen des soziokulturellen und biologischen Geschlechts sowie die vorhandene Konstruktion eines Ichs überschritten werden können. Dass die Schwangerschaft mental unabhängig vom biologischen Geschlecht stark beeinflusst wird, verdeutlicht sich am Beispiel von Frauen, die scheinschwanger gehen, oder auch solchen, die tatsächlich schwanger sind, aber aufgrund eines immensen Verdrängungsprozesses bis kurz vor der Geburt kein Bewusstsein hiervon haben. In dieser Hinsicht kann man folglich von einer Differenzierung der Geschlechter absehen.

Geschlechtsspezifische Verknüpfungen lassen sich weiter dekonstruieren, wenn man beachtet, dass sich eine Person unabhängig von ihrer Biologie in Anführungszeichen „männlich" oder „weiblich" fühlen kann. Dass sich die Wahrnehmung von biologischen Gegebenheiten innerhalb einer kulterell geprägten Konstruktion des Geschlechts abspielt, führt Judith Butler in *Das Unbehagen der Geschlechter* detailliert aus. (Butler: 1991, 37-49). Dem würde ich nun anfügen, dass dies ebenfalls für die Entstehung unserer Gedanken im Sinne von Gefühlen und Phantasien zutrifft. Im Extremfall kann sich ein Unbehagen mit diesen Identitätsvorgaben in Form von transsexuellen Bestrebungen zeigen, bis hin zum Wunsch nach einer operativen Geschlechtsumwandlung, während Transvestiten mehr spielerisch in andersgeschlechtlicher äusserer Aufmachung vorübergehend in die Rolle des anderen Geschlechts schlüpfen. Die Phantasie, gerade in einem anderen Geschlecht zu sein, als jenem, das einem biologisch und gesellschaftlich zugefallen ist, wird jede Person kennen, nicht zuletzt als implizite Kehrseite des gesellschaftlich zuerkannten Geschlechts. Kommt man biologisch betrachtet als Mann zur Welt, wird man als Mann sozialisiert, beeinflusst von einer langen Geschichte, was dieses Mannsein alles beinhaltet. Dasselbe gilt auch für Frauen, nur findet dort eine andere Konstruktion mit einem anderen geschichtlichen Background statt. Sicher wäre es verfehlt zu sagen, dass die Biologie keine Rolle spielt, aber diese Differenz hilft uns nicht, das grosse Mysterium aufzulösen, was es letztlich bedeutet, ein Mann oder eine Frau zu sein. Wenn es bei Transsexuellen und Transvestiten in erster Linie um den Wunsch geht, die Spiele, Gewohnheiten und teilweise auch die Sexualität des anderen Geschlechts ausleben zu dürfen, sind Schwangerschaftsphantasien sicher etwas Subtileres, da sie sich in einem psychischen Bereich abspielen, der sich nicht unbedingt äusserlich manifestieren muss.

Nun gibt es verschiedene Möglichkeiten, weshalb ein Mann überhaupt Schwangerschaftsphantasien entwickeln kann. Im folgenden werde ich insbesondere auf den in den Statistiken mit Vorliebe behandelten Fall von männlichen Schwangerschaftsphantasien eingehen, bei welchen Männer — meist heterosexuelle Familienväter — während der Schwangerschaft ähnliche Symptome wie eine werdende Mutter entwickeln. Generell sollen Väter hierbei eine intensivere geistig-seelische Besinnungsphase erleben, während Mütter doch mehr mit den körperlichen Veränderungen konfrontiert und beschäftigt sind. Ähnlich wie bei schwangeren Frauen kann es auch bei werdenden Vätern zu Übelkeit, übermässigen Essgelüsten und Stimmungsschwankungen kommen. Im sexuellen Bereich scheint es die Phantasie der Männer zu irritieren, dass plötzlich auch noch eine Drittperson zugegen ist, bis hin zu Ängsten, beim Geschlechtsverkehr das Ungeborene zu verletzen, oder selbst einen Schaden davonzutragen. Psychoanalytisch wird diese Auslegung ergänzt durch die Vermutung, dass Partner während der Schwangerschaft die Tendenz haben, ihre Frau mit ihrer Mutter zu identifizieren, sodass die Sexualität von Inzestängsten beeinflusst wird. Auch ohne Betonung einer ödipalen Konstellation, lässt sich mit Sicherheit sagen, dass diese neun Monate ein kreatives Feld für Phantasien sind, zumal klar ist, dass etwas anders sein wird, aber es ist unklar was und ebenso ungewiss, wie dieses Neue, das in die Welt kommt, sein wird. Oft werden diese Symptome bei Männern gesellschaftlich weniger ernst genommen, mit der Begründung, dass sie ja nicht in biologischem Sinne schwanger sind, während von einer schwangeren Frau beinahe erwartet wird, dass sie mit Gefühlsschwankungen und besonderen Essgelüsten zu rechnen habe. Ebenfalls als Produkt von geschlechtsorientierten Phantasien ist die Tatsache zu betrachten, dass Väter, je nachdem ob sie Vater einer Tochter oder Vater eines Sohnes werden, nach der Geburt bei Töchtern kürzer im Kreissaal bleiben und weniger Bemerkungen machen, als bei Söhnen. Bei Söhnen scheinen Väter wiederum mit ihren Ängsten konfrontiert zu werden, sie könnten selber homosexuell sein oder ihre Söhne es werden, sodass sie zögern, diese zu wickeln, zu streicheln und zu küssen. (Mayer, Liebich: 1994, 147). Auch diese Statistik weist auf den Einfluss von spezifisch männlichen Phantasien hin, rsp. Phantasien, die sich innerhalb eines Diskurses abspielen, der geprägt ist von einer heterosexuellen Hegemonie, welche die herkömmliche Differenz der Geschlechter fortsetzt. Der in diesem Kontext nicht uninteressanten Verbindung von Homosexualität und Schwangerschaftsphantasien wurde insbesondere in psychoanalytischen Studien nachgegangen. Freud pathologisierte im Fall des „Wolfsmannes" die Schwangerschaftsphantasie als Wunsch nach dem Verzicht auf die Männlichkeit, um auf diese Weise die Liebe des Vaters zu gewinnen und ihm ein Kind schenken zu können. (Freud: 1994, 193). Freud ignoriert in dieser Deutung, dass eine Schwangerschaftsphantasie nicht zwingend Teil der weiblichen Identität sein muss, insofern wird seine Pathologisierung fragwürdig. Dass männliche Schwangerschaftsphantasien gesellschaftlich akzeptiert und in Ritualen konkret integriert sein können, vermag ein Vergleich mit anderen Kulturen zu verdeutlichen. (Zapperi: 1984, 137).

Generell zu behaupten, Männer litten unter Gebärneid, scheint ebenso zweifelhaft wie die Unterstellung eines generellen Penisneides auf Seite der Frauen. Vielmehr lese ich aus den geschlechterübergreifenden Phantasien, dass herkömmlich „männliche" und „weibliche" Anteile bei beiden Geschlechtern vorkommen und insofern von einer generellen, mehr oder weniger bewussten multisexuellen Veranlagung ausgegangen werden kann. Biologische Differenzen können nur interpretiert werden und dies geschieht stets in Bezug auf damit einhergehende Vor- und Nachteile innerhalb eines Machtgefüges. Männliche Schwangerschaftsphantasien weisen darauf hin, dass wir mit der Phantasie nicht nur in sexuellem Sinne, sondern weit umfänglicher, die eigenen Körperzonen überschreiten können, zumal wir unsere Identität nicht nur auf uns selbst gründen, sondern immer im Kontext unserer Handlungen, Beziehungen und psychischen Verfassungen. (Perko: 1993, 72). Hierzu gehört auch unser Verhältnis zur Schwangerschaft und zur Geburt, das, so möchte ich mit meinen Ausführungen abschliessend betonen, je nachdem, gerade als männlich oder weiblich bezeichnet werden kann.

Quellennachweise

Butler, Judith, *Das Unbehagen der Geschlechter*, Frankfurt am Main 1991.

Fischer-Homberger, Esther, *Geschichte der Medizin*, Berlin 1977.

Freud, Sigmund, *Zwei Kinderneurosen. Studienausgabe*, Frankfurt am Main 1969.

Irigaray, Luce, *Speculum. Spiegel des anderen Geschlechts*, Frankfurt am Main 1980.

Mayer, Christian, Liebich, Daniela, *Wenn Mann ein Kind bekommt. Was werdende Väter in der Schwangerschaft erleben*, Freiburg in Breisgau 1994.

Perko, Gudrun, *Aufschlüsse der Einbildungskraft. Auswirkungen und Wirkungsweisen der Phantasie*, Pfaffenweiler 1993.

Pieper, Annemarie, "Der kreis(s)ende Gott der Philosophen", in: *Basler Zeitung Magazin Nr. 7*, (1996) pp. 6-7.

Schmid, Wilhelm, *Die Geburt der Philosophie im Garten der Lüste. Michael Foucaults Archäologie des platonischen Eros*, Frankfurt am Main 1987.

Zapperi, Roberto, *Der schwangere Mann. Männer, Frauen und die Macht*, München 1984.

Britta HERRMANN / Walter ERHART

XY ungelöst: Männlichkeit als Performance

Spätestens seit Sigmund Freud zu Beginn des 20. Jahrhunderts das "Rätsel der Weiblichkeit" als lösenswerte Aufgabe in den Mittelpunkt des Interesses rückte, avancierte Männlichkeit im Gegenzug zu einer Größe, die scheinbar nur wenig Überraschungen zu bieten hatte. Sie präsentiert sich fortan als erforschter "Kontinent", den auch die Psychoanalyse als erstes entdeckt und vermessen hat (Rhode-Dachser: 1991). Zu Anfang des 21. Jahrhunderts sind die Seiten vermutlich vertauscht. Während wie einst im 18. und 19. Jahrhundert vornehmlich Frauen und Weiblichkeit im Fokus der Forschung (und nun vor allem im Fokus der Forscherinnen) stehen, scheint Männlichkeit heute umgekehrt zu jenem 'dunklen Kontinent' geworden zu sein, den Freud für die Weiblichkeit gleichsam reserviert hatte.

Ging Freud noch davon aus, daß Männlichkeit in der psychosexuellen Entwicklung beider Geschlechter als 'primär' anzusetzen ist und von Frauen zugunsten von Weiblichkeit explizit 'verdrängt' werden muß (z.B. Freud: 1981, Freud: 1991), so findet sich auch dieses Verhältnis mittlerweile revidiert: Sowohl in (natur-)wissenschaftlichen Beschreibungen (Badinter: 1993) als auch in soziologischen Bestandsaufnahmen (Tiger: 1999, Faludi: 1999) und in populärwissenschaftlichen Abhandlungen (Farrell: 1993, Horrocks: 1994) wird Männlichkeit als sekundär, als nachträgliche Deformation, als Problem behandelt und beschrieben. Mit den ungelösten Problemen eines vermeintlich 'ersten' Geschlechts (Frevert: 1991) aber, das auch in den Archiven und im Erkenntnisinteresse der *gender studies* stets auf die 'zweite' Position verwiesen blieb, sind eine Reihe offener Fragen verbunden. Deshalb entstehen neue (Er-)Forschungsprogramme: *men's studies, masculinity studies*.

"XY ungelöst": Von den Chromosomen bis zu der in Abrede gestellten Zukunft 'des' Mannes (der heute gängige Slogan "Die Zukunft ist weiblich" impliziert diesen Zukunftsverlust ebenso wie der einstige Ruf nach 'neuen Männern für das Land') stehen derzeit jedoch nicht allein männliche Gegebenheiten und Entitäten auf dem Prüfstand, sondern all jene Formen und Praktiken des performativen Handelns, in die sich die Kategorie des Geschlechts jenseits aller starren Geschlechterdichotomien mittlerweile verwandelt hat (vgl. Sedgwick: 1992, Parpart: 2000). Wurde Weiblichkeit bereits seit Jahrhunderten in die Nähe der Verstellungkunst, der Schauspielerei und Maskerade gerückt, so 'verstellt' gerade dies den Blick darauf, daß *performance* eine besonders (auch) für moderne und postmoderne Männlichkeit notwendige Geschlechter-Praxis bezeichnet. Im folgenden wird diese These kursorisch entfaltet, und dies führt anhand einer Reihe ganz unterschiedlicher Beispiele in verschiedene Bereiche der (Geschlechter-)Kultur: in die Theorie, in die Popkultur von Videoclips (Madonna, Prince) und Film, sowie in die deutsche Literatur des 20. Jahrhunderts (von der Neuen Sachlichkeit über Peter Weiss bis zur deutschen Gegenwartsliteratur).

1. Doing gender, doing masculinity

Wie so oft in Zeiten des politisch-gesellschaftlichen Umbruchs wird in der Alltagskultur neuerdings überall mit den Muskeln gespielt und eine 'starke' Männlichkeit inszeniert – sei es im Musikbereich, im Film oder in der neuen deutschen Literatur. Freilich ahnen wohl viele: Hier wird in der Tat 'gespielt' und 'inszeniert' – mit oder ohne ironische Brechung. Der Begriff der Inszenierung verweist nicht allein darauf, daß Männlichkeit sozial konstruiert ist und sich etwa in Form von "Männerphantasien" (Theweleit: 1980) oder als *machismo* (Cornwall/Lindisfarne: 1994, 12-18) zeigt – all dies dürfte inzwischen zu den Gemeinplätzen der *gender studies* und der Männlichkeitsforschung gehören (Bußmann/Hof: 1995). Wie 'Performativität' und *performance* zielt die 'Inszenierung' von geschlechtsspezifischen Praktiken auf eine grundlegende Doppelung von Geschlechter-*enactment* und Geschlechter-*embodiment*: Praktiken dessen, was im Englischen *doing gender* heißt und sich im Deutschen vielleicht nur unvollkommen übersetzen ließe mit "als Geschlecht auftreten oder handeln".

Doing gender – auch dies dürfte mittlerweile Konsens der Geschlechterforschung sein – stellt kein beliebiges und im männlichen Fall lustvoll und mächtig ausgeübtes Rollenspiel dar, auch keine bewußte oder willkürliche Wahl angesichts eines (postmodernen) Angebotes im 'Supermarkt der Geschlechtsidentitäten' (Hirschauer: 1993b, 56). Von den äußeren Manifestationen der Männlichkeit, ihren Zeichen, Ritualen, Kommunikationen und Gemeinschaftsformen, hat die historische Männlichkeitsforschung daher den Blick seit kurzem auf die eher verborgenen und 'inneren' Aspekte dieses männlichen Handelns gelenkt[21]: Die symbolische Geschlechterordnung bringt neben Machtverhältnissen immer auch "*gelebte* Denk-, Gefühls- und Körperpraxen" (Maihofer: 1994, 259) hervor, die sich mittels einer Liste abrufbereiter männlicher Stereotypen (vgl. Mosse: 1996) kaum analysieren oder gar entschlüsseln lassen dürften. In der Somatisierung bestimmter kultureller Geschlechternormierungen bildet sich vielmehr jener komplizierte Komplex heraus, den Pierre Bourdieu 'Habitus' genannt hat, gleichsam ein zweiter Körper, der den ersten überlagert, ein "*corps socialement différencié* du genre opposé" (Bourdieu: 1998, 29).[22]

Rein biologisch unterscheidet sich der Männerkörper vom Frauenkörper bis in den Chromosomensatz hinein nur geringfügig. Das Geschlecht wäre daher eher als Variation denn als Opposition zu erfassen (vgl. Fausto-Sterling: 2000). Auch der Körper jedoch ist – seit die Geschlechterforschung in die Schule von Judith Butler

---

[21] Überblicke über dementsprechende Forschungsergebnisse finden sich in den Sammelbänden von Brod/Kaufman: 1994, Kühne: 1996, Erhart/Herrmann: 1997, Dinges: 1998. Pointiert dazu: Filene: 1987, Tosh: 1998, Lengwiler: 1998. Zu einer Geschichte der (amerikanischen) Männlichkeit vgl. Rotundo: 1993, Kimmel: 1996.

[22] Zur möglichen Produktivität der Bourdieuschen Theorie für die *gender studies* vgl. auch Krais: 1993; Meuser: 1994.

gegangen ist – performativ hervorgebracht, d.h. durch Sprache und kulturelle Praxis gesetzt, gedeutet und fortlaufend produziert (Butler: 1991). Denn wie groß oder klein der biologische Unterschied der Geschlechtskörper auch immer sein mag: Soziale Praktiken bestehen jedenfalls nicht darin, solche Körper als vorgängige 'natürliche' Größen bloß zu formen, in kulturelle Konstrukte zu überführen und ihnen dann eine (nur eine) geschlechtliche Identität zuzuordnen. Statt die Opposition von 'Natur' und 'Kultur', *sex* und *gender* lediglich zu verschieben, zu verkleinern oder auf Restgrößen zu verlagern, kommt es vielmehr darauf an, jenseits der Alternative von ewiger Fortdauer und erhofftem Ende der Geschlechterdifferenz das 'Unentschiedene' dieser Grenzziehung festzuhalten und das gleichfalls unentschiedene Zusammenspiel physischer, somatischer und psychischer Aspekte zu beobachten, also die Artikulation *von* Geschlechterdifferenzen zu thematisieren statt das Reden *über* die Differenz fortzuführen (Butler: 1997). An die Seite des *embodiment* von Geschlecht tritt somit das *enactment* eines Körpers und einer Geschlechtsidentität. Im Falle der Männlichkeit dürfte dies zumindest ebenso vielfältig und doppelbödig sein, wie es die kulturhistorisch durchleuchtete und jüngst auch poststrukturalistisch nobilitierte Litanei über das 'Rätsel' und die 'Maskerade' der Weiblichkeit stets vorgeführt haben (Vinken: 1992, Weisberg: 1994).

Als männlich aufzutreten (*acting male* [23]) und wie ein Mann zu handeln (*act like a man*) verweist auf eine performative Strategie, die sowohl auf den Sexus (*male*) als auch auf das Genus zielt. Wer zu einem bestimmten Zeitpunkt in einer bestimmten Kultur als ein bestimmtes Geschlecht 'durchgeht', beispielsweise als Mann, der muß weder notwendigerweise den Körper eines Mannes haben (und dazu gehört längst mehr als jenes sogenannte primäre Geschlechtsmerkmal, das in der Psychoanalyse zugleich als Symbol der Ganzheit fungiert), noch muß dieser Körper von Geburt an als männlich bezeichnet oder sozialisiert worden sein – zahlreiche Untersuchungen über Transsexuelle und Transvestiten haben dies gezeigt (Lindemann: 1993a, Hirschauer: 1993a, Young: 1999). Dennoch – oder eben deswegen – wird gerade der moderne (postmoderne?) Männerkörper neuerdings als ein männlicher Körper permanent inszeniert, und zwar mit Techniken, die für den 'medikalisierten' Frauenkörper (Honegger: 1983) längst untersucht sind: Körperdisziplin (Bodybuilding und Diät), kosmetische Chirurgie ('Waschbrettbauch'), das Spiel und die Maskerade von Kleidung und Entkleidung (Jeans und nackter Oberkörper), Hautschmuck (Tatoos und Goldkettchen), ostentative Verweise auf das dem Blick gerade noch entzogene Geschlechtsorgan, Demonstration sexueller Potenz, aber auch sexueller Verfügbarkeit (vgl. Bordo: 1999). *Doing sex* ist ein nicht zu unterschätzender Teil des *doing gender*, besonders im Hinblick auf Männlichkeit.

Um tatsächlich als männlicher Mann wahrgenommen zu werden, muß der biologische Körper in einen gleichsam indexikalischen Ausdruck des Geschlechtsunterschiedes verwandelt werden. Dies aber entspricht eben nur zum Teil

---

[23] So lautet nicht zufällig auch der Titels eines Buches über Männlichkeit im Film: *Acting Male. Masculinities in the Films of James Stewart, Jack Nicholson and Clint Eastwood* (Bingham: 1994).

dem, was Bourdieu als naturalisierte Somatisierung geschlecht-licher Herrschaftsverhältnisse (Bourdieu: 1997, 166ff.), Butler als Sedimentierung von Geschlechternormen (Butler: 1991, 206) und Gesa Lindemann als soziale Strukturiertheit passiver Leiberfahrungen (Lindemann: 1993b, 50) bestimmt haben. Vielmehr ist diese Indexika-lisierung des Körpers auch Teil einer *aktiven* Darstellung, die durch Regeln und Normen geleitet ist.

Das entsprechende Regelwissen mag einerseits zwar durch Bezeichnungs-praktiken inkorporiert sein, andererseits wird es aber mimetisch angeeignet und vorgeführt. Zwischen Präsentation und Repräsentation gibt es dabei immer wieder Möglichkeiten der Verschiebung, die auf die Konstruiertheit des Geschlechts oder die Geschlechtermaskerade verweisen können. Ob dies tatsächlich und zwangsläufig die unterstellte Subversion nach sich zieht, ist allerdings zunehmend fraglich.[24] Vielmehr muß man wohl davon ausgehen, daß Geschlechterakte selbst "stilbildende Aktivitäten" sind (Hirschauer: 1993b, 59): Der prozessuale Charakter dient zum einen dazu, die Geschlechterdichotomien und die Geschlechtsidentitäten jeweils den historischen, kulturellen und sozialen Gegebenheiten anzupassen[25]; zum anderen bedeuten Formen der Durchkreuzung, Transgression und Neupositionierung der binären Geschlechteranordnung eben nicht eine Aufhebung der Dichotomie, sondern eine "Denknotwendigkeit auf ihrer Basis" (Hirschauer: 1993b, 60) – und zuweilen sogar deren Fortschreibung bis ins Klischee.

Gilt Weiblichkeit schon seit längerem als das 'verstellte' Geschlecht, als Maskerade und Produkt männlicher Phantasien, so werden neuerdings die Strategien männlicher Geschlechtskonstruktion offen zur Schau getragen. Wie jede Form der Repräsentation zielt auch die der Männlichkeit überdeutlich auf zwei Momente: auf Vergegenwärtigung eines kulturell geprägten phantasmatischen Modells sowie auf dessen individuelle Darstellung und Nachahmung (Mimesis). Die verfehlte oder gelungene mimetische Aneignung bedient sich dabei verschiedener Strategien, aber nur im Falle des Mißlingens werden sie meist auch offenbar. Wenn Männlichkeit zur Zeit nicht zuletzt in der Unterhaltungsindustrie verstärkt als eine solch mißlingende Form der Mimesis vorgeführt wird – als Parodie, als Travestie oder als decouvrierte Mimikry –, so mag dies einerseits darauf hinweisen, daß die Repräsentation von Männlichkeit nur (noch) bedingt funktioniert, daß aber genau diese Reibung zwischen geschlechtlicher Erwartungshaltung und ihrer Ent-täuschung sowohl Frauen als auch Männern ein gewisses Vergnügen bereitet – ein ökonomisch durchaus einträgliches. Andererseits könnte das Vergnügen gar nicht so subversiv angelegt sein und vielmehr daher rühren, daß gesellschaftlich zur Zeit (noch) verworfene Formen von

---

[24] Zur Relativierung des subversiven Potential von *drag* und Transvestismus s. bereits Butler: 1993. Zu Kritik und Diskussion vgl. etwa Landweer: 1993, Landweer: 1994 und Hark: 1998.

[25] *Acting male* wird z.B. vom biologischen Mann je nach Alter, physischer Konstitution, sozialem Rang, Kulturation usw. verschieden aussehen, wird – unabhängig von der sexuellen Orientierung – innerhalb einer Männergruppe anders ausfallen als innerhalb einer Frauengruppe usw.

Männlichkeit auf diese Weise als Spektakel präsentiert und mit Genuß (wieder) konsumiert werden können – dies ebenfalls von Frauen *und* Männern. Offenbar befriedigt die Erkenntnis (und die Wiederholung) der Geschlechtskonstruktion ein gesellschaftliches Bedürfnis. Analog zur Weiblichkeit (Riviere 1994) erweist sich nun plötzlich Männlichkeit als Maskerade, als das In-Szene-Setzen eines maskulinen Originals, das es nicht gibt und das performativ immer wieder neu erfunden werden muß (vgl. zu diesem Thema auch Fabricius: 1999). In Anlehnung an Simone de Beauvoirs Diktum, man werde als Frau nicht geboren, man werde dazu gemacht, wird heute oft davon gesprochen, daß auch (und gerade) Mann-Sein ebenfalls kein mit der Geburt erworbener Zustand ist, sondern einen fortlaufend produzierten Geschlechtscharakter darstellt (Frevert 1996). Analog dazu mag jedoch ein weiterer – und späterer – Merksatz geschlechtertheoretischer Weiblichkeitsforschung für das 'andere' Geschlecht zutreffen, und so ließe sich mit Jacques Lacan formulieren: *L'homme n'existe pas*. Während der Feminismus jedoch längst gezeigt hat, daß die Projektion des weiblichen 'Anderen' (der unvollkommenen Kopie) sich an die Stelle des 'Eigenen' (des Originals) setzt, scheint das Verhältnis in Bezug auf die neue Männlichkeit komplizierter zu sein (falls dies für Weiblichkeit nicht genauso gilt, wofür u.a. Chantal Mouffe plädiert, Mouffe: 2000). Wem ist diese Männlichkeit das 'Andere' und wo ist es angesiedelt? Die kulturellen Geschlechter-positionen sind ja nicht invertiert, Weiblichkeit und Männlichkeit haben nicht den Platz gewechselt. Dagegen liegt die Vermutung mehr als nahe, daß sich – als feministische Errungenschaft – das vermeintlich 'Andere' nicht mehr so ohne weiteres ins Weibliche ausgrenzen läßt, daß gleichsam eine Geschlechtsremigration[26] stattfindet, bei der männliche Maskeraden nicht nur zuweilen entlarvt, sondern auch neu besetzt werden können – vom biologischen Geschlecht 'Frau' ebenso wie vom biologischen 'Mann'.

2. *Mimesis und Männlichkeit*

Beschreibt der auch im Titel dieses Bandes benannte Plural in "Männlichkeiten" nur ein Geschehen der Oberfläche? Zeigen sich lediglich historisch und sozial differenzierte Ausformungen dessen, was stets als geschlechtliche Rollenverteilung wahrgenommen wurde, oder bedeutet dieser Plural vielmehr, daß es *die* Männlichkeit nicht gibt, daß auch das männliche Geschlecht und seine Identität nicht 'eins' ist (nach Irigaray: 1979)?

Von der Einheit und dem gemeinsamen Ursprung der Männlichkeit mußten wir bisher jedenfalls – mit Klaus Theweleit – ausgehen. Psychisch, psychoanalytisch und sozialpsychologisch entstünde Männlichkeit demzufolge nach einem stets gleichen

---

[26] In Anlehnung an Stefan Hirschauer, der den Begriff "Geschlechtsmigration" vor allem auf Frauen bezieht, welche die Position ihres sozialen Geschlechts verlassen, um männliche Positionen einzunehmen – eine Geschlechterwanderung, die aufgrund der asymmetrischen Geschlechterhierarchie kaum je die umgekehrte Zielrichtung verfolgt (Hirschauer: 1993b; 63f.).

und nur geringfügig variierten Drehbuch, einem monotonen und gewaltsamen Prozeß, in dem fließende Körper in mehr oder weniger identische Körperpanzer verwandelt werden (Theweleit 1980). Schenken wir den uns vertrauten "Männerphantasien" Glauben, dann befindet sich Männlichkeit tatsächlich in einer schon lang andauernden Krise, in der Geschichte einer zähen Endlosschleife von aufbrechenden Körperpanzern und heillosen Re-Maskulinisierungen (vgl. Theweleit 1995, 40-70).

Richten wir den Blick hingegen auf gegenwärtige Modelle des *enactment* und der *performance* – nicht als Oberfläche, sondern als Realisierung und Materialisierung von Geschlecht und Geschlechternormen – dann sehen wir eine andere Form der Endlosschleife: eine permanente Nachahmung und Mimikry von Männlichkeitszeichen.[27] Wenn Männlichkeit beginnt, sich zu artikulieren und zu agieren – in der Kindheit, im Kopieren von Leinwandhelden und Rockmusikern, im ständigen Bemühen, ein Mann zu sein und vor allem zu bleiben –, dann zeigt sich das 'Projekt Männlichkeit' (wie Geschlechtswerdung überhaupt) als identifikatorisches Begehren, das sich der Nachahmung, der Maskerade und des Schauspiels bedient.

Heißt Männlichkeit imitieren immer: einen Körperpanzer ausbilden? Oder bedeutet eine solche psychosexuelle Fixierung nicht gerade: den Prozeß der identifizierenden Wiederholung einstellen? Der Begriff der Mimikry spielt seit geraumer Zeit eine große Rolle im *postcolonial discourse*: Er bezeichnet eine Nachahmung ohne Original, ein 'Uneigentliches' ohne 'Eigentliches', eine zweite und dritte Natur ohne Ursprung – zugleich eine Vervielfältigung des Kopierten, eine Demontage der Einheit (Taussig: 1993, Bhabha: 1994). Nachahmung ist eine der entscheidenden Praktiken im Selbstentwurf, im Spiel und im Kampf der Geschlechter – mit jeweils unterschiedlichen Funktionen. In der Imitation werden Weiblichkeit und Männlichkeit performativ, aber auch produktiv, denn jeder Epigone produziert eine Differenz zwischen Original und Kopie – "a difference that is almost the same, but not quite" (Bhabha 1994, 86).

Deshalb ist es heute nicht nur möglich, mit Eve K. Sedgwick (Sedgwick: 1997) und Judith Halberstam von einer *Female Masculinity* (Halberstam: 1998) zu sprechen, sondern notwendig, in Analogie dazu gleichsam 'Male Masculinities' zu denken: nachgeahmte und gerade dadurch 'uneigentlich' gewordene Männlichkeiten, "almost the same, but not quite". Längst ist die Performativität von Geschlecht, von beiden Geschlechtern, ein Bestandteil des kulturellen, zumindest aber des akademischen Allgemeinwissens geworden. In Anlehnung an Austins Theorie der Sprechakte (Austin: 1972) scheint der illokutionäre und performative Charakter von Geschlecht theoretisch längst hinreichend begründet und untermauert worden zu sein. Doch was bereits beantwortet scheint – "How to do things with gender" (Austin: 1972) – bleibt als Fragestellung bestehen. *Wie* nämlich dieses Handeln aussieht und *was* im einzelnen dabei (re)präsentiert wird, wie also Performativität in *performance* überführt

---

[27] Der Begriff der 'Mimesis' ist in den Überlegungen zu Geschlecht und Performativität derzeit unterbestimmt, dürfte aber sehr hilfreich sein: vgl. Goltermann 1998.

wird[28]: Dies ist – neben anderem – das eigentliche Feld von *masculinity studies*, die sich nicht damit begnügen wollen, die Konstruiertheit des männlichen Geschlechts nur zu behaupten und die Zeichen einer äußerlich 'starken' und 'mächtigen' Männlichkeit bloß vorzuführen oder zu kritisieren (Easthope: 1992, Berger/Wallis/Watson: 1995).

Wenn sich geschlechtliche Identität (aber nicht nur geschlechtliche) am Schnittpunkt von Kollektivität und Individualität sowie der Inkorporation sozialer Praxis als Körper-*performance* entwickelt, dann könnte man die an demselben Schnittpunkt angesiedelte Populärmusik als eine dafür besonders bereitgestellte Praxis bezeichnen. Der Rockkritiker und Soziologe Simon Frith bezeichnet in diesem Sinn Musik sogar als eine Metapher für Identität, weil sowohl Musik als auch das Selbst sich als besondere Organisationsformen "sozialer, physischer und materieller Kräfte" denken lassen (Frith: 1999, 152). Kein Wunder also, daß seit fast fünfzig Jahren beinahe nirgendwo das Geschlecht so deutlich verhandelt und (heterosexuelle) Männlichkeit so offensichtlich in Szene gesetzt wird wie auf den Bühnen der Rockmusik (Frith: 1992, 181f. Bechdolf: 1997). Und nirgendwo werden auch die Strategien männlicher Maskerade und *performance* sichtbarer zitiert (vgl. Pfeil: 1995).

Nicht zuletzt wegen der vielfach beobachteten filmischen und semiotischen Umsetzung gegenwärtiger Theorien zur Performativität von Geschlecht hat sich die amerikanische Rocksängerin und *performance*-Künstlerin Madonna einen Ruf auch unter *gender*-Theoretikerinnen erworben (vgl. Schwichtenberg: 1993). Madonnas *shows* und Videofilme setzen nicht allein die Maskeraden von Weiblichkeit in Szene und präsentieren sie – wie im Falle der Fotoserien von Cindy Sherman – als Versatzstücke, Arrangements und Dekonstruktionen weiblicher Geschlechterzeichen; sie vertauschen zugleich die binären Geschlechter-Codes, arrangieren sie neu und machen sich nicht selten ununterscheidbar. In ihrer Bühnenshow zu *Express Yourself*[29] zitiert Madonna zunächst Fritz Langs *Metropolis*: Marlene-Dietrich-Hosen und Monokel verweisen auf die zwanziger und dreißiger Jahre, das industriale Design der Bühne und die als Arbeiter verkleideten männlichen Tänzer imitieren das *setting* und Personal des Films (vgl. Morton: 1993).

Madonnas *performance* zitiert und inszeniert die kulturellen Geschlechteroppositionen zunächst mit einer Choreographie der bloßen Inversion: im räumlichen Arrangement von Frauen (oben) und Männern (unten), Individuen (Frauen) und Masse (Männer)[30] sowie in der Verteilung der Kräfteverhältnisse. Zur Verszeile "You need a big strong hand to lift you to the higher ground" zieht Madonnas *persona* auf der Bühne einen der muskulösen Tänzer 'zu sich' hoch. Über

---

[28] Zur gegenwärtigen Bedeutung von *performance* in der Kunst und auf dem Theater vgl. Fischer-Lichte 2000.

[29] Ein Mitschnitt dieser Bühnenshow aus Madonnas Tournee von 1992 ist im Konzertfilm *Truth or Dare* zu sehen, in Deutschland auch bekannt unter dem brillant übersetzten Titel *In bed with Madonna*.

[30] Zur semiotischen Verknüpfung von Weiblichkeit und 'Masse' in der Moderne vgl. Huyssen: 1986.

diese Verkehrung der beiden Geschlechter hinaus setzt Madonna den eigenen Körper als Ausstellungs-fläche einer "semiotischen Collage" ein (Morton: 1993, 214), die Zeichen der Männlichkeit und der Weiblichkeit ineinander blendet: (Männer?-)Anzug in Kombination mit Marlene-Dietrich-Hose, betont sichtbares *Bustier*, Griff in den Schritt (zugleich wohl ein Michael Jackson-Zitat),[31] Entblößung der bustierbetonten Brust als geschlechtlich zweideutige Aktion (Modeschau à la Gaultier und Zur-Schau-Stellung eines muskulösen Frauenkörpers), Einsatz eines Monokels als Ausdruck des *male gaze*.

Auf diese Weise präsentiert Madonna ihre Figur zugleich als Subjekt und als Objekt des männlichen Blicks. Sie spielt Fritz Langs *Master of Metropolis*, agiert als Herrenmensch, der hier allerdings nicht die Arbeitskraft seiner Sklaven ausbeutet, sondern deren sexuelle Potenz. Im Musikvideo zeigt sich Madonna auch in stereotyp-'weiblichen' masochistischen Posen, in der Bühnenperformance diffundieren sexuelle und geschlechtliche Grenzen durch ebenso stereotype 'männliche' Posen in nachgestellten Kopulationsszenen, bei denen Madonna jeweils einen der Tänzer 'penetriert'. Nebenbei wird dabei gleichsam die Bandbreite der Geschlechts- und Geschlechterakte durchgespielt: von buchstäblich ver-kehrten heterosexuellen über transsexuelle bis zu homosexuellen Positionen. Madonnas *performance* führt keine Frau vor, die einen Mann spielt oder als Mann wahrgenommen werden will. Sie präsentiert vielmehr eine Frau, die eine Frau spielt, die einen Mann spielt. Dabei werden einerseits Inszenierungsmodelle von Männlichkeit mimetisch nachgeahmt und simuliert – und zwar *sex* und *gender* gleichermaßen. Anderseits aber repräsentiert *Express Yourself* keine transsexuelle oder transvestische *show*, denn ebenso wie Männlichkeit findet sich auch Weiblichkeit ausgestellt. Ein scheinbar authentischer Frauenkörper wird bis auf das *dessous* entblößt und offeriert doch nur das Schauspiel der Weiblichkeit – ein in Männlichkeit übergehendes dazu. Ein solches Bühnegeschehen übersetzt Judith Butlers Theorie der Performativität in szenische *performance*: Die körperlichen und verkörperten Geschlechtsmerkmale werden zu Metaphern, die jedem biologischen Geschlecht zur Verfügung stehen, gerade weil sich dahinter nichts 'Eigentliches' verbirgt.[32] Geschlecht wird zu einem Ensemble rhetorischer Figuren, die von Madonna in Rede und Gegenrede, Zitat und Dementi arrangiert werden.[33]

---

[31] Über die Herkunft dieses Zitats herrscht in der Forschung allerdings Uneinigkeit: "Rap musicians (and, aping them, Madonna) have made crotch grabbing a common cultural code for sexual power and virility" (Bordo: 1999, 25).

[32] In der Bühnenshow zu dem Lied *Like A Virgin*, tragen die Männer denn auch umgeschnallte 'Busen': buchstäblich überspitzt durch ihre lange Kegelform, dienen sie unübersehbar als Zeichen des geschlechtlichen Verweises und der geschlechtlichen Simulation.

[33] Dem entspricht übrigens auch die Tatsache, daß *Express Yourself* musikalisch zwei verschiedene Tonlagen miteinander vermischt. Der geschlechtlich markierte Körper und seine performative (Re-)Inszenierung als Geschlecht bedienen sich auch hier zweier Zeichensysteme, die nicht notwendig synchron zueinander verlaufen müssen (Morton: 1993, 226-229).

Was Madonnas Auftritt bereits auf den ersten Blick zeigt, läßt ein weiterer *videoclip* nur in verdeckter Form erkennen: *Cream* von Prince. Erschienen im Jahr 1991, könnte dieser *clip* Madonna in einigen Arrangements als Negativfolie zu ihrer eigenen Bühnenshow (1992) gedient haben. Hinweise darauf geben die Tänzerinnen in *Cream*, die ein für das Genre Rockmusik geschlechtsspezifischeres Pendant zu Madonnas Tänzern bilden und die dabei zudem tatsächlich in jenen Dessous auftreten, die Madonna und ihre beiden Sängerinnen, wie manches andere eben auch, gerade verkehrt vorführen: *dessus* nämlich (über der Hose).

Vordergründig bebildert das *Cream*-Video lediglich misogyne und klischeehafte Männerphanatsien. Halbnackte Frauen offerieren sich als weibliche Sexualobjekte, die den (selbstverständlich bekleideten) Männern buchstäblich zu Füßen liegen, und Großaufnahmen weiblicher Gesichter mit lasziven Blicken setzen bekannte filmische Techniken des männlich-voyeuristischen Begehrens ein. Doch nur scheinbar spiegeln die sexuellen Anspielungen in Wort und Bild – genau anders als bei Madonna – heterosexuelle 'Normalität' wider. Der betonte Einsatz von Weichzeichnern und entsprechenden Farben führt zu einem Verfremdungseffekt, der ironische Distanz herstellt und das Geschehen als eine äußerst künstliche Inszenierung kennzeichnet, sogar in die Nähe des artifizellen Kitsch eines Jeff Koons rückt. Wer sich in der Rockgeschichte auskennt, identifiziert zudem verschiedene Zitate, Metaphern und Camouflagen in einem misogynen *acting male*, das nicht zuletzt Jimi Hendrix und James Brown für die Musikbühne erfunden haben.

Zu solchen filmischen und musikalischen Formen der uneigentlichen Rede und der 'intertextuellen' Verweise gesellen sich Mode- und Geschlechter-Codes, welche die vorgeführte maskuline *performance* als Mimikry ausweisen: Princes Spagateinlagen auf Stöckelschuhen mit hohem Absatz, seine hohe Stimme, seine grazilen Gesten und lasziven Augenaufschläge, dazu Frisur und Kleidung, die den Sänger zum skopophilen Objekt werden lassen – insgesamt vermittelt diese Selbsinszenierung "an aura of snarling virility commingled with doe-eyed femininity" (Garelick: 1998, 158). Der Blick des Publikums richtet sich demnach auf einen Männlichkeits- Darsteller, der – analog zu Madonna – als Subjekt und als Objekt des Begehrens agiert und dabei die 'klassischen' Objekte des *male gaze*, die Tänzerinnen, buchstäblich in den Schatten der geschlechtlichen Wahrnehmung stellt. In frühen Bühnenauftritten trägt Prince konsequenterweise selbst die Strapse und Dessous. Aber auch in *Cream* verkörpert die Figur von Prince offenbar keinen Mann, der als Mann durchgehen soll (*passing as a man*), sondern einen Mann, der einen heterosexuellen *machismo* mimt und diese Mimesis dabei ausstellt: mit Zeichen, die sich überlagern und sowohl heterosexuelle als auch homo- und transsexuelle Decodierungsversuche ermutigen.

Unverkennbar ist die *persona* von Prince – auch außerhalb dieses Videos – dem Dandy um 1900 nachgebildet: "[...] Prince Rogers Nelson demonstrates how the dandy fused with the woman onstage to create contemporary media stars" (Garelick: 1998, 154). Auf diese Weise präsentiert sich eine moderne Figuration von Männlichkeit, bei der die Abweichung von 'normaler' Männlichkeit und die Ambiguität geschlechtlicher Kodierung gleichsam Programm geworden sind

(Feldman: 1993). Als Medienstar den voyeuristisch-sexualisierten Blick der Kamera befriedigend, bedient und ironisiert der Darsteller Prince die Geschlechter-Klischees, zitiert wie Madonna die Strategien männlicher *performance* und führt sie dabei als eine Form der Uneigentlichkeit vor: Fragmente einer Körpersprache, die gerade nicht inkorporiert ist, sondern den Körper als Bühne und als Ausstellungsfläche benutzt.

Das Ineinanderblenden von Geschlechter-Positionen führt in diesen beiden Videos zu keinem klar erkennbaren Ziel. Es ist weder Strategie zur Wiedererrichtung hegemonialer Männlichkeit noch eine bloße Zur-Schau-Stellung männlicher Krisensymptome. Vielmehr gleichen sie dem Spiegel eines sozialen Raumes, in dem Männlichkeiten sowohl als Mimikry sichtbar werden als auch lustvoll eingesetzt werden. Die vorgeführten *performances* entlarven Männlichkeit, weil sie die soziale und synchrone Verbindung von *enactment* und *enbodiment* entkoppeln. Sie lassen aber divergierende Männlichkeitskonzepte zugleich produktiv werden, indem sie das theoretisch gängige Muster einer verdrängenden und bloß erzwungenen, einer sekundären oder gar naturfernen Männlichkeit in Frage stellen und deren Zeichen in ein Repertoire an Gesten und Verkörperungen überführen, das nun plötzlich beiden oder mehreren Geschlechtern zur Verfügung steht (Erhart: 2000).[34]

3. Männlichkeit – ein Traum

Auf die Verbindung von Bühne, Theater und Geschlecht ist bereits mehrfach hingewiesen worden (vgl. etwa Aalten: 1997, 41-58, Salomon: 1997). Nicht zuletzt Judith Butler hat ihre Theorie von *gender* als performativem Akt an subkultuellen Tanzdarstellungen und Travestien exemplifiziert (Butler: 1993, 121-140). Zugrunde liegt diesen Beispielen von Geschlechter-konstruktion allerdings immer ein impliziter Pakt mit dem Zuschauer, der sich als doppelter, vielleicht sogar "schielender Blick" (in Anlehnung an Weigel: 1988) bezeichnen ließe: Man sieht den Darsteller und die *persona* oder den 'Charakter' (Salomon: 1997, 16), registriert die Differenz zwischen dem Geschlechter-*embodiment* und dem Geschlechter-*enactment*. In ironischen oder parodistischen Darstellungen wie denen von Prince oder Madonna wird diese Differenz deutlich ausgestellt, sogar auf der Ebene des *enactment* noch einmal verdoppelt. Doch auch *performances*, die darauf abzielen, als ein bestimmtes Geschlecht (sei es das 'andere' oder das vermeintlich 'eigene' des Sexus) durchzugehen, beziehen ihre Dynamik und ihre Schwierigkeiten aus diesem 'kleinen Unterschied' zwischen Verkörperung und mimetischer Aneignung. Scheinbar natürlich gegeben, kann das Geschlecht doch verfehlt werden. Genau darin aber manifestiert sich "the phantasmatic attempt to approximate realness, but it also exposes the norms that regulate realness as *themselves* phantasmatically instituted and sustained." (Butler: 1993, 130)

---

[34] Gesondert zu untersuchen wäre dabei noch die potentielle Verknüpfung von *gender* und *race* in den *personae* des farbigen Prince und der weißen Madonna.

Gleichermaßen eine Einheit der Differenz, bildet das Zusammenspiel von phantasmatischem und 'realem' Geschlecht, Ich und Nicht-Ich im Grunde ein hysterisches Modell (von Braun: 1990); und es dürfte wohl kein Zufall sein, daß Hysterie lange Zeit als *das* Beispiel geschlechtlicher Verstellungskunst und Schauspielerei schlechthin galt (vgl. etwa Decker: 1977, 76f., Porter: 1993, 251). Sigmund Freud war der erste, der seine Aufmerksamkeit weniger auf die Erscheinungen als vielmehr auf die Erzählmuster der Hysterie richtete. Nach 1968 rückten bekanntlich feministische Intellektuelle und Literaturwissenschaftlerinnen das Verhältnis von Geschlecht und Erzählen erneut in den Blick mit der Absicht, das hysterische Sprechen als subversives Potential gegenüber der patriarchalen Sprach- und Denkordnung fruchtbar zu machen (vgl. Herrmann: 1999). Läßt die Synonymisierung von Hysterie und Weiblichkeit schon im 19. Jahrhundert den bereits vor Freud diagnostizierten hysterischen Mann als unmännlich, eben als weiblich erscheinen (Link-Heer: 1988, 364-397), so avanciert Hysterie im späten 20. Jahrhundert erneut zu einem Ort spezifisch weiblicher Artikulation (Showalter: 1997, 86-94). Der Blick auf das Geschlecht, "das nicht eins" ist (Irigaray), verkennt jedoch, daß auch das männliche Geschlecht keinen "Singular Mann" bildet (Hirschauer 1993b, 64; ähnlich Erhart/Herrmann: 1997, 24), und während die Konzepte einer 'weiblichen Ästhetik' oder einer *écriture féminine* darauf abzielen, in Anlehnung an Autoren der Moderne das Konzept von Polyphonie, Polysemie und lustvoller *jouissance* fruchtbar zu machen, scheint die Vorstellung von einer 'männlichen Schreibweise' auf das genaue Gegenteil zu verweisen: Härte und Stabilität statt Verflüssigung, (symbolische) Ordnung statt Desorganisation und Entgrenzung.

In diesen Oppositionen schreibt sich ein kultureller und literarischer Männlichkeitsentwurf fort, wie er explizit nach dem ersten Weltkrieg formuliert wurde – als jene *ordre froid* nämlich, die den Habitus der Neuen Sachlichkeit bestimmt. Einerseits manifestieren sich deren "Verhaltenslehren der Kälte" (Lethen: 1994) in einem männlichen Körperentwurf und in einer psychosexuellen Struktur, die sich gegen weiblich konnotierte Auflösungserscheinungen panzert (Theweleit: 1980, Bd.1); andererseits jedoch markieren sie eine kulturelle Gegenbewegung zu einer als bedrohlich (weiblich) empfundenen Moderne. Entsprechend formiert sich der neue Text/Körper der Literatur: "Die Neue Sachlichkeit ist männlich", erklärt Kurt Pinthus 1929, und statt weiterhin "feministische Weichlichkeit" aufzuweisen, zeigt sich diese männliche Literatur "hart, zäh, trainiert, dem Körper eines Boxers vergleichbar" (zit. nach Baureithel: 1993, 30). Bereits drei Jahre zuvor weist Arnolt Bronnen in die gleiche literarische Richtung und verspricht, daß seine Generation "ruhige, ernste und männliche Stücke schaffen wolle" (zit. nach Baureithel: 1993, 30).

Einst Vertreter der expressionistischen Bewegung, sind die vatermordenden Söhne Pinthus, Bronnen und ihre Zeitgenossen offenbar erwachsen – männlich – geworden: eine ödipale Erfolgsstory. Hinter der Maskulinisierung der Literatur und dem Wunsch nach einer *écriture masculine* aber steckt die Strategie, gleich einer ganzen kriegsgeschädigten Männergeneration mit ihren hysterischen "Kriegszitterern" eben diese Erfolgsgeschichte zu suggerieren – nicht immer mit Erfolg. So konzediert zwar schon der Zeitgenosse Béla Balàzs in seiner Replik auf Kurt Pinthus, daß die Neue Sachlichkeit eine "notwendige Reaktion auf eine feminin-schwülstige Gefühlsduselei und auf das hysterische Wehgeschrei der expressionistischen Jünglingsliteratur" (Balàzs: 1929, 969) darstelle; Balàzs sieht darin aber nur eine vorgetäuschte Männlichkeit, eine habituelle Maskerade: "Es ist die Literatur einer seelischen Müdigkeit. [...] Eine gestählte Schwäche also, Impotenz mit Haltung, eine Attitüde der Männlichkeit" (Balàzs: 1929, 969f.).

"Männlich oder kriegsblind?" Innerhalb dieser beiden Alternativen, mit denen Balàzs seinen Artikel überschrieben hat, muß 'man(n)' sich offenbar positionieren: entweder als Ödipus, der die Kastrationsdrohung (die Blendung) letztlich abwehrt, oder als Hysteriker. Alles Dritte ist weder männlich noch unmännlich, sondern bloße Nachahmung. Erst seit kurzem widmet sich die Forschung der Genese des ödipalen (phallischen) Männlichkeitskonzeptes aus den Freudschen Hysteriestudien und weist auf die Bedeutung der Ödipustheorie für die Ausklammerung 'defizienter' (kastrierter) Männlichkeiten im 20. Jahrhundert hin (Smith: 1997, 82), zu denen neben jenen von Hysterikern etwa auch die von Künstlern und Juden gehören (Gilman: 1993a). Das Geschlecht, 'das eins ist', entsteht so erstens in einem Verdrängungsprozeß und als Gegenkonzept zu einer 'verdoppelten', hysterischen Weiblichkeit, welche zudem metaphorisch die Moderne verkörpert. Zweitens verlagert sich der Ort der Geschlechter-*performance* von dem Schauspiel des hysterischen Körpers, der mit seinen Bögen, Figuren und Hautzeichen zu lesen ist wie eine Schrift, in ödipale Erzählungen und in eine Literatur, die sich als männlicher Textkörper mit dem Ziel neu formiert, dezidiert nicht weiblich-hysterische Schauspiele, sondern "ruhige, ernste [...] Stücke" zu produzieren.

Nach dem zweiten Weltkrieg führt nicht zuletzt Peter Weiss das Scheitern der ödipalen Erzählung vor. Sein Prosastück *Abschied von den Eltern* (1961) erzählt die Geschichte einer verfehlten Mannwerdung: Im klassischen Dreieck von überdominanter Mutter und einem (auch geschlechtlich) abwesenden Vater, erlebt sich das Erzähl-Ich innerlich gespalten, als männliches Ich und weibliches Nicht-Ich. Dabei weist die Ich-Figur jene klassischen Merkmale der Hysterie auf, wie sie bereits um 1900 in psychiatrischen Lehrbüchern zu finden sind (etwa Kraepelin: 1904, 684-720): Der Held hat Angstträume und 'Alpdruck', er leidet unter Somnambulismus, Aphasie - und Impotenz (Weiss: 1991, 81/82, 129).

Trotz mehr oder weniger expliziter Verweise auf den "aufragende[n] Phallus" (Weiss: 1991, 96), gelingt es dem Erzähler auf zweifache Weise nicht, die geschlechtliche Verdoppelung zu überwinden und "mein neues Leben als Mann beginnen" (Weiss: 1991, 129). Zunächst scheitert die narrative Strategie, den hysterischen Diskurs in einen ödipalen zu überführen und den mannhaften Abschied von den Eltern einzuleiten (vgl. Herrmann: 2001, 68-89). Stattdessen mündet die Erzählung in eine zirkuläre Struktur, die das Ende der Geschichte und den vermeintlichen Aufbruch des Sohnes an den Textanfang zurückbindet: die Erzählung dreht sich buchstäblich im Kreis, der Abschied bleibt aufgeschoben.

Zweitens mißlingt aber innerhalb der Textebene auch der Versuch des Erzählers, die Männlichkeitsrituale der nationalsozialistischen Umgebung zu imitieren. Beeindruckt von der virilen Männlichkeit des Fritz W – er "war in allem ein Gegensatz meines Vaters, er war kraftvoll, lebhaft, seine Sprache witzig und drastisch, er war [...] intim und vital in seiner Annäherung an meine Mutter" (Weiss: 1991, 48) – versucht der Erzähler, sich selbst in einen solchen potenten Mann (und Gegenentwurf des – jüdischen – Vaters) zu verwandeln. In einem Traum entwickelt der Erzähler nicht nur männerbündnerische bis homoerotische Phantasien (52), sondern nimmt Teil an den gewalttätigen Praktiken seiner Altersgenossen aus der Hitlerjugend, bis er sich in einen der Anführer verwandelt: "Ich wurde zu Friederle" (53). Der Traum aber, "zu den Starken" zu gehören, wird in dem Moment jäh zerstört, in dem die Ich-Figur von ihrer halbjüdischen Identität erfährt. Mit dieser doppelten Genealogie hat der Erzähler für die angestrebte Männlichkeit das falsche Geschlecht (vgl. dazu auch Gilman: 1993b, 49-92), der Virilitätsnachweis ist mißglückt, die Mimesis 'arischer' Männlichkeit gerät zur entlarvten – und letztlich unmöglichen – Mimikry.

Beinahe vierzig Jahre später könnte man David Finchers Film *Fight Club* (USA 1999) als eine Antwort auf Peter Weiss lesen: Wie in dessen Prosastück gibt es auch hier einen durchgehenden Erzählermonolog, in dem sich unterschiedliche Zeit- und Wirklichkeitsebenen vermengen, Fiktion und Realität, Erinnerung und Gegenwart ineinander fließen. Und wie der Protagonist bei Weiss leidet auch in *Fight Club* der namenlose Held unter massiven Schlafstörungen. Um diese zu bekämpfen, besucht er willkürlich Selbsthilfegruppen, die mit seinem Problem vordergründig nichts zu tun haben – solche für Hodenkrebspatienten etwa. Als "Rupert" nimmt er hier die Identität jener Männer an, die mit dem Verlust ihrer Manneskraft, mit Kastration und Busenwachstum zu kämpfen haben. Für kurze Zeit bessern sich "Ruperts" Schlafprobleme. Die mimetische Anverwandlung dieses Ortes einer nicht-phallischen Männlichkeit gelingt jedoch nur bis zu dem Moment, in dem eine Frau, Marla, in der Männergruppe auftaucht. Gleichsam parodistisch spiegelt sie "Ruperts" Inkorporation und decouvriert sie als Mimkry. Sie macht offensichtlich, was vorher verdeckt ist: "Rupert" hat den falschen (phallischen) Körper für seine Inszenierung. Solange "Rupert" sich zugleich als kastriert *und* als phallisch unversehrt erfahren kann, erlebt er gerade in dieser paradoxen Männlichkeit eine Befriedigung, die man leicht als prädipale Ganzheit bezeichnen könnte (Fabricius: 2001, 401). Doch der Film weist über das psychoanalytische Instrumentarium als Beschreibungsmodell hinaus: "Nicht einmal Babies schlafen so gut" (0.08.23-0.08.25). Statt als Rückkehr in ein prädipales Stadium läßt sich "Ruperts" Verdoppelung als eine Überschreitung psychoanalytischer Dichotomien lesen, gleichsam als Rückeroberung des Verdrängten und als Versuch, "die psychoanalytische Schreckgestalt der Kastration zwar nicht ganz abzutun, aber doch erst einmal provisorisch zu ignorieren" (Smith 1997: 70).

Mit der Vertreibung aus der Selbsthilfegruppe aber verändert sich die Experimentalanordnung der Männlichkeit. Die zuvor verkörperte Einheit der Differenz verwandelt sich von einem hysterischen Identitätsmodell in ein schizophrenes, und das männliche Individuum wird – wie einst bei Jekyll and Hyde[35] – zu einem 'Dividuum': an die Seite des vorgeblich kastrierten "Rupert" tritt sein phantasmatisches und phallisches *alter ego* Tylor Durden, ein anarchischer Kämpfer und 'wild man' von sexueller Hyperpotenz. Zusammen gründen die beiden den "Fight Club", einen Boxclub, der einer ganzen Generation von vaterlosen Mutter-Söhnen ihre 'Männlichkeit' zurückerstatten soll.

Die schizoide mann-männliche Spaltung wiederholt einerseits die Freudsche Anordnung und bildet damit das dezidierte Gegenmodell zu jener neurotischen Männlichkeit, wie sie Peter Weiss beschreibt. Andererseits wird "Rupert" sich am Ende gegen sein phantasmatisches Männlichkeitsdouble durchsetzen, indem er sich selbst durch einen Schuß verstümmelt und den phallischen 'Anderen' dabei zerstört. *Fight Club* führt demnach das Projekt der Errichtung einer virilen Männlichkeit und einer funktionierenden Männergesellschaft vor (vgl. Fabricius: 2001) – um es im letzten Moment (übrigens erneut wegen Marla) scheitern zu lassen. Dabei unterliegt der Erzähler zwar den gleichen Symptomen wie der Hysteriker – zuweilen muß sich "Rupert" vergewissern, ob er träumt oder wacht: "Schlief ich? Hatte ich geschlafen? Ist Tylor mein Alptraum oder bin ich seiner?" (1.44.30-1.44.36) –, doch produziert seine Strategie der Verdoppelung eben nicht "das Weibliche in mir" (Weiss) sondern, ganz ödipal, das 'Männliche in mir'. Und dies verkörpert sich in genau der Figur, die Pinthus als mimetisches Vorbild für die Literatur bestimmt hat: der des Boxers. Mit Bizeps, Waschbrettbauch und Prügeln, mit Ehrencodex und Schweigeritual, mit *homosocial desire* und *male bonding*, schließlich auch mit faschistoiden Führerstrukturen und para-militärischen Aktionen heißt es nun für die Mitglieder des "Fight Clubs", sich boxend einer bislang fragwürdigen Identität zu versichern: "Wir sind immer noch Männer." – "Ja, wir sind Männer. Männer. Genau das sind wir." (0.03.37-0.03.42)

4. Noch einmal: Männlichkeit in der Schrift

Auch in der neuen deutschen Literatur hält das Modell des Boxers wieder Einzug. Forderte Kurt Pinthus einst "Wirklichkeit" und einen harten,"naturhaft-derbschlächtigen" Stil (Balàzs: 1929, 970; Baureithel: 1993, 31), so antwortet darauf die Literatur nach 1989 mit einem "Hardcore-Realismus", der in dieser Hinsicht offenbar nichts zu wünschen übrig läßt und in den Feuilletons enthusiastisch gefeiert wird: als "prall und plastisch", "rüde", "voll Stolz und Härte" und mit "so viel Gegenwart" wie kaum jemals zuvor.[36] Kein Traum also. Gegen die "Knabenwindelprosa" (Zaimoglu: 1999), gegen die "Schlappschwanz-Literatur" und ihre "lauwarmen Geschichten"

---

[35] ("Rupert") "Sicher hast du den Eindruck, ich hätte zwei Seiten, wenn du mit mir zusammen bist." – (Marla) "Zwei Seiten? Du bist Dr. Jekyll und Mr. Arsch." (1.52.34 – 1.52.38)

[36] Die Zitate sind den Klappentexten von Kraussers Roman *Fette Welt* und Zaimoglus *Kanak Sprak* entnommen, die Rezensionen der "Allgemeinen Zeitung", der "Lübecker Nachrichten" und aus dem "Spiegel" zitieren.

(Biller: 2000, 49) – gemeint ist die Prosa eines Benjamin von Stuckrad-Barre, Benjamin Lebert oder auch eines Rainald Goetz – setzen Autoren wie Feridun Zaimoglu und Maxim Biller wieder auf "Flammenhärtung durch *counsciousness*" (Zaimoglu) und auf eine "Härte", die bereit ist, konsequent und "so brutal, daß das Blut spritzt, die letzten Fragen zu stellen" (Biller).[37] Willkommen im "Fight Club".

Am Ende des 20. Jahrhunderts taucht also die wahre Männlichkeit zumindest rhetorisch wieder ins Stahlbad ein. Für den performativen Akt des *parler homme* wird der Körper nicht zur Bühne, sondern verwandelt sich erneut in Schrift. Forderte Hélène Cixous für die *écriture féminine* noch ein Schreiben mit der 'weißen Tinte' der Muttermilch und aus einer weiblichen Ökonomie des Begehrens heraus[38], so zeigt sich nun das maskuline Gegenmodell. "Kommt, ihr schönen Mädchen, ich schreib euch ein Gedicht zwischen die Brüste, mit weißer Tinte [...]", deklariert der Erzähler und "Poet" in Helmut Kraussers 1992 erschienenen Roman *Fette Welt* (Krausser: 1997, 88); und der verhinderte Schriftsteller und Nobelpreisträger in Thomas Brussigs Roman *Helden wie wir* (1995) erzählt die Geschichte des Mauerfalls als "Geschichte meines Pinsels" (Brussig: 1998, 7). Auch Männlichkeit in der Schrift scheint im Kampf um den Phallus – haben, wenn schon nicht sein; zu sein vorgeben, wenn nicht haben – vor allem zwei Strategien performativer Aneignung zu kennen: demonstratives Muskelspiel und sexuelle Hyperbeln.

"Männlichkeit? Phallisches? Gerade das wird alles lesbar sein." (Cixous: 1980, S.72). Lesbar, und damit schreibbar. Jedoch bildet Männlichkeit auch und gerade in der Literatur und in der Schrift weniger den Ausdruck eines spezifischen Körpers, seines *embodiments* und seiner Ökonomie, sondern konstituiert sich erneut aus rhetorischen Figuren eines *acting male*.

Quellennachweise

Aalten, Anna, "Performing the Body, Creating Culture", in: Kathy Davis (Hg.), *Embodied Practices. Feminist Perspectives on the Body*, London u.a. 1997, S. 41-58.
Austin, John L., *Zur Theorie der Sprechakte (How to Do Things with Words)*, Stuttgart 1972.
Badinter, Elisabeth, XY. *Die Identität des Mannes*, München, Zürich 1993.

---

[37] Auch für die Literatur zu Beginn des 21. Jahrhunderts läßt sich noch mit Bela Balàzs fragen: "Und was hat das mit Männlichkeit zu tun? Die sensible Feinheit des analystischen Nachspürens und Einfühlens ist, wenn man schon bei solchen Geschlechtskategorien bleiben will, eine eminent männliche Qualität [...]. Nicht von der Literatur selbst ist hier die Rede, sondern von der Literaturpolitik, die getrieben wird. Nicht von den Autoren, sondern von ihrer besonderen Bewertung. Es muß einmal gesprochen werden von der gefährlich amerikanisierten Verrohung des berliner [!] Literatur- (und Theater-) Betriebs [...]" (Balàzs: 1929, 970f.).

[38] Kritisch dazu: Lindhoff: 1995, S.122-128 und Weber: 1994, S.30-32.

Balàzs, Bela, "Männlich oder kriegsblind?", in: *Die Weltbühne* 25 (1929), H.26, S. 969-971.

Baureithel, Ulrike: "Masken der Virilität. Kulturtheoretische Strategien zur Überwindung des männlichen Identitätsverlustes im ersten Drittel des 20. Jahrhunderts", in: *Die Philosophin* 4 (1993), H.8, S. 24-35.

Bechdolf, Ute, "Verhandlungssache 'Geschlecht'. Eine Fallstudie zur kulturellen Herstellung von Differenz bei der Rezeption von Musikvideos", in: Andreas Hepp, Rainer Winter (Hg.), *Kultur – Medien – Macht. Cultural Studies und Medienanalyse*, Opladen 1997, S. 201-214.

Berger, Maurice, Wallis, Brian, Watson, Simon (Hg.), *Constructing Masculinity*, New York, London 1995.

Bhabha, Homi K., "Of Mimicry and Man. The Ambivalence of Colonial Discourse", in: Homi K. Bhabha, *The Location of Culture*, London, New York 1994, S. 85-93.

Biller, Maxim, "Feige das Land, schlapp die Literatur. Über die Schwierigkeiten beim Sagen der Wahrheit", in: *Die Zeit* 16 (2000), S. 47-49.

Bingham, Dennis, *Acting Male. Masculinities in the Films of James Stewart, Jack Nicholson and Clint Eastwood*, New Brunswick 1994.

Bordo, Susan, *The Male Body. A New Look at Men in Public and in Private*, New York 1999.

Bourdieu, Pierre, "Die männliche Herrschaft", in: Irene Dölling, Beate Krais (Hg.), *Ein alltägliches Spiel. Geschlechterkonstruktion in der sozialen Praxis*, Frankfurt a.M. 1997, S. 153-216.

Bourdieu, Pierre, *La domination masculine*, Paris 1998.

Braun, Christina von, *Nicht-Ich. Logik, Lüge, Libido*, Frankfurt a.M. 1990.

Brod, Harry, Kaufman, Michael (Hg.), *Theorizing Masculinities*, Thousand Oaks, London, New Delhi 1994.

Brussig, Thomas, *Helden wie wir. Roman*, Frankfurt a.M. 1998.

Bußmann, Hadumod, Hof, Renate (Hg.), *Genus. Zur Geschlechterdifferenz in den Kulturwissenschaften*, Stuttgart 1995.

Butler, Judith, *Das Unbehagen der Geschlechter*, Frankfurt a.M. 1991.

Butler, Judith, *Bodies That Matter. On The Discursive Limits of "Sex"*, New York, London 1993.

Butler, Judith, "Das Ende der Geschlechterdifferenz?", in: Jörg Huber, Martin Heller, *Konturen des Unentschiedenen*, Basel, Frankfurt a.M., Zürich 1997, S. 25-43.

Cixous, Hélène, "Wer singt? Wer veranlaßt zu singen? Wer wird besungen? Wer ruft – wer nennt sich selbst 'Orpheus'?", in: Hélène Cixous, *Weiblichkeit in der Schrift*, Berlin 1980, S. 58-107.

Cornwall, Andrea, Lindisfarne, Nancy, "Dislocating Masculinity. Gender, Power and Anthropology", in: Andrea Cornwall, Nancy Lindisfarne (Hg.), *Dislocating Masculinity. Comparative Ethnographies*, London, New York 1994, S. 11-47.

Decker, Hannah S., *Freud in Germany. Revolution and Reaction in Science 1893-1907*, New York 1977.

Dinges, Martin (Hg.), *Hausväter, Priester, Kastraten. Zur Konstruktion von Männlichkeit in Spätmittelalter und Früher Neuzeit*, Göttingen 1998.

Easthope, Anthony, *What a Man's Gotta Do. The Masculine Myth in Popular Culture*, New York, London 1992.

Erhart, Walter, Herrmann, Britta (Hg.): *Wann ist der Mann ein Mann? Zur Geschichte der Männlichkeit*, Stuttgart, Weimar 1997.

Erhart, Walter, "Männlichkeit als Kategorie der postmodernen Kondition", in: Ingeborg Hoesterey, Paul Michael Lützeler (Hg.), *Räume der Postmoderne. Zur Interrelation der Diskurse*, Tübingen 2000, S. 127-146.

Fabricius, Tobias, "Männlichkeit als Maskerade. Zu Byrons Poetik in 'Don Juan'", in: Kati Röttger, Heike Paul (Hg.), *Differenzen in der Geschlechterdifferenz / Differences within Gender Studies. Aktuelle Perspektiven der Geschlechterforschung*, Berlin 1999, S. 187–201.

Fabricius, Tobias, "Pa(ar)thologie: Kulturtext, Körperschrift und männliche Homosozialität in David Finchers Film 'Fight Club'", in: Annegret Heitman, Sigrid Nieberle, Barbara Schaff, Sabine Schülting (Hg.), *Bi- Textualität. Inszenierungen des Paars*, Berlin 2001, S. 395-410.

Faludi, Susan, *Stiffed. The Betrayal of the American Man*, New York 1999.

Farrell, Warren, *The Myth of Male Power. Why Men are the Disposable Sex*, New York u. a. 1993.

Fausto-Sterling, Anne, *Gender Politics and the Construction of Sexuality*, New York 2000.

Feldman, Jessica R., *Gender in the Divide. The Dandy in Modernist Literature*, Princeton 1993.

Filene, Peter, "The Secrets of Men's History", in: Harry Brod (Hg.), *The Making of Masculinities. The New Men's Studies*, London, Sydney, Wellington 1987, S. 103-119.

Fischer-Lichte, Erika, "Performance-Kunst und Ritual: Körper- Inszenierungen in Performances", in: Gerhard Neumann, Sigrid Weigel (Hg.), *Lesbarkeit der Kultur. Literaturwissenschaft zwischen Kulturtechnik und Ethnographie*, München 2000, S. 113-129.

Freud, Sigmund, "Der Untergang des Ödipuskomplexes", in: Sigmund Freud, *Beiträge zur Psychologie des Liebeslebens*, Frankfurt a.M. 1981, S. 51- 156.

Freud, Sigmund. "Die Weiblichkeit", in: Sigmund Freud, *Neue Folge der Vorlesungen zur Einführung in die Psychoanalyse*, Frankfurt a.M. 1991, S. 110-132.

Frevert, Ute, "Männergeschichte oder die Suche nach dem 'ersten' Geschlecht", in: Manfred Hettling, Claudia Huerkamp, Paul Nolte, Hans-Walter Schmuhl (Hg.), *Was ist Gesellschaftsgeschichte? Positionen, Themen, Analysen*, München 1991, S. 31-43.

Frevert, Ute, "Soldaten, Staatsbürger. Überlegungen zur historischen Konstruktion von Männlichkeit", in: Thomas Kühne, *Männergeschichte. Geschlechtergeschichte. Männlichkeit im Wandel der Moderne*, Frankfurt a.M., New York 1996, S. 69-87.

Frith, Simon, "Musik und Identität", in: Jan Engelmann (Hg.), *Die kleinen Unterschiede. Der Cultural Studies-Reader*, Frankfurt a.M., New York 1999, S. 149-169.

49

Frith, Simon, "The Cultural Study of Popular Music", in: Lawrence Grossberg, Cary Nelson, Paula Treichler (Hg.), *Cultural Studies*, New York, London 1992, S. 174-182.

Garelick, Rhonda K., *Rising Star. Dandyism, Gender, and Performance in the Fin de Siècle*, Princeton 1998.

Gilman, Sander L., "The Image of the Hysteric", in: Sander L. Gilman u.a., *Hysteria Beyond Freud*, Berkeley 1993, S. 345-452 (Gilman 1993a).

Gilman, Sander L., *Freud, Race, and Gender*, Princeton, New Jersey 1993 (Gilman 1993b).

Goltermann, Sabine, "Doppelgänger ihrer selbst. Überlegungen zur Mimesis und Männlichkeit am Beispiel der deutschen Turnbewegung, 1860- 1900", in: *traverse* 5 (1998), H.1, S. 113-125.

Halberstam, Judith, *Female Masculinity*, Durham, London 1998.

Hark, Sabine, "Parodistischer Ernst und politisches Spiel. Zur Politik in der Geschlechterparodie", in: Antje Hornscheidt, Gabriele Jähnert, Annette Schlichter (Hg.), *Kritische Differenzen – geteilte Perspektiven. Zum Verhältnis von Feminismus und Postmoderne*, Opladen 1998, S. 115-139.

Herrmann, Britta, "Das uneinige Geschlecht: *history*, her story, Hysterie – Erzählen, Körper, Differenz", in: Kati Röttger, Heike Paul (Hg.), *Differenzen in der Geschlechterdifferenz / Differences within Gender Studies. Aktuelle Perspektiven der Geschlechterforschung*, Berlin 1999, S. 169-186.

Herrmann, Britta, *Töchter des Ödipus. Zur Geschichte eines Erzählmusters in der deutschsprachigen Literatur des 20. Jahrhunderts*, Tübingen 2001.

Hirschauer, Stefan, "Dekonstruktion und Rekonstruktion. Plädoyer für die Erforschung des Bekannten", in: *Feministische Studien* 2 (1993), S. 55-67 (Hirschauer 1993b).

Hirschauer, Stefan, *Die soziale Konstruktion der Transsexualität. Über die Medizin und den Geschlechtswechsel*, Frankfurt a.M. 1993 (Hirschauer 1993a).

Honegger, Claudia: "Überlegungen zur Medikalisierung des weiblichen Körpers", in: Arthur Imhof (Hg.), *Leib und Leben in der Geschichte der Neuzeit*, Berlin 1983, S. 203-214.

Horrocks, Roger, *Masculinity in Crisis*, New York 1994.

Huyssen, Andreas, "Mass Culture as Woman. Moderninsm's Other", in: *After The Great Divide. Modernism, Mass Culture, and Postmodernism*, Bloomington 1986, S. 44-62.

Irigaray, Luce, *Das Geschlecht das nicht eins ist*, Berlin 1979.

Kimmel, Michael S., *Manhood in America. A Cultural History*, New York u.a. 1996.

Kimmel, Michael S., *The Gendered Society*, Oxford 2000.

Kraepelin, Emil, *Psychiatrie. Ein Lehrbuch für Studierende und Ärzte*, Bd.2, 7. Aufl., Leipzig 1904.

Krais, Beate, "Geschlechterverhältnisse und symbolische Gewalt", in: Gunter Gebauer, Christoph Wulf (Hg.), *Praxis und Ästhetik. Neue Perspektiven im Denken Pierre Bourdieus*, Frankfurt a.M. 1993, S. 208-250.

Krausser, Helmut, *Fette Welt. Roman*, Reinbek 1997.

Kühne, Thomas, *Männergeschichte. Geschlechtergeschichte. Männlichkeit im Wandel der Moderne*, Frankfurt a.M., New York 1996.

Landweer, Hilge, "Kritik und Verteidigung der Kategorie Geschlecht. Wahrnehmungs- und symboltheoretische Überlegungen zur sex/gender-Unterscheidung", in: Feministische Studien 2 (1993), S. 34-43.

Landweer, Hilge: "Jenseits des Geschlechts? Zum Phänomen der theoretischen und politischen Fehleinschätzung von Travestie und Transsexualität", in: Institut für Sozialforschung (Hg.), *Geschlechterverhältnisse und Politik*, Frankfurt a.M. 1994, S. 139-167.

Lengwiler, Martin, "Aktuelle Perspektiven der historischen Männlichkeitsforschung im angelsächsischen Raum", in: *traverse* 5 (1998), H. 5, S. 25-34.

Lethen, Helmut, *Verhaltenslehren der Kälte. Lebensversuche zwischen den Kriegen*, Frankfurt a.M. 1994.

Lindemann, Gesa, *Das paradoxe Geschlecht. Transsexualität im Spannungsfeld von Körper, Leib und Gefühl*, Frankfurt a.M. 1993 (Lindemann 1993a).

Lindemann, Gesa, "Wider die Verdrängung des Leibes aus der Geschlechterkonstruktion", in: *Feministische Studien* 2 (1993), S. 44-54 (Lindemann 1993b).

Lindhoff, Lena, *Einführung in die feministische Literaturtheorie*, Stuttgart 1995.

Link-Heer, Ursula, "'Männliche Hysterie'. Eine Diskursanalyse", in: Ursula A. J. Becher, Jörn Rüsen (Hg.), *Weiblichkeit in geschichtlicher Perspektive. Fallstudien und Reflexionen zu Grundproblemen der historischen Frauenforschung*, Frankfurt a.M. 1988, S. 364-397.

Maihofer, Andrea, "Geschlecht als hegemonialer Diskurs. Ansätze zu einer kritischen Theorie des 'Geschlechts'", in: Theresa Wobbe, Gesa Lindemann (Hg.), *Denkachsen. Zur theoretischen und institutionellen Rede vom Geschlecht*, Frankfurt a.M. 1994, S. 236-263.

Morton, Melanie, "Don't go for Second Sex, Baby!", in: Cathy Schwichtenberg (Hg.), *The Madonna Connection*, Boulder, San Francisco, Oxford 1993, S. 213-235.

Meuser, Michael, *Geschlecht und Männlichkeit. Soziologische Theorie und kulturelle Deutungsmuster*, Opladen 1998.

Mosse, George L., *The Image of Man. The Creation of Modern Masculinity*, New York 1996.

Mouffe, Chantal, "Hegemony, Power and the Political Dimension of Culture", in: Bundesministerium für Wissenschaft und Verkehr in Wien und Internationales Forschungszentrum Kulturwissenschaften (Hg.), *The Contemporary Study of Culture*, Wien 2000, S. 47-52.

Parpart, Nadja, *Geschlecht und Kontingenz. Zur Zerstreuung des anderen Geschlechts im Feminismus*, Frankfurt a.M. 2000.

Pfeil, Fred, *White Guys. Studies in Postmodern Domination and Difference*, London, New York 1995.

Porter, Roy, "The Body and the Mind, the Doctor and the Patient: Negotiating Hysteria", in: Sander L. Gilman u.a., *Hysteria Beyond Freud*, Berkley 1993, S. 225-285.

Rhode-Dachser, Christa, *Expedition in den dunklen Kontinent. Weiblichkeit im Diskurs der Psychoanalyse*, Berlin u.a. 1991.

Riviere, Joan, "Weiblichkeit als Maskerade", in: Liliane Weisberg (Hg.), *Weiblichkeit als Maskerade*, Frankfurt a.M. 1994, S. 34-47.

Rotundo, E. Anthony, *American Manhood. Transformations in Masculinity from the Revolution to the Modern Era*, New York 1993.

Salomon, Alisa, *Re-Dressing the Canon. Essays on Theatre and Gender*, London, New York 1997.

Schlaffer, Hannelore, "Philosophie und Pornographie. Erlösungsmodelle von Sloterdijk, Kittler, Duerr, Theweleit", in: *Merkur* 54 (2000), S. 1132-1139.

Schwichtenberg, Cathy (Hg.), *The Madonna Connection*, Boulder, San Francisco, Oxford 1993.

Sedgwick, Eve K., "Gender Criticism", in: Stephen Greenblatt, Giles Gunn (Hg.), *Redrawing the Boundaries. The Transformation of English and American Literary Studies*, New York 1992, S. 271-302.

Sedgwick, Eve K., "Mensch, Boy George, du bist dir deiner Männlichkeit ja unglaublich sicher!", in: Walter Erhart, Britta Herrmann (Hg.), *Wann ist der Mann ein Mann? Zur Geschichte der Männlichkeit*, Stuttgart, Weimar 1997, S. 353-361.

Showalter, Elaine, *Hystorien. Hysterische Epidemien im Zeitalter der Medien*, Berlin 1997.

Taussig, Michael, *Mimesis and Alterity. A Particular History of the Senses*, New York, London 1993.

Theweleit, Klaus, *Männerphantasien*, 2 Bde., Hamburg 1980.

Theweleit, Klaus, *Das Land, das Ausland heißt. Essays, Reden, Interviews zu Politik und Kunst*, München 1995.

Tiger, Lionel, *The Decline of Males*, New York 1999.

Tosh, John, "Was soll die Geschichtswissenschaft mit Männlichkeit anfangen? Betrachtungen zum 19. Jahrhundert in Großbritannien", in: Christoph Conrad, Martina Kessel (Hg.), *Kultur & Geschichte. Neue Einblicke in eine alte Beziehung*, Stuttgart 1998, S. 160-206.

Vinken, Barbara (Hg.), *Dekonstruktiver Feminismus. Literaturwissenschaft in Amerika*, Frankfurt a.M. 1992.

Weber, Ingeborg, "Poststrukturalismus und 'écriture féminine': Von der Entzauberung der Aufklärung", in: Ingeborg Weber (Hrsg.), *Weiblichkeit und weibliches Schreiben*, Darmstadt 1994, S. 13-50.

Weigel, Sigrid, "Der schielende Blick. Thesen zur Geschichte der weiblichen Schreibpraxis", in: Inge Stephan, Sigrid Weigel (Hg.), *Die verborgene Frau*, Berlin 1988, S. 83-137.

Weisberg, Liliane (Hg.), *Weiblichkeit als Maskerade*, Frankfurt a.M. 1994.

Weiss, Peter, *Abschied von den Eltern*, in: Peter Weiss, *Werke in sechs Bänden*, Bd.2, Hg. vom Suhrkamp-Verlag in Zusammenarbeit mit Gunilla Palmstierna-Weiss, Frankfurt a.M. 1991.

Young, Antonia, *Women Who Become Men. Albanian Sworn Virgins*, New York 1999.

Zaimoglu, Feridun, "Knabenwindelprosa. Überall wird von deutscher Popliteratur geschwärmt. Aber sie ist nur reaktionäres Kunsthandwerk. Eine Abrechnung", in: *Die Zeit* 47 (1999), S. 56.

3. MASCULINITIES/MASKULINITÄTEN: VISUELLE REPRÄSENTATION

Klaus RIESER
Feminized Men or Non-Hegemonic Masculinity

Barbara STRAUMANN
The Masculine Space of *North by Northwest,* or: Mapping the Vicissitudes of Masculinity as Performance

Stefan BRANDT
Acting Heroes: Heroes, Homos, and the Postmodern in Recent Hollywood Cinema

Veronika GROB
Fear of Falling: White Middle Class Masculinity in
Joel Schumacher's *Falling Down*

Elisabeth SCHAEFER-WUENSCHE
Rolling into History: Time and Community in Spike Lee's *Get on the Bus*

Elisabeth BRONFEN
'Masculinity; see under crisis:' Die Verfilmungen der Teena Brandon (*Boys Don't Cry*)

Barbara STRAUMANN

The Masculine Space of *North by Northwest*, or Mapping the Vicissitudes of Masculinity as Performance

[M]aps bring to light the *internal* logic of narrative: the semiotic domain around which a plot coalesces and self-organizes.[39]

In the case of *North by Northwest* (1959), the formulation of a plot idea appears to have been a particularly difficult process. When weeks of pondering, "two months of back-and-forth ping-ponging of ideas" had not produced a storyline, the scriptwriter Ernest Lehman expressed his ambition in the following laconic way: "All I want to do is write the Hitchcock picture to end all Hitchcock pictures." Asked by Alfred Hitchcock what this would mean, he shrugged. "Something with wit, glamor, sophistication, suspense, many different colorful locals, a real movie movie." In the completed film as well as in the writing process, many different locales (rather than "colorful locals")[40] actually turned out to be the determining function. According to Lehman's recollection, the shoreline started to come off when Hitchcock "murmured wistfully, 'I always wanted to do a chase across the faces of Mount Rushmore'" and then "one day" said that he "'always wanted to do a scene [...] where our hero is standing all alone in a wide open space and there's nobody and nothing else in sight for three hundred and sixty degrees around, as far as the eye can see... and then along comes a tornado. No place to run.'"[41] As already hinted at by the title's northwesterly direction, the plot of *North by Northwest* (1959) is indeed largely structured by movement through space, the geographical trajectory of Thornhill's odyssey as well as the prominent sites visited; among others a number of elegant Manhattan buildings such as the Plaza Hotel near Central Park, the United Nations Building, the Grand Central Station, followed by the Twentieth Century Limited Train along the Hudson to Chicago, an out-of-the-way bus stop on a vast and empty plain of fields in Indianapolis, a Frank Lloyd Wright house, and, finally, the Mount Rushmore National Memorial with the gigantic portraits of the American presidents Washington, Jefferson, Lincoln and Roosevelt. Thus Franco Moretti's definition of space as instrumental plot function is particularly pertinent to this film. Space is predominant in the sense that all the episodes and scenes are dependent on particular places, sites,

---

[39] Franco Moretti: *The Atlas of the European Novel 1800-1900*. London, New York: Verso, 1998, p. 5.

[40] Possibly Lehman already means 'locales' by using 'locals' in the obsolete meaning of 'places, localities' rather than the more usual 'inhabitants of a particular locality.'

[41] Ernest Lehman: "Introduction." *North by Northwest*. London: Faber & Faber, 1999, vii-xi, pp. vii-ix.

and landscapes, which, far more than mere settings, create the particular shape of this plot and its encodings.

In fact, the space traversed by Roger Thornhill (Cary Grant) in the course of his odyssey is encoded as American terrain the iconicity of which renders it a landscape of 'national importance.' Given the film's recurrent tongue-in-cheek treatment of various sites (see for example Thornhill's disguise as one of the porters in La Salle Street Station, Chicago, or the chase over the presidential faces on Mount Rushmore), *North by Northwest* can be seen as a running gag about a number of particular American landscapes. Without discounting the film's sophisticated, sparkling wit and buoyant flippancy, I would like to argue, however, that the jocular playfulness of this supposed light comedy is juxtaposed by a dark undercurrent. Although the manic hyperactivity and surfaceness of the film's language seek to deny it, this sombre crosscurrent is explicitly referred to by the allusion of its title to Hamlet's line "I am but mad north-north-west."[42] This intertextual reference alludes to the 'space' of literature as well as fantasy and hence invites us to read the film's space not so much as a mimetic rendition of American landscape but rather as a psychic reality. At the same time it brings into play doubts and discontent triggered, as in *Hamlet*, by the sense that "all is not well" in the nation state. In fact my wager is that, very much along the lines of *Hamlet*, *North by Northwest* acts out a discontent with the nation's body politic as well as a crisis in masculinity, both of which are articulated in spatial terms.

At first sight, *North by Northwest* appears above all to be an excellent illustration of Barthes's claim that narration and "the Oedipus" are coterminous,[43] as well as of Bellour's contention that "all Hollywood narratives are dramatizations of the male oedipal story, of man's entry into the social and Symbolic order."[44] In other words, the

---

[42] *Hamlet*, II.2. 374. For a reading that highlights the intertextual references to *Hamlet*, see Stanley Cavell's text
"North by Northwest" (*A Hitchcock Reader*. Ed. Marshall Deutelbaum, Leland Poague. Ames, Iowa: Iowa State University Press, 1986, 249-264).

[43] "At all events, without wanting to strain the phylogenetic hypothesis, it may be significant that it is at the same moment (around the age of three) that the little human 'invents' at once sentence, narration, and the Oedipus." (Roland Barthes: "Introduction to the Structural Analysis of Narratives." In: *Image, Music, Text*. London: Fontana, 1977, 79-124, p. 124.) There are a great number of readings of *North by Northwest* along oedipal lines; see for example Lesley Brill ("North by Northwest and Romance." *The Hitchcock Romance: Love and Irony in Hitchcock's Films*. Princeton, New Jersey: Princeton UP, 1988, 3-21), Robin Wood ("North by Northwest." *Hitchcock's Films Revisited*. New York: Columbia University Press, 1989, 131-141), and, above all, Raymond Bellour well-known analysis in "Le blocage symbolique" (*L'analyse du film*. Paris: Edition Albatros, 1979, 131-246).

[44] Tania Modleski: *The Women Who Knew Too Much: Hitchcock and Feminist Theory*. New York, London: Routledge, 1989, p. 45. Modleski refers to Janet Bergstrom's interview of Bellour ("Alternation, Segmentation, Hypnosis: Interview with Raymond Bellour." *Camera Obscura*, 3-4 (1979): 93.) Also note Bellour's emphasis on the oedipal trajectory in "Le blocage symbolique."

purpose of Roger Thornhill's journey seems to lie in the substitution of his overly present mother for the young and attractive Eve Kendall. In more abstract psychoanalytical terms, Roger has to overcome his excessive attachment to the maternal first love object in order to invest his libidinal energy in a second, more mature object choice, thus following the classical Oedipal trajectory as it is described by Freud. This Oedipal model delineates of course a masculine or even masculinist trajectory, in which the two female characters figure exclusively as functions of Thornhill's evolving maturation. This is rendered quite explicit by the fact that both women are (ultimately) called Mrs Thornhill, i.e. they are largely defined by their relation to the male protagonist, who exchanges the first Mrs. Thornhill for the second. The masculine inflection of this scenario is further underpinned by Miss Kendall's name: by encountering Eve, Roger steers towards woman and femininity as such.

In the concrete terms of the plot, Roger's maturation is represented as a straight development from irresponsible to responsible behaviour. In the establishing shots, Roger presents himself as a brash, fast-talking, and overconfident Madison Avenue advertising executive and a notorious playboy who not only lives purely on the surface but who also shows himself to be highly inconsiderate as he cheats two people out of their cab. However, in the course of his journey, the twice divorcé and heavy drinker suddenly finds himself seriously involved in and committed to romance and "togetherness," which come to replace his superficiality. However, the "pop-psychological"[45] explicitness of this straight trajectory suggests that it is not quite to be taken at face value. I am not denying that this configuration is in fact deployed by the film. But, apart from my doubts about the journey's semantic value as a trope of self-discovery (I will say more about this later), I am skeptical that it is above all the direction towards romance that is at stake.[46]

---

[45] Fredric Jameson: "Spatial Systems in North by Northwest." *Everything You Always Wanted to Know About Lacan But Were Afraid to Ask Hitchcock*. Ed. Slavoj Zizek. London, New York: Verso, 1992, 47-72, p. 48.

[46] As a contrast to my reservations about the romance plot see Lesley Brill, who begins his study *The Hitchcock Romance* with a reading of *North by Northwest* as a romance quest. Rather than stressing the romance element in my reading of the film, I should like to point out that, in the historio-cultural context of *North by Northwest*, the separation from the mother is in fact highly significant – yet not so much in oedipal terms but rather in relation to the threat of 'momism.' According to Michael Rogin, American postwar culture was obsessed by the fear that a strong maternal attachment prevented mother's boys from growing into responsible citizens, for 'momism' was aligned with communism and so-called un-American activities (Michael Rogin: "Kiss Me Deadly: Communism, Motherhood, and Cold War Movies." *Ronald Reagan, the Movie and Other Episodes in Political Demonology*." Berkeley, Los Angeles, London: University of California Press, 1988, 236-273). For a reading of *North by Northwest* focusing on the threat of 'momism,' see Robert J. Corber: In The Name of National Security: Hitchcock, Homophobia and the Political Construction of Gender in Postwar America (Durham, London: Duke UP, 1993, 190-218). See also Steven Cohan on "[t]he dread that the American male's emotional dependency [...], which led to his social as well as personal irresponsibility [...], [...] made him unduly dependent upon a woman (his mother) and, consequently, susceptible to pernicious

Quite in keeping with Roger's orientation towards surfaceness (not only is he an advertising executive but he also leads a superficial way of life), the film language of *North by Northwest* displays a wealth of surfaces. The film's opening credit sequence features a single-color two-dimensional screen with "rectangular outlines, resembling film frames."[47] After a while the grid is transformed into the window frames of a Manhattan high-rise office block[48] the mirror facade of which reflects the offscreen traffic on the street below. In a self-reflexive gesture, "the world conjured up announces itself as [...] the reflection of a world projected on the flat and receptive screen."[49] This artificial surfaceness is then enhanced by a plethora of reflections and artificial rear projections as well as the plot's harping on deceptions, mistaken identities, theatricality and performance. Actually the film's emphasis on surface is so pervasive that it can be read as a figuration not only of Thornhill's superficiality but of the (supposed) surfaceness of the American culture of the fifties at large.

However, as observed by Keane, the self-reflexive film language of *North by Northwest* – though beginning "in flatness" – "opens to depth," onto a disturbing knowledge, I should like to add, which the self-reflexive surfaces are grounded upon. Although Thornhill declares that the O of his trademark R.O.T. signifies 'nothing,' the attentive viewer comes to realize that R.O.T. does not simply mean 'nothing' (*rot!*) but that it simultaneously hints at the fact that (as in Hamlet's Denmark) something is

---

influences (Communism)" ('The Spy in the Gray Flannel Suit." *The Masculine Masquerade: Masculinity and Representation*. Eds. Andrew Perchuck & Helaine Posner. Cambridge Massachusetts, London: MIT Press, 1995, 43-62, p. 48; a somewhat longer version in Steven Cohan: *Masked Men: Masculinity and the Movies in the Fifties*. Bloomington, Indianapolis: Indiana UP, 1997, 1-33). Cohan's reading of *North by Northwest* forms a major source of inspiration for my own text.

[47] Marian Keane: "The Designs of Authorship: An Essay on *North by Northwest*." *Wide Angle*, 4:1 (1980): 44-52, p. 49.

[48] Interestingly enough, it is the reflecting facade of the Seagram Building, a typical piece of postwar architecture designed by Mies van der Rohe and built shortly before *North by Northwest* was made, that we are shown.

[49] Ibid. Similar to the *Hamlet* allusion mentioned above, this self-reflexive *mise-en-scène* of the film underlines that what is going to be mapped by *North by Northwest* is a fantasmatic projection rather than a mimetic rendition of American space. As pointed out by Corber (193), the opening titles by Saul Bass, featuring "a series of intersecting lines, clearly intend[...] to invoke a map or graph [...]." As the frame dissolves into the shot of the glass and steel facade, the grid is gradually filled by the reflection of the hectic traffic below. Yet as pointed out by Corber, "[t]he mirrorlike surface of the facade that emerges from the intersecting lines functions *as a screen on which the images of the busy street below are not so much reflected as projected*" (emphasis added). As it literally projects images onto a screen, the credit sequence thus forms a self-referential statement of the film about the status of its representations. Also note that the grid-structure is repeated by the design of the Rushmore cafeteria (floor, windows) as well as by the parallel lines carved systematically into the rock of the monument.

*rot*ten in this Cold War culture.[50] Thus rather than reading Roger's journey as a trope of Oedipal self-discovery, I suggest that we consider it as a symptomatic performance and articulation of cultural discontents.

Roger's traveling forms a resilient metaphor as it is reminiscent of the symptoms at play in a certain epidemic of wandering. Towards the end of the 19th century, the hotshot neurologist and former student of Charcot, Dr. Albert Pitres and his student Philippe Tissié witnessed the spread among lower and middle class Bordeaux males of a compulsion to set out for the road. An increasing number of "mad travelers," also called "fugueurs," peopled their ward.[51] Perhaps Tissié was particularly attentive and responsive to their symptoms as he was himself an enthusiastic cyclist and a prominent figure in the emerging cycling tourism.[52] At any rate, he devoted his thèse *Les Aliénés voyageurs* to the case of Albert Dadas, supposedly the first patient to suffer from the traveling epidemic, which evolved in a niche between criminal vagrancy and emergent romantic tourism. The mental disorder of the fugueur involved the repeated compulsion to set out and walk for weeks. During their protracted wandering that took some of them to such faraway places as Moscow and Constantinople, mad voyagers would often lose their identity papers. When stopped, arrested and checked by the authorities, they could neither remember who they were nor where they came from. In a sense then, 'pathological tourism' and its concomitant amnesia allowed a certain group of men (employed, emplaced, lower and middle class) to take flight not only from boredom but also from their identity, which was imposed upon them by social norms and control, particularly by the surveillance practices of the police and the military.

According to Ian Hacking, compulsive traveling is a "highly gender-specific" practice[53]; during much of our cultural history, females quite obviously could not move freely on the road without being regarded as 'loose' women. A release for men

---

[50] See Cavell's suggestion: "Thornhill's identifying 'rot' as his trademark [...] irresistibly suggests to me Hamlet's sense of something rotten" (253). It is from Eric Santner's rereading of Walter Benjamin's text "Zur Kritik der Gewalt" that I derive the notion of symbolic rottenness (Eric Santner: *My Own Private Germany: Daniel Paul Schreber's Secret History of Modernity*. Princeton, New Jersey: Princeton UP, 1996; Walter Benjamin: "Zur Kritik der Gewalt." *Gesammelte Schriften II.1*. Eds. Rolf Tiedemann & Hermann Schweppenhäuser. Frankfurt am Main: Suhrkamp, 1997, 179-203.) Santner develops the intriguing argument that in the late 19th century a "crisis of investiture" comes to articulate itself in the individual's relation to institutional authority. As a result of their sense that something is rotten in the law, subjects (mostly masculine as well as socially empowered) do not see themselves in a position to maintain their symbolic mandates. However, whereas Santner is interested in the analysis of paranoid fantasy structures which are developed as a result of a vacuum in the symbolic law, I am here more interested in the hysterical negotiation of a historio-cultural crisis in the symbolic.

[51] On the so-called "mad travelers," see Ian Hacking's book *Mad Travelers: Reflections on the Reality of a Transient Mental Illness* (Charlottesville, London: University Press of Virginia, 1998).

[52] This is Hacking's suggestion, pp. 14-18.

[53] Hacking, p. 50.

who "are curiously powerless in the face of their daily lives," the hysterical fugue "relieves them of responsibility" and offers them "an escape over which they have no control"[54] – they are overcome by a compulsion and, after having traversed considerable distances, cannot remember anything. In fact, their excessive wandering is reminiscent of feminine hysteria, which, according to the image traditionally disseminated by medical discourse, can be accounted for by the unhooking and the consequent wandering of the discontent uterus through the patient's body.[55] In contrast to feminine hysteria, the mad travelers, propelled towards distant places, leave their homes; they do so in order to articulate – like the feminine hysterics – that, in every respect, they do not feel at home. While, in order not to be marked as a 'loose' woman, the feminine hysteric has to act out her displacing discontent within the parameters of her bodily confinement to the domestic space, the masculine hysterical fuguer articulates his alienation in spacious landscapes. Although, thanks to his spacious enactment of his discontent, he can escape the confinement of domestic space, his wandering – just as the symptoms of feminine hysteria – is a recourse to speaking his distress and incapacitation with his body as symbolic language fails. In short, his traveling symptoms are, according to Hacking, "the bodily expression of male powerlessness."[56]

I invoke the mad travelers for several reasons. For one thing, the plot of *North by Northwest* bears a distinct masculine stamp as it is shaped to a great extent by Thornhill's obsessive traveling activities.[57] In other words, "the semiotic domain around which [the] plot coalesces and self-organizes" is encoded as masculine, on the one hand, by the larger trajectory of movement and traveling and, on the other hand, by the particular sites visited, which map a masculinity in crisis. Roger's journey evokes the notion of (male) travel as a trope for moral development; yet, more importantly, in traversing paradigmatic American spaces, it traces a hysterical fugue in response to a sense that something is 'rotten' in Cold War culture. In fact, Thornhill's flight takes its point of departure in a discontent with control and surveillance practices in the 1950s. It is not by accident that, in the Oak Bar, he should get up at the very moment in which the name 'George Kaplan' is pronounced. Similar

---

[54] Ibid.

[55] The notion of hysteria as articulating a discontent with and hence a critique of symbolic systems is developed by Elisabeth Bronfen in her book *The Knotted Subject: Hysteria and Its Discontents* (Princeton, New Jersey: Princeton UP, 1998).

[56] Hacking, p. 49.

[57] Of course, I am not referring to the actual involvement of the sexes in empirical fugue and travel towards the end of the 19th century and the 1950s, respectively. What I am trying to emphasize instead is the gendering of movement and travel, which needn't coincide with actual travel instances. The (en)gendering of these encodings is particularly evident in the shaping of feminine and masculine hysteria by medical discourses. Note that, during much of the plot journey, the feminine traveler, Eve Kendall, is indeed encoded as a "loose" *femme fatale* with an overly active sex life.

to the fugueur, Thornhill is at this moment interpellated; the signifier 'Kaplan' promises to offer a welcome escape from hegemonic norms of masculinity and the tensions inherent in some of these normative expectations. Yet while Thornhill is drawn towards the empty signifier 'Kaplan,' he simultaneously seeks to avoid the intrusion into his subjecthood when both the spies and the counterintelligence agents force Kaplan's name and identity upon him. In a sense then Roger Thornhill's travel narrative functions not unlike road movies, which "set[...] the liberation of the road against the oppression of hegemonic norms."[58] Yet in contrast to the outlaw rebel in the road movie, Thornhill is not a fugitive from the law. Quite on the contrary, his journey is to be read as a hysterical negotiation of the symbolic law and its particular historio-cultural figurations and interpellations. His wandering is so resilient precisely because of its incessant oscillation between a flight from and an embrace of the symbolic law and its codes.[59]

According to Ayako Saito, Thornhill's manic hyperactivity denies something fundamentally disturbing.[60] One could equally argue that the jocular, ironic and sometimes cynical overgarrulity of his incessant commentaries functions as a means of maintaining a sort of safe distance. And yet Thornhill's wandering can simultaneously be said to openly stage and articulate a discontent that is closely linked with the tenuousness of the nation's construction, notably with the fallible representatives of the national symbolic order, i.e. the government agents, who act as ruthlessly as the spy racket and do not shrink from sacrificing citizens in the name of national security.[61] Yet along with his discontent with the national symbolic order and its obscene undersides, Thornhill is also troubled by the war of the sexes and the question of masculine identity in this constellation. To be more precise, Thornhill finds himself having to fight on two fronts at the same time. On the one hand, he stands in a relation of simple opposition to both the spies and the government agents, while, on the other hand, he is involved in the more opaque antagonism between the sexes. Yet, as I will argue, this opposition and antagonism veil another, probably even more disturbing antagonism, namely a crisis in masculine identity.

---

[58] Steven Cohan & Ina Rae Hark: "Introduction." *The Road Movie Book*. Eds. Steven Cohan & Ina Rae Hark. London, New York: Routledge, 1997, 1-14, p. 1.

[59] Note that when first threatened by the secret agents he does not report them to the police but instead flees as if he were himself indeed a guilty fugitive from justice, while later on, at the auction sale, he poses as a troublemaker to attract police attention.

[60] Ayako Saito: "Hitchcock's Trilogy: A Logic of Mise en Scène." *Endless Night: Cinema and Psychoanalysis, Parallel Histories*. Ed. Janet Bergstrom. Berkeley, London, Los Angeles: University of California Press, 1999, 200-248, pp. 204, 215-216, 218.

[61] Asked how long Thornhill is going to survive as the live decoy Kaplan, the 'Professor,' i.e. the head of the national counterintelligence, dryly answers "[t]hat's his problem" (Lehman, 66). The UN diplomat Townsend is killed as a direct result of the mix-up of Thornhill and the counterintelligence's fictive decoy and later the government agents are willing to sacrifice Eve Kendall.

In its second half, *North by Northwest* offers us a scenario which carries all the marks of a perfectly happy end since all oppositions and antagonisms eventually seem to be magically sublated. In the scene in question, Roger and Eve meet in the romantic setting of a secluded pine grove. Finally, the enigmatic and treacherous *femme fatale* has turned completely transparent and all the obstacles to the final union of the two seem to have been removed. This is underpinned by the scene's symmetrical choreography – initially positioned next to a car at the very left and the very right of the frame respectively, Eve and Roger slowly move towards each other until they arrive at the centre of the frame, at which moment the camera switches from a longshot to a medium shot to focus on their intimate "togetherness." This symmetrical movement appears to dispute Lacan's dictum "entre l'homme et la femme ça ne va pas." Suggesting that there could indeed be an untroubled relation between the sexes, the scenario thus functions as a heterotopia, i.e. as a site at which a utopian hope has been realized. Although they are "outside of all places", heterotopias – according to Foucault – are by no means separate from the "normal" cultural spaces. Instead they constitute real places – places that do exist and that are formed in the very founding of society – which are something like counter-sites, a kind of effectively enacted utopia in which the real sites, all the other real sites that can be found within the culture, are simultaneously represented, contested, and inverted.[62]

However, this heterotopic moment of romance is framed by other scenarios which set off its artificial *mise-en-scène* and cast a shadow over the protective fiction of romance and its phantasmatic message that there can in fact be an unproblematic relation between the sexes on the one and between the subject and public apparatuses on the other hand. In what follows, I will therefore discuss a number of particular scenes and sites which interrogate this wishfulfilling message in particularly poignant manners.

The perhaps most haunting sites of *North by Northwest* are George Kaplan's hotel rooms. They exert a haunting power both because they are uninhabited and thus phantomatic sites and because, like foreign bodies, they wander over a vast expanse of space, across several states. They incite Thornhill to his obsessive traveling and actually determine his itinerary. However, they displace him not only in a concrete literal but also a figurative and psychic sense. What Thornhill's visit to one of Kaplan's rooms suggests is that masculine identity is perhaps but an effect of masquerading practices.

In our cultural imaginary, masquerade has always been aligned with femininity, or, to be more precise, femininity has been deemed coterminous with masquerade. This is not only the case since Rivière's and Lacan's seminal theoretical arguments that, in order to emerge under the feminine function in patriarchal and thus masculine symbolic systems, the subject has to adopt masquerading practices to an extent that

---

[62] Michel Foucault: "Of Other Spaces." *Diacritics* 16.1 (1986), 22-27, p. 24.

there is no difference whatsoever between femininity and masquerade.[63] In other words, masquerade does not mask a primary authentic identity but it constitutes feminine subjectivization and gender identity a such. In a less critical way, femininity has for a long time been stereotypically synonymous with simulation, deception, duplicity and multiplicity, in short, with histrionic performance, which lets masculinity appear as the One, the universal, the authentic and the unmarked. This alignment was reinforced and epitomized in and by the medical discourse about feminine hysteria. For example in the pictures taken at the clinic La Salpêtrière, it becomes evident that Jean-Martin Charcot, the leading neurologist in the second half of the 19th century working on hysteria, clearly privileged patients whose theatrical gestures and poses would attract and impress the audience of his famous Tuesday lectures, during which he used to display his hysterics in a lecture theatre.[64] Yet this powerful cultural iconography should not keep us from asking whether masquerade is indeed limited to femininity. In fact, in *North by Northwest*, Kaplan's 'personal belongings' stored in his hotel rooms evoke the suspicion that masculine gender identity may be equally dependent upon masquerade and performance. Room 769 at the Plaza Hotel New York derives its haunting quality not only from Kaplan's missing body but also from the fact that, contrary to its blatant absence of a guest, it so openly displays a plethora of personal items. Although Kaplan has not been seen for days, his material objects and traces insist on the room's inhabited state.

There are two twin beds, neatly made up, but the rest of the room looks lived-in. There is an open suitcase on the floor with a few shirts and some soiled socks in it. On a chair is a three-day stack of well-read New York newspapers. The dresser top is strewn with masculine odds and ends – an electric shaver, a pair of military brushes monogrammed 'G.K.', a half-empty pint of Canadian club, several scribbled

---

[63] Joan Rivière: "Womanliness as a Masquerade." *Formations of Fantasy.* Eds. Victor Burgin, James Donald & Dora Kaplan. London, New York: Methuen, 1986, pp. 35-44; first published in *International Journal of Psychoanalysis* 10 (1929); Jacques Lacan: "The Meaning of the Phallus" [1958]. *Feminine Sexuality: Jacques Lacan & the Ecole Freudienne.* Ed. Juliet Mitchell & Jacqueline Rose. Trans. Jacqueline Rose. Houndmills, Basingstoke, London: Macmillan, 1982, 74-85, p. 84. See also Harry Brod's "The Masculine Masquerade," an excellent overview of the development of 'masquerade' as a critical term (*The Masculine Masquerade: Masculinity and Representation.* Eds. Andrew Perchuk & Helaine Posner. Cambridge Massachusetts, London: MIT Press, 1995. Catalog of *The Masculine Masquerade*, an exhibition organized by Helaine Posner and Andrew Perchuk at the MIT List Visual Arts Center, Cambridge, Massachusetts, January 21-March 26, 1995).

[64] About the iconography of the Salpêtrière see George Didi-Huberman's seminal study *Erfindung der Hysterie: Die photographische Klinik von Jean-Martin Charcot* (trans. Silvia Henke, Martin Stingelin & Hubert Thüring. München: Fink, 1997 [1982]; particularly pp. 152-153, 251-253).

reminders: 'Call Wilson', 'Laundry Friday', 'Wire Ambassador East confirming reservation', 'Mahdi of Pakistan'. [...][65]

Together with the suits in the closet, Kaplan's "masculine odds and ends" conjure up an uncanny absence-presence. At the same time, however, they insist in their reference to a figure endowed with a more or less distinct identity. This effect is enhanced by a ridiculously arbitrary but decisive detail, namely the evidence of Kaplan's dandruff that Thornhill finds on the comb. Kaplan's dandruff forms a trace which, for the very reason that it seems to be so completely contingent, insists on the personal uniqueness of Kaplan. To (en)gender identity, thus the suggestion of this scene, it appears sufficient to supplement a name with a couple of arbitrary accessories and metonymical traces. This notion becomes even more disturbing in hindsight when it becomes clear that room 769, presumably along with all the other Kaplan hotel rooms, was nothing but a stage setting, that Kaplan himself is a set-up.

However, Kaplan and his hotel rooms represent more than the simple semblance designed by the counterintelligence office. In fact, at stake in room 769 is not only Kaplan as a contrivance of clues but also a more fundamental knowledge regarding masculine gender identity. As a kind of crypt, Kaplan's hotel room stores the notion that there is nothing 'authentic' at the core of the masculine subject, that – as much as femininity – masculine gender identity is dependent upon signs and performance. As Judith Butler argues so persuasively, "the inner truth of gender is a fabrication and [...] a true gender is a fantasy instituted and inscribed on the surface of bodies."[66] As it does not embody a coherent and continuous self, the gendered body has an ontological status only insofar as its reality is constituted by multiple acts of (en)gendering such as certain gestures and desires. These are *"performative* in the sense that the essence or identity that they otherwise purport to express are *fabrications* manufactured through corporeal signs and other discursive means."[67] In other words, these performative acts and gestures retroactively create the semblance of "an interior and organizing gender core"[68] which they pretend to express. Gender identity is thus not masked by performance but in fact fully dependent on it.[69] When he accuses Thornhill of masquerading and qualifies his performance as "expert playacting" and then again as "over-play[ed]," Vandamm, the head of the spy racket, does not grasp the full implications of performative practices. He correctly diagnoses Thornhill as enacting multiple roles. First you're the outraged Madison Avenue man who claims

---

[65] This is the stage direction for the scene of Thornhill's visit of room 769 in Ernest Lehman's screenplay (47), which is somewhat more explicit in its details than the actual scene in the film.

[66] *Gender Trouble: Feminism and the Subversion of Identity* (New York, London: Routledge, 1990, p. 136.

[67] Ibid.

[68] Ibid.

[69] Although the film features several disguises (Vandamm as Townsend, Thornhill as Kaplan), these masquerading practices simply supplement the more radical notion of performance that is simultaneously at stake.

he has been mistaken for someone else. Then you play a fugitive from justice, supposedly trying to clear his name of a crime he knows he didn't commit. And now, you play the peevish lover, stung by jealousy and betrayal.[70]

Vandamm's notion of masquerade and performance is, however, limited to Cold War spy games and accordingly he insists on knowing that 'Thornhill' is actually a fictitious figure fashioned to mask the real person Kaplan. Thus, according to Vandamm, performance and masquerade distort or veil (the expression of) a primary identity, while, in the Butlerian, more radical notion of performance, the relation of expression and performance is reversed to the effect that performance constitutes the ground of identity so that, without constantly reiterated acts of performance, there is no identity nor subjectivity.

Indeed, rather than veiling a 'true' identity, Roger's polished performances "redefine[...] his personality as the site of repeated identity displacements."[71] In the course of his odyssey, Thornhill is not only dislocated spatially but also in terms of his identity. To suit the particular requirements of the various scenarios, he has to constantly re-negotiate and readjust his persona according to different notions of masculinity. At one point an overly confident Madison Avenue executive, divorcé and womanizer, alcoholic, infantile mother's boy, he then successively turns into a kidnap victim, murderer, vulnerable fugitive, lover, porter, troublemaker, decoy impersonator, gallant rescuer and, finally, a fiancé, future husband-to-be and prospective breadwinner. Although some of these roles can be embodied at the same time, others are incompatible and thus displace one another in time and according to place as well as interpellating agency so that Thornhill's journey, rather than a way to self-discovery, reveals a lack of core identity, a "play of signifying absences that suggest but never reveal, the organizing principle of identity as a cause."[72] Instead of leading to maturation, his multiple performances point out that "[t]here is no gender identity behind the expressions of gender; that identity is performatively constituted by the very 'expressions' that are said to be its results."[73]

This, of course, is a far more unsettling perspective than the one implied by Vandamm's notion of masquerade as a strategy of disguise. And indeed, *North by Northwest* shows so very insistently how empty and brittle supposedly 'true' (gender) identities are. In fact, as Thornhill's case demonstrates, identity can boil down to the

---

[70] Lehman, p. 125.

[71] Cohan, p. 56.

[72] Butler, p. 136.

[73] Butler, p. 25. See also the following passage in *Gender Trouble* (p. 141): "If gender attributes [...] are not expressive but performative, then these attributes effectively constitute the identity they are said to express or reveal. The distinction between expression and performativeness is crucial. If gender attributes and acts, the various ways in which a body shows or produces its cultural signification, are performative, then there is no preexisting identity by which an act or attribute might be measured; there would be no true or false, real or distorted acts of gender, and the postulation of a true gender identity would be revealed as regulatory fiction."

question of not who you are but where you are so that identity becomes a matter of your temporary whereabouts, of a contingent proximity to the enunciation of a name, and the acts you come to perform from this particular site and interpellation. Due to his temporary presence in the Oak Bar at a particular moment, Thornhill is forced to enter into incessant negotiations in the course of which his identity emerges as an unstable assemblage of acts. Each one of his roles and acts is contingent upon a particular site so that his identity performance proves to be as dynamically discontinuous as his incessant displacement. In fact, his performance is indeed not so different from Kaplan's constant refashioning of the self, in which his place of origin is subjected to an incessant wandering. On June sixteenth, you checked into the Sherwyn Hotel in Pittsburgh as a *Mr George Kaplan of Berkeley, California*. A week later you registered at the Benjamin Franklin Hotel in Philadelphia as *Mr George Kaplan of Pittsburgh*. On August eleventh you stayed at the Statler in Boston. On August twenty-ninth *George Kaplan of Boston* registered at the Whittier in Detroit. At present, you are registered in room seven ninety-six at the Plaza Hotel in New York as *Mr George Kaplan of Detroit* – [...] In two days, you are due at the Ambassador East in Chicago – [...] And then at the Sheraton-Johnson Hotel in Rapid City South Dakota.[74] Thornhill insists vis-à-vis the Professor that, in contrast to Kaplan, he is not and will not function as a decoy – "I'm an advertising man, not a red herring! I've got a job, a secretary, a mother, two ex-wives and several bartenders waiting for me, and I don't intend to disappoint them all and get myself slightly killed by playing the man in the gray-flannel cloak and-dagger."[75] Yet in spite of Thornhill's remonstrance, Cohan's question "what makes one identity (Roger's, say) any more real than another (Kaplan's)?"[76] is extremely well put. Again, its being undecidable underpins the performative character of any gender identity.

In contrast to Vandamm, Thornhill the advertising executive is predestined to possess insight into the discursive effects of performance practices and gender identity as a semiotic activity in particular. He actually explains to his secretary that "[i]n the world of advertising there is no such thing as a lie, Maggie. There is only The Expedient Exaggeration." Furthermore, he asks her "Do I look a little heavish to you?" And, adept as he is at manipulating appearances, he immediately thinks of a remedial strategy. "I *feel* heavish. Put a note on my desk in the morning. 'Think thin.'"[77] These statements are quite in keeping with Thornhill's professional affiliation as is Eve's characterization of him: "You're an advertising man, that's all I know. You've got taste in clothes ... taste in food – [...] And you're very clever with words. You can probably make them do anything for you... Sell people things they don't need... Make women

---

[74] Lehman, p. 21-22; emphasis added.

[75] Lehman, p. 141.

[76] Cohan, p. 51.

[77] Lehman, p. 6.

who don't know you fall in love with you..."[78] In short, Thornhill is clearly encoded as belonging to a new professional-managerial class which, according to Cohan, controls representations and manipulates signs and images. Yet, as I will argue, this power is ambivalent in Thornhill's case. Instead of attenuating anxieties about the performative character of masculine gender traits, it actually renders these anxieties more acute.

North by Northwest in fact stages what Harry Brod calls "the profound but repressed cultural anxiety over gender identity in the 1950s."[79] To be more precise, Thornhill's professional affiliation refers to the change in historio-cultural paradigms which, fifty years later, allow Susan Faludi to speak of "the betrayal of modern man," namely the shift of the typical male postwar workplace from production to white-collar work and alienating corporate identity as well as the fear of the decay of virility in a cold war without armed conflicts. As pointed out by Steven Cohan, "the emerging power base of postwar America," i.e. the coalition of college-educated media and managerial professionals, to which Thronhill belongs, developed as a direct result of this major shift, especially in urban economy, from production to consumption, "the bedrock of the United States's postwar domestic economy."[80] Already in his contemporary book *The Lonely Crowd: A Study of the Changing American* (1950), David Riesman remarks that "[t]here is a decline in the numbers and in the proportion of the working population engaged in production and extraction – agriculture, heavy industry, heavy transport – and an increase in the numbers and the proportions engaged in white-collar work."[81] This new middle-class segment was constituted by "people who manipulated symbols rather than made things, whose stock in trade consisted of their organizational, technical, conceptual, or verbal skills."[82] Cohan points out that, although lacking the homogeneity and coherence of a class in the strict sense, this new social group yielded a hegemonic influence on American society and culture and, by making the lower classes orient themselves towards middle-class values, produced what later came to be seen as the complacent fifties consensus culture. However, it becomes clear in Cohan's description that this professional class, the power of which relied mainly on its control over the representations and images it commodified, was at the same time haunted by its own semiotic influence. In fact, this new social group accompanied its own semiotic activities with a considerable mistrust of representation. Even within the new class itself, there were virulent attacks on Madison Avenue hucksterism, the professional misuse of representation, and

---

[78] Lehman, p. 87.

[79] Brod, p. 17-18.

[80] Cohan, p.53, 54.

[81] In Cohan, p. 55.

[82] Jackson Lears: "A Matter of Taste: Corporate Cultural Hegemony in Mass-Consumption Society." *Recasting America: Culture and Politics in the Age of Cold War*. Ed. Lary May. Chicago: University of Chicago Press, 1989, p. 50; quoted in Cohan, 53.

advertisers were "accused of equating substance and packaging – and then suspected of doing even worse: selling an empty package to an unsuspecting public."[83]

Importantly enough, the paradigm shift from production to consumption affects not only the power over images in general but, in particular, the relation between representation and masculinity. At once catalyst and product of consumerism, the new class of professionals has to subject themselves to a culture of performance, i.e. their own regime of signs. In public relations, outer appearance becomes vital for successful business performance and, indeed, the Roger Thornhill figure embodies a looked-at-ness which is not only due to the visual organization of the cinematic medium.[84] To promote his aims, professional as well as private, Thornhill himself has to be both a manipulator of words and appearances and a product of polished performance. Over his body, then, substance and packaging come to be literally conflated or, in other words, masculinity is absorbed in(to) consumerism.[85]

Here, then, lies the crux of masculinity in consumerist culture. While consumerism, together with mass culture, had been aligned with femininity from the beginning of modernity (think of Emma Bovary's consumerist excesses), masculinity relied heavily on hard production work, combat in armed conflicts or, alternatively, the art of High Modernism.[86] If, as Huyssen shows, mass culture and hence consumerism are

---

[83] Cohan, p. 53.

[84] During much of the film we do nothing but observe the changing expressions of Thornhill / Grant and / or the agile movement of his body under danger. Then there is the joke about Thornhill's / Grant's face. "I know," Thornhill / Grant says removing his sunglasses and glancing at Kendall / Saint across the table, "I look vaguely familiar to you. [...] You feel you've seen me somewhere before. [...] Funny how I have that effect on people. Something about my face...." The immediate familiarity Thornhill's face provokes in Eve harps, of course, on Grant's star image. In another scene, Roger is stopped by the woman through whose hospital room he trespasses because she desires to get a good look at him. See also James Naremore ("Cary Grant in *North by Northwest* (1959)." *Acting in the Cinema*. Berkeley, Los Angeles, London: University of California Press, 1988, 213-235), who emphasizes, in his description of Grant's body in performance, the spectacle of the star.

[85] See Cohan on Thornhill's gray flannel suit which renders him "instantly recognizable as the 'original' representative of 'his kind,' the professional-managerial coalition that emerged within the middle class to dominate the entire culture during the postwar era": "Much of the significance of The Man in the Gray Flannel Suit had to do with the way advertising, increasingly directed toward male shoppers as well as female ones, revised what had been presumed to be an absolute gender divide: masculine production versus feminine consumption. [...] The Man in the Gray Flannel Suit was perceived as the agent of this disturbing – but also, everyone recognized, economically advantageous – absorption of masculinity into consumerism; what is more, he himself came to personify the corresponding conflation of substance and packaging" (52). Also note Brod's suggestion that the changes of postwar economy turn "the male body from a site of production to a site of consumption [...]" (19).

[86] Even Gustave Flaubert, who so willingly submits to and indulges in dreams and fantasies common among young women ("je suis dans les rêves de jeune fille jusqu'au cou") and who claims "Madame Bovary – c'est moi!", wishes to transform his beloved Louise Colet into "un hermaphrodite sublime," while he believes that he has himself overcome the "whitish fat" of

perceived as "the other of modernism, the specter that haunts it, the threat against which high art has to shore up its terrain,"[87] matters become more complicated once this opposition collapses as it is the case in both *North by Northwest* and the social culture of the fifties at large. However, the break-down of the prevalent cultural dichotomy of masculine production and feminine consumerism does not only provoke a fear of being engulfed by a supposedly feminized and feminizing mass culture (which actually had been there all along, supporting the dichotomy) and a consequent erosion of virility. The troubling impact of everybody's absorption into consumerist culture is rather the suspicion it evokes that social culture as a whole is permeated by performativity.

Thus the radical message of *North by Northwest* is not so much that masculine figures are emasculated through the film's concern with performativity, though performance is so bound up with the cultural construction of femininity,[88] but rather that the (admittedly) disturbing notion of gender as performance cannot be deflected onto the feminine figures. The film does go to great lengths to encode Eve as a duplicitous character; before turning into the transparent lover and wife-to-be, she is featured as promiscuous seducer, dangerous siren, and deceiving *femme fatale*. When, in the Rushmore cafeteria set-up of a theatre-within-the-theatre scene, Eve 'shoots' Roger with blanks, this is to suggest not only that Eve is a histrionic actress but that, in fact, she is empty at her core and thus ready to impersonate any role offered to her.[89] 'Eve,' her forename, is significant in this respect as it suggests that her ruthless shape-shifting coincides with the 'true' nature of femininity as such. However, this simple alliance is called into question as the gendered opposition masculine genuineness vs. feminine fakery is shown not to hold (any longer). As it has become evident in Roger's case, masculine action proves to be as performative as Eve's agency. In the cafeteria it is not just Eve who shoots fake bullets, but Roger complies with her put-up job, at once impersonating Kaplan and letting himself, in a completely convincing performance of vulnerability, fall to the ground in answer to her fire. One can make the reasonable claim that this particular scene in the Mount Rushmore cafeteria marks a turning point in the plot of *North by Northwest* since "it results in Roger Thornhill's recuperation of a full-fledged male hero who rather acts than reacts" as it "finally

femininity that jeopardizes virility; "c'est à force de patience et d'étude que je me suis débarrassé de toute la graisse blanchâtre qui noyait mes muscles." In Gustave Flaubert: *Correspondance*. Three Volumes. Edited and annotated by Jean Bruneau. Paris: Gallimard, 1973, 1980, and 1991; 3/31852, 20/3/1852, 12/4/1854, and 26 or 27/7/1852.

[87] Andreas Huyssen: "Mass Culture as Woman: Modernism's Other." *Studies in Entertainment: Critical Approaches to Mass Culture*. Ed. Tania Modleski. Bloomington: Indiana UP, 1986, 188-207, p. 200.

[88] See Rivière; Cohan, p. 58; Tania Modleski in *The Women Who Knew Too Much: Hitchcock, Feminism, and the Patriarchal Unconscious*. New York, London: Routledge, 1988, pp. 33-34.

[89] This is also suggested by the fact that, while Vandamm's mistress, she accepts the offer of the secret service to work as an undercover agent surveilling Vandamm's un-American activities.

achieves the 'demise' of George Kaplan, the fictional identity."[90] Equally one could make the point that Roger, who has so far only been reacting, turns to make his own decisions and to take action accordingly, notably "to go after Eve in his own name and on his own authority."[91] Although he never spells it out explicitly, Cohan's stimulating reading suggests that, although *North by Northwest* proposes this plot model, it simultaneously performs a contrarious knowledge. If we take the notion of gender identity as performance seriously, there is no reason then to assume that "the heroic masculinity Roger displays in rescuing [Eve] is meant to be read as the genuine article."[92]

This is not to suggest that Roger's or, for that matter, Eve's performative acts are mere fakery, but rather that neither of them is more real than the others. The point is precisely that performance is the only genuineness there is. Although "representations without an origin beyond the act of representation itself,"[93] performative acts are real and 'authentic' in that they articulate discontents and antagonisms and, in so doing, produce 'genuine' subjectivity. In other words, performance is a critical socio-cultural practice as its reiterative acts open up a distance, a gap which points to the fact that not any one performative act 'is it.' As they are not congruent expressions of some preexisting ontological core which would organize and coordinate them, the performative acts enact an incessant missing which insists on a fundamental lack. Being far more than a phoney bogus scene, Roger's fall in the cafeteria is real and authentic in its reference to the tenuousness and vulnerability of masculine identity, which result from the lack of an organizing core.

Matters are complicated as this lack goes together with a plethora of conflicting and regulatory images of masculinity. In the fifties one of these normative images is the tough masculinity which the Cold War warrior is required to embody in order to guarantee national strength and security. Thus masculinity and nation come to stabilize each other as they stand in a mutual relation of stable representation. However, the homeostasis of both masculinity and the nation is jeopardized by the tough warrior's uncanny spectre, namely the dependent, immature and irresponsible male (particularly the mother's boy) of consumerist culture. In contrast to the tough masculinity claimed by the Cold War, consumerist economy demands 'softer' qualities which can be reconciled with the emphasis of fifties culture on family values. Notably family fathers are supposed not only to fulfil the breadwinner function but also – especially as members of the middle class, which distinguishes itself by what it consumes – to both provide a family home and help furnish it with the desirable objects and fashionable gadgets such as refrigerators and TV sets. As this excess of

---

[90] Cohan, p. 44.
[91] Ibid.
[92] Ibid.
[93] Cohan, p. 58.

normative demands shows, masculinity is marked by overdetermination,[94] which leaves Roger Thornhill, despite his deft semiotic manipulations, utterly powerless. Though a controller of signs, he is haunted by these masculine images to the effect that he cannot but act out their conflicting demands in his incontinuous performance of diverse identities. [95] However, the lack of a core organizing gender identities appears to cause even more (gender) trouble than the overdetermination of masculinity through conflicting images and demands. The lack of such a core clashing with the gender difference enacted in the discursive domain of the cultural symbolic gives rise to the suspicion that there is something rotten in the regulatory fiction of the binary gender divide. Particularly the absorption of masculinity into the sphere of consumption puts the normative binarism that engenders identities into question. Masculinity and its activity no longer stand for "[h]uman law in its universal existence" which, according to Hegel, "is, moves, and maintains itself by consuming and absorbing into itself the separatism of the Penates, or the separation of independent families presided over by womankind, and by keeping them dissolved in the fluid continuity of its own nature." [96] In consumerist culture, masculinity can no longer successfully preserve the community's universal interests qua repression of its "hostile principle" or "internal enemy," namely "womankind in general," which stands for the particular and the individual as it "changes by intrigue the universal end of government into a private end, transforms its universal activity into a work of

---

[94] For a discussion of the contemporary debate on the "exquisite contradiction of the fifties conformity" (52) which troubles masculine identity, see Cohan, 48.

[95] Robert J. Corber regards Thornhill's identity as far less problematic. Emphasizing the Oedipal trajectory as well as the middle-class nuclear family as normative formation in Cold War ideology, he argues that in the course of the plot Thornhill succeeds in jettisoning his mother, thus overcoming his over-dependence on his mother as well as his concomitant "lack [of] a fixed stable identity" (191). Thanks to his opposition to the homosexually encoded "Communist agent" Vandamm, "he begins to occupy a more stable and unitary subject position" (191). As Thornhill subscribes to national security interests and simultaneously internalizes the rules of straight Oedipal desire, "his entry into full masculinity [...] and his patriotic duty are mutually reinforcing" (192). Thus, Corber argues, "North by Northwest shows that the construction of gender and national identity anchored and guaranteed each other in postwar America" (Corber, 191-218). The film certainly invokes the relation between (masculine) identity and the nation. But, as I should like to suggest, it does so in order to articulate a discontent with the contradictions inherent in the national symbolic as well as in masculine identity. Although he mentions Eve's violation of the hegemonic rules governing female sexuality in the fifties, Corber appears to take gender identity for granted rather than to consider it as troubled. Furthermore, Corber emphasizes that throughout the film "the American government remains in control" (196) without discussing the obscenity of this control nor Thornhill's discontent with the fallibility of the government representatives.

[96] G. W. F. Hegel: Phenomenology of Spirit. Trans. A. V. Miller with analysis of the text and foreword by J. N. Findlay. Oxford, New York, Toronto, Melbourne: Oxford UP, 1977, pp. 287-88. I would like to thank Jan Freitag for his inspiring idea to relate Hegel's passages on the necessity of the war to Butler's notion of gender trouble and the thesis that the performance of gender difference can be understood as articulating an unresolvable antagonism.

72

some particular individual and perverts the universal property of the state into a possession and ornament for the Family."[97] Instead virility is itself 'consumed' by consumerist culture, which feeds on the individual pursuit of happiness in materialistic terms so that the boundaries between a universal masculinity and the feminine "internal enemy" collapse.[98]

The breakdown of gender boundaries as well as the 'homelessness' of masculine subjectivity are resiliently brought to the open in the well-known scene in which Thornhill, exposed to utter vulnerability on an endless plain of fields without covers, is all of a sudden attacked by a crop-dusting plane. The completely flat landscape is reduced to an iconic simplicity and prototypical midwestern all-Americanness which remind us of *the* foundation myth of the American nation as well as of American masculine subjectivity, namely the westward shifting of the frontier as a result of the progressing civilization of both nature and the native population in the 'Wild West.' At the same time, the barrenness of the fields is reminiscent of a combat zone, the waste- and no-man-land of a field of conflict. Yet in contrast to the cowboy, whose isolated but somehow dignified and even glamorous loneliness and wandering are bound up with his paradoxical compulsion to return again and again to the wilderness and hence to turn his back on the civilized community, on whose foundation and consolidation he is constantly working but of which he can nevertheless have no part of, the urban figure Thornhill is completely displaced in this vast expanse of land, which is liminally positioned between nature and culture. In the nostalgic genre of the western, the privileged representatives of civilized life in the family as well as in larger communities are women, while the masculine figures, secretly afraid of "the separatism of the Penates," the domestic space presided over by femininity, leave home as they see this feminine space as a source of corrupting effeminacy and particularity, luring them away from virile independence. In keeping with Hegel, who juxtaposes the particularity of feminine domestic space with war, "the absolute freedom of the ethical self from every existential form,"[99] Michael Wood suggests that the cowboy and the soldier simply replace community "by corporate masculine adventures, of which war is the most common and most easily available."[100] So the soldier and the cowboy go to war or return to the wilderness, respectively, in order to embrace the homogenous male bond in the simple opposition of the front and the frontier, thus leaving behind the unresolvable antagonisms of the gender trouble at home.[101]

---

[97] Hegel, p. 288.

[98] Note that due to the emphasis of fifties consumerism on the acquisition of homes, home equipment and domestic appliances (such as TV sets, refrigerators and vacuum cleaners), the consumerist culture of the fifties is effectively a domestic culture.

[99] Hegel, p. 289.

[100] Michael Wood: *America in the Movies.* New York: Columbia University Press, 1989, p. 43.

[101] Wood (40-41) describes the masculine necessity to flee from home in spite of the American dream of the home in vivid terms. "Home is what we know we ought to want but can't really

However, in the case of Roger Thornhill, the impossibility of this scenario is played out. Exposed on the plain of fields, he is actually involved in a masculine combat action but the simple opposition scenario is tainted as he is all alone without the support of an all-male group of brothers-in-arms. And, more importantly, the simple opposition is disturbed by the superimposition of the antagonistic war of the sexes. After all it is Eve Kendall who dispatches him to this dangerous site, at which 'mother nature' (*womb*) is perverted into a fatal trap (*tomb*). As a 'double agent' in the literal sense, that is as spy and lover, she blurs the boundaries between private and public, between feminine domestic space and masculine combat zone. Neither is there a home from which Thornhill could escape in order to reinstate boundaries nor is there a front informed by simple oppositions and male bonding with which he could find refuge. Instead, as suggested by the superimposition of Eve's face onto the plain of fields, this seemingly empty landscape is flooded with gender trouble, notably the question of gender identity and the relation between the sexes. This flooding indicates that antagonistic relations cannot be delegated to and thus delimited to a feminine figure or a feminine location; as a result, there is no other option than the performance of discontent which propels Thornhill on his journey.

When, in the final scene, the spectacular chase over the monumental presidential faces, all relations are translated into simple oppositions, this is only to attenuate the disturbing antagonisms. Boundaries are only seemingly reinstated as Kendall transforms into a victim whose sacrifice is in turn prevented by the now gallant rescuer Thornhill. Yet, as a matter of fact, the scenes harping on Roger's vulnerability still linger and the film's emphasis on performativity prevent us from considering this simple and transparent relation between victim and triumphant hero as a true expression of interior cores informing stable gender identities. Furthermore, we have no guarantee that Thornhill's rescuing feat actually succeeds, that the beloved object does not – as in Hitchcock's previous film *Vertigo* (1957) – fall to death but can indeed

---

take. America is not so much a home for anyone as a universal dream of home, a wish whose attraction depends upon its remaining at the level of a wish. The movies bring the boys back but stop as soon as they get them back; for home, that vaunted all-American ideal, is a sort of death, and an oblique justification for all the wandering that kept you away from it for so long." He then quotes Cavell's observation that "'[w]hen the man (in the movies) goes home to his wife, [...] his life is over. [...] In a thousand other instances, [...] the marriage must not be seen, and the walk into the sunset is into a dying star: they live happily ever after – as long as they keep walking" (Stanley Cavell, *The World Viewed: Reflections on the Ontology of Film*. Cambridge Mass., London: Harvard UP, 1979 [1971], 49). In his classic study *Love and Death in the American Novel* (Illinois State University: Dalkey Archive Press, 1997 [1960]), Leslie Fiedler develops a similar argument for the American novel (see in particular the chapter "The Failure of Sentiment and the Evasion of Love" (337-390). The idyllic site where the American male feels at home "cannot be [...] city or village, hearth or home; for isolation is the key, the non-presence of the customary – in the words of Henry James, 'the absence of what he didn't want.' And what 'he' especially doesn't want is *women*!" Thus Fiedler goes on to argue, "[i]n America, the earthly paradise for men only is associated, for obvious historical reasons, with the 'West'; and it is possible to regard the classic works which we've been discussing, in this sense, as 'Westerns'" (Fiedler, 355).

be saved. When, during Roger's struggle to help Eve precariously hanging over the abyss on the rock ledge, the two agonized faces in close-up all of a sudden dissolve into the relaxed honeymoon faces as well as his addressing her as "Mrs. Thornhill" and pulling her up to the top bunk in the Pullman, this superimposition has so phantasmatic a quality that Hartman's suggestion is completely convincing that "[t]he last image of Roger's and Eve's bedding down may be a fantasy flash,"[102] a literal cliff-hanger which keeps us in suspense as to the status of Eve's survival. Similarly, the tenuousness of the sexual relation is underpinned by the fact that the pair's consolidation is viable only by virtue of a joint fight against an outer enemy, namely Vandamm and his brutal accomplices, on the one, and the representative of the national counterintelligence, the 'Professor,' on the other hand; two parties, in short, which, in their ruthless fight over "government secrets," are both willing to sacrifice the lives of innocent citizens.

In this scene, gender antagonisms are replaced by an opaque foreign body that subtends the national symbolic system. The film arrives at the 'navel' of the nation insofar as the chase over the Rushmore Monument, a site commemorating the national fathers and thus the nation's origin, hints at the precariousness but also the rottenness of the nation as a symbolic construction. In other words, the symbolic national landscape – in the form of the Mount Rushmore National Memorial, *the* symbolic representation of the political representatives of the national law *par excellence* – reverts into a dangerous overpresence of real matter. The fatal precipices literally reveal the void of the Real that subtends any symbolic construction, or, in Jameson's reading, the spatial end of the world,[103] which is reminiscent of the boundary in Truman's world in *The Truman Show*. Yet whereas in *The Truman Show*, there is a manipulating big Other operating from another world, there is no *sujet-supposé-à-savoir* here that could intervene (in time) to avert moments of catastrophe – quite on the contrary, the fallible father- and author-figures are themselves the cause of fatal catastrophes as they engage in irresponsible scriptwriting. What we are shown instead is the gaping abyss that underlies the nation's symbolic fiction. The glossy surface displayed in the opening sequence returns as the rough amorphous material of the monument, overpresent and grotesquely distorted, as it is seen in overproximity and as it points to the real abyss, the site at which the costs of an irresponsible and violent scriptwriting and the fallibility are visibly brought to the fore.

Although the crisis in masculine gender identity is at this point substituted by the full display of the cause of Roger's hysterical discontent with the symbolic representatives of the national law, we are nevertheless forced to realize that the relationship between Roger and Eve is dependent upon a mediating third term, notably the national symbolic law. This is already hinted at in the heterotopic *tête-à-*

---

[102] Geoffrey H. Hartman: "Plenty of Nothing: Hitchcock's *North by Northwest*." *The Yale Review* 71(1981): 13-27.

[103] Jameson, p. 61; also see Cavell: "To fall from Mount Rushmore, as I am imagining it, would be to fall off the earth, down the vast edges drear of the world" (1986: 262).

tête in the pine grove, where the pair is visually linked by a symmetrical *mise-en-scène* but where they are simultaneously overtopped by the monumental faces in the background. Yet their dependence on a third term becomes even more conspicuous when, during their struggle on the monument, they are completely dwarfed by the overwhelming symbolic structure. In fact, I would go so far as to argue that their "togetherness" is rendered possible only by the intrusion of the state, i.e. the symbolic mediation of a disturber of love. To consolidate their relation, the two lovers need to stand in opposition to a third term in order to forget the antagonistic gender troubles, while the protective fiction of love and romance veils the crisis in masculinity. It is, furthermore, significant that, in spite of the fifties obsession with domesticity and family values, we are never offered a representation of a home. In Jameson's words, the concept of the intimately private that the film seeks to "'produce' or 'construct' [...] need never be tested, since – ideal marriage – it lies beyond the closure of the film and thus beyond representation."[104] Or, in a somewhat more radical way of putting it, we could draw the conclusion that Roger and Eve – so as to stay a couple – mustn't ever arrive at home. The only provisional 'home' they may inhabit is "as limited and as evanescent as that collapsing upper berth in the Pullman, which can always be folded away without a trace. The berth is, however, not a statement, or a symbol, or a proposition; but rather a problem."[105] So they have to continue their endless quest, re-negotiating symbolic codes and confronting fallible fathers as well as America's inner and outer enemies, never to arrive home – neither spatially nor psychically – but instead forced to be always on the move, to keep forever wandering in antagonistic spaces.

---

[104] Jameson, p. 52.
[105] Ibid.

Klaus RIESER

Feminized Men or Non-Hegemonic Masculinity?

This article is concerned with the question how best to conceptualize non-normative masculinity on the movie screen, as it is represented by marginalized men – soft, hysterical, childish, transgender. In particular, it inquires inhowfar it makes sense to consider such men to be feminized by the filmic text or whether we should rather see them as variants of manhood. Finally, an attempt is made to theorize beyond the masculine / feminine binary.

In the 1980s and 1990s, feminist film theory has increasingly moved away from the original psychoanalytical concepts that had connected male figures almost invariably to power (voyeurism, sadism) and female figures to passivity (being an object of the gaze). Instead, various critics have pointed out that also men can be masochistic, subordinated, and / or the object of a cinematic gaze. However, many of these critics have claimed such men to be feminized, a tendency that in my opinion raises a number of questions: Is femininity always the property of a powerless object? Are male figures on the screen who do not belong to hegemony – because they are Jewish, black, young, hysterical, or gay - really feminized by the movie-machine (the apparatus and the codes of mainstream narrative film)? If not, what then about men who really seem to be feminine, such as transvestites, or transgender persons? Moreover, since the aim of this analysis is not just terminological clarification but also political it will also trace questions that arise for feminism and pro-feminist men's studies:

Is it analytically and politically correct if femininity encompasses men? Is it helpful to consider male gender rebels to be aligned with the feminine or is it better to identify them as non-hegemonic but still men? These and related questions will be traced in the following pages. I will first introduce the topic through some quotes, which use the term feminization or femininity in regard to male characters on the screen. I will then argue under what circumstances I consider this terminology and the conceptualizations related to it acceptable or useful. Then I will turn to a criticism of this position by pointing out five main problematic areas associated with it: binarization; reduction of the complexity of masculinity; male usurpation of a female position; heterosexism; and equaling femininity with victimhood and passivity. Finally, I will present concepts which point beyond feminization by breaking with sex / gender dualism: Gilbert Herdt's concept of a third sex, Eve Kosofsky Sedgwick's model of masculinity and femininity as orthogonal to each other and Chris Straayer's queer interventions in direction of multivalency and bi-sexed identity. Critical and theoretical texts that deal with non-normative men very often claim them to be feminized. To illustrate this tendency, I here present a few such instances, far from attempting to be exhaustive. Interestingly, the term is already employed in one of the foundation texts on masculinity in film, a seminal article by Steve Neale. In this article, Neale applies Laura Mulvey's famous psychoanalytical theorems (active male gaze -

passive female object of the gaze) to an interrogation of masculinity. He remarks that Rock Hudson's body is sometimes the object of an erotic look in films, but does not consider this fact to counter Mulvey's system. Instead, he claims that "... Hudson's body is *feminized* in those moments, an indication of the strength of those conventions, which dictate that only women can function as the objects of an explicitly erotic gaze. Such instances of 'feminization' tend also to occur in the musical..." (1983, 18).[106] Unfortunately, Neale fails to specify in what the feminization consists, so that it might be a circular argument: 'woman' in patriarchal cinema means passivity and therefore a passive male has to be feminized. But not only men who function as spectacle, such as dancers in the musical have been considered to be feminized. The same has been claimed, for example, regarding the romantic hero, who, Gledhill argues, "is in many ways like her [the heroine] - he is feminised" (1995, 82), and of any young man: "The male youth can be considered as feminized because he is not yet fully mature and he presents an ambivalent figure..." (Branston: 1995, 31). Others see a feminization of the Jews in Schindler's List – "Schindler's List perpetuates the image of a weak, feminized Jew, the passive figure so negatively described by Otto Weininger, and later, Bruno Bettelheim, at the expense of truth." (Doneson, 145), of the Woody Allen persona (Rowe: 1995), or even of a powerful action film bad guy: According to Branston, in the film *In the Line of Fire* the killer Leary (played by John Malcovich) is feminized vs. the securely masculine hero Horrigan (played by Clint Eastwood).

As even this cursory listing reveals, I tend towards a critique of the term feminization, particularly when the use is not substantiated or reflected. But before an elaboration of this criticism I would like to point out the instances where I have found the concept put to convincing use.

That is, first of all, the case when femininity in men is not simply seen as synonymous with a lack of power, but more substantiated. I am referring above all to effeminate (woman-identified) men, transgenders and transsexuals – to men, that is, who identify themselves with femininity or womanhood – and, by extension, to their filmic representations.[107] In other words, the term can be appropriate when referring to cultural symbols of femininity (gestures, clothes, etc), instead of being linked without reflection to passivity and objecthood. Movie examples range from films about effeminate men (*Torch Song Trilogy*) via crossdressing / transvestite films (*Some Like It Hot; Paris Is Burning; Priscilla, Queen of the Desert*), to transgender / transsexual films (*The Crying Game; M. Butterfly*; Divine films). To better work with this concept of

---

[106] The italics and the single quotation marks qualifying the term "feminization" are Neale's, an indication perhaps that he is himself doubtful about this interpretation.

[107] A very interesting study of cultural gender codes on the "opposite" sex has been provided by Judith Halberstam in her book *Female Masculinity* (1998), which concerns itself however, with masculinity in women, not femininity in men, as this paper does. Another major work that should be mentioned is Rebecca Bell-Metereau's historical study of *Hollywood Androgyny* (1993). For a short discussion of the terms "sissy" (young effeminate man), "effeminate", "woman-identified", "feminine" compare Doty: 1991.

femininity in men a suggestion by Alexander Doty may be particularly useful: In his article on Pee-Wee Herman, he defends gay male femininity against criticism of anti-feminism claiming that we should distinguish it from straight female femininity. This opening up of femininity into plurality and allowing one of these to be accessible to males qualifies the term feminization and therefore makes it both more complex and more precise. This has become more and more relevant, since transvestism, cross-dressing and transsexuality – all relating to femininity and feminization in/of men - have made a strong impact on the mainstream in the 1990s in very ambivalent but often quite astonishing ways. For example as a quite recent phenomenon we can witness mainstream narrative films which introduce male-to-female transgender persons in central positions, whose queer identity is revealed to the audience only in the course of the film. *The Crying Game* has become a media event because of this and *M. Butterfly* plays in a similar way with audience expectations and 'misreadings'. In both cases we can claim the men to be feminine, partly I think because they are feminized by cultural as well as filmic codes, and partly because these processes are reflected upon by the texts themselves. Particularly in *M. Butterfly* (witness the title!) imperialistic/cultural assumptions are blamed for the misrecognition on the part of the protagonist. Moreover, this imperialistic feminization of Song (the Chinese man who plays a woman in Chinese opera and for Rene, the French diplomat) is precisely *not* only attached to passivity. In fact, it is revealed in the end that the male French protagonist himself is drawn to passivity and being an object of the gaze.

Similarly, if it is made clear that by 'feminization' one refers above all to a patriarchal strategy, it may be employed to great use. For films do indeed use signals of femininity (dress, posture, etc.) as a means of marginalization. This can be explained by the fact that the non-conform has to both be sometimes presented (although at other times repressed) *and* kept under control. Moreover, the various marginalizations in society are interrelated, even to some degree interchangeable from the point of view of the center. Or, to put it differently, the various subordinations reinforce each other. Asuman Suner, for example, in a reading of *M. Butterfly*, deals with the feminization of the colonized and the colonization of the feminine as intertwined modes of the Orientalist discourse which serves to center the Western white male subject. Thus sexual preference, gender, and race are all pegged to each other under patriarchy: Asians may be seen as softly feminine, gays as screaming wannabe women or inverts (women in male bodies), and women as close to racial others in belonging to the realm of the natural rather than the white male realm of the cultural. Conversely, dominant masculinity tries to distinguish itself for its identity *at the same time* from the mother ('I am not a child'), women ('I am not a woman') and from the gay man (' I am not gay'). In such conceptualizations-awareness of multiple forms of marginalization combined with a reading of feminization strategies – the term feminization not only is acceptable but may indeed be illuminating (e.g. for a reading of the high pitched voice of black comedians such as Eddie Murphy, Chris Tucker and others). Even supermacho men may be feminized/marginalized as can be witnessed in the male hysteria of action comedies such as *Rush Hour*, which present little more than a surfacing of what in 'serious' action film boils under the surface. The most obvious strategy in this regard is indeed a hysterizising (feminizing in patriarchal terms) of a male (usually racially coded) character. Various subordinations can actually be played out against each other, when, for example, the hysterical (feminized) black spews forth sexist remarks.

However, the cultural logic of our gender system also runs much deeper, and I want to acknowledge even the nowadays much discounted concept of the gendered nature of the cinematic apparatus. In this case I find Mulvey's argument still valid, which sees the cinema's favoring of distance, and therefore voyeurism and fetishism as intricately aligned to masculinity while femininity is culturally coded with closeness.[108] Thus if a character is to be presented outside normative masculinity it will be presented not as a purveyor of the distanced gaze but rather 'too close' to the objects of his desire, and accordingly functions as non-male in the apparatus to be legible at all. Cinema functioning as a part of the binary machine of gender under patriarchy, it is in this way possible to refer to the deviation from normative masculinity in film as a feminization.

Finally, I want to acknowledge the use of 'feminine male' and 'feminization' within explicit theoretical grids as for example Rodowick's categorization of Freudian terms. Rodowick's complex systematic goes far beyond simple duality, as it encompasses not only 'masculine:feminine' but also the diversity of lived experiences ('men-women'), ideological binarism ('man/woman'), medical discourse that allows for deviation but still sticks to two normative concepts ('male ... female'), and the sexual drive, which in Freudian terms encompasses 'active <-> passive.' Moreover, Rodowick points out that in Freudian thought (in contrast to everyday use) 'masculine' and 'feminine' pertain to men *and* women, because *both* are present in every human subject. 'Masculine:feminine' therefore refers to object choice and fluid patterns of sexed identification.

Another very illuminating use of the Freudian system in all its complexity can be found in *Male Subjectivity at the Margins*, the highly impressive work of Kaja Silverman. Amongst other things, she develops a theory of male masochism in the cinema, distinguishing between moral (e.g. Christian) masochism and sexual masochism, which following Freud she calls "feminine masochism". Her highly theoretical analysis helps explain, for example, how one kind of masochism can be culturally revered (for example that of martyr figures such as Rambo in captivity) while another (sexual surrender to women) is marginalized. According to Silverman, this is the case because the former "variety of masochism [is] in no way incompatible with virility" (1992, 10). She goes further by claiming that not only are some masochistic figures exemplary, but that, in fact, "only the narrowest of borders ... separates normative male subjectivity from masochism" (1992, 363). On the other hand, the sexual masochist, according to Silverman "a feminine yet heterosexual male

---

[108] For an introduction to apparatus theories see for example Mast: 1992.

80

subject" (1992, 212) is culturally marginalized because he is tainted with femininity.[109] These complex positionings of femininity and the high degree of reflexivity in the Silverman text make her use of the term with regard to male subjects not only acceptable, but simply fascinating. However I am still reluctant regarding this use. Not within her analysis, where it is entirely convincing, but if were to be applied in a more popular manner. That is, I am convinced only within the theoretical apparatus she uses, but doubtful of the applicability to common political action, perhaps even to general film analysis.

A Critique of Feminization

After this brief overview of possible employments of 'feminization' I will now present some arguments against usage of the term and the theoretical structures it implies. My criticism is based on five major dangers I see inherent in a use of feminization, namely that it reinforces a binary sex/gender system; reduces the complexity and contradictive nature of masculinity; hides male usurpation of a female position; can be heterosexist; and finally, equals femininity with passivity and victimization.

The first claim, that feminization is binarizing is perhaps the most obvious one. The term may be employed in a system which in certain ways transgressed binarism – such as Rodowick's presented above, but in and of itself it binarizes by implying that what is not masculine has to be feminine. One might also claim that feminization is binarizing on another level, namely in that it enforces the sex-gender split: In insisting on the sex-gender distinction with a freer floating of the gender (feminized men vs. masculine men), sex is presented as less variable and biology thereby raised to the level of destiny. For the theoretical faults of such a position Judith Butler has provided the ultimate criticism in *Gender Trouble*, where she makes a call for a constructivist conceptualization of sex just as much as gender. In other words, the concept of gender inherent in calling non-hegemonic men 'feminized', makes it seem as something simply taken up or put on by society, like a piece of clothing over a more immutable sexual body, rather than a process that reaches into the smallest nooks of our identities. Moreover, I claim that however strenuous the connection of gender (femininity in men) to biological sex may be conceptualized by theoreticians, in most cases the double binarism feminine-masculine and female-male lead to a normalization of their coincidence, implying if not denoting the feminine to belong to the female order and the masculine to the male. I am thus arguing that in difference to 'feminization' and the exclusive focus on masculine-feminine it implies we should follow Brod's suggestion that in analyzing masculinity we need at least two axes: the male-female axis and one that follows the hierarchy between men. I am of the opinion

---

[109] In a similar argumentative stance Silverman also claims that homosexuality cannot be analyzed in isolation from sexual difference, that, in other words, the gay man is always to some extent related to femininity (34, 346).

that many men (particularly mass-mediated images of men) who are not in the normative fold differ as much if not more on this latter male-male axis as on a male - female one, a fact obscured by reducing marginalization, subordination, oppression or simply *difference* to 'feminization.' As a filmic example of these remarks I would point out Pee-Wee Herman in *Pee-Wee's Big Adventure* who – as many comedians – can be considered feminized only in relation to normative masculinity but not in relation to the other characters in the film. Instead, in his interaction with a female character he can be quite 'manly' and in those with a male convict to whom he seems to be attracted mostly shy or childish. In any case, both interactions speak loudly against reading Pee-Wee as a woman or even in the position of a woman. Similarly, the shifting relation between the 'small', 'soft' Asian (Jackie Chan) and the 'hysterical' black man in *Rush Hour* and their relations to other characters contradict a reading of either as feminized.

The second point of contention I have with the term 'feminization' is connected to the above argument against binarizing. I am convinced that to call non-normative men feminized reduces the complexity and contradictory nature of masculinity. I would argue first of all that such men, from super-puffed-up body builders to softies are so diverse and contradictory in themselves that they should not be reduced to a labeling such as feminized. Moreover, 'normal' (normative) masculinity is not simple and uniform either. If indeed – as Silverman convincingly claims – masochistic masculinity is only distinguished by the narrowest border from normative masculinity, does it then makes sense to call the one feminized and conceive of the other as a stable core of masculinity rather than a tenuous - albeit multiply sustained - construction? In fact we should return the diversity and the resultant friction to the concept of masculinity rather than including it into an Othered 'femininity'. The Elvis persona may serve as an historical example: He became famous for offering his body as spectacle, which, however, hardly feminized him. On the contrary, as Fred Pfeil points out, Elvis shocked precisely as a *male* sexual object for a primarily female gaze. This 'scandal' could only have been one for patriarchy and struck right at home in masculinity, which is where it belongs and against which non-normative behavior should be turned. Similarly, Robyn Wiegman in her article "Feminism, 'The Boyz,' and Other Matters Regarding the Male" warns against a feminist reinscription of the feminization of Uncle Tom: "For the African American male is not a symbolic woman, no matter how intense the process through which a chain of social and specular being is inscribed along the lines provided by sexual difference. If lack must be consigned, if the black male must be physically, psychologically, and/or symbolically castrated, then his construction in the guise of the feminine evinces not simply an aversion to racial difference but a profound attempt to negate masculine sameness, a sameness so terrifying to the cultural position of the white masculine that only castration can provide the necessary disavowal" (1993, 179).

Even in cases where a feminization seems to be quite obvious, we should employ analytical caution, because it might be an instance of a male usurpation of a female position. For example, Kathleen Rowe, who at one point in her paper uses the term 'feminization' later argues: "The apparent feminization of the sensitive male does not undo sexual difference but reauthorizes male power by denying women the very specificity of their being" (1995, 186). In such cases, the patriarchal system transgresses its own boundaries in an attempt to shore up its power. Another example for such an usurpation of a feminine position is the male public tears that have been analyzed by Maurizia Boscagli. Boscagli points out how mass-mediated male tears such as Clint Eastwood's in *Unforgiven* and those to which Gulf War General Schwarzkopf admitted on television, are not a true change of masculinity but an appropriation of positions that have hitherto been defined as female. They are actually melodramatic signs of emotionality that appropriate the position provided by melodrama without a concurrent change of gender dynamics or hierarchy. "Male tears are not a chosen feminization, or a form of androgyny, a case of postmodern gender bending" (Boscagli: 1992, 67). On the contrary, they serve to exclude women. "The individual case of a man crying in private (almost secretly until he is 'discovered' and revealed but not exposed by the TV camera) is elevated to the dignity of universal exemplum and made into an essence – the inner quality of masculinity – where masculinity equals humanity once again" (1992, 71). In particular, Boscagli points out how this recuperation of the private and of authentic feeling for the male – far from feminizing him – maintains the gender split: "While a man who cries is a human being, a woman who cries is a woman. By crying she loses her humanity only to become gendered and 'particular' again" (1992, 75). A similar process of usurpation can also be analyzed to underlie many films with homosocial settings that include no or only alibi women. In these male-only settings feminized men by allowing for the necessary emotionality, for example, serve to better seal off the system, rather than open it up.

The use of 'feminization' to explain media images of non-conformist masculinity can also be heterosexist. As is well known, there is a long tradition of seeing homosexuals as inverts. Presented with the challenge homosexuality poses to a binary gender system (there are only men and women and they desire each other), patriarchy sometimes has responded by simply taking same-sex desire as indication for a wrong gender identity. This view of (male) homosexuality as a 'female soul enclosed in a male body' (*anima muliebris in corpore virili inclusa*) was codified by Karl Friedrich Ulrichs in the nineteenth century. [110] Originally intended to make homosexuality 'natural' and thus defensible it is nevertheless highly problematic, since it has co-constructed the idea of THE homosexual as an identity distinguished from heterosexuals. Also, it reinscribes patriarchal definitions of femininity and simply runs into theoretical problems, when men desire men without seeing themselves as women. Feminization is also heterosexist in that allows variation only in the gender field while maintaining a rigid sex (male-female) system. As Butler has pointed out, this reduction to sex is a reduction to sexuality and ultimately to reproduction (biological destiny). That is, binary patriarchal sex/gender society, according to

---

[110] Herdt: 1994, 75. For an in-depth discussion of this notion compare Hekma: 1994.

Butler, is first and foremost based on a refutation of homosexuality and only thereafter on a male-female split. Using feminization thus leads us right back to the two sexes and circumscribes, indeed obliterates space for variation on the level of sexuality and gender, as it is posed by gay, lesbian and other queer desires and identifications.

To illustrate the point from another angle, it is instructive to look at an argument by Kelly Hankin, who has analyzed some heterosexual male movie personae as representations of butch lesbians. What she has to say about these male icons of butchness makes it clear that 'feminization' does hardly come close to defining their non-conformity to hegemonic masculinity. According to Hankin elements that make a man such a representative for butch are: a) differing from and resisting the heterosexual economy (for example, by fighting for lesbian and gay rights); b) *ambiguous* gender (not feminine, that is, unless we equal femininity with ambiguity); c) an outsider/rebel position and stance; and d) nonphallic attributes (softness, etc.), this last being the only characteristic that relates to feminization at all. While Hankin does not explicitly focus on whether such men are feminized, implicitly her whole argument runs counter to such a view. For example, she claims as a necessary corollary for a butch-man that he exhibits desire is desirable for a femme, that, in other words, he should exhibit enough butch/masculine traits and desires. This butch male does not seem feminized to me, but rather a figure *related* to normative masculinity without being complicit or identical with it. Hankin precisely mentions that such a butch-man is often one who *plays* with male signals, such as a 'typical' male stance, a taking on of masculine identity (most likely with a knowledge of it being a masquerade). Hankin's most surprising example for a butch male symbol is perhaps that of Johnny Cash - but surprising only if we still think in feminization terms rather than the elements Hankin has pointed out. For then the macho, but troubled and outsider masculinity that Cash embodies - prison, alcohol, women - becomes understandable as an icon for butch identity. In short, in analyzing gender in film we should look at various processes of marginalization (race, class, gender, queer, etc.) and resistant readings.

Finally, in terms of feminist analysis - where practically all the works I am referring to are situated, including those that use 'feminization' - the term is questionable, since it equals femininity with passivity and/or victimhood. In many instances it does not refer to such supposedly feminine characteristics as higher voice, emotionality, wearing women's clothes, sexual interest in men (as mentioned earlier, these are hardly unproblematic either), but precisely to a positioning under power, to a depowerment: being treated as an object, being dependent, etc. This is particularly problematic because it is usually not made clear which textual code (hermeneutic, cultural, etc.) the term refers to and what definition of gender (power relation, social role, identity, etc.) is employed. Rarely is made clear whether by using 'feminized' these authors refer to a strategy of submission concurrently devaluing the man *and* femininity, to cultural traits such as 'feminine' behavior, or even to supposedly 'real', innate characteristics. Such uses of the term 'feminization' tend to mask power by hiding it behind supposed gender identity issues or, worse, by linking submission to cultural codes of femininity. In other words, if femininity were universally understood as purely social in a multidimensional field of identities, the term feminization might be acceptable, and similarly, if by femininity we all understood patriarchal oppression of women. However, neither is the case, not in the general public, and not in academic writing. Therefore to call male subordination or passivity as femininity or feminization is highly problematic. As Carol Siegel has put it in a critique of Silverman's analysis of male masochism: "Where feminine can only mean passive/receptive and heterosexual can only mean male-dominant, female dominance must be both culturally represented and read as feminization of man. Thus the term 'feminine masochism' [referring to male sexual masochism] effectively erases the woman's desire in the S/M scenario because the man occupies the feminine place" (1995, 87).

In some cases, moreover, passivity and divestment of power can be better understood as regression (to a childlike stage) than as feminization. For while patriarchal texts often attempt to relate regression to femininity, if the text is looked at carefully enough, the regressed character is actually quite distinct from adult femininity. Quite clearly, for example, Pee-Wee Herman's sex/gender pranking – as often in comedy - is channeled through regression (love of his bike, giggling, etc.) and is therefore to some extent outside the binary masculine-feminine machine. A similar example occurs in *Rush Hour* where at one point the two 'action heroes' argue whose daddy was the better policeman – a clear allusion to a child's claim to power - 'my daddy can beat up your daddy'.

As the above arguments have shown, I regard it as important to clearly distinguish between and reflect the use of the various terms that are applicable to the gender world of narrative film: femininity, queerness, subordination, non-normative masculinity, passivity, transgender, etc. However, I consider it equally important to search for ways to theorize beyond academically and politically correct terminology. In the following pages I will therefore present three approaches which all seek to overcome the restrictions inherent in the usual sex-gender and masculinity-femininity concepts.

Beyond the Sex/Gender and Masculine/Feminine Dichotomy

One way to think beyond sexual binarism has found a major representation in a volume entitled *Third Sex, Third Gender*, edited by Gilbert Herdt. Historical and anthropological research presented in this volume point to a variety of sexual/gender identities outside the male-female, masculine-feminine system. For example, as most researchers agree, in the West before the seventeenth century, a one-sex paradigm (male with female inside) predominated. This was gradually replaced in the seventeenth century by a new model with three sexes (male, female, hermaphrodite) but only two genders, a system in which the choice of a wrong sexual partner constituted sodomy but not a separate gender identity (cf. Trumbach: 1994). Later this system developed into a two sex - two gender system which attempted to exclude a third, illegitimate gender, of adult, passive, transvestite, effeminate men (called 'mollies' in England) and by the eighteenth century also sapphist women, or 'tommies'. It was based on this idea of the molly, that Karl Heinrich Ulrichs in 1862 argued for same-sex orientation as a third sex under his already mentioned rubric of a woman trapped in the body of a man (cf. Van der Meer: 1994). Finally, around 1900, these processes lead to the third sex/gender category of *homosexuals* understood mostly as feminine men and masculine women (cf. Hekma: 1994). In my opinion, what emerges from the accounts in Herdt's volume is that both sex and gender are culturally defined – underlining thereby what Butler in a very different approach has also claimed – and that both exhibit a highly shifting nature, noticeable particularly in the long run.[111] This multiplicity of sex and gender categories has far reaching consequences for the analysis of non-normative men in film. For these mass-mediated men (soft men, transvestites, transgender) are not necessarily feminized if we really embrace the possibility of a third or fourth or more sexes or genders. My criticism of Herdt and some other contributors to the volume is that their opening up of frozen sex/gender binarism is limited to offering a third category, the danger being that a third term can easily be a receptacle for what binarism cannot retain. On the basis of the historical and anthropological research presented in Herdt it seems to me adapt to conceptualize not three sexes but rather sex/gender as on the one hand bound and fixed by social discourse or ideology but on the other as multifaceted and fluid.

Eve K. Sedgwick, one of the preeminent theoreticians of queerness, has provided another interesting approach beyond feminization, which goes even further in the direction of multiplicity. The analytic system presented in her article "Gosh, Boy George, You Must Be Awfully Secure in Your Masculinity," is based on sociological work by Sandra Bem. They point out that masculinity and femininity are not on a scale as is commonly assumed but are better understood as orthogonal to each other. Therefore, less manly does not mean more womanly and vice versa, as ideology would have us assume. Rather, Sedgwick points out that we have to conceive gender as – at least, I would add – a two-dimensional system in which femininity and masculinity are independent variables. [112] Beyond the ideological reductive concept of womanly – manly, represented by the line from upper left to lower right, this model shows us that there are instead an infinite number of sex/gender positions. Fascinatingly, there are, according to Bem, many people who score high on both the femininity and masculinity scale, while others score low on both. Moreover, and perhaps most importantly for our purposes, she found out that, "a high score on either of them does not predict a low score on the other" (Sedgwick: 1995, 16). In other

---

[111] In other cultures sex/gender is sometimes more malleable still as various contributions of anthropological research in Herdt, for example on the Native American *berdache* or the Indian *Hijras* reveals.

[112] *At least* two-dimensional, because to adequately represent real life gender we would have to figure in the dynamic aspect: change, fluidity, and gender as process.

words, a lack of traditional masculine traits 'emasculates' a man, but does not necessarily feminize him.

Finally, I would like to turn to work by Chris Straayer as another fascinating road-sign beyond the sex/gender and the masculine/feminine distinction in direction of multivalency.[113] In an analysis of temporary transvestite films (usually called crossdressing films), Straayer focuses on the double structure of most of these films: While the diegetic characters believe in the masquerade of the protagonist, the audience sees behind it. Straayer does not, however, focus on the ideological, binarizing effect – that the gender behind the disguise is the supposedly 'real' gender (presented usually as the real sex vs. the gender disguise). Instead, she looks at the *overlap* of these two genders. Thereby she pulls into visibility a gender confusion particularly noticeable in the bivalent kiss (a kiss before the disguise is lifted), which is *both* straight and gay, depending on which gender we choose to read. Or, alternatively, one can say that in this instance the transvestite character is both genders – the diegetic and the extra-diegetic – at the same time: masculine *and* feminine.

In another article, Straayer takes such a splicing together of sex and gender identities even further, drawing out a historical trajectory that leads to a culturally powerful figure, for which she coins the term 'She-man'. To summarize, Straayer constructs roughly the following genealogy: feminist theory (Doane, Cixous, Irigaray, and others) and feminist performance (e.g. Lynda Benglis, Carolee Schneemann) have from the basis of a patriarchal coding of femininity as sexuality recast female sexuality along the lines and beyond the phallic femme (connected to masquerade) and the medusan femme (female sexuality as multiple). Consecutively, the development of music video has brought a reconfiguring of gender presentation, giving women more authorship and bringing men to enter the languages of sensuality and exhibitionism. Another source of influence for the development of the She-man was video art in its affinity with performance art. In result, from the eighties onward we can witness a number of She-men, particularly in video art and music videos, but increasingly also in other cultural forms. What is particularly relevant for our purposes here is that according to Straayer the She-man is not simply a cross-dresser, a transvestite or a gender bender, much less a feminized man. "It should be noted that, although gay audiences may have more to gain from the She-man's radical display of gender and sex constructions, the She-man is not a gay figure, nor an effeminate male, nor a hermaphrodite. The She-man, as enacted by both gay and straight performers, is a fully functional figuration signifying woman/man" (1990, 276-77). According to Straayer, in media feminine signals (dress, behavior, etc.) have come to mean female sexuality and therefore the She-man through taking up a feminine garb and behavior becomes more than a gender transgressor, combining both the male and the female sex. That is, he goes way beyond feminization because the sex taken on is an

---

[113] Apart from the articles mentioned below, see also her book *Deviant Eyes, Deviant Bodies*, where she develops these motifs in a wider context.

amplification of his own and therefore a deeper (and higher) combination. But it is also *not* feminization for he does not 'become woman.' Rather he remains male and manly and masculine, *and* he takes on female and womanly and feminine – and thereby becomes powerfully sexy.

My main criticism of Straayer is that her argument of a sexual rather than just gender transformation while very alluring is underdeveloped theoretically, resting on eclectic examples from art or music videos. For example, analyzing Dead or Alive's music video "Save You All My Kisses" she claims that "[t]he contradictory reactions of [the] diegetic audience emphasize and confirm the She-man as simultaneously female and male" (1990, 276), while these reactions might just as well be ambivalence towards *gender*-mixing (feminine and masculine). Similarly, she claims that "As he [Mike Monroe of Hanoi Rocks] performs both male and female gestures – in makeup and androgynous clothing – a doubling of sexes occurs which increases sexuality and produces a bi-sexed rather than bisexual image" (1990, 277), as though gesture were more biological and less social then make-up or dress. However, while I would dispute Straayer's claim that the She-man's mixing of feminine and masculine gestures produces necessarily a female-plus-male *bi-sex*, what matters for our purposes is that the doubling of signals in fact *increases* the sexuality and power of the figure, rather than divesting him of it. That is, the She-man's feminization is also a masculinization, and it is a going beyond both without destroying these categories. It is as though through a skillful play with these contradictory aspects, such bi-figures achieve a higher plane. This can actually be combined with Sedgwick's analysis, namely what she calls 'gendery'. She points out how a butch or masculine style (short hair in her case) did not make her necessarily more butch or masculine, but rather – by serving as a threshold effect – more gendery. The difference between the two arguments is that Sedgwick contrary to Straayer does not claim a sexual bivalence. But what they have in common is the thinking beyond binarism: The figures they analyze are both/and and neither/nor.

To conclude, I want to repeat that we do not have much to gain by conceiving of non-normative men as 'feminized' but quite a lot to loose. Particularly when the term used unreflected, in an aside manner. But just abandoning the term is not enough; we rather have to theorize beyond the masculine/feminine duality of patriarchal culture. For if we open up the concepts of sex and gender into multidimensionality and multivalency, as particularly Sedgwick and Straayer do, new sex/gender spaces appear on our social horizon that may be disquieting for those who want to maintain the seeming stability of a two-gender system but ultimately harbor the chance for a broadening of *all* gender positions.

Sources

Bell-Metereau, Rebecca, *Hollywood Androgyny*, 2. ed., New York 1993.

Bem, Sandra L., "The Measurement of Psychological Androgyny", in: *Journal of Consulting and Clinical Psychology* 42 (April 1974), pp. 155-62.

Bem, Sandra L., "The Theory and Measurement of Androgyny: A Reply to the Pedhazur-Tetenbaum and Locksley-Colten Critiques", in: *Journal of Personality and Social Psychology* 37 (June 1979), pp. 1047-1054.

Boscagli, Maurizia, "A Moving Story: Masculine Tears and the Humanity of Televised Emotions", in: *Discourse* 15.2 (Winter 92), pp. 64-79.

Branston, Gill, "... Viewer, I Listened to Him ... Voices, Masculinity, *In the Line of Fire*", in: Pat Kirkham, Janet Thumim (eds.), *Me Jane: Masculinity, Movies and Women*, New York 1995, pp. 37-50.

Brod, Harry, "Masculinity as Masquerade", in: Andrew Perchuk, Helaine Posner (eds.), *The Masculine Masquerade: Masculinity and Representation*. Cambridge, Mass. 1995.

Butler, Judith, *Gender Trouble: Feminism and the Subversion of Identity*, New York 1990.

Doneson, Judith E., "The Image Lingers: The Feminization of the Jew in *Schindler's List*", in: Yosefa Loshitzky (ed.), *Spielberg's Holocaust: Critical Perspectives on Schindler's List*. Indiana 1997.

Doty, Alexander, "The Sissy Boy, The Fat Ladies, and The Dykes: Queerness and/as Gender in Pee-Wee's World", in: *Camera Obscura* 25-26 (Jan/May 1991), pp. 125-143.

Gledhill, Christine, "Women Reading Men", in: Pat Kirkham, Janet Thumim (eds.), *Me Jane: Masculinity, Movies and Women*, New York 1995, pp. 73-93.

Halberstam, Judith, *Female Masculinity*. Durham 1998.

Hankin, Kelly, "A Rebel without a Choice?: Femme Spectatorship in Hollywood Cinema", *The Velvet Light Trap* 41 (Spring 1998), pp. 3-18.

Hekma, Gert, "'A Female Soul in a Male Body': Sexual Inversion as Gender Inversion in Nineteenth-Century Sexology", in: Gilbert Herdt (ed.), *Third Sex, Third Gender: Beyond Sexual Dimorphism in Culture and History*, New York 1994, pp. 213-240.

Herdt, Gilbert (ed.), *Third Sex, Third Gender: Beyond Sexual Dimorphism in Culture and History*, New York 1994.

Kirkham, Pat, Thumim, Janet, (eds.) *Me Jane: Masculinity, Movies and Women*, New York 1995.

Mast, Gerald et al., (eds.) *Film Theory and Criticism: Introductory Readings*, 4. ed., New York 1992.

Mulvey, Laura, "Afterthoughts on 'Visual Pleasure and Narrative Cinema' Inspired by Duel in the Sun", in: *Framework* 6.15-17 (1981). (repr. in: Constance Penley (ed.), *Feminism and Film Theory*, New York 1988, pp. 69-79)

Mulvey, Laura, *Visual and Other Pleasures*, Houndsmills 1989.

Mulvey, Laura, "Visual Pleasure and Narrative Cinema", in: *Screen* 16.3 (Autumn 1975). (repr. in: Constance Penley (ed.), *Feminism and Film Theory*, New York 1988, pp. 57-68.)

Neale, Steve, "Masculinity as Spectacle: Reflections on Men and Mainstream Cinema", in: *Screen* 24.6 (Nov-Dec 1983), pp. 2-16. (repr. in: Steven Cohen, Ina Rae Hark (eds.), *Screening the Male: Exploring Masculinities in Hollywood Cinema*, London 1993, pp. 9-20.)

Pfeil, Fred, *White Guys: Studies in Postmodern Domination and Difference,* London 1995.

Rodowick, David N., *The Difficulty of Difference: Psychoanalysis, Sexual Difference and Film Theory,* New York 1991.

Rowe, Kathleen, "Melodrama and Men in Post-Classical Romantic Comedy", in: Pat Kirkham, Janet Thumim (eds.), *Me Jane: Masculinity, Movies and Women,* New York 1995, pp. 184-193.

Sedgwick, Eve K., *Epistemology of the Closet,* Berkeley 1990.

Sedgwick, Eve K., "Gosh, Boy George, You Must Be Awfully Secure in Your Masculinity", in Maurice Berger et al. (eds.), *Constructing Masculinity*, New York 1995, pp. 11-20.

Siegel, Carol, *Male Masochism: Modern Revisions of the Story of Love,* Bloomington 1995.

Silverman, Kaja, *Male Subjectivity at the Margins,* New York 1992.

Straayer, Chris, *Deviant Eyes, Deviant Bodies: Sexual Re-orientations in Film and Video,* New York 1996.

Straayer, Chris, "Redressing the 'Natural': The Temporary Transvestite Film", in: *Wide Angle* 14.1 (Jan 1992), pp. 36-55.

Straayer, Chris, "The She-Man: Postmodern Bi-Sexed Performance in Film and Video", in: *Screen* 31.3 (Summer 1990), pp. 262-280.

Suner, Asuman, "Postmodern Double Cross: Reading David Cronenberg's *M. Butterfly* as a Horror Story", *Cinema Journal* 37.2 (Winter 1998), pp. 49-64.

Trumbach, Randolph, "London's Sapphists: From Three Sexes to Four Genders in the Making of Modern Culture", in: Gilbert Herdt (ed.), *Third Sex, Third Gender: Beyond Sexual Dimorphism in Culture and History*, New York 1994, pp. 111-136.

Van der Meer, Theo, "Sodomy and the Pursuit of a Third Sex in the Early Modern Period", in: Gilbert Herdt (ed.), *Third Sex, Third Gender: Beyond Sexual Dimorphism in Culture and History,* New York 1994, pp. 137-212.

Wiegman, Robyn, "Feminism, 'The Boys,' and Other Matters Regarding the Male", in Steven Cohen, Ina Rae Hark (eds.), *Screening the Male: Exploring Masculinities in Hollywood Cinema,* London 1993, pp. 173- 193.

Filmography:

Boys Don't Cry (Kimberly Pierce, USA 1999)
Crying Game, The (Neil Jordan, UK 1992)
In the Line of Fire (Wolfgang Petersen, USA 1993)
M. Butterfly (David Cronenberg, USA 1993)
Paris Is Burning (Jennie Livingston, USA 1990)
Adventures of Priscilla, Queen of the Desert, The (Stephan Elliot, AUS 1994)

Rocky Horror Picture Show, The (Jim Sharman, UK 1975)
Schindler's List (Steven Spielberg, USA 1993)
Some Like It Hot (Billie Wilder, USA 1959)

Stefan BRANDT

Acting Heroes: Heroes, Homos, and the Postmodern in Recent Hollywood Cinema

"The modern hero is no hero, he *acts* heroes," Walter Benjamin tells us (1973, 97). In recent Hollywood cinema, this statement seems more relevant than ever. Instead of a monolithic, homogenous concept of heroism we are faced with a wide range of heroes and anti-heroes all playing their part in the show of postmodernity. The term 'acting heroes' refers to both the film hero who executes rather than plausibly incorporates the myth and to the actor himself who clearly performs and *acts* heroes. The classic film trailer "Clint Eastwood IS Dirty Harry" seems rather comical today. To totally identify an actor with the mythic hero he embodies is like believing in Santa Claus or assuming that babies are found in the cabbage patch. The actor as an integral entity seems to be just as dead as the proverbial author in the Foucauldian argument. The playful intertextual reference to various circulating myths and cultural ideas has gradually replaced the illusion of essence, truth and universality that was once associated with the hero figure. The hero has stepped out from the movie screen and has entered not only postmodern culture, but also our mind. He has become, more and more, a product of our cultural symbolic production and the machinery of our imagination.

This inevitably leads us to question if such a thing as a 'sharply defined' concept of heroic masculinity really exists in modern day America (or, more bluntly speaking, if it has ever really existed). From a 1990s standpoint, one would have to answer this question with a distinct 'no'. Many of the traditional ideas on masculinity that have formed the consciousness of young Americans from the turn of the century up until the 1990s seem rather outdated in the present. But have these ideas ever 'really existed' in a clear-cut, monolithic form? A closer look at the 'great' American heroes in film shows that most of the prominent figures consist of multi-faceted, sometimes contradictory aspects. For example, Rudolph Valentino is — in his screen presence — both aggressive male invader and a rather passive object of desire. Even the screen character embodied by Gary Cooper — the archetypal model of the super-cool 'yup-and-nope-hero' — bears, as James Naremore has competently shown, elements of a domineering masculinity as well as elements of a coquettish, even narcissistic femininity.

In the American culture of the beginning 21st century this contestedness and ambiguity of the concept of masculinity seems more obvious than ever. Almost all major Hollywood stars, ranging from Arnold Schwarzenegger to Wesley Snipes, from Dustin Hoffman to Patrick Swayzee, have played characters in which the traditional male stereotypes have been transformed into a charade. It seems almost a cliché today to claim that the modern hero is a composite figure. On the other hand, there has been a strong revival of archaic figures since the mid 1980s. It started with Sylvester Stallone's unforgettable impersonation of Vietnam war hero John Rambo and ending up with various Bruce Willis and Jean Claude Van Damme movies in which the hero fights for liberty and world peace with his bare fists and a machine gun. Films like Ted Kotcheff's FIRST BLOOD (1982) and John McTiernan's DIE HARD (1988) have often been understood as sounding the bell for a new round of (re-) masculinization in American culture.

The typical character in these films is certainly not free from irony — he often seems more like an "excessive parody of an ideal" (Tasker: 1993, 1) —, but the narrative built around these figures is in many cases much too serious and loaded with the viewer's expectations to be taken as mere irony. My thesis is that both serious and comic elements blend together in these characters in a performative fashion. I will argue that the ideological element is often privileged in favor of the goal to create a more 'imagined' than 'real' cultural consensus. In a time characterized by a deep sense of insecurity and crisis on the side of many men, it seems important to revive traditional models of strong masculinity in order to rescue the average male from his *anomie*.

This element of 'crisis' can be easily detected in many depictions of masculinity in mainstream cinema. In Tarantino's PULP FICTION, for example, masculinity is characterized as a concept constantly under siege. The old formula that "the heroic man is always physically beaten, injured and brought to breaking point" (Smith: 1995, 81) is miraculously rediscovered here. The 'real man' is an endangered species in this view. He is at the same time exposed to the deconstruction of his own myth and reinvented as a new creature who can withstand the challenges which await the 'new man' on the eve of the millennium. The vision of the manly hero as a 'body triumphant' is also very vivid in this kind of cinematic fiction.

However, this conventional way of constructing masculinity stands in a sharp contrast to the emerging discourse of deconstructing gender. In postmodern theory (and also often in modern cultural practice), gender identity is viewed as a dynamic and therefore ambiguous product of performative acts (Butler: 1990, 270-82). What these opposing versions of the masculine self have in common is that they both stress the function of masculinity as a spectacle for cultural self-fashioning. The male figure is, in these presentations, always a show, a sometimes all to clear signifier for a seemingly timeless 'essence' of naturalness. Also, there is an element of explicitness about what it means to be a man (a clarity that can be undermined on the sub-level of the texts). These figures seem simply to be predestined to operate as consoling fantasies in the minds of a new generation that yearns for new heroes. But is the figure of the 'new American hero' really all that 'new'? There is, of course, no definite and simple answer to this question. It can probably only be answered by saying 'yes' and 'no'. The supposed antithesis between 'male body in crisis' and 'body triumphant' which many critics still claim to be valid for modern depictions of masculinity (Tasker: 1993, 109-131) does not really help in understanding the dynamic and contradictory structure of modern heroism. There is no 'either or', but rather an 'as well as' when it comes to constructions of masculinity in modern culture. Masculinity can be seen here as a vehicle for negotiating certain beliefs, conflicts and paradoxes which seem to be relevant at a given point in time. The film heroes embodied by Bruce Willis and John

93

Travolta are, in this view, complex answers to problems articulated by culture and can therefore be read as aesthetic dictionaries for the whole gamut of behavioral, sensory and visual possibilities that are existent in a culture. The contradictoriness of these heroes is no criterion of exclusion, it rather is an integral part of their dynamic structure and is closely connected to the aesthetic effect that the viewer will experience while watching these heroes.

The long battle of constructing and deconstructing masculinity finally reached a symbolic climax in the 1990s. The stance which Hollywood cinema currently takes is just as paradoxical as it is nostalgic. While standing in a long tradition of validating mainstream masculinity, movies like PULP FICTION (1994) and Luc Besson's THE FIFTH ELEMENT (1997) also partially distance themselves from these roots. Heroic manhood is rehearsed and at the same time ridiculed.

Luc Besson's THE FIFTH ELEMENT (1997) is a good example for this double discourse. In the movie, Bruce Willis plays Korben Dallas, a cab driver and American Everyman who, in the year 2214, is asked by the government of the United States to save the world. The Willis character seems to be the paradigm of the American hero. He is masculine, healthy, brave, strong-willed and almost Herculean in his ability to master the most difficult situations. Compared with the other figures, he is recognizably the only one who can cope with the task of saving the world. The character is both comical and serious, the perfect hybridized figure that appeals to action fans and intellectuals alike. The marketing for the film was almost completely based on Bruce Willis's hero persona. One of the movie posters for THE FIFTH ELEMENT depicts him at the center of the picture radiating confidence and charisma.

The aesthetic structure of this sharp-contrast photograph relies almost exclusively on the centeredness of the hero from which the other objects seem to originate. Like the metaphorical sun, Bruce Willis is the focal point of this universe. The flying space cars that emerge at both the bottom and the top of the picture seem as though they are beams coming from an imaginary center. The position of the two other figures, Milla Jovovich and Gary Oldman, at the upper left and the lower right of the poster also suggests such a focus. This configuration is echoed in the narrative structure of the movie. The film starts with a nightmare of the main protagonist, Korben Dallas, and ends with the realization of his romantic dreams.

The aesthetic structure of this sharp-contrast photograph relies almost exclusively on the centeredness of the hero from which the other objects seem to originate. Like the metaphorical sun, Bruce Willis is the focal point of this universe. The flying space cars that emerge at both the bottom and the top of the picture seem as though they are beams coming from an imaginary center. The position of the two other figures, Milla Jovovich and Gary Oldman, at the upper left and the lower right of the poster also suggests such a focus. This configuration is echoed in the narrative structure of the movie. The film starts with a nightmare of the main protagonist, Korben Dallas, and ends with the realization of his romantic dreams.

Significantly, the film still which was most often used in reviews employs precisely the same radial configuration. Here, the hero stands in the midst of grim-faced aliens whose machine-guns are directed at him from many different directions. Again, the hero is in the center of the action. But there is a certain tension in this picture that cannot be observed in the movie poster. The hero is obviously a prisoner here. Both his hands are lifted, and the ape-mouthed aliens are pointing their guns at him. But the threatening pose quickly resolves into absurdity. Although clearly superior in number, the aliens need five or six big guns to hold the hero giving their action a note of ridiculousness. And even though Willis lifts both of his hands like a prisoner-of-war, his posture seems anything else but helpless or passive. Since we know from similar movies (with or without Bruce Willis) that a true hero "can be destroyed but never defeated" (to pick up the famous Hemingway line), the only question that remains is *how* he will rescue himself from the unfortunate situation. Nonetheless, the photograph plays with the notion of male vulnerability. This notion is clearly hinted at here, but at the same time neutralized through the hero's confident aura and especially his cocksure smile. This smile tells us that the hero will, once again, master the situation. The film still can be seen as a *mise-en-abyme*, a bottomless, repetitive image for the leitmotif of the wounding/rescue pattern that occurs throughout the whole movie. While the narrative is often completely confusing and even illogical, the concept of the heroic male safely guides us through the plot. "Without his familiar face and sanity," one critic wrote, "THE FIFTH ELEMENT would be completely unwatchable" (Denby: 1997, 63). Significantly, the hero's identity in THE FIFTH ELEMENT is established through his interplay with other figures. It is especially through the representation of non-heroic masculinities that Korben Dallas's own, heroic personality constitutes itself. The signifiers of effeminacy that emerge from these male supporting characters are used, in the Derridean sense, as indicators of a 'productive non-presence' that foreshadows the hero's true masculinity (1982, 11). This interplay between the center and the periphery has the potential of either stabilizing or deconstructing the concept of heroic masculinity. On the one hand, the lead character's tough guy performance comes across as very masculine; on the other hand we are continuously reminded that masculinity is a fragile concept which can be easily deconstructed. No wonder critic David Denby calls the sad crowd of losers in

THE FIFTH ELEMENT "a carnival of geeks" (1997, 63). Even the movie's smallest figures, for instance Ruby Rhod's unmistakably queer co-workers, are vivid instructions on how a man should *not* be. The traditional concept of heroism is continually reaffirmed through signifiers of a symbolic order which knows basically only two types of men: 'real' men and mollycoddles — Bruce Willis and the rest of men. Bruce Willis is 'Mr. Dynamite Dandy' after all: tough, but with a touch of softness. His movie persona encapsulates both elements of the macho character from DIE HARD as well as elements from his wise-guy character in the TV series MOONLIGHTING. It even holds child-like characteristics that we remember from baby Mikey in LOOK WHO'S TALKING (1989) whose voice was Willis's. In this sense, the Willis persona in THE FIFTH ELEMENT is a kind of hybrid construction, a palimpsest which presents the material in a new form while it still echoes its original meaning. Out of the oscillating tension between the different meanings and images of masculinity in the movie, Bruce Willis emerges as both an anchor of stability and a decentralizing impulse towards dissent. However, as Dennis Bingham claims in his book *Acting Male*, the "'gentling' of white masculinity" can be read as a "strategy for holding on to power during shifting times" (Bingham: 1994, 4). In an era determined by concepts of role reversal and sexual 'indeterminacy', it seems to be important for a culture to draw a line between chaos and order, between sexual anarchy and the imagined well-functioning structure of social practice and 'real life'.

There is probably no other movie that attempts to play with the notion of the 'crisis of masculinity' as accurately as Quentin Tarantino's PULP FICTION (1994). Men are 'real men' in this movie, and women are once again these little playthings who are best suited as either sexual objects or loving housewives. But, sure, everything is just a spoof, a merely intellectual negotiation of genres and cultural stereotypes. "Tarantino's gangsters," one critic assures us, "are not 'real.'" (Denby: 1995, 228). Another critic claims that "the general tone of Tarantino's work is a rejection of anything resembling the 'real' world" (Dowell: 1995, 4; cf. Indiana: 1995, 108). Strange that a movie which purports to be 'not real' in almost every respect, should allude so masterfully to very real structures in our mind. To act heroes, it seems, also means to act out the viewer's perception. In her foreword to the movie's screenplay, Manohla Dargis draws a parallel between the drastic images of corporeality in the movie and the complexity of the (mainly male) film characters. Bone-shattering, skin-splitting, blood-spurting, Tarantino's cinema of viscera is written on the flesh of outlaw men and women, all of whom are far more complicated than their underworld types would suggest. (1994, 1).

Is there anything more real than flesh and blood? While PULP FICTION is formally redundant with allusions to all sorts of conventions and hoary clichés from gangster and kung-fu movies, it is far from looking at these texts in merely referential terms. What is recovered in PULP FICTION, is not so much the semiotic heritage of these texts, as their lived cultural agenda. The camaraderie of males which is shown in the movie clearly echoes the fundamental patterns of Western thought (cf. Derrida: 1989 [1978], 110). These patterns, especially the notion of the 'true hero' or the 'true man' are portrayed as still valid in contemporary fiction even though their contestedness is continuously pointed out. This becomes very clear in the famous male rape scene when Butch (played by Bruce Willis) rescues the male mafia boss from the two queers. Set in the dungeon-basement of a pawnshop, the scene reenacts heroic masculinity in its most paradigmatic way: while emphasizing the strength of heterosexual male bonding, the scene identifies the abysses of masculinity, namely homosexuality and effeminacy, as the common enemy of all heroes. It is only in the context of this 'dark side' of maleness that the true hero can emerge. The homosexual rape that occurs in the dungeon functions as a signifier of the 'Other' which the true hero must distinguish himself from. After having freed himself from the sadists' bonds, Butch suddenly hesitates; he decides that he can't leave Marsellus, his mortal enemy, in a "situation like that" (screenplay, 128). In order to release Marsellus from the rapists he selects the largest weapon the pawnshop has to offer: not the hammer, not the chainsaw, not the Louisville slugger, but a "magnificent" Samurai sword (screenplay, 128).

This is 'acting heroes' at its finest. The hero plays one warrior after another, finally rescuing the person he hates the most in an act of homosocial bonding among heterosexuals. Heroic masculinity is presented here as a performance with a shrill ideological twist. In the final scene of this episode we are confronted with a triumphant Butch roaring away on the Harley owned by the dead homo. But couldn't it be that Tarantino is simply showing us the absurdity of male bonding in his film? Isn't he exposing the hyper-masculinity that lies at the basis of male sexual politics? In a flashback scene which is positioned before the rape scene we see the young Butch who is being given a gold watch which was transported from one male ancestor to the other and finally held in his father's anus while he was a prisoner in Vietnam. This same watch is the very reason why Butch returns to his house and finally ends up with a ball gag in the Mason-Dixon Pawnshop. With the 'gold watch' anecdote, the film "titillate[s] with subversive possibility" (hooks: 1995, 66), but then "everything kinda comes right back to normal" (ibid). The film purports to generate a niche for male self-irony here, but by reinventing the very same myths it pretends to be deconstructing, it wastes this possibility in the same breath. Yeah,l ike it's really funny when Butch the hypermasculine phallic white boy — [...] who comes straight out of childhood clinging to the anal-retentive timepiece of patriarchal imperialism — is exposed. [...] As the work progresses, little Butch is still doing it for Daddy — a real American hero. (ibid., 65-66) In its almost paranoid fear of the anus, PULP FICTION resembles other films from the 90s that have discovered the theme as a symbol for the contestedness of modern masculinity. "The anus," writes William Ian Miller, "[is] more than any other orifice [....]. [I]t is the gate that protects the inviolability, the autonomy, of males" (1998, 100). In Tony Kaye's AMERICAN HISTORY X (1998), the moral awakening of the bad boy hero (Edward Norton) is depicted as a process of being humiliated, physically abused and finally raped. The anal intercourse, in both films, constitutes the ultimate evil which either kills the hero or transforms him forever. In AMERICAN HISTORY X, the hero survives the offense; also, he undergoes a painful process of catharsis after which he is saner, more human, and, most importantly, more heroic than before.

To 'act heroes' in contemporary Hollywood cinema means not only playing with the mythic notions of heroism, but also deploying the ideological potential which is implied in the myth. Masculinity is not a sacred concept anymore. Even in those Hollywood movies which clearly advocate traditional masculinity, the danger of a deconstruction of maleness is clearly shown. By choosing performance over essentialism, Hollywood cinema offers us both the consoling illusion of a transhistorical heroism and the semiotic potential for a new, alternative masculinity. What we make of this, is ultimately *our* choice.

Filmography

AMERICAN HISTORY X, USA, 1998, (R), New Line Cinema, P: Turman-Morissey Company, D: Tony Kaye, S: David McKenna, C: Edward Norton (Derek Vinyard), Edward Furlong (Danny Vinyard), Avery Brooks (Bob Sweeney), Stacy Keach (Cameron), Guy Torry (Lamont), Ethan Suplee (Seth).
THE FIFTH ELEMENT, USA, 1997, (PG-13), Columbia Pictures, P: Patrice Ledoux, D: Luc Besson, C: Bruce Willis (Korben Dallas), Milla Jovovich (Leeloo), Gary Oldman (Zorg), Chris Tucker (Ruby Rhod), Ian Holm (Cornelius), Brion James (General Munro).
PULP FICTION, USA, 1994 (R), Miramax Films, P: Lawrence Bender, D: Quentin Tarantino, S: Quentin Tarantino & Roger Roberts Avary, C: John Travolta (Vincent Vega), Samuel L, Jackson (Jules), Uma Thurman (Mia Wallace), Bruce Willis (Butch), Ving Rhames (Marsellus Wallace).

Sources

Adams, Michael, "Pulp Fiction", in: Magill, Frank Northen (ed.), Magill's Cinema Annual, Englewood Cliffs 1994, pp. 470-472.
AMERICAN HISTORY X, *Original Screenplay*, prepared By David McKenna, School of Cinema and Television at the University of Southern California 1996, 12/17.
Benjamin, Walter, *Charles Baudelaire: A Lyric Poet in the Era of High Capitalism*, London 1973.
Bingham, Dennis, *Acting Male: Masculinities in the Films of James Stewart, Jack Nicholson, and Clint Eastwood*, New Brunswick 1994.
Creed, Barbara, "From Here to Modernity: Feminism and Postmodernism", in: *Screen* 28,2 (1987), pp. 47-67.
Dargis, Manohla, "Foreword", in: *Pulp Fiction: A Quentin Tarantino Screenplay*, (Stories by Quentin Tarantino and Roger Avary), New York 1994, pp. 1-2.

Denby, David, "Pulp Fiction", in: Keogh, Peter (ed.), *Flesh and Blood: The National Society of Film Critics on Sex, Violence, and Censorship*, San Francisco 1995, pp. 227-231.

——, "Hack Work", in: *New York* 30,19 (May 19, 1997), p. 63.

Derrida, Jacques, *Writing and Difference*, [*L' écriture et la différence*, trans, Alan Bass, 1976], London 1978.

——, 1989, "Structure, Sign, and Play in the Discourse of the Human Sciences", [Trans, Alan Bass, 1978], in: Lodge, Davi (ed.), *Modern Criticism and Theory. A Reader*, London, New York 1989, pp. 108-123.

Dinshaw, Carolyn, "Getting Medieval: PULP FICTION, Gawain, Foucault", in: Frese, Dolores Warwick, and O'Keefe, Katherine O'Brien, *The Book and the Body*, Notre Dame, Ind., 1997, pp. 116-163.

Dowell, Pat, "Pulp Friction, Two Shots at Quentin Tarantino's PULP FICTION", (with John Fried), in: *Cineaste* 21,3 (1995), pp. 4-5.

Fried, John, "Pulp Friction, Two Shots at Quentin Tarantino's PULP FICTION", (with Pat Dowell), in: *Cineaste* 21,3 (1995), pp. 6-7.

Gerzon, Mark, *A Choice of Heroes: The Changing Face of American Manhood*, 2. ed., Boston, New York & London 1992.

hooks, bell, "Cool Tool", in: *Artforum* discussion "Pulp the Hype on the Q, T", 33,7 (March 1995), pp. 63-66, 108.

Indiana, Gary, "Geek Chic", in: *Artforum* discussion "Pulp the Hype on the Q, T", 33,7 (March 1995), pp. 63-66, 108.

Jeffords, Susan, *Hard Bodies: Hollywood Masculinity in the Reagan Era*, New Brunswick 1994.

Miller, William Ian, *The Anatomy of Disgust*, Cambridge, Mass., London, England, 1998.

Naremore, James, *Acting in the Cinema*, 2 ed., Berkeley, Los Angeles, London 1990.

Pulp Fiction: A Quentin Tarantino Screenplay, (Stories by Quentin Tarantino and Roger Avary), New York 1994.

Silverman, Kaja, *Male Subjectivity at the Margins*, New York & London 1992.

Simpson, Mark, *Male Impersonators: Men Performing Masculinity*, London 1994.

Smith, Gavin, "'When you know you're in good hands': Quentin Tarantino interviewed by Gavin Smith", in: *Film Comment* 30,4 (1994), pp. 32-38; pp. 40-43.

Smith, Paul, "Eastwood Bound", *Constructing Masculinity*, Ed, Maurice Berger, Brian Wallis, and Simon Watson, New York, London 1995, pp. 77-97.

Tasker, Yvonne, *Spectacular Bodies: Gender, Genre and the Action Cinema*, London and New York 1993.

Welsh, James M, 1998, "The Fifth Element", in: Magill, Frank Northen (ed.), *Magill's Cinema Annual*, Englewood Cliffs 1994, pp. 186-188.

Willis, Sharon, "The Fathers Watch the Boys' Room", *Camera Obscura* 32 (1993/94), pp. 40-73.

Veronika GROB

Fear of Falling
White Middle-class Masculinity in Joel Schumacher's *Falling Down*

Joel Schumacher's highly controversial film *Falling Down* zooms in on the rage of a white, male, middle-class citizen who has lost both his job and his home. Since D-FENS - this is the hero's telling name we glimpse from his license plate - is unable to come to terms with this double loss, he develops the fixed idea of forcing his way „home", he will do so more and more violently, from downtown Los Angeles to Venice Beach, where his ex-wife, who inflicted a restraining order upon him, lives with their little daughter. However, D-Fens' identity is not only threatened by the loss of his job and home; as a heterosexual, white, middle-class male he has also lost his place in a society split by political discourses of ethnicity and gender, i. e. by so-called identity politics. D-FENS' opponent, police officer Prendergast - the other white, male, middle-class protagonist in the movie - succeeds at least in identifying the runner of amuck when he sees a giant advertisement (he remembers D-FENS passing in front of it) that recommends a sun lotion with the slogan „White is for laundry". The ad displays significantly a tanned Asian woman disfigured by a little graffiti man who is crying for help between the model's breasts. Could there be a more succinct way of alluding to the theme of *Falling Down*?

In his study on „Whiteness" Richard Dyer (1997) has convincingly discussed how whites and especially white males have occupied the so far unmarked, ‚blank' territory of universalism. In American society, which is more and more divided by various interest groups, whiteness finally becomes visible as a particular social category among others. However, the dehistoricised and depoliticised ideology of universalism is more complex in contemporary America. If we metaphorise the subject as a knotted one, i. e. as determined by a variety of discourses, languages and orders, the alleged neutral position also has to be conceived of as a nodal point condensed in the figure of the white, heterosexual, middle-class male (i. e. coloured people are marked while whites are not, femininity is marked while masculinity is the norm, etc.). Therefore D-FENS' problem boils down to him being an „unemployed protagonist desperately in need of an identity politics for white males" (Davis, Smith: 1997, 27).

Is this not precisely what is at stake in the issue of „Masculinities"? That is to say, it is time to make the so far unmarked position of males finally visible, a position which, until now, has presented itself as the standard and the norm. It is not surprising then that today's unmasking of the so far neutral position of white masculinity always already entails an identity crisis for white men. Rowena Chapman and Jonathan Rutherford point out that [f]or men who were promised recognition and a secure place in the world there lies ahead a frightening prospect: that masculinity will be shorn of its hierarchical power and will become simply one identity among others.

(quoted in Pfeil: 1995, ix)[114]*Falling Down* is highly relevant in this context since the film focuses exactly on the specific problems the neutralised position of white middle-class men entails. The formerly neutral, universal category of white middle-class males no longer provides a ground for the articulation of identity. As it appears, there is only one possible identification left for Schumacher's hypernormal hero D-FENS: „the American Way of Life". The subtlety of the movie, which renders the reproaches of fascist tendencies futile, lies precisely in the fact that its hero does not try to secure his identity with abstract categories such as race or nationalism but through the more elusive but no less ideological notion of the „American Way of Life" with its founding concepts of multiculturalism, political correctness and freedom of speech. This has confused a considerable number of the film critics. They praise the movie because it depicts white males as a particular interest group; at the same time they criticize it for collapsing the problems of white males with those of America in general, and thus for re-universalising the white man's position. However, what else is there for the white male in crisis to cling to if not to the abstract idea of America he so long dominated? D-FENS' working clothes - he is a ‚white collar' worker - not only imply an analogy between D-FENS and his opponent, police officer Prendergast, who, by the way, also suffers from an identity crisis, but, moreover, relate him to a third character, a black man. D-FENS encounters the latter in front of a financial institute, where the black demonstrates against the denial of a loan with a sign-board and its slogan „NOT ECONOMICALLY VIABLE". Later D-FENS will take over this slogan and literally integrate it into his own discourse. However, unlike the black man he remains unable to articulate his problems from a social perspective. Jude Davis and Carol R. Smith have correctly pointed out, the difference hinted at through the iconic status of this black protester who can refer to a long tradition of protest: The African American, the film implies, has a discourse developed through the struggles against racism and for civil rights which enables him to understand his oppression and to protest against it. By comparison, D-FENS has no way of understanding his own situation. Instead of being able to locate himself with respect to a history of oppression and its contestation, and/or to establish an identity with others in the same condition, D-FENS experiences his loss of job, wife, home and daughter as an inexplicable victimisation which he is powerless to resist or to put into words. (Davis, Smith: 1997, 34) This scene then proposes that ethnical differences could be transcended in order to restore identification on an economic basis. From such a perspective *Falling Down* can be read as a return to the demands of the good old class struggle. And as a hint that the America of the nineties is very different from the America of the sixties when the white middle-class was flourishing and communism was *the* political enemy.[115] The

---

[114] It should of course be stressed that this applies to the position of *white* males only. The same could not possibly be said with respect to non-white males.

[115] D-FENS is a child of the Cold War. Not only is he a former employee of an armament factory, but the movie shows this also in numerous references to Vietnam and in the general nostalgia for the sixties. D-FENS is longing for his home in Venice Beach and for times in which

central theme of Schumacher's movie however, and the central means by which the movie articulates the white male crisis is that of violence. As a consequence, it has been frequently criticized for its alleged justification of fascist tendencies. But *Falling Down* is more complex. The movie's subtlety lies precisely in the fact that D-FENS does *not* attempt to secure his identity by means of abstract categories such as race or nationality but through the more elusive albeit no less ideological notion of the „American Way of Life" which encompasses aspects of multiculturalism, political correctness, and freedom of speech. I have already pointed out that D-FENS reacts to the threat of losing his place in society as the head of a family, as a white-collar worker and as a patriot in a desperate attempt to retain it. The problem is that in doing so he loses the vital distance to the American dream, while literally traversing it on his odyssey through Los Angeles. Slavoj Zizek has never ceased pointing out that fantasy is precisely the form of representation that seeks to veil the fundamental impossibility of a clearly defined identity. As such, fantasy is not opposed to, but the very condition of reality, its innermost support. But because behind fantasy there is only a fundamental impossibilty, it cannot be interpreted but just traversed in order to experience the fact that there is nothing behind it. And this is exactly what *Falling Down* focuses on: its hero D-FENS comes too close to the fantasy of the American dream and, therefore, forfeits it irrevocably. In a sense, then, the runner of amuck is more American than America and, ultimately, *Falling Down* is literally a film about the „American Way of Life".

On the formal level, the collapse of fantasy is represented by means of several radically overblown close-ups. Opening by focusing on clearly delineated sign systems such as traffic signs the movie already shows us in its first scene what happens when the crucial distance to the symbolic breaks down. In a radical close-up, a flashing arrow indicating a detour loses its meaning as a signpost. We recognize only a threatening blinking of single lamps. Every sign is of course based on its materiality but this materiality has to be suspended in order for the sign to mean something. Losing the distance in a short circuit D-FENS loses sight of the whole signifying aspect of the sign and is left with its massive material presence, which is part of the real. D-FENS is now literally stuck in the jam of the signifying process. What this scene really shows is the fact that signs can signify anything as long as they

---

Ameria's enemy was easy to denominate. But the analogy to the Cold War could also lead further, because D-FENSE turns exactly then into a monstrous threat to society when he changes his clothes and transforms into a GI. In Vietnam too, the war was justified with reference to the protection of the „American Way of Life" but was negotiated territorially. And as D-FENS finally thinks he is coming home, as a veteran so to speak, he has to find out that his home is not his home anymore. His wife did not wait for him and his neighbourhood was colonialized: instead of an ice cream parlor there is now a „West-American-New-Age-Kind-Of-Thing"; this being in analogy to the veterans of the Vietnam War, who met a changed country when coming home. America is unable to reintegrate its homeless and alienated soldiers who transgressed various frontiers of morality and violence for their country; a story numerously recounted.

don't signify themselves. If this happens, and that is the crucial point, they lose all meaning and we cannot speak of signs anymore. As a literary theorist one could of course say that D-FENS is a poet because poetry is exactly defined as the quest for the unnameable, for the unmediated word in its materiality. However, art is only about a cautious transgression of the symbolic and thus avoids falling into the delusion of poetic ecstasy. How much more horrific must it be for this white-collar worker to encounter the real without the protecting parentheses of a work of art!

In one of the brilliant core scenes of *Falling Down*, the hero, packed with automatic weapons, enters a Whammy Burger joint to have a late breakfast. On his way to the restaurant's entrance, D-FENS crosses a huge burger painted onto the parking lot. This is a wonderful illustration of how fantasy cannot be interpreted but only traversed. Once inside the restaurant, our hero engages in a threatening dispute with the employees whether or not it is too late for breakfast. Eventually he orders a burger from the lunch menu, for his anger only to return when opening the box:

"You see, that is what I am talking about...." *to the employees* "Turn around, look at that! *advertising picture of a burger above their heads.* You see what I mean: it is plump, it is juicy, it is three inch thick. Now, look at this miserable, squashed thing. Can anybody tell me what is wrong with this picture? *To the frightened customers* "Anybody?"

What D-FENS encounters here is the „miserable squashed thing", which is left after the fantasy has been traversed and which has to be registered as part of the real. It is no coincidence that this scene hints at a similar one in Terry Gilliam's *Brazil*, in which the guests of a first-class restaurant get wonderful colour pictures of the chosen meal and are served a disgusting grey mash. Without the frame of fantasy the world presents itself in its horrifying massive materiality.

D-FENS' having come too close to the American fantasy (epitomized in the burger) has catastrophic consequences for his last refuge, the „American Dream", the position from which he hoped to defend his threatened identity and to regain his home. Owing to this overproximity, he loses the frame of fantasy, the protecting screen which veils the real and constitutes reality. Since this scene can be said to mirror the movie as a whole, it is only consequent that D-FENS after having lost the support of fantasy ends in an impasse. Going West, as American men always have done, he finally reaches at the pier of Santa Monica the outermost point of America, where he gets shot and literally falls out of America, i. e. his dead body falls into the sea.

To sum up, losing one's frame of fantasy and encountering the real can have fatal consequences. But *Falling Down* not only shows us a hero who unveils America's innermost horrific kernel which has to be abjected in order to constitute a coherent reality. The subject of violence is highlighted in yet another way. In her book *Powers of Horror*, Julia Kristeva refers to the process of delineating identity as „abjection" and opposes it to the „abject", which has to be located beyond representation and identity; indeed, it is the non-object caused by jouissance. Abjection, then, designates the process of demarcation from this horrific Other. It is an act necessary for the constitution of both individual and collective identities; although inevitable it is also a violent act. Moreover, in a worst case scenerio it might well occur that the one who abjects in order to defend his own and the American identity as a whole turns into a figure who threatens society and must himself be abjected.

This turning point occurs exactly in the middle of the film when D-FENS commits his only murder and kills a misogynous, homophobe, and xenophobe neo-Nazi. His opponent, police officer Prendergast takes on the role of protecting society. In the beginning of the movie Prendergast finds himself in fact in a situation very similar to that of D-FENS: he has lost all his dreams and even quit his job under pressure from his wife. In the end, though, he is able to reconstitute himself as a male subject over the dead body of D-Fens.[116] At the same time he re-inforces gender difference by for the first time silencing his wife, who has been constantly nagging him: „Amanda, shut up, and you have dinner ready and waiting for me!" While D-FENS is eventually defeated because the G. I.-uniform he puts on after the murder of the Nazi is not appropriate for that specific time and place, Prendergast acts appropriately, although violently, in the name of the law.[117] As a result, he could be interpreted as the saviour of the white male hero. But Prendergast is, of course, an ambivalent hero. It is the merit of the movie to show that he can only re-secure his identity through the use of violence and thus to demonstrate that the delineation of identity is a highly ambiguous process.

Film referred to

Falling Down, directed by Joel Schumacher; featuring: Michael Douglas, Robert Duvall, Barbara Hershey, Rachel Ticotin, etc.; Warner 1993.

Sources

Benjamin, Walter, *Zur Kritik der Gewalt,* Frankfurt a. M. 1997, pp. 179-203.
Davis, Jude, Smith, Carol R., *Gender, Ethnicity and Sexuality in Contemporary American Film,* Edinburgh 1997.
Dyer, Richard, *White,* London 1997.

---

[116] Speaking in Julia Kristeva's terms Prendergast's abjection is successful while D-FENS transgresses the border, for which Kristeva also uses the metaphor of falling:

There, I am at the border of my condition as a living being. My body extricates itself, as being alive, from that border. Such wastes drop so that I might live, until, from loss to loss, nothing remains in me and my entrie body falls beyond the limit - *cadere*, cadaver. (Kristeva: 1982, 3)

[117] This hints at the genuinely problematic status of the symbolic law. And, in fact, Walter Benjamin, in his essay on the critique of violence, refers precisely to the police as his privileged example. In the police, the law collapses with its uncanny reverse which illustrates Benjamin's thesis that there is always something rotten in law (Benjamin: 1997).

Kristeva, Julia, *Powers of Horror: An Essay on Abjection*, New York 1982.
Pfeil, Fred, *White Guys: Studies in Postmodern Domination and Difference*, London 1995.
Zizek, Slavoj, *The Plague of Fantasies*, London, New York 1997.

Elisabeth SCHAEFER-WUENSCHE

Masculine Atonement at the Century's End: The Million Man March and Spike Lee's Narrative

There is an increasingly conservative and hostile climate growing in America towards the aspirations of Black people and people of color for justice. The 'Contract with America,' proposed by the Republicans and thus far agreed to by the Congress is turning back the hands of time, depriving the Black community of many of the gains made through the suffering and sacrifice of our fellow advocates of change during the '50s and '60s. (Farrakhan: 1996b, 150)

Authored or rather authorized by Louis Farrakhan, the most prominent representative of the Nation of Islam (NOI),[118] these sentences proclaim a deep, ongoing crisis and the threat of a powerful attempt to reverse that which is seen as progressing and progressive: time and the political and social gains made along with the movement of time. The words quoted are the opening statement of a document entitled "The Vision for the Million Man March," calling for a march of African American men in Washington, D.C., on October 16, 1995.[119] Farrakhan's "Vision Statement" came at the beginning of a national economic upsurge that appeared, however, to by-pass those African American communites which had been most severely affected by neoliberal policies. Unemployment and poverty in many urban neighborhoods, accompanied by a soaring rate of incarceration of their male and, increasingly, their female population, had come to provide a stark contrast to the affluence of a growing black middle-class. A widening economic rift had started to visibly undermine the coherence implied in

---

[118] The Nation of Islam (NOI) is a syncretistic, fundamentalist African American faith community, founded in the 1930s. Its teachings significantly diverge from those of orthodox Islamic denominations, and in an international context it has therefore retained the status of a religious sect. The NOI's most famous minister/spokesman was Malcolm X, who left the Nation after a pilgrimage to Mecca and was assassinated shortly afterwards. During the 1980s the figure of Malcolm X started to acquire the status of a national pop-culture icon. Infamous for its race-based theories of evolution and its eschatology, as well as its anti-semitic and homophobic rhetoric, the NOI nevertheless exerted considerable influence on cultural nationalisms of the 1960s, on the Hiphop culture of the 1980s and '90s and on versions of Afrocentrism. Since the 1990s Louis Farrakhan has started to leave the rigid political separatism of his earlier years, and his rhetoric has assumed a more conciliatory tone. For a discussion of the Nation of Islam and its leaders, cf. e.g. Mattias Gardell, *In the Name of Elijah Muhammad: Louis Farrakhan and the Nation of Islam* (1996), Louis A. DeCaro, *Malcolm and the Cross: The Nation of Islam, Malcolm X, and Christianity* (2000), and Frank Kelleter, *Con/Tradition*.

[119] Speaking of "the suffering and sacrifice of our fellow advocates of change" implies a significant shift in self-positioning. Farrakhan now assumes a place next to those who struggled in the Civil Rights Movement of the 1950s and '60s, a movement the NOI and its representatives polemically disclaimed at the time.

the notion of a black community.[120] While Farrakhan's "Vision Statement" stresses the destructive consequences of recent political decisions for African Americans in general, it argues that it is black men who have been most severely affected.
The epitome of these major challenges to the Black male and our community is this mounting force of hate being built against our people, particularly Black men. We, therefore, have deemed it necessary in this critical hour to call for one million disciplined, committed, and dedicated Black men, from all walks of life in America, to march in Washington, D.C. – showing the world a vastly different picture of the Black male. (Farrakhan: 1996b, 151) The vision statement is a public document of what critics have called the "endangered Black male narrative," a narrative which, they argue, deflects, marginalizes, and ignores "the many ways in which race, class, and gender also endanger the lives of Black women" (Harris: 1999, 57). Yet, statistics on black male incarceration, discrimination in the criminal justice system, and the number of fatal police shootings – even ardent critics of the march concede this – help to strengthen the wide support of this narrative. Enacting black masculinity by marching with a million black men and representing black masculinity to the world, are explicitly linked in Farrakhan's statement. But if difference is called upon twice – black men "from all walks of life" are invited to participate, and they are supposed to create "a vastly different picture" – difference is at the same time negated through a language anchored in the collective singular. During the march, the text assumes, a picture will emerge that truthfully represents an imagined oneness, "the Black male," a oneness which is perhaps most emphatically appealed to in the act of naming the event the Million Man March.
My discussion of masculinity will be informed by race, an oscillating category still speaking through its absence in parts of European discourse on gender. Practically discarded in the sciences, race nevertheless continues to map global geographies. It has remained a tenaciously powerful, if empty paradigm of division that grounds itself in visibility – skin color, hair, and facial features are its most salient signifiers – and in metaphors of blood. Race, as it is enacted in the United States, may still determine the color of blood, declaring it to be either black or white. A meta-binary is thus created that intersects with and sometimes overshadows further agents of difference, gender and class being the most prominent.[121] Two commemorations of the Million Man March will become the foils for my discussion of masculinity as *raced*. The first is an anthology edited by two coorganizers of the march, Haki R. Madhubuti

---

[120] I use the term community in the concrete sense of neighborhood and in the sense of an imagined community whose reality and even desirability is, however, a topic of public debate. I have discussed the semantics of community more extensively in "Rolling into History: Time and Community in Spike Lee's *Get on the Bus*."

[121] Historically, racial theory has of course distinguished between more than two races. I would like to argue though that in the U.S. the black-white binary has been the most unsurmountable one, potentially subsuming further racial divisions.

and Maulana Karenga.[122] Aside from commentary, this mostly celebratory collection also contains a number of documents of the march, among them Louis Farrakhan's "Vision Statement," "The Black Woman's Statement of Support for the Million Man March," and Farrakhan's speech at the march.[123] The second commemorative text is the film *Get on the Bus*, directed by Spike Lee, who is arguably the most visible African American filmmaker of the past two decades. While I will focus on an African American context, *raced* masculinity could of course also refer to white American masculinity, which is still often placed in a realm beyond race in public debate. Although Farrakhan's "Vision Statement" tends to locate the causes of disintegration and destruction outside the African American community, the day of the Million Man March is declared "A Holy Day of Atonement and Reconciliation." While atonement presumes the sinfulness of all human beings, in this gender-determined context it concretely implies former misdeeds committed by African American men. The causes of desolation are thus at least partially relocated within the community and, specifically, within its male constituency. Even among supporters of the march, the term atonement caused critical concern. Maulana Karenga's retrospective comment attempts to secularize and politicize the march's motto: "My task in the Mission Statement, as I understood it, was to expand the concept of atonement from simply an internal posture of spiritual purification and a public posture on confession to a personal and social posture of self-criticism and self-correction around issues of social/ethical practice" (Karenga: 1996, 5). Yet, even Karenga's words affirm the need for African American men to publicly admit faults committed in the past. A more fundamental criticism is voiced by Clarence Walker who states that many of those who participated in the march constituted the part of the community that had indeed "nothing to atone for" (C. Walker: 1996, 5).

Calling for men to congregate in Washington D.C. creates the need to address those who are also members of the community, but are not invited to participate, black women. The "Vision Statement" pleads: "We are asking the Black woman, particularly our mothers, to be with our children teaching them the value of home, self-esteem,

---

[122] In a tradition enacted since slavery, both men use chosen names. Former slaves often selected names from the pantheon of the U.S. founding fathers, especially those of George Washington and Thomas Jefferson. Cultural nationalisms of the 1960s and '70s and Afrocentrist influences of the following decades have provided strong impulses to adopt and adapt Arabic names as well as names from various African languages. For a critical discussion of Afrocentrism, cf. Clarence Walker, *We Can't Go Home Again*.

[123] Other anthologies thematizing the Million Man March are Garth Kasimu Baker-Fletcher's *Black Religion after the Million Man March* and Devon W. Carbado, *Black Men on Race, Gender, and Sexuality*. Many of the articles included in Baker-Fletcher share the Afrocentrist leanings of Madhubuti's and Karenga's volume. Further publications from the 1990s which focus on African American men and black masculinity are a collection of essays by John Wideman, entitled *Fatheralong*, Marcellus Blount, George P. Cunningham (eds.), *Representing Black Men*, Herb Boyd, Robert L. Allen (eds.), *Brotherman: The Odyssey of Black Men in America*, and Daniel J. Wideman, Rohan B Preston (eds.), *Soulfires: Young Black Men on Love and Violence*.

family, and unity; and to work with us to ensure the success of the march and our mission to improve the quality of life for our people." (Farrakhan: 1996b, 151) Perhaps even more than the call for atonement, the relegation of women to family and home, grounded in the elevation of women's reproductive capacities and their nursing duties, provoked a heated public debate. Among the most well-known critics whose political activism goes back to the 1960s and '70s were Angela Davis and Amiri Baraka [LeRoi Jones]. A commentary by Ron Daniels acknowledges the impact of the gender debate and states: "Hence, the March leadership has grappled with the issue of whether the March would promote patriarchy or partnership" (Daniels: 1996, 108).[124]

The march's all-male agenda was indeed softened up; a "Black Women's Task Force" was created, and there was the attempt to focus upon the day's second motto. The "Holy Day of Atonement and Reconciliation" was also to be a "Day of Absence," of absence from school, work, sports, entertainment, and consumption. Church services and community activities were called for, and leadership in these activities was ascribed to women. Still, for many critics, the second motto tended to further reinscribe the traditional dialectics of male public presence and high visibility vs. female absence and invisibility. "The Black Woman's Statement of Support," part of the packet which could be ordered from the organizing committee, repeats and reaffirms the arguments of the "Vision Statement," but it is more poignant about the necessity of atonement, capitalizing the verb "atone" and printing it in bold-face: The Black man must recognize and unconditionally Atone for the absence, in too many cases, of the Black male as the head of the household, positive role model and builder of our community. / The Black man must Atone for and establish positive solutions to the abuse and misuse of Black women and girls. ("Black Woman's Statement of Support," 156) While the second point is rather straightforward in its reference to abuse of black women and girls and its demands for "positive solutions," the first point made seems to imply that black men have forsaken their position as "the head of the household" and are obliged to unconditionally atone for their absence from this pre-ordained place. The theme of the absent father in African American families has been brought up in a wide spectrum of arguments. This spectrum ranges from John Edgar Wideman's reflections on the historically loaded complexities of father-son-relationships,[125] to the accusation of female-centered family structures as producing social pathologies among black boys and men, an argument which culminated in

---

[124] Anthony Paul Farley, however, claims that gender-segregation policies were necessary: "Black men and women together would have been transgressive in a way that would not have constituted an antispectacle. Women and men together would have made the march a family affair. A black family march would have been another civil rights protest, not an antispectacle" (Farley: 1999, 75) To Farley, the theme of atonement actually gave the march "a feminist edge" (75).

[125] Cf. John Edgar Wideman's *Fatheralong*. Father-son-relationships are a theme in much of Wideman's work.

Daniel Patrick Moynihan's study in the 1960s.[126] While the women's statement of support would hardly blame African American women for the desperate economic conditions of a large number of black families,[127] the demand for the "Black male as head of the household" does repeat, with a difference, the call for a return of the law-giving father underlying so many claims for family values voiced by white conservatives. Authors of the women's statement of support are not named, but a "National Black Women's Endorsement Roster" is added, containing the names of two celebrities, of civil rights activist and organizer Rosa Parks who is given the title "Mother," and of poet/writer Maya Angelou. Both women figured prominently as speakers at the march and both are quoted with their own readings of Farrakhan's call, readings that do not, however, question his granting of leadership to black men.

The language of the march relies on a fixed and transparent referential relation between language and a given object-world, considered the real world. Yet, aware of its inventive power, this language also grants agency to words and expects them to create that object-world. The black community is thus called upon as a given entitiy, predetermined and contained through boundaries drawn by descent. At the same time, the texts quoted aim to bring forth this community by calling together its male constituency. Like the notion of the real world, the semantics of man and male seem stable, existing beyond place and time. A salient connotation of man and male as well as manhood[128] is the claim to a specific position in family and society at large, a position which implies male responsibility. Assumed to be religiously or, in a broader sense, metaphysically authorized, the moral foundation of this responsibility is not questioned. As for its metaphors and rhetorical strategies, Farrakhan's call for atonement and many responses of those who followed it employ the language of an African American Protestant Christianity, a language that has also been an important facet of the NOI's syncretistic reinvention of Islam. In his critical reflections on the march, Victor Anderson speaks of a conversionist ideology, one that puts "emphasis on repentance, separation, sanctification, and a summons toward the moral transformation of one's racial self-consciousness" (Andersen: 1998, 19).[129] Through the inclusion of different faith communities and political groups, the Million Man March

---

[126] Cf. Paula Giddings's discussion of the Moynihan Report, *When and Where I Enter*, pp. 325 ff.

[127] The feminization of poverty of course applies across race and ethnicity. Jesse Jackson states in his speech: "The poor are mostly White, female, and young. They put a Black face on poverty, and it's open season for all in that class" (Jackson: 1996, 35).

[128] In their introductory essay "What Does Man Want?" Ulf Reichhard and Sabine Sielke use the terms manhood and masculinity as quasi-synonyms. I would like to argue that in its vague connotations manhood tends to rely more securely on nature, biology, religion, while the term masculinity is quite often part of a more critical rhetoric. But depending on context, both terms of course overlap.

[129] Anthony Farley celebrates the aspects of atonement and conversion as confessing to the sins of patriarchy and converting from "the black role" of submitting to white phantasies (Farley: 1999, 76).

110

and its texts create a setting where an African American (civil) religion is presented to a national public, a composite wholeness that celebrates its plurality while remaining grounded in assumptions of male responsibility as leadership.[130]

According to the editors, the title of a 1988 issue of *Camera Obscura*, "Male Trouble," "refers not so much to men in trouble, but to the 'idea of masculinity itself (which) is both theoretically and historically troubled'" (quot. in Caldwell: 1996, 133). Despite repeated references to the construction of male images in the media, the Million Man March and many of its texts – those which preceded it and those which celebrated it in retrospect – focus on men in trouble, while avoiding the theme of a troubled masculinity. A critical discussion of black masculinity and its history, one may assume, would have indeed clashed with many ideological assumptions providing the platform for the march and its choreography.[131] The end of Farrakhan's long speech consisted of a pledge the men were asked to repeat. Adapting the ten commandments, the men were to embrace each other and solemnly promise that they would strive to love their brother as they love themselves, improve themselves in all realms of life, strive to build themselves up economically, and raise their hand against nobody, except in self–defense. The fifth and sixth commandments explicitly refer to violence in the realms of gender and sexuality: I, (name), pledge from this day forward I will never abuse my wife by striking her or disrespecting her, for she is the mother of my children and the producer of my future. I, —— , pledge from this day forward I will never engage in the abuse of children, little boys or little girls, for sexual gratification; I will let them grow in peace to be strong men and women for the future of our people. (Farrakhan: 1996b, 29) The theme of domestic violence and sexual abuse, explicitly dealt with in African American literature, has provoked heated debates. Authors have been criticized as inviting white voyeurism and affirming racist stereotypes. The public acknowledgement of social pathologies through a communal repetition at the march, one may argue, enters a tabooed domain. At the same time, the pledge objectifies women as possessions whose value lies in their capability – and destiny – to bear the black man's future. Moreover, the semantics of respect may, depending on context, well imply hegemonic power relations. Difference is named as sameness: woman as wife as mother; man as husband as father. Very explicitly, the (complete) nuclear family and thus heterosexuality as unquestioned and unquestionable norm constitute the only platform from which the assembled men are allowed to speak. To Victor Anderson, the communal vows do not transgress protective traditions but inscribe "on the conscience of every black man a history of

---

[130] Cf. also Frank Kelleter's discussion of American civil religion, pp. 87ff. It is problematic to generalize about the gender politics of the many speeches held at the march and the many celebratory articles written. But despite Maulana Karenga's "Mission Statement" which called for partnership, the tenor of the march's documents does support a degree of generalization.

[131] Alice Walker's contribution to the Million Man March anthology, although surprisingly uncritical as to Farrakhan's speech, is among the few texts in the collection to explicitly thematize masculinity and gendered religion.

self-hatred" (Anderson: 1998, 20). Anderson also stresses that in the list of black male failures which require atonement, homophobia (and the insistence on the nuclear family makes this only logical) remains silent. If conventions of masculinity appear threatened by the changes of the preceding decades, the pledge tries to overcome possible anxiety by proclaiming an agenda for the new millennium, an agenda that promises to restore security. The march's rhetoric of responsibility also evokes the language of the Promise Keepers, "a conservative Christian group that espouses a traditional vision of family life rooted in the idea that men should take on the responsibility of leadership in both the family and the general community" (Harris: 1999, 67, ann. 13). Clarence Walker states, "If the Promise Keepers offer black and white men the possibility of getting in touch with their 'inner man' for spiritual revewal, this march did not offer much more" (C. Walker: 1995, 5). Cornel West, who participated in but did not speak at the march, mentions deep disagreements with Farrakhan. Yet, the antiracist agenda that he and speakers like Jesse Jackson so strongly support – an agenda which was very much part of the march's momentum – recreates a traditional hierarchy of issues. Class, gender and sexuality become secondary to race(ism). "If we can target white supremacy, then the other crucial issues of poverty, maldistribution of wealth, corporate power, patriarchy, homophobia an[d] ecological abuse will be brought into daylight? Why so? Because race matters so much in American society" (West: 1996b, 99). The demands of black feminists that the whole spectrum of oppression be focused upon instead of foregrounding race and subsuming other forms of injustice, seem to be erased in this rhetoric.

Knowing about the power of representation in the context of a highly visible public event, Farrakhan's "Vision Statement" claims that the media have been particularly destructive in their globally disseminated images of black men as a threat to society. Two narratives emerge, an African American narrative of the endangered black male, which functions as an antithesis to the second and more powerful narrative, that of the threatening black male. Farrakhan names the conduits of white mis-representation, "movies, music and other communications technologies throughout the world" (Farrakhan: 1996c, 151). Spike Lee's film *Get on the Bus*, I will argue, assumes the task of representation as "truthful fiction," a fiction which does not claim to be representative of a given whole. It draws awareness to its textual status and, in opposition to Farrakhan's call, argues against the notion of a collective "Black man." While the theme of black men in trouble is very much part of the film, troubled black masculinity is its main focus. Yet, if black masculinity is represented as visibly heterogeneous and plural – one should speak of masculinities – much of the film's rhetoric envisions a healing of the deep crisis through the moral restoration of securely gendered spaces in family and community.

Released on October 16, 1996, *Get on the Bus* celebrates the first anniversary of the Million Man March which is presented as a historic event. Through its title, the film turns cultural memory, especially the memory of the Civil Rights Movement, into a request, into a call for participation, for involvement, for change grounded in self-reliance. While the film was distributed by Columbia, it was independently financed by a group of black men, and this information is visualized at the beginning, in an iconography which fuses elements of graffity and rusty brown colors connoting slavery. *Get on the Bus* is introduced as a "15 Black Men Production." It thus identifies itself as an investment by African American men in images and stories, in a history of their own. The fundraising – one of the investors was scriptwriter Reggie Rock Bythewood – and the filmmaking under the restrictions of a low budget are recalled as a challenging communal endeavor: "It was about working as a team, and I believe our efforts are up there on the screen" (www.spe.sony.com 3). All who were involved had high expectations about the film's impact, and actor Ossie Davis, featured prominently in the narrative, is quoted as predicting: "I have a feeling that what we've done here will make cinematic history just as it's making cultural and social history" (www.spe.sony.com 4). *Get on the Bus* indeed won an award at the Berlin Film Festival 1997 for "exemplary ensemble acting of the whole team."[132] But the high expectations raised, failed at least in one decisive realm; the film drew no enthusiastic audience, it was unsuccessful at the box office. Moreover, *Get on the Bus* has not found its place in what Wahneema Lubiano refers to as "the Spike Lee discourse," a discourse spanning a wide spectrum of journalistic and academic responses. The film's plot is easily told: Twenty men board a chartered bus in South Central Los Angeles to join the Million Man March in Washington D.C.[133] Crossing the continent from West to East, they go on a pilgrimage – biblical motives are consistently evoked – and this pilgrimage reverses historical routes. It reverses the trajectory of the Puritan pilgrim fathers who landed at Plymouth Rock, one of the founding texts of an America imagined as white and male. It also reverses the colonizing movement of white settlers. Finally, and very importantly for the narrative, the West-East pilgrimage reverses the routes of the Middle Passage, the passage of enslaved Africans across the Atlantic to an ill-boding future in the New World. The bus with its narrow space – although there are quite a few empty seats, there is little room to move – becomes a vessel, a ship headed towards a future that holds promises. There are many trials and tribulations to be overcome on this "historic journey," as one of the passengers, the oldest and revered member of the group, the prophetic Jeremiah Washington, calls it. In metaphors rewording the Civil Rights Movement, the audience eventually learns that it is the act of getting on the bus which is important, not the arrival, which is suspended. The men

---

[132] This foregrounding of communal achievement raises the question of authorship, and although Lee's filmmaking is usually discussed as auteur cinema, it is debatable whether one should speak of *Get on the Bus* as Spike Lee's narrative. Yet, aside from the intensity of his involvement in making the film, I consider the product itself to be a part of Lee's "body of work" which projects, as Douglas Kellner points out, "a distinctive style and vision" (Kellner: 1997, 76).

[133] It is actually difficult to tell the number of men on the bus.

113

never make it to the march,[134] because Jeremiah suffers a heart attack and dies in a hospital. Those who remain with him get to watch the march on television.

The journey's start, South Central Los Angeles, is associated in the public mind with gang wars and an explosive riot. But the actual point of departure is the First AME (African Methodist Episcopalian) Church, signifying a history of community building and diasporic Christianity. A banner across the church's front announces its support of the march and pronounces it to be an ecumenical endeavor. Ghetto voyeurism and promises of a sensationalist commodification of black masculinity are discouraged in this imagery.[135] Moreover, the men who approach the bus embody difference, difference of age, class, religion, political persuasion, and, as the audience will learn soon, sexuality. A middle-aged man named George, one of the drivers, calls the passengers to get on the bus and "ride into history."[136] He will emerge as an integrative leader, a Moses-figure. George lays out the rules: no guns, no illegal substances, and – no women. Women, one might argue, become illegal substances here. Yet, the rhetoric of exclusion is phrased in a way that divests the link between masculinity and the male body of its assumed naturalness. Introducing himself to the men, a kind of prologue to the film's narrative, George pleads, "I trust that none of you men are women" and thereby admits that gender visibility can be treacherous. One of the men might indeed be a woman.[137] On these shifting premises an insult is meant to deter non-members from intruding into the journey's desired community of true men. In case any of the men on the bus are women, they are called "some of the ugliest broads" George has ever seen, a punishment of possible gender transgression and an attempt to recreate the security of a single gender identity. Then anatomy is reassuringly called upon through forbiddance, no pissing on the toilet seat. The interjection from one of the men that George sounds just like his mother, seemingly suggesting an inversion of gender roles, is taken up and carried further by an answer immersed in history. George asserts that on this bus he is indeed the mother, and then he playfully pretends to take his belt and promises punishment in case the rules are not obeyed. The figure of the punishing father, central to a Judeo-Christian tradition, becomes the figure of the punishing mother. While one might claim that the masculinity of George/the mother is reasserted through the threatening belt, such a reading becomes uncertain in a context of race and family structures of a New World diaspora. In a long history of women-centered families in African American

---

[134] The plot is somewhat confusing, since it first suggests that a group of men do make it to the Mall but then implies that they did not. The script, however, explicitly states that none of the men participated in the march.

[135] This reading does not support Reggy Rock Bythewood's polemical description of a ghetto setting, cf. Bythewood: 1996, 1.

[136] Page numbers will only be indicated, if the quotations are identical with the script.

[137] Bythewood's script works with vernacular implications. George (Charles Dutton) was supposed to say: "I trust that none of you are on the rag, so we don't have to worry about that" (Bythewood: 1996, 7).

communities, narratives of the lawgiving and punishing mother who is at the same time nurturing, quite often displace the loaded image of the father. It has been an ongoing debate whether this position of women can be reduced to being a consequence of the absent father – an absence attributable to a history of slavery and institutionalized racism – or whether it is also an effect of traditionally different enactments of family structures. How easily the concept of cultural difference may slip into clichés, however, is demonstrated when the men who are slowly getting to know each other, tell tales about their worst childhood punishment. The concluding remark to these tales is: "White mothers lecture, black mothers kick ass." Yet, the figure of the absent father is concretely embodied, and becomes a strong presence among the men assembled. Evan Sr., admitting to his many years of absence as father, is conjoined with his son, Evan Jr. It was the father who forced the young man to get on the bus, the son having been sentenced by a judge to be tethered for 72 hours, and the two remain shackled to each other for most of the bus ride. While the film stresses the desired dialogic nature of father-son-relationships, meanings of fatherhood oscillate. Visually as well as verbally they take up a large space in the desired wholeness of black masculinity.

A prayer is spoken before the journey starts. Jeremiah Washington asks for God's assistance, calling the men "pilgrims on a bus bound for glory" and expressing his hope that they will return "a better man."[138] His words are grounded in religious metaphors of empowerment that link the Old Testament, European Christianity, and the African diaspora. Jeremiah names men who are ascribed the status of prophetic leaders and martyrs: Moses, Noah, Malcolm, and Martin.[139] An inclusive African American Protestant Christianity provides space for Islam, not only through the name of Malcolm X, but also, as part of the film's narrative, through one of the passengers, a young orthodox Muslim. Comparable to the ecumenical assembly at the march, Islam and Christianity do not oppose each other on this journey.

The men's decision to go to the march is commented on by two critical female voices, voices which are, however, kept off the bus. There is a young woman in a BMW convertible, driving her partner Gary to the bus stop. She calls the march "sexist and exclusionary." But the evolving argument drifts off into questions of skin color and ends with the promise that Gary who is firmly determined to attend the march, will be part of CNN news. The second criticial voice is heard during a brief encounter at a stop during the journey. On being told that the men are going to the Million Man March, two young women engage in a lively dispute. While the scene demonstrates that the march is indeed a contested project, it stresses that there is also strong female support. Yet, the critical voices heard before and during the journey remain without consequences and seem to evaporate as soon as the men board the bus. Aside from

---

[138] The script reads: "If nothing else oh Lord, we pray that after this trip, each and every one of us become more of a man than we were before" (Bythewood: 1996, 9).

[139] With the juxtaposition of Malcolm X and Martin Luther King, the film repeats the gesture of Spike Lee's earlier film *Do the Right Thing*.

George as mother, women travel on the bus as stories and as images contained in photographs that are proudly displayed. The long ride across the continent – a ride which provides ample time for bonding as well as dispute – affirms Robert Reid-Pharr's argument that "Women act only as conduits by which social relations, relations that take place exclusively between men, are represented" (Reid-Pharr, 356). Cultural critic Paul Gilroy judges harshly: The bus journey provides Lee with a legitimate means to exclude women so that he can do what he does best: explore the tortured contours of the black man's being in the the modern world. The film thus owes something to that genre of military movies in which men can confidently become intimate with one another without the distractions women would represent. (Indeed, this mutual tenderness seems somehow to require the banishment of women.) (Gilroy: 1996, 17-18)

Women as conduits help to keep relations between the men within a secure realm. A hot debate emerges whether it is a sign of a healthy masculinity to cheat on one's girlfriend or wife. While some of the men admit that they have cheated, it is not declared a manly thing to do, rather a masculine lapse. Possible slipping from homosocial to homosexual relations is averted through this discourse. Still, the topic of homosexuality looms large in the narrative. A gay couple in the process of breaking up is among the passengers, and the two men become a focus of attention. Different positions are taken by the travelers, ranging from friendly support to violent homophobia. Jeremiah, the old man, relies on biblical judgment, although he has his own thoughts that make him skeptical of any exclusionary practices. But his reference, "The Bible says it's an abomination," quotes the most authoritative of texts. It places homosexuality and the homosexual into the realm of abjection, forcing it/him beyond boundaries and declaring it/him unassimilable.[140] At the same time, abject homosexuality traveling on the bus challenges that which it cannot be part of, a black masculinity imagined as heterosexual by nature. In a society where for centuries a rigidly delineated if unmarked whiteness has provided a mooring for power, blackness, Robert Reid-Pharr argues provocatively, is refused its own boundaries. It thus faces the specter of being boundaryless, "[...] there is no normal blackness to which the black subject [...] might refer" (Reid-Pharr: 1997, 353). On the bus, the repeated attempt to draw boundaries around blackness on the basis of skin color and the racial status of the mother is shown as highly destructive.[141] Gary, a member of the Los Angeles police force, was raised by his white mother, and his membership in the

---

[140] Jeremiah refers to Leviticus 18: "Thou shalt not lie with mankind as with womankind: it is abomination." Cf. also Julia Kristeva, *Pouvoirs de l'horreur*, 9ff, 122f.

[141] Enactments of race have a widely differing history in the former slave-holding societies of the Americas. One important facet of racial mythology in the U.S. was the infamous "one-drop-rule," declaring that one drop of black blood places makes a person black. In the racial imagination whiteness thus became synonymous with uncontaminated purity. As a consequence, the legal categories *Negro* or *of color* did and the current terms *African American* and *black* do not necessarily imply dark skin.

black community is challenged by Flip, the loudmouthed aspiring Hollywood star. Flip's polemics are criticized, most explicitly by Jeremiah who becomes an authoritative teller of history. What remains unsaid in the dispute over the historical privileges of light skin color and the boundaries of blackness is the legal definition of a person's status as free or enslaved in the antebellum South. Slavery statutes declared that a person followed the condition of the mother, a rule upholding the rationality of a slave-holding economy and implicitly granting white men sexual access to black women. Race thus ruptured the structures of patrilinearity that American society took for granted.[142] Since sexual access to white women was denied to black men – this does become part of the controversy between Flip and Jeremiah – it came to signify a position of power, a history still weighing on "mixed-race" couples. Reconceptualizing black masculinity necessarily implies an act of redefining, of drawing at least provisionary boundaries. It is the creation of livable boundaries around a redeemed masculinity capable of countering oppression, which may be considered one if not the ultimate goal of the men's pilgrimage.

A very concrete reason for atonement and for the necessity of the Million Man March, the film repeatedly stresses, is violence in the domestic sphere, as well as in the public space of the street. Still, violence is allowed to enter the negotiations of difference among the men. Like the talk about and the photographs of women, violent homophobia attempts to keep homosexuality beyond the boundaries of blackness. "To strike the homosexual, the scapegoat, the sign of chaos and crisis, is to return the community to normalcy, to create boundaries around blackness, rights that indeed white men are obliged to recognize," Robert Reid-Pharr claims (Reid-Pharr: 1997, 354). Violence against the homosexual, the argument implies, is not disruptive but rather normalizes that which is outside of whiteness. Only a violent insistence on normalcy will create a definition of black masculinity binding for white men, those whom Eldridge Cleaver considered the controllers of black masculinity. The film shifts this attempt at drawing boundaries. While the man who openly professes his homosexuality is verbally struck, is labeled as sissy, as abject, physical blows are aimed at the "man in the relationship," the tough ex-marine Kyle, who at first refuses to let his sexuality become a topic, but then stands up, talks back, appropriates the catalog of insults, and is prepared to fight.[143] His masculinity, the scene suggests, exceeds that of Flip, the violent homophobe. As an expression of ultimate anxiety, Flip accuses Kyle of slipping back and forth between homo- and heterosexuality, of feeling "butch" about everybody. While butch might simply be read as an ascription of sexual aggressiveness, Flip's act of (un)naming Kyle, I would like to suggest, acts as a queering label. Feminizing and remasculinizing him at the same time, it signifies

---

[142] For a discussion of the ruptures caused by the Middle Passage and slavery, cf. Hortense Spillers, "Mama's Baby, Papa's Maybe."

[143] To the big surprise of the men, Kyle is also a Republican, claiming that blacks are kept in perpetual dependence by the Democrats and their handouts, another demonstration of the film's effort to subvert "packaged" identities.

ultimate sexual transgression. Kyle, who is in excellent physical condition and goes into a martial arts stance, accompanies his blows with the names of famous black men. Langston Hughes and James Baldwin are mentioned, the poet laureate of Harlem and the writer in exile whose work thematizes homosexuality.[144] Another fighting name is that of Dennis Rodman, the basketball star who for years publicly celebrated his play with gender boundaries. The surprise of the by now beaten homophobe about Dennis Rodman's gayness misses the aspect of willful transgression entirely. Kyle's vicious blows, it seems, are meant to revenge those black writers whose sexuality was either met with silence or whose gay or queer texts were excluded from the corpus of black literature. Moreover, the pain caused by the blows seems to revenge those black athletes who were (and still are) forced to negate any sexual preferences outside a rigid heterosexual norm. With the names of Hughes, Baldwin, and Rodman, *Get on the Bus* participates in a discourse on black masculinity that stresses the utter necessity of integrating gender and sexuality into an antiracist agenda.[145] Like the critical voices of the women, however, queerness as the denial of a clearly delineated sexual identity, remains inconsequential in the film, it is not allowed to remain part of the narrative.

The fight is enacted as a ritual and, as other scenes, digresses from the script. In Bythewood's text it functions as an example of masculine aberration, a demonstration of the men's definite need for atonement. In the film, however, ambivalence reigns. Some of the men try to prevent the fight, and indeed, the combatants have to get off the bus, enacting a reversal of the film's loaded title and indicating a point of crisis in their pilgrimage. But if those who cheer the combatants on, are a minority, the whole group builds a circle around the two. The ritual is documented by one of the younger passengers, film student Xavier. Xavier's ubiquitous camera recalls the intrusive gaze of the film camera that remains invisible, and one might argue that a self-critical, slightly ironic stance towards film and photography, but especially towards documentation with its insistence on closeness to its object is taken. Suggesting redemption and catharsis, the righteous one who has decided to stand up in a manly way for his homosexuality, wins. He is thereby granted a place, albeit a marginalized one, a minority position, within black masculinity. Whether this also includes his non-macho former lover who does not physically respond to the insults hurled at him, remains a question the film does not ask. Flip, the fasttalking aggressor, gets punished for his homophobia. Indeed, in what is perhaps the only instance where Louis Farrakhan's rhetoric is criticized, the march is ironically called an opportunity for the NOI's leader himself to atone for his homophobia. Being on the bus, being committed and part of a movement which situates itself in the tradition of the Civil Rights Movement, should mean – the integrative voice of George is very clear about this – to come together across difference. At the same time, heterosexuality as a normative realm of stability remains unquestioned.

---

[144] Baldwin's writing as well as his sexuality were scathingly commented upon by Eldridge Cleaver, cf. "Notes on a Native Son" in *Soul on Ice*, 96ff.

[145] Cf. the contributions in Marcellus Blount and George Cunningham and in Devon Carbado.

Spending three days in the narrow confinement of the bus confronts the men with a lot of empty time. Statements about their motivation to go to the march, elicited and meticulously documented by Xavier, open up spaces for the life stories that are eventually told. Confession as a paradigmatic text for the extraction of truth about lives provides an impetus for many of the autobiographic stories shared. "Under the pressure of feminism and gay politics, and as a result of the demand of advanced capitalism for new kinds of workers," Constance Penley and Sharon Willis assert, "men are being asked to respond as men in new and different ways" (Quot. in Caldwell 133). Feminism, as opposed to homosexuality, is kept off the bus, but its presence in the world outside remains vocal. It is Jeremiah Washington, prophet and figure of the past, whose story provides an elaborate example of the fate of a man marked by age as too inflexible to respond to the demands of globalization. Troubled masculinity and men in trouble are two facets of *raced* lives that can hardly be separated.

Music as diegetic and non-diegetic sound becomes an agent of bonding and of historical commentary. It is a celebration of James Brown's unabashed macho funk "Papa Don't Take No Mess," which literally gets the bus rolling out of South Central. If performing James Brown's song from the mid-'60s is also readable as taking a rebellious stance against an oppressive status quo, it definitely subverts the somber request for atonement made in Farrakhan's call as well as in Jeremiah's prayer. It is no surprise that the only passenger who wears the attire of the NOI (black suit, white shirt, bow tie) does not join in this performance. He actually remains a muted stranger until the men reach Washington D.C, a silence indicating ambivalence towards the NOI or demonstrating an unwillingness to deal more thoroughly with the group. Evan Jr., the youngest of the men, is another passenger who does not join the men and refuses to get involved in this sharing of masculine history. James Brown's sounds and the Rap of the early 90s which Evan Jr. is listening to through his earphones, are tightly connected through the celebrated blackness of their sounds and their hyperbolic masculinity, but in the bus they clash as the music of father and son.[146] Leaving the urban sprawl of Los Angeles, the men join in a rapped roll call which, after the James Brown warm-up, intensifies the experience of a black male community of sound. The generation gap evident before is at least temporarily closed. Among the unsettling aspects of the film's soundtrack is a smooth rendering of Bob Marley's "Redemption Song" by Stevie Wonder, which accompanies the ritual fight. Marley's diasporic lyrics are hardly audible though, and the sound adds to the scene's ambivalence.

The ritual of violence, seemingly supported as well as critiqued by the music, claims a difference to those spectacles that have become an integral part of media narratives on black masculinity. Gang-violence is a salient theme in Lee's film, yet, the

---

[146] Rap is silenced and dismissed as noise by the father's authority, but it accompanies the film as part of the soundtrack. The fact that Rap has extensively sampled James Brown is lost on both father and son.

fighting scene itself seems to counter the "hood"-films of the 1990s, a genre that took up aspects of the Blaxploitation (exploitation of blackness) movies of the 1970s.[147] In the Hollywood-invented "hood," fights are hardly fist fights, instead, guns keep a physical distance between the opponents. Masculinity thus either means heroic loneliness, or masculine bonding takes place within the gang as extended family. The fighting in *Get on the Bus* in its close contact between male bodies – violence might be mingled with eroticism here – thus almost seems to evoke nostalgia for a time when strong men resolved conflicts with their fists and the homosocial bonds of the male community were actually strengthened. Moreover, unlike the gunfights which leave dead bodies in their wake, this fight seems to leave no wounds. The faces are cleansed of any traces left by the blows, bodies do not seem to be injured. Still, along with the life-stories of the young orthodox Muslim Jamal and the policeman Gary, the fight evokes the narrative of the endangered black male. Perhaps the film introduces a touch of irony, however, through the spotted owl painted on the side of the bus, an animal that has officially been declared an endangered species. The closure of the fighting scene is not Flip's defeat, but the communal search for the lost son, Evan Jr., who has run away from his father while the men are watching the fight. When Evan Sr. finally catches up with his son, his claim to fatherhood, i.e. to authority, is met with fierce resistance. But after a long talk on the cold ground, father and son are reunited and get on the bus together.

Anti-semitism becomes a topic and so does white liberalism as barely masked white prejudice. Stranded in the desert with a broken axle, the men's journey seems to have found an early end, but another, more comfortable bus is sent. The new driver, Rick, is white and Jewish. Rick eventually decides to leave the group, to literally get off the bus, his gesture proclaiming a difference between this ride and the Civil Rights Movement. Again, the film avoids any differentiated statement when the driver justifies his decision by referring to the anti-semitic rhetoric of Farrakhan. Instead, Rick withdraws into polemic clichés. Arguing against affirmative action and insisting that O.J. Simpson is guilty, he repeats a public discourse that has recreated a chasm between black and white voices. Bringing up the O.J. Simpson verdict, the narrative indeed touches upon a highly sensitive issue, O.J. Simpson's name signifying the explosive reciprocal reinforcement of race and gender divisions. Historically, whiteness and masculinity have been closely linked to positions and enactments of power, moreover, Jewishness has highly charged connotations in the film industry. With the figure of the Jewish bus driver some of these inscriptions are undermined,

---

[147] Among the most well-known films of the "hood"-genre are *Boyz 'n the Hood* (1991) and *Menace II [to] Society* (1993). Blaxploitation movies with cult status are *Shaft* (1971) and *Superfly* (1972). A follow-up of *Shaft* was released in 2000, but despite its focus on action it seems a tame recycling of a celebrated '70s black machismo which became coded as inherently transgressive.

yet, no dialogue emerges.[148] Only a short sequence, inserted into the narrative as TV-coverage, presents documentary footage of the Million Man March. While there are some panoramic views of the perhaps more than a million men who came to Washington, one does not see or hear Louis Farrakhan. His paramilitary, uniformed guard, the Fruit of Islam is shown, however. What the film also shows is the larger than life picture of poet/writer Maya Angelou who addresses the assembled men with a poem. Her words seem to prefigure the words spoken at the end of the film. Hers are metaphors of kinship, welcoming the men at the Mall as sons, cousins, grandsons, nephews. In the film's final words, words of exhortation spoken by George and followed by a prayer, the hope is expressed that the boys who got on the bus have turned into men. In the rhetoric of gendered life-histories, George's words suggest that the journey has been an initiation to manhood and has achieved the existential transformation hoped for. Again, the family becomes the trope of black connectedness. Black men are connected, reconnected it seems, to women as mothers, wives, sisters, and daughters. George's words seem to affirm Paul Gilroy's warning that at a certain point "the trope of the family begins to look like a desaster for black femininism" (Gilroy: 1992, 307). The projection of a responsible black masculinity anchored in family and community attaches itself to an imagined past as a space where the boundaries of gender were securely drawn.

Victor Anderson's critique of black antiracist intellectual traditions is especially significant for the end of the film: Anderson speaks of a "pervasive preoccupation [...] with the classical, heroic virtues of courage, manliness, strength, self-determination, and racial loyalty" (Anderson: 1998, 21). Like the march, whose choreography and topics it takes up, the film wants to reestablish categories, but unlike the rhetoric of the march, it is willing to integrate challenges and to negotiate boundaries. Concrete political demands are avoided, however, and visions of a better future thus tend to remain vague, subject to appropriation for very different ends.[149] At the same time, it is the fissures and ambivalences, the ironic collisions and narrative flaws, which, aside from the intensity of improvised dialogues and the amount of attention given to black homophobia, offer flickers of a more radical interrogation of masculinity.

The Million Man March, it has been argued, was appropriated by those who participated: "Farrakhan made the call – but the March belongs to us all" (Daniels: 1996, 112–13). The front cover of the commemorative anthology shows an aerial view of the huge expanse of space taken up by the men assembled at the Mall, creating an iconography of black manhood as nationhood. But the book's back as well as some photographs inside the volume depict the attentive faces of women attending the march. Some of the womem are obviously the wives and daughters of the speakers, but others simply seem to have decided that they would attend the march without

---

[148] Farrakhan made at least a rhetorical effort to reach out to members of the Jewish community in his speech, and Maulana Karenga's "Mission Statement" mentions Judaism in a catalog of religions providing spiritual and ethical traditions. Cf. the discussion in Anthony Farley, 76.

[149] Jesse Jackson's speech may have been the most politicized statement of the march.

invitation. Moreover, most of the commentary stresses that the participants indulged in the peacefulness of the assembly and that Farrakhan's speech was by no means the core of the event.[150] With its insistence on the importance of fatherhood and its avoidance of Farrakhan's speech, the film about the march at least partially affirms Henry Louis Gates's conclusion: "No, the day did not belong to Farrakhan; it belonged to a million black fathers and their sons" (Gates: 1996, xix).[151] Quite obviously, Farrakhan's attempt to appropriate the masculine legacy of the Civil Rights Movement proved less successful than the strong response to his call might have suggested. Clearly, however, the march and many of its texts including Lee's film try to reclaim the patrilinearity ruptured by slavery and the century to follow. There has been a continuity of gender-related marches organized or at least supported by the NOI. The Million Man March was followed by the Million Woman March in Philadelphia on October 25, 1997, an event which drew fewer celebrities and consequently generated less media-attention than the men's march.[152] As a commemoration of the fifth anniversary of the Million Man March, the NOI, still under the leadership of Farrakhan, called a Million Family March with an agenda accessible on the Nation's webpage. In this document, the institution of the family appears as a universal, organic unit, grounded in the founding texts of the Bible and the Koran. Definitions of family are not given, since its timeless, unshifting meaning is taken for granted.[153] However, unlike the call for the Million Man March, the agenda claims to make concrete political demands and does not foreground male leadership.[154]

Black men in trouble and a troubled black masculinity have been topics of African Americans texts since the slave narratives of the 19th century. They were salient

---

[150] In the heated debates over the event and its long-term benefits, this indulgence was criticized as a mere celebration of good feelings. Anthony Pinn makes a similar statement about Spike Lee's film: "The process [of connecting and of transformation during the travel to the march] is redemptive. Ideally this is what happens, but the good feelings generated by a film quickly fade" (Pinn: 1998, 66).

[151] Cf. also Gates's essay on Louis Farrakhan, "The Charmer."

[152] Furthermore, there was the mostly middle-class Million Mom March to push for gun control, and on August 26, 2000, a "Redeem the Dream" march took place, protesting racial profiling and police brutality.

[153] While conceding the NOI's essentialist vision of race, gender, and sexuality, Anthony Farley stresses the history of the NOI as a rescuing mission: "Perhaps, despite itself, it has rescued the black body from its identity as the *black* body" (Farley: 1999, 80).

[154] Due to the highly contested status of the NOI, media coverage of the Million Family March differs widely from the NOI's own reporting on the event. This is brought up by Farrakhan himself in his interview on the Tom Joyner Morning Show, cf. www.millionfamilymarch.com, "Latest News & Information Updates." The interview also demonstrates the shift towards the more inclusive stance that Farrakhan has started to take. This shift may also include gender politics.

themes of Richard Wright's *Native Son* and Eldridge Cleaver's *Soul on Ice*. [155] Slavery and institutionalized racism in a New World diaspora provided social and economic conditions that kept bringing forth the trope of a continuing or a recurring crisis. Since the hegemonic position which gender hierarchy granted to white men was not or only partially granted to African American men, there has been a tradition of focusing on men as the primary targets and victims of race(ism), and the crisis has tended to be couched in gendered terms. Decades of critical interventions, especially by African American women – heterosexual and lesbian [156] – and gay men have challenged this narrative. Moreover, their voices have of course intersected with the interrogations of masculinity in American academic and general public realms. If the Million Man March's request for atonement, a language taken up in parts of Lee's film, was grounded in the spiritual and religious/political affiliations of the march's organizers, it is readable also as a retrospective gesture, a way of looking back at a century whose problem was predicted to be the "color line" (Du Bois: 1989, xxxi). Beyond the millenarianism of the NOI, [157] the language of atonement may have has lost some of its weight after the turn of the century. But despite the high visibility of successful black men, it seems that oppressive realities – the rate of incarceration and police shootings are only two deeply unsettling aspects – as well as ongoing critiques of masculinity keep providing the ground for the trope of a crisis, of black men in trouble and of a troubled black masculinity.

Sources

Anderson, Victor, "Abominations of a Million Men," in: Garth Kasimu Baker-Fletcher (ed.), *Black Religion After the Million Man March*, pp. 19-26.
Baker-Fletcher, Garth Kasimu (ed.), *Black Religion After the Million Man March*, Mayknoll, NY, 1998.
Bythewood, Reggie Rock, *Get on the Bus!* Atlanta, GA, 1996, <http://www.scriptshop.com>.
"The Black Woman's Statement of Support for the Million Man March," in: Haki R Madhubuti, Maulana Karenga (eds.), *Million Man March / Day of Absence*, pp. 155-157.
Boyd, Herb, Robert L. Allen (eds.), *Brotherman – The Odyssey of Black Men in America*, New York, 1995.
Blount, Marcellus, Cunningham, George P. (eds.), *Representing Black Men*, New York, London, 1996.

---

[155] Cf. also Ulf Reichhardt and Sabine Sielke, 564, annot. 9.

[156] African American women have spoken up and written on race and gender since the 19th century, but pervasive criticism of black masculinity became a theme of public debate only after the 1960s.

[157] Cf. also Martha F. Lee, *The Nation of Islam: An American Millenarian Movement* (1996).

The Bible, Authorized Version. The Bible Society, Oxford.

Caldwell, Brian, "Muscling in on the Movies: Excess and the Representation of the Male Body in Films of the 1980s and 1990s," in: Tim Armstrong (ed.), *American Bodies: Cultural Histories of the Physique*. Sheffield, 1996, pp. 133-140.

Carbado, Devon W. (ed.), *Black Men on Race, Gender, and Sexuality: A Critical Reader*, Durham, NC, 1999.

Cleaver, Eldridge, *Soul on Ice*, 1968, New York, 1992.

Daniels, Ron, "The Million Man March: From Patriarchy to Partnership," in: Haki. R Madhubuti, Maulana Karenga (eds.), *Million Man March / Day of Absence*, pp. 108-109.

Du Bois, W.E.B., *The Souls of Black Folk*, 1903, New York, 1989.

Farrakhan, Louis, "Day of Atonement," in: Haki. R Madhubuti, Maulana Karenga (eds.), *Million Man March / Day of Absence*, pp. 9-28.

——, "Million Man March Pledge," in: Haki. R Madhubuti, Maulana Karenga (eds.), *Million Man March / Day of Absence*, p. 29.

——, "The Vision for the Million Man March," in: Haki. R Madhubuti, Maulana Karenga (eds.), *Million Man March / Day of Absence: A Commemorative*, pp. 150-153.

Gates, Henry Louis, Jr., Introduction: "Camp Meeting," in: Daniel J. Wideman, Rohan B Preston (eds.), *Soulfires: Young Black Men on Love and Violence*, xvii-xxiii.

——, "The Charmer," *The New Yorker*, April 29, 1996, pp. 116-131.

Giddings, Paula. *When and Where I Enter: The Impact of Black Women on Race and Sex in America*, New York, 1988.

Gilroy, Paul, "Million Man Mouthpiece," in: *Sight and Sound*, August 1997, pp. 16-18.

——, "It's a Family Affair," in: Gina Dent (ed.), *Black Popular Culture*, Seattle, 1992, pp. 303-316.

<http://www.spe.sony.com/movies/getonthebus/production.html>

<http://www.millionfamilymarch.com>

Harris, Luke Charles, "My Two Mothers, America, and the Million Man March," in: Devon W. Carbado (ed.), *Black Men on Race, Gender, and Sexuality*, pp. 54-67.

Jackson, Jesse L., "Remarks before One Million Men," in: Haki R. Madhubuti and Maulana Karenga (eds.), *Million Man March / Day of Absence*, pp. 32-36.

Karenga, Maulana, "The March, the Day of Absence and the Movement," in: Haki R. Madhubuti and Maulana Karenga (eds.), *Million Man March / Day of Absence*, pp. 5-7.

Kellner, Douglas, "Aesthetics, Ethics, and Politics in the Films of Spike Lee," in: Mark A. Reid (ed.), *Spike Lee's Do the Right Thing*, Cambridge, England, 1997, pp. 73-106.

Kelleter, Frank, *Con/Tradition: Louis Farrakhan's Nation of Islam, the Million Man March, and American Civil Religion*, American Studies – A Monograph Series 84, Heidelberg, 2000.

Kristeva, Julia, *Pouvoirs de l'horreur*. Paris, 1980.

Lee, Spike (dir.), *Get on the Bus*, A 15 Black Men Production / Forty Acres & a Mule / Columbia Pictures, 1996.

——, *Do the Right Thing*, Forty Acres & a Mule / Columbia Pictures, 1989.

Lubiano, Wahneema, "'But Compared to What?': Reading Realism, Representation, and Essentialism in *School Daze, Do the Right Thing*, and the Spike Lee Discourse," in: Marcellus Blount, George P. Cunningham (eds.), *Representing Black Men*, pp. 173-204.

Madhubuti, Haki. R. and Maulana Karenga (eds.), *Million Man March / Day of Absence: A Commemorative Anthology – Speeches, Commentary, Photography, Poetry, Illustrations, and Documents*, Chicago, Los Angeles, 1996.

Pinn, Anthony B., "Keep on Keepin' On: Reflections on *Get on the Bus* and the Language of Movement," in: Garth Kasimu Baker-Fletcher (ed.), *Black Religion After the Million Man March*, pp. 58-67.

Reichardt, Ulf, Sielke, Sabine, "What Does Man Want? The Recent Debates on Manhood and Masculinities," in: Ulf Reichardt, Sabine Sielke (eds.), *Engendering Manchood, Amerikastudien – American Studies* 43 (1998), pp. 563-575.

Reid-Pharr, Robert, "Tearing the Goat's Flesh: Homosexuality, Abjection, and the Production of Late-Twentieth-Century Black Masculinity," in: Eve Kosofsky Sedgwick (ed.), *Novel Gazing: Queer Readings in Fiction*, Durham, NC, 1997, pp. 353-76.

Schäfer–Wünsche, Elisabeth, "Rolling into History: Time and Community in Spike Lee's *Get on the Bus*, in: Patrick B. Miller, Therese Frey Steffen, Elisabeth Schäfer-Wünsche (eds.), *The Civil Rights Movement Revisited: Critical Perspectives on the Struggle for Racial Equality in the the United States*, Münster, Hamburg, 2001, pp. 147-164.

Spillers, Hortense, "Mama's Baby, Papa's Maybe: An American Grammar Book," *Diacritics* 17 (Summer 1987), pp. 68-81.

Walker, Alice, "What the Day Was Like for Me," in: Madhubuti, Haki. R. and Maulana Karenga (eds.), *Million Man March / Day of Absence*, pp. 42-43.

Walker, Clarence, *We Can't Go Home Again: An Argument about Afrocentrism*, Oxford, New York, 2001.

——, "March to 'No' Where," in: *Red Pepper*, December 24/25 1995 (quot. from ms.).

West, Cornell, "Why I'm Marching in Washington," in: Madhubuti, Haki. R. and Maulana Karenga (eds.), *Million Man March / Day of Absence*, pp. 37-38.

——, "Historic Event," in: Madhubuti, Haki. R. and Maulana Karenga (eds.), *Million Man March / Day of Absence*, pp. 98-99.

Wideman, Daniel J., Rohan B Preston (eds.), *Soulfires: Young Black Men on Love and Violence*, New York, London, 1996.

Wideman, John Edgar, *Fatheralong: A Meditation on Fathers and Sons, Race and Society*, New York, 1994.

Elisabeth BRONFEN

'Masculinity; see under crisis:' Die Verfilmungen der Teena Brandon

Was ist eine Sexual Identity Crisis?

"Why do you run around with girls instead of guys, being you are a girl yourself? Why do you make girls think your are a guy," fragt der verblüffte Sheriff Laux die junge Frau, die eine Klage wegen Vergewaltigung gegen ihre Freunde Tom Nissan und John Lotter eingereicht hat. "I haven't the slightest idea," antwortet die traumatisierte Teena Brandon. Doch er bleibt beharrlich bei seiner skeptischen Haltung und fragt als nächstes: "You go around kissing other girls?' worauf sie ihm zaghaft erklärt, "The one's that know about me." Er kann diesen merkwürdigen Fall noch immer nicht verstehen, und fragt weiter: "The ones, the girls that don't know about you, thinks you are a guy. Do you kiss them?" Nun versucht Brandon auszuweichen und fragt ihn seinerseits: "What does this have to do with what happened last night?" Spätestens an dieser Stelle wird für diejenigen, die dieses Verhör nachträglich auf Band hören - und das bedeutet nach der Ermordung Teena Brandons durch ihre Vergewaltiger - deutlich, dass der Sheriff und die Klägerin nicht die selbe Sprache sprechen. Der Vertreter des Gesetzes braucht einen Diskurs, der vor dem Gericht standhalten kann, die vergewaltigte und zusammengeschlagene Frau will hingegen über psychische und physische Verletzungen sprechen. So erklärt Sheriff Laux der sich sträubenden jungen Frau: "Because I'm trying to get some answers so I know exactly what's going on. Now, do you want to answer that question for me or not." Darin jedoch liegt genau das Problem. Es wird nicht möglich sein, in diesem tragischen Fall, bei dem es um Selbstentwürfe geht, die auf fatale Weise entgleisten, eine eindeutige Antwort zu erhalten. Wieder versucht Teena Brandon auszuweichen: "I don't see why I have to," denn sie will gerade keinen zwingenden Zusammenhang zwischen diesem Gewaltakt und ihrem *cross-dressing* als Mann festlegen. Ein letztes Mal greift der Vertreter des Gesetzes auf jene normativ regulierenden Sprachkodes zurück, die für die Hybridität des *transgendered subjects* keine Begriffe kennen. "The only thing is, if it goes to court, that question is going to come up in Court. And I'm gonna want an answer for it before it goes to court. See what I'm saying?" Endlich benennt Teena ihre Schwierigkeit mit seinen Fragen in der einzigen Sprache, die sie dafür finden kann: "I have a sexual identity crisis." Nun ist der Sheriff derjenige, der nicht versteht. Auf seine Bitte, "You wanna explain that?" antwortet sie jedoch nur, "I don't know if I can even talk about it."

Der Fall Teena Brandon wurde zwei Mal verfilmt - das erste Mal von Susan Muska und Greta Olafdottir als *The Brandon Teena Story*, 1998 in Berlin und in Vancouver als bester Dokumentarfilm prämiert. Das zweite Mal von Kimberly Pierce als Spielfilm mit dem Titel *Boys Don't Cry* (1999), für den die beiden Schauspielerinnen Hilary Swank und Chloë Sevigny Oscarnominierungen erhielten, und erstere die Auszeichnung auch bekam. Bei der im Folgenden unternommenen vergleichenden Lektüre dieser beiden Filme geht es mir darum herauszuarbeiten, welches Narrativ über diese tragische Figur des *transgendered subject* jeweils festgemacht wird, wobei beide Filme um die Frage kreisen was es bedeutet, eine *sexual identity crisis* zu haben. Brisant an dieser Fallgeschichte scheint mir jedoch vorallem der Umstand, dass der Fall Teena Brandons jene als *gender trouble* von Judith Butler formulierte Vorstellung von Geschlechtsidentität als Performance in ein neues Licht rückt. Die amerikanische Philosophin hatte mit ihren Ausführungen zur kulturellen Konstruktion jeglicher sexueller Geschlechtlichkeit eine Unterscheidung von Sexualität und *gender* vorgeschlagen. *Gender* - so ihr Postulat - stellt eine Verkörperung dar. Zu einer geschlechtlich markierten Identität kommt man nur, indem man ein Idealbild zu verkörpern sucht, das eigentlich niemand bewohnt. Gleichzeitig gibt es aber auch keine Identität vor oder jenseits dieser kulturellen Prägung. *Gender* ist somit immer schon *troubled*, weil es um die eigene konstruierte Verkörperung weiss.[158] Hatte man der amerikanischen Philosophin nach Veröffentlichung ihres Buches vorgeworfen, sie würde in ihrem Plädoyer für eine ironische Aneignung der Gesten des Geschlechts das Reale des Körpers übersehen, und die subversive Kraft des *cross-dressing* zu stark auf der Ebene der Repräsentation ansiedeln, öffnet der Fall Teena Brandon tatsächlich einen Einblick darin was es bedeuten könnte, wenn das Insistieren auf einem radikalen Aufbrechen der Grenze zwischen Männlichkeit und Weiblichkeit am materiellen Körper bis zur letzten Konsequenz durchgeführt wird. Teena Brandon bestand nämlich hartnäckig darauf, dass sie kein lesbisches Subjekt sei, sondern ein Mann, im weiblichen Körper gefangen. Sie identifizierte sich ausschliesslich mit einer *middle-american masculinity*, doch tat dies - wie Muska und Olafdottir in ihrem Dokumentarfilm betonen - aus der Sensibilität einer Frau heraus. Die Mädchen mochten sie, weil Teena Brandon genau wusste, was Frauen wollen.

Mit anderen Worten, während sie am eigenen Körper *gender trouble* inszenierte - und zwar als Spiel mit der Grenze der Geschlechterdifferenz, die im Augenblick ihrer Verflüssigung diese auch ganz deutlich aufscheinen lässt - unterminierte sie auch die radikale Antinomie zwischen Mann und Frau. Denn wenn Weiblichkeit sowie Männlichkeit gerade dadurch ihre kategoriale Bestimmung erhalten, dass sie nur als Gegensatz Bedeutung einnehmen können, und somit das Beharren auf einer radikalen, unüberschreitbaren Differenz zwischen den Geschlechtern jeglicher Geschlechtsdefinitionen im Kern innewohnt, verkörpert ein *transgendered subject* wie Teena Brandon gerade die Brüchigkeit dieser Differenz. Sie ist eine Frau im anatomischen Sinne, sie empfindet als Frau, bzw. sie kann sich in die Wünsche und Erwartungen der von ihr umworbenen Frauen nahtlos hineindenken, weil diese

---

[158] Siehe Judith Butler, *Gender Trouble. Feminism and the Subversion of Identity* (New York/ London: 1990), sowie den Ausstellungskatalog des Guggenheim Museum *Rose is a Rrose is a Rrose. Gender Performance in Photography*, hrsg. von Jennifer Blessing (New York: 1997).

Phantasien ihr als Frau vertraut sind. Gleichzeitig gibt sie sich in ihrer Kleidung und ihrem Gebärden als Mann aus und identifiziert sich zudem - im Sinne einer symbolischen Anrufung (Althusser) - mit der männlichen Position. Dabei löscht sie aber die Antinomie zwischen Männlichem und Weiblichem aus, wenngleich sie in ihrer Selbstdarstellung an dieser unüberbrückbaren Unterscheidung auch festzuhalten sucht. Sie will nämlich gerade nicht als lesbisches Subjekt andere Frauen lieben, sondern als männliches Subjekt. Die Geschlechterdifferenz liegt somit auf der Oberfläche der Selbstdarstellung, verdeckt aber ein geheimes gegenseitiges Verständnis zwischen Teena Brandon und ihren Liebhaberinnen. Gleichzeitig kann dieses Spiel nur solange durchgehalten werden, als ein Minimum an Geschlechterdifferenz aufrechterhalten bleibt: Solange die Männer, an denen Teena Brandon sich orientiert, meinen, sie sei eine von ihnen, und solange die jungen Frauen, um die sie wirbt, sich zumindest vormachen können, sie sei dem Bereich der Männlichkeit zuzuordnen, um somit die tatsächlich stattfindende Homosexualität auszublenden. In dem Augenblick jedoch, in dem diese Fiktion als solche entlarvt wird, und somit ein Minimum an gesellschaftlicher Konsistenz, die vom heterosexuellen Regime abhängig ist, nicht aufrecht erhalten bleibt, bricht eine *category crisis* aus, auf die scheinbar nur mit Gewalt reagiert werden kann. Denn in einem wesentlichen Punkt behält Judith Butler natürlich Recht. Nicht jedes *cross-dressing* muss notwendigerweise immer schon subversiv sein. Von Filmen Wie *Tootsie* oder *Some Like it Hot* erklärt sie, "Indeed, one might argue that such films are functional in providing a ritualistic release for a heterosexual economy that must constantly police its own boundaries against the invasion of queerness, and that this displaced production and resolution of homosexual panic actually fortifies the heterosexual regime in its self-perpetuating task."[159]

Meine vergleichende Lektüre der beiden Filme ist jedoch darauf angelegt, Butlers theoretische Position selbst zu beunruhigen. Denn es geht mir vornehmlich darum aufzuzeigen, dass das von Teena Brandon verkörperte *transgendered subject* nicht nur ein *heterosexual regime* im Bezug auf Geschlechteridentitäten in Frage stellt, sondern auch ein *homosexual regime* unterläuft. Ihre Fallgeschichte dient nämlich der Festlegung sowohl heterosexueller wie homosexueller Normen, und zwar deshalb, weil beide Diskurse von einer einfachen Opposition zwischen Männlichkeit und Weiblichkeit ausgehen, und nicht von der jegliche sexuelle Beziehung innewohnenden Antinomie, egal ob es sich um heterosexuelle oder homosexuelle Beziehung handelt. Lässt sich für Differenz als einfache Opposition verstanden immer eine Auflösung feststellen, muss man hingegen beim antinomischen Denken von einer unlösbaren Inkommensurabilität ausgehen, die unabhängig von allen Versuchen der Schlichtung sich immer weiter perpetuiert, und somit, wie Wlad Godzich diese Denkfigur beschreibt, einem verbietet, eine 'ground of communality' vorauszusetzen, die die

---

[159] Judith Butler, *Bodies that Matter. On the discursive limits of "Sex"* (New York/ London: 1993); 126. Siehe auch Michel Foucault, *History of Sexuality. An Introduction. Vol. I* (New York: Vintage 1990).

Gegensätze - beispielsweise die zwischen Männlichkeit und Weiblichkeit - als einfache Gegenüberstellung nebeneinander, und zwischen ihnen vermitteln könnte. Daraus ergibt sich laut Godzich auch die Notwendigkeit von Geschichtserzählung, denn er folgert: "the solution to antinomy is narrative, because it answers to a recognition of the antinomy. Narrative is a mode of intervening that preserves rather than solves the antinomy, and does so in such a manner as to allow a sense of history and agency to evolve."[160] Diese Definition von Narration, die die Antinomie der Geschlechterdifferenz sichtbar macht ohne sie zu schlichten, leitet meine eigenen Gedanken zu den beiden filmischen Geschichten, die am Fall Teena Brandons festgemacht wurden, und zwar gerade deshalb, weil es eine Fallgeschichte ist, in der die Protagonistin für die sexuelle Identitätskrise, die sie am eigenen Leib erfährt, und die sie ihren Mitmenschen vorführt, keine erklärenden Worte finden kann. An diesem *transgendered body* - so die Wette, um die es mir im folgenden geht - finden wir in Godzichs Sinne eine die Geschlechterdifferenez betreffende Antinomie verkörpert, die zwar in keine totalisierende Erklärung - sei sie juristisch oder klinisch - aufzulösen ist, wenngleich sie durchaus als Quelle für fiktionale Narrationen dienen kann.

Eine Home Romance

Danny Leigh hat in *Sight and Sound* von diesem Ereignis behauptet, "It sounds like supermarket tabloids and Jerry Springer, salaciousness and and tragedy neatly wrapped and headed for Movie of the Week. In late 1993 petty criminal Tenna Brandon was found dead in a decrepid farmhouse just outside Falls City, Nebraska. The killers, John Lotter and Thomas Nissen, turned out to be ex-con acquaintances of Teena's girlfriend, a factory worker two years his junior named Lana Tisdel. Except that wasn't quite the whole story, and it's certainly not what inspired the front-page delirirum. What became clear only after the event was that Brandon Teena was actually Teena Brandon, a young woman who for most of her brief adult life had passed as male ... Sex, death and transgression in the Midwestern dustbowl: flawless hard copy." Auf seine Frage an die Regisseurin, ob ein Teil ihres Anliegen darin bestanden hatte, diese Geschichte den *tabloids* wieder wegzunehmen, antwortet Kimberly Pierce: "Absolutely. The coverage was focused almost exclusively on the spectacle of a girl passing as a boy, without any understanding of why a girl would want to pass. And I thought that was dangerous." Sie wollte der verstorbenen Teena Brandon stattdessen auf eine Weise cinematisch darstellen, "that was universally understood. " Aus diesem Grund wählte sie auch das Genre des Liebesmärchens: "If I show the audience every detail, they're going to hate me. The minute you tell it like a fairy tale, they're so happy." Diese Fokussierung auf eine traditionslastige Art, eine Fallgeschichte cinematisch umzusetzen, brachte jedoch auch folgendes Problem mit

---

[160] Wlad Godzich, aus einem Vortragsmanuskript über emergente Literatur und Bessie Head.

sich: Im gleichen Zuge, in dem Kimberly Pierce tatsächlich die Antinomien, auf denen Teena Brandons *cross-dressing* beruht, in ihrem Film hervorhebt - nämlich die Inkommensurabilität zwischen Männlichkeit und Weiblichkeit, die sich auf so tragische Weise als widersprüchliche symbolische Anrufungen im Falle dieses *transgendered subject* kreuzten - greift sie gleichzeitig auf ein Narrativ zurück, in dem es um eine einfache Opposition, und somit um eine lösbare Differenz geht: der Familienroman, der sich als Heimatroman entpuppt.[161] Die Unmöglichkeit für das *transgrendered subject*, sich in einer geschlechtlichen Definition gänzlich beheimatet zu fühlen wird übersetzt in eine Geschichte, in der es um geo-kulturelle Zugehörigkeit geht. Die von Brandon kultivierte Vorstellung, sie würde in die Gemeinde von Falls City gehören, weil sie das Gefühl hat - "everything suddenly seemed to fit" - wird ihr in *Boys Don't Cry* deshalb zum Verhängnis, weil ihr diese Illusion, ein *home* gefunden zu haben, gänzlich zu verdrängen erlaubt, wie sehr es für die von ihr gelebte Antinomie der Geschlechtlichkeit keine Lösungen geben kann - zumindest nicht im *middle America*. Apodiktisch formuliert: Die *home story*, die sie als ihre Version des Familienromans des Neurotikers in Falls City kultiviert, indem sie sich sowohl Lanas Familie als auch diesem Ort verschreibt, erlaubt ihr, jenes Gesetz des Symbolischen zu verwerfen, das ihr als *transgendered subject* keinen Ort zuschreiben möchte, bis die für diesen geographischen Ort charakteristischen Vorurteile, die Menschen wie sie kategorisch ausschliessen, sie schliesslich doch einholen, und zwar in der Form von Vergewaltigung und Mord.

Nicht zufällig beginnt *Boys Don't Cry* nachts, während einer Autofahrt. Brandon blickt in den Rückspiegel und lächelt. Sie scheint angekommen zu sein, an dem Ort im Symbolischen, der mit Lacan gesprochen das Schild 'Männer' trägt.[162] Sie weiss, dass sie zu schnell fährt. Doch sie freut sich darüber, dass sie gerade ein Auto überholt hat, mit dem sie und ihre Freunde ein Wettrennen eingegangen sind. Durch ihr rasantes Autofahren erhofft sie sich eine doppelte Anerkennung - von Lana und den anderen Frauen, weil sie sich wie ein typischer Nebraska-Boy verhält; von Tom und John, weil sie ihre Waghalsigkeit erfolgreich nachahmt. Plötzlich bemerkt sie die Lichter eines Polizeiautos und ihr Lächeln erstarrt; nicht nur, weil sie schon wiederholt von der Polizei angehalten und festgenommen worden ist, sondern weil sie ahnt, dass diese symbolische Instanz ihre transgressive Einbildungswelt gefährden könnte. Es wird

---

[161] In seinem Aufsatz "Der Familienroman der Neurotiker" (1909), *Gesammelte Werke* 7 (Frankfurt a. Main: 1941) beschreibt Freud die Wunschfantasie, man sei ein Findelkind auf der Suche nach seinen wahren Eltern, die höher und edler seien als die eigenen. Für Kimberley Peirces Film lässt sich dieses Muster folgendermaßen umformulieren. Die junge Teena Brandon fühlt sich einer Waise entsprechend entfremdet in der geschlechtsspezifischen Rolle, die ihr zugewiesen wurde, und entdeckt in der Familie ihrer Geliebten Lana ein neues Zuhause, was mit der Annahme einer anderen - von ihr als edler begriffenen - sexuellen Identität einher geht. Die in Falls City angesiedelte Liebesgeschichte bietet also im doppelten Sinne einen befriedigenden Schutz - eine Familiengeborgenheit und eine neue Heimat, wo bei beide Zugehörigkeiten als Chiffren für die Annahme der männlichen Identität fungieren.

[162] Siehe Jacques Lacan, *Le Séminaire XX. Encore* (Paris: 1975).

dann tatsächlich auch so kommen. Diese Anfangssequenz der nächtlichen Autofahrt, die wir im Verlauf des Films noch einmal sehen werden, ist zugleich auch die Peripeteia von *Boys Don't Cry*. Der Führerschein, mit dem Teena Brandon sich gegenüber der Polizei ausweist, trägt zwar einen männlichen Namen, da man sich in den USA nennen darf, wie man will. Doch die kodierte Nummer, die ebenfalls auf dem Führerschein steht, lässt die Polizei sofort erkennen, dass es sich bei Brandon Teena um eine Frau handelt, und mit der öffentlichen Preisgabe dieser Information kommt dann die ganze Tragödie, die Brandon das Leben kosten wird, ins Rollen. Für diesen Wendepunkt in der Filmhandlung lässt sich jedoch noch ein weiterer Aspekt hervorheben. Das Umkippen von Traum in Alptraum ist nicht nur dadurch vorprogrammiert, dass Brandons gesamte Selbstinszenierung als Nebraska-Boy auf Lügen und Diebstahl beruht. Kimberly Peirces Verfilmung macht durch den doppelten Einsatz dieser nächtlichen Autofahrt - als Anfangssequenz und Wendepunkt - auch sichtbar, dass eine selbstentworfene Geschlechtsidentität von genau der symbolischen Autorität notwendigerweise eingeholt wird, deren Anrufung sie verweigert. Denn Brandon weiss, dass sie gesellschaftlich als Frau angerufen ist; eine Erkenntnis, die ihr nicht nur von den Behörden eingeprägt wird, sondern auch von ihrem schwulen Freund Lonny, der ihr mit Ausdruck versichert, sie sei kein Mann, auch wenn sie sich so kleidet. Brandon widersetzt sich genau dieser symbolischen Anrufung und hält eine eigene, autopoetisch geschaffene Identität dagegen - die der Männlichkeit. Die Tragik dieser Fallgeschichte besteht demzufolge in einer auf das Selbst gerichteten Fetischisierung. Brandon weiss zwar, dass sie eine Frau ist, zieht es aber vor, in ihrer psychischen Realität die Phantsievorstellung zu privilegieren, sie sei ein Mann.[163] Man könnte auch sagen, sie nimmt Judith Butlers *gender trouble* ernst, denn da sie der eigenen Einbildungskraft mehr Gewicht und Wichtigkeit einräumt als den sie definieren und reglementierenden symbolischen Gesetzen, will sie auch bis zum Schluss nicht einsehen, warum man die symbolische Anrufung nicht eigenmächtig neu aushandeln kann. Nur fehlt ihr, im Gegensatz zu denen von Judith Butler besprochenen *cross-dressers* der Harlem Balls jegliche Ironie, und somit jegliche Distanz zu ihrer spezifischen Aneignung einer *middle-american masculinity*.

Ihr Freud Lonny hingegen steht ein für genau das Gesetz, dass ihn als homosexuellen Mann auch von der amerikanischen Normalität ausschliesst, und versucht deshalb, Brandons Selbstentwurf zu stören. In einer der ersten Szenen des Films schneidet er ihr die Haare, während sie stolz und glücklich in den Spiegel blickt und mit ihren Fingern durch die kurzen Haare streift. Er fragt sie spöttisch, als wolle

---

[163] Siehe Sigmund Freuds Schriften zur Weiblichkeit, "Einige psychische Folgen des anatomischen Geschlechtsunterschieds" (1925), *Gesammelte Werke XIV* (Frankfurt a. Main: 1948), "Die Weiblichkeit" (1933). In: *Neuere Folge der Vorlesungen zur Einführung in die Psychoanalyse*. *Gesammelte Werke XV* (Frankfurt a. Main: 1944), .in denen er die Bisexualität als den ursprünglichen Zustand des Mädchens beschreibt, der im Verlauf der Entwicklung zur erwachsenen Weiblichekeit aufgegeben werden muss.

er dieses narzisstische Selbstbild wieder zurechtrückten: 'So you're a boy. Now what.' Nachdem die Brüder der Mädchen, mit denen sie in Lincoln begonnen hat, auszugehen, hinter ihre Masquerade kommen und sie deshalb verfolgen, findet eine weitere Auseinandersetzung im Wohnwagen des Freundes statt. Brandon will hartnäckig daran festhalten, dass die männliche Erscheinung ihrem sexuellen Selbstverständnis gänzlich entspricht, und kann deshalb nicht verstehen, warum sie solche Schwierigkeiten bekommt: "I don't know what went wrong," erklärt sie Lonny, der ihr antwortet "You're not a boy. That's what's wrong. Why don't you admit you're a dyke." Sie bleibt jedoch beharrlich bei ihrem antinomischen geschlechtlichen Selbstverständnis: "I'm not a dyke". Ihr Problem liegt tatsächlich darin, dass ihre Mitmenschen eine eindeutige Klassifikation ihrer Geschlechtsidentität wünschen, während ihr *cross-dressing* diese Art Eindeutigkeit auf mehrfache Weise verunmöglicht. Sie will nämlich die eigene geschlechtliche Hybridität so wenig gelten lassen wie die jungen Männer, die sich dagegen wehren, dass eine Frau sich ihre gesellschaftliche Identitätsrolle aneignet. Das Problem liegt also darin, dass für Brandon die Darbietung ihres *gender-bendings* ausschliesslich als Wahrheit begriffen wird, und nicht - wie dies für die Harlem *drag ball culture*, über die Butler schreibt, der Fall ist - als parodistisches Spiel. Wiederholt taucht Lonny, der seine Homosexualität offen lebt und sich deshalb auch der gesellschaftlichen Sanktionen, die ihn in *middle America* treffen können, bewusst ist, als die Instanz der symbolischen Vernunft auf: Eine Warnung, die Brandon nicht annehmen möchte, oder vielleicht auch nicht annehmen kann. Nachdem Brandon in einer Kneipe Candice und deren Freunde John und Tom zufällig trifft, und dort während seines ersten Männerkampf seine Aneignung der Männlichkeit mit den herrschenden Männlickheitskonzept des amerikanischen Mittelwesetens messen kann, landet sie in Candices Wohnung ausserhalb Falls City; jenem Ort, an dem sie wenige Wochen später ihren Tod finden wird. Von dort aus ruft sie Lonny an und erklärt ihm, sie wüsse nicht wo sie sei, wüsse auch, dass sie sich nur immer mehr in Netz an Fehlern und Lügen verstrickt: "My life is a fucking nightmare. I got this big court date coming up next week and I don't have any place to stay." Darauf macht Lonny ihr das vernünftige Angebot "now come straight to my house. No more stopping in bars. No more stealing, and no girls." Doch Brandon hegt eine Gefühlsambivalenz. Sie weiss von ihren hoffnungslosen Verstrickungen mit dem Gesetz, ist aber gleichzeitig stolz darauf, sich mit dem Kratzer im Gesicht auch die Marke jener wahren *white middleclass masculinity* ergattert zu haben, und im fröhlichen Blick, mit dem Candice, die gerade aufgestanden ist, ihren Gast begrüsst, scheint diese junge Frau ihr auch das Gelingen ihrer gerade erfolgreich getesteten Aneignung von Männlichkeit zu versprechen. Später wird Brandon seinem Freund Lonny Photos von Lana und ihren Freunden zeigen, als wären dies Dokumente seiner geglückten Ankunft in Falls City, und somit am Ort namens Männlichkeit, worauf Lonny ein letztes Mal das Gesetz der Vernunft geltend zu machen versucht: "They hang faggots there". Brandon besteht jedoch sowohl darauf, dass sie in Falls City eine neue Existenz aufbauen kann, wie auch auf der Schönheit ihrer neuen Geliebten. Weil Lana den Pfand in Brandons

Erlösungsphantasie darstellt ist sie auch unfähig, den sarkastischen Unterton Lonnys Kommentar zu hören, der lakonisch bemerkt: "if you like white trash." Tatsächlich enthält nämlich von Anfang an das Zusammentreffen von Lana und Brandon in einer Bar eine phantasmatische Komponente, folgt es doch den Gesetzen jenes literarischen Topos, den Mladen Dolar als fatale Liebe auf den ersten Blick beschreibt: "To put it roughly, the subject, in its insertion in the social, is subject of a choice, but a forced one, and of a loss. The example is also designed to demonstrate the price one has to pay for the entry into symbolic...Love, in its many various forms, has this mechanism of forced choice always attached to it. To put it simply, one is compelled to choose love and thereby give up the freedom of choice, while by choosing freedom of choice, one loses both".[164]

Eigentlich hätte Brandon mit einem Lastfahrer nach Lincoln zurückfahren sollen, doch in dem Augenblick, in dem Lana angefangen hat, mit ihren Freundinnen Karioke zu singen, ist sie wie in einem zauberhaften Bann gefangen. Darin fängt Kimberly Pierce mit ihrer Inszenierung dieser Szenen den Kern dessen ein, was für Dolar in dem Topos der Liebe auf den ersten Blick auf dem Spiel steht: "A young hero quite *by coincidence* and *through no endeavor of his* meets a young girl in some more or less extraordinary circumstances. What happened unintentionally and by pure chance is in the second stage recognized as the realization of his innermost and immemorial wishes and desires. The contingent miraculously becomes the place of his deepest truth, the sign of fate given by the Other. It is the Other that has chosen, not the young man himself who was powerless...It turns out that the pure chance was actually no chance at all: the intrusion of the unforeseen turned into necessity, the *tyche* turned into the *automaton*. The moment of subjectivation is precisely that moment of suspension of subjectivity to the Other (fate, providence, eternal plan, destiny, or whatever one might call it), manifesting itself as the pure contingency of the Real".[165] In diesem Austausch von Kontingenz durch Schicksal liegt natürlich, wie Freud dies in seinen Bemerkungen zur Kästchenwahl festgehalten hat, auch die Wendung zum *fairy tale*, die Kimberly Pierce erlaubt, aus einem historischen Ereignis eine allgemein verständliche mythische Umschrift herzustellen.[166] Diese Wendung ins Märchenhafte erlaubt ihr zudem, genau jene Antinomien der geschlechtlichen Identität, die in der Teena Brandon Geschichte auf so unheimliche Weise zum Vorschein traten, in eine Entlastungsgeschichte umzuwandeln. Die fatale Handlung, die nach dem ersten Blickaustausch zwischen den beiden schicksalhaften Liebenden ihren Lauf nehmen wird ist eine, in der Brandon sich nicht mehr helfen kann. Er muss immer wieder zu seiner Geliebten zurückkehren, auch wenn es ihn das Leben kosten. Darin verhält er sich tatsächlich einem ganz spezifischen amerikanischen Männlichkeitsbild konform,

---

[164] Mladen Dolar, "At First Sight." Sic 1. Gaze and Voice as Love Objects, Hrsg. Renata Salecl und Slavoj Zizek (Durham: 1996), 131.

[165] Dolar, "At First Sight", 131.

[166] Siehe Sigmund Freud, "Das Motiv der Kästchenwahl" (1913). *Gesammelte Werke X* (Frankfurt a. Main: 1946).

nämlich dem Held des klassischen *film noir*. Mit diesem explizit eingesetzten filmischen Intertext weist Kimberly Pierce ihrerseits darauf hin, wie sehr jegliche Männlichkeitsbilder als kulturelle, und zudem als medial erzeugte und vertriebene zu verstehen sind.

Auch die von Chloë Sevigny gespielte Lana hat etwas von der klassischen *femme fatale*, und unterscheidet sich somit gänzlich von der realen Lana Tisdal, die in der *Teena Brandon Story* selbst zu Worte kommt. Sie läuft wie in Trance durch die Szenen des Films hindurch, meist unter dem Einfluss von Drogen und Alkohol, während ihr ganzes Verhalten von einem einzigen Wunsch geprägt ist - der Flucht aus dieser beklemmenden Kleinstadt. Die unheimliche Identifikation zwischen den beiden Liebenden liegt demzufolge darin, dass beide in ihrem Begehren für den Anderen immer von einem narzisstisch geprägten Phantasiebild ausgehen, das den Wunsch nach einer anderen Lebenssituation widerspiegelt. Brandon ist von Lana fasziniert, weil sie ihr eine Verortung in der ersehnten Männlichkeit verspricht, während Lana von Brandon hingerissen ist, weil an ihr das Versprechen scheinbar festgemacht werden kann, sich aus der Trägheit des Kleinstadtlebens zu befreien. Denn Brandon hatte sich ihr vorgestellt als jemand, der auf dem Weg nach Memphis, Tenessee sei, mit Familienangehörigen in Hollywood. In der *mock rodeo* Szene, in der Brandon sich von John an das offene Ende eines Trucks festbinden lässt, um dann wie auf einem Pferd stehend, herumgefahren zu werden, macht Kimberly Pierce sowohl deutlich, wie unterschiedlich Brandon und Lanas Einschätzung dieses Ortes sind, als auch die Tatsache, dass die Faszination, die sie für einander empfinden, an genau dem Bild festzumachen ist, das sie sich von Falls City haben. Für Brandon ist es eine wunderbare Welt, weil sie sich hier scheinbar erfolgreich *middle american masculinity* performativ sich aneignen kann. Auf Lanas zynische Antwort, warum sie sich auf das lächerliche Rodeo-Spiel eingelassen hat antwortet Brandon: "I just thought that's what guys do around her." Für Lana hingegen ist dieser Freizeitsport ein paradigmatisches Beispiel dafür, warum sie Falls City so dringend verlassen möchte.

In einer Szene kommt die merkwürdige Mischung von selbst-ironischer Aneignung von Männlichkeit und einer beunruhigenden Ernsthaftigkeit, die gerade das Spielerische des *cross-dressing* verleugnet, besonders eindrücklich zum Ausdruck. Brandon bereitet sich auf seinen Besuch bei Lana vor, der in dem bereits besprochenen Autorennen und der Konfrontation mit der Polizei seinen narrativen Abschluss finden wird, sodas letzteres wie ein von Pierce verstandener kritischer Kommentar zu dieser narzisstischen Spiegelszene zu verstehen ist. Am Morgen der Feier nimmt Brandon eine Dusche, und kehrt dann in das Schlafzimmer, das ihr Candice, bei der sie vorübergehend wohnt, zur Verfügung gestellt hat, zurück. Sie hat sich ein Badetuch um den nackten Körper gewickelt, und blickt kurz in den Spiegel, der an der Schranktüre ihres Zimmers befestigt ist, als wolle sie diesen Körper nicht wahr haben. Dieser Eindruck wird zudem dadurch unterstützt, dass Kimberley Pierce uns zeigt, wie Brandon mit schmerzhaft verzogenem Gesicht sich ein Tampon einführt, dann verzweifelt nach einem geheimen Versteck für die Hülse sucht, da sie, aus Furcht in ihrer Weiblichkeit entdeckt zu werden, diese nicht einfach in den Mülleimer werfen kann. Daraufhin breitet sich auf dem Bett jene Utensilien aus, mit denen sie die Maskerade der Männlichkeit anlegt: Die Mullbinde, die sie sich um den Oberkörper bindet, der Socken, den sie sich in ihre Unterhose steckt. Sie weiss, sie ist eine Frau, doch die Annahme dieser symbolischen Anrufung ist so schmerzlich, wie das Einführen des Tampons. Das Abbinden der Brüste und das Hinzufügen eines Penis wird noch mit einem sturen Ernst vollzogen, der sie ihre Verwandlung kritisch im Spiegel prüfen lässt. In dem Augenblick jedoch, in dem es um die Haarfrisur, geht, die ihr das ersehnte imaginäre Selbstbild unzweifelhaft zu bestätigen scheint, strahlt sie. Scherzhaft erklärt sie ihrem Spiegelbild: "I'm an asshole," und bringt somit sowohl die Freude über die geglückte Maskerade, also auch ihr Wissen um den Trug, den sie verkörpert, lustvoll zum Ausdruck. Die Schutzdichtung scheint intakt, und der im Hollywood Kino geschulte Betrachter ist zudem an zwei für das amerikanische Männerbild der 80er Jahre brisanten Spiegelszenen erinnert: Einerseits Robert De Niro in *Taxidriver*, der mit entblösstem Oberkörper eine Waffe gegen sein Spiegelbild richtet, und wiederholt sein Selbstbild fragt: "You talking to me," und andererseits Richard Gere in *American Gigolo*, der seine *designer outfits* auf seinem Bett ausgebreitet hat, und diese lustvoll und stolz betrachtet: beides Inszenierung eines Versuches, den Lieb so auszustatten, dass sich über die Bewaffnung eine Schutzdichtung gegen die jeder Selbstkonstruktion innewohnenden Antinomien errichten lassen.

In *Boys Don't Cry* wird Brandon in der Reaktion ihrer Freunde nach dem plötzlichen Auftauchen der Polizei während dem nächtlichen Autorennen jedoch jene Komponente einer *white middle american masculinity* erfahren, die sie sich weder aneignen möchte, noch die sie richtig einschätzen kann. Nachdem die Polizei sie wieder verlassen hat bricht John in einen fast psychotischen Wutanfall aus, dessen ungezügelte Brutalität proleptisch auf die Vergewaltigung und den Mord hinweisen. Brandon und Tom, sowie Candice, der das Auto eigentlich gehört, müssen aussteigen und zu Fuss weiter gehen. Nur Lana und deren Mitarbeiterin dürfen im Auto bleiben, weil Tom bereit ist, diese beiden zur Fabrik zu fahren, wo sie Nachtdienst haben. Tom versichert dem erstaunten Brandon, der diesen dramatischen Gefühlsumschwung nicht versteht, Tom hätte "no impulse control". Auf die Vorführung jener nach aussen gerichteten männlichen Gewalt, die nur den *masculine wannabe*, nicht aber die Frauen erstaunt, da ihnen dieser Aspekt der *middle-american masculinity* durchaus bekannt ist, erfährt Brandon dann das Gegenstück an männlicher Gewaltausübung - die Selbstzerstümmelung. Mit Tom sitzt sie, nachdem sie Candice nach Hause gebracht haben, an einem Lagerfeuer, das sie abseits der Landstrasse errichtet haben. Tom steckt seine Hand ins Feuer und fragt Brandon, ob auch sie das schon ausprobiert hätte. Sie verneint seine Frage, worauf er sein Taschenmesser öffnet, sich das Hemd nach oben zieht, und sie fragt, ob sie sich je mit einem Messer selbst geschnitten hätte. Wieder verneint sie die Frage, sichtlich erschüttert darüber, dass Tom dabei Lust empfinden kann, sich Schmerz zuzufügen. Tom erklärt ihr, dieser Schmerz würde ihm helfen, seine Aggression gegenüber anderen in den Griff zu bekommen, zeigt ihr daraufhin die Narben auf seiner rechten Wade, und fügt hinzu, er und John hätten das als Wettbewerb im Gefängnis gemacht, wobei er immer tiefer schneiden konnte als sein Freund. Mit dieser Aussage will er ihr seine Männlichkeit demonstrieren, und bietet ihr herausfordernd sein Messer an. "Try it," meint er lakonisch, worauf sie zögerlich antwortet, die Worte sichtbar vorsichtig wählend: "I guess I'm a pussy compared to you." Auf diese Vorführung der Wunden eines selbst zugefügtem Schmerz fällt ihr nichts anderes ein, weil die auf andere wie auf das Selbst gerichtete Gewalt ein Aspekt des in Nebraska dominanten männlichen Kodes ist, den sie in ihrer *transgendered identity* gar nicht übernehmen möchte. Stattdessen greift sie gleichzeitig wie Tom zur Bierflasche, eine für sie durchaus akzeptable Geste der Männlichkeit, doch damit macht Kimberley Pierce nicht nur sichtbar, dass im Vergleich mit Tom Brandon eine "pussy" (ängstlich) ist. Es findet mit der Wahl dieses Ausdruckes zudem noch ein weiterer proleptischer Hinweis auf die tragische Handlungsauflösung statt. Brandon wird in kürzester Zeit tatsächlich ausschliesslich als *pussy* (Frau) wahrgenommen, und auf diese genitale Bedeutung reduziert werden. Denn *middle american masculinity* kommt als Paket, das man entweder ganz oder gar nicht annimmt wird: Jedes Abweichen von der *white trash* Norm wird als nicht-männlich begriffen, und bei dieser Grenzziehung befinden sich schwule Männer wie *cross-dressed* Frauen auf der anderen Seite der Demarkationslinie; was gleichbedeutend damit ist, dass sie zum Freiwild werden, an dem diese rigide Vorstellung von Männlichkeit in Form von *gay-bashing* immer wieder zementiert wird. Lonny käme nicht auf die Idee, in Falls City leben zu wollen, da er von männlicher Gewalt als Antwort auf seine vermeintlich abweichende sexuelle Präferenz ausgeht. Deshalb mahnt er seine Freundin auch, "They hang faggots there." Brandon hingegen kultiviert eine romantische Blindheit, die sich ebenso den Kodes männlicher Gewalt versperrt wie den symbolischen Gesetzen einer reglementierten Geschlechtsidentität überhaupt. Kimberly Pierce verdeutlicht diese hartnäckige Blindheit bei ihrer Protagonistin dadurch, dass sie Brandon Falls City kurz verlassen lässt, um in Lincoln bei der Gerichtsverhandlung zu erscheinen, bei der Brandons Autodiebstähle und Fälschungen verhandelt werden sollen, sich dort aber nicht meldet, als sie aufgerufen wird, und stattdessen zurück in die Liebesbeziehung zu Lana flieht. Man könnte das mit Mladen Dolar auch formulieren als eine Flucht aus der Verantwortung in die Kontingenz des Schicksals, die ihr erlaubt, ihr Phantasieleben gegenüber der doppelten Bestrafung, die ihr durch die symbolische Ordnung droht, zu privilegieren: Gegen eine Geldbusse und gegen die sie kränkende Verordnung, sie müsse ihre anatomische Weiblichkeit leben.

Wie bereits erwähnt wurde beruht auch diese Liebesgeschichte auf einer Blindheit gegenüber der Antinomie, die ihrem Begehren eingeschrieben ist. Für den Drehbuchautor von *Boys Don't Cry* Andy Bienen spielte nämlich die Verkreuzung von *family romance* und *home romance* bei der Umarbeitung des Falls in eine fiktionale Geschichte eine zentrale Rolle. Einerseits hat Johns Eifersucht auf Brandon, die im Mord enden wird, ihren Anfang darin, dass er in Brandon eine Bedrohung für sein Heim sieht; eg. in der Ersatzfamilie, die Lana und deren Mutter seit seinem Gefängnisaufenthalt für ihn verkörpern. Andererseits wird in der Phantasievorstellung Brandons, sie hätte bei Lana und ihrer Mutter ein seinen

Bedürfnissen gänzlich entsprechendes Zuhause gefunden jene Aporie im Selbstverständnis dieses *transgendered subject* sichtbar gemacht, die auch die tragische Universalität dieser Geschichte ausmacht. Brandon will gerade an dem Ort sein neues *home* errichten, um die bislang erfahrende Lücke im familiären Glück zu tilgen, an der für ihn die Ankunft unmöglich ist. In einer Kernszene des Films verkündet Lana ihrem Liebhaber, sie hätte gerade ihren Job gekündigt, um mit ihm nach Memphis zu gehen. Erstaunt versucht Brandon ihr diese Fluchtphantasie wieder auszureden. Sie legen sich gemeinsam auf Lanas Bett und Brandon beschreibt ihr, wie er sich ihr gemeinsames Glück vorstellt; nicht im fernen Memphis, sondern hier im Herzen Nebraskas: "I've been thinking we could just start our own trailer park right here in Falls City." Lana, die sie nichts sehnlicher wünscht, als diese Kleinstadt zu verlassen, fragt ihren Geliebten, ob es sich bei dieser Vorstellung darum handelt, dass sie sie nicht begleiten wolle. Brandon missversteht sie bewusst, und antwortet mit einem Hochzeitsantrag. "I'll marry you right now." Es folgt ein harter Schnitt. Brandon, Lana und ihre Mutter sitzen in der Küche beim Frühstück. Lanas Mutter überreicht ihrer Tochter ein Kuvert, dass dem Stempel des Falls City Traffic Courts trägt: die Busse für das Überschreiten der Geschwindigkeitsgrenze während die nächtlichen Autofahrt. Lanas Mutter setzt an, ihre Tochter zu beschuldigen, doch Brandon nimmt ihr das Kuvert aus der Hand, demonstriert seine Männlichkeit mit der Erklärung, er würde sich darum kümmern, und macht sich auf den Weg zum Gerichtshof, wo bei seinem Versuch, diese Busse zu bezahlen, seine Geschlechtsidentität von den Behörden erkannt, und diese dann als Zeitungsmitteilung von Lanas Freunde erfahren wird.

Bezeichnenderweise hören wir aus dem Off den Rest des Heimatromans, den Brandon in seinem Liebesroman mit Lana erreichen will, während wir seinen Gang zum Gerichtsgebäude sehen: "The thing about the trailer part is, we'll have picknick tables, we'll be playing music and have bar-b-ques every night, and we'll invite our friends, Candice, Kate, your Mom, even Tom and John, if they don't kill each other first, and best of all, we'll have our own airstrip." Das Schild *Hunt County Court House* weist also nochmals auf den ironisch kritischen Blick Kimberley Peirces hin, ist es doch die Materialisierung genau jedes Polizeisignals, das am Anfang des Films ihre Heldin, wenn auch nur für einen kurzen Augenblick, aus ihrem selbstverliebten Tagtraum hat aufwachen lassen. Die Vermutung liegt nahe, dass die Regisseurin mit der monumentalen Aufnahme des Gerichtsgebäudes als architektonische Materialisierung des symbolischen Gesetzes einen Verweis auf Louis Althussers Parabel zur symbolischen Anrufung visualisiert. Als Kernbeispiel für den Prozess der symbolischen Anrufung hatte Althusser bekanntlich eine Szene gewählt, in der ein Mensch die Strasse entlang läuft und auf den Ausruf eines Polizisten sich 180° um die eigene Achse dreht. Als Zeichen, dass er diese symbolische Anrufen verstanden und angenommen hat, antwortet der Betreffende darauf hin: "ja ich bin es." Laut Althusser ist jedoch ein zweiter Schritt notwendig, bevor man von einem gänzlich symbolisch angerufenen Subjekt sprechen könnte, der zweite anerkennende Satz nämlich: "ja, ich nehmen den Ort ein, den ihr mir zuweist".[167] Kimberly Pierces Anspielung an Althussers Formel ist jedoch deshalb bezeichnend, weil Brandon zwischen diesen beiden Antworten verharrt. Sie kennt zwar die symbolische Anrufung, die ihr die weibliche Position innerhalb eines symbolischen Feldes zuweist, auf dem es eine klare Demarkationslinie zwischen Männlichkeit und Weiblichkeit gibt. Im Gefängnis von Falls City muss sie diese sie kränkende Beschränkung auf ihre weibliche Identität auch konkret annehmen, und zwar, indem sie in die Frauenabteilung eingeliefert wird. Dennoch ist sie nicht bereit diese ihr vom symbolischen Gesetz zugewiesene kränkende Position auch als ihre psychische Heimat anzuerkennen. Die Position einer ausschliesslichen Weiblichkeit, und daran geknüpft eine eindeutige Absage an ihre Männlichkeit, kommt für sie nicht in Frage. Stattdessen wählt sie die Einstellung, die für sie immer im Gegensatz zur symbolischen Anrufung gestanden hat: Sie wählt das Gesetz der romantischen Liebe als tragisches Schicksal, um die Kränkungen der symbolischen Gesetze gesellschaftlicher Kodes auszublenden. Doch damit liefert sie sich auch der Kontingenz einer realen Tötung aus, die ihrerseits jene psychische Tötung, die eine Festlegung auf ihre Weiblichkeit für sie bedeuten würde, bis zur radikalen Konsequenz durchspielt.

Durchaus im Sinne des *film noirs* erscheint Lana von Brandons hartnäckiger Insistenz, ihre romantische Glücksvorstellung um jeden Preis durchzusetzen, angesteckt zu sein, und geht deshalb auch auf die Selbsttäuschung ihres Geliebten ein. Sie holt Brandon aus dem Gefängnis heraus, und verteidigt ihre doppelte geschlechtliche Identität gegenüber ihrer Familie, die auf einer eindeutigen sexuellen Zuschreibung beharrt. Lana will an die Wahrheit der Inszenierung ihres Geliebten glauben, und versichert Brandon, "I know you are a guy," teilweise, um Brandons performative Aussage zu stützen, teilweise aber auch, um ihrerseits an der Phantasie festzuhalten, sie könnte von der sich anbahnenden Katastrophe verschont mit Brandon aus Falls City fliehen. In ihrem gegenseitigen Liebeswahn übersehen beide, dass gegenüber dem Fremdkörper, der mit dem Anspruch, er hätte eine *sexual identity crisis* sich die Gesten der *middle-american masculinity* aneignet, die vermeintlich natürlichen Vertreter dieser Männlichkeit diesen Begriff schützen müssen. Denn wenn jeder sich diese Kategorie zu eigenen machen kann, verliert sie ihre differenzträchtige Bedeutung, und somit ihre Kraft, innerhalb der Gemeinschaft konsistenzstiftend zu sein. Um diese über die sexuelle Differenz verhandelte gesellschaftliche Stabilität zu bewahren verrät zuerst Candice ihren Freund, denn auch ihre Selbstdefinition ist durch eine Verflüssigung der Grenze zwischen Männlichkeit und Weiblichkeit bedroht. Bezeich-nenderweise unter der Schirmherrschaft der Mutter, die ihnen den Aufenthaltsort Brandons verrät, gehen John und Tom dann zu einer Sprache der Gewalt über, deren Ziel es ist, den Fremdkörper des *transgendered subject* eindeutig als weiblichen festzulegen, um somit die Geschlechtergrenze erfolgreich zu ziehen und bewachen zu können. Ihre verbrecherische Transgression wird demzufolge auch nicht

---

[167] Louis Althusser, Ideologie und ideologische Staatsapparate (Hamburg/ Westberlin: 1977).

als kriminelle Tat von ihnen begriffen, denn in ihren Augen, wie auch in den Augen der weiblichen Mitglieder dieser Gemeinschaft, handeln sie eigentlich nur wie richtige Männer, bestrafen im Namen einer Aufrechterhaltung der gesellschaftlich sanktionierten Männlichkeit, und sind deshalb auch berechtigt, sich gegen jegliche Form von perverser Abweichung zur Wehr zu setzen. Innerhalb der von ihnen Vertretenen Logik einer eindeutigen Zuweisung von Geschlechteridentität zählt nur die Realität des Körpers: die öffentlich entblössten Genitalien Brandons, die sie in einer Steigerung der Demütigung dann anschliessend im geheimen schänden. In diesem doppelten Vergreifen am Körper des *transgendered subject* lässt sich somit eine Spiegelverkehrung jener performativen Haltung erkennen, mit der Brandon ihre Männlichkeit deklarierte. Tom und John vergewaltigen Brandon wie eine Frau, um ihr - und gleichzeitig auch sich selber - davon zu überzeugen, dass sie sei eine Frau ist. Hier steht nicht die wörtliche Deklaration für eine Handlung ein, sondern die Handlung autorisiert die wörtliche Deklaration: diese Person ist eindeutig kein Mann.

In *Boys Don't Cry* wird das Verhör zwischen Sheriff Laux und Teena Brandon, das am Anfang dieses Aufsatzes bereits zitiert worden ist, inszeniert, jedoch lässt Kimberly Pierce bezeichnenderweise den letzten Satz weg. Ihre Teena Brandon hat nämlich durchaus Worte für ihre *sexual identity crisis* - die entrückte Sprache des schicksalhaften Liebhabers des *film noir*. Auch nachdem ihr klar geworden ist, dass John und Tom für sie eine tödliche Bedrohung darstellen, weil sie sie bei der Polizei angezeigt hat, flieht Brandon nicht. Im Gegenteil, sie kehrt an den Anfangsort dieser zum Alptraum gewordenen *home romance* zurück, zum Schuppen neben dem Haus ihrer Freundin Candices. Dort gesteht sie Lana nicht nur alle Lügen ein, auf der ihre Selbstdarstellung basieren; die Tatsache, dass sie nicht von fernen Staaten kommt, sondern selber Nebraska nie verlassen hat. Doch benennt sie auch nochmals die Aporie ihrer Vertrautheit mit dem Ort, der nie ihr *home* werden kann. Auf Lanas Frage "what were you like before all this, were you like me, a girl-girl," antwortet sie, sie sei zuerst so etwas gewesen, dann eine Art *boy-girl*: "then I was just a jerk. Its wierd. Finally everything felt right." Weil sie diesem Gefühl der Zugehörigkeit vertraut, und nicht der Vernunft, bleibt sie anschliessend in der Scheune, und wartet dort auf die Geliebte, die nochmals nach Hause gegangen ist, um ihre Koffer zu packen. Wie die Helden des *film noir* träumt sie verzückt davon, mit dieser Frau aus der Welt sie kränkender symbolischer Gesetzen in die Heterotopie der ausserweltlichen Liebe zu flüchten.[168] Und wie im *neo-noir* erweist sich dieser Fluchtort als Bühne für den Liebestod des Helden, nicht aber für seine *femme fatale*. Nachdem nicht nur Lana, sondern auch John und Tom aufgetaucht und bei Candice eingedrungen sind, versucht Brandon die wütenden Männer davon abzuhalten, den Frauen Gewalt anzutun, wird dabei zusammen mit Candice erschossen, während Lana gezwungen

---

[168] Siehe Michel Foucault, "Andere Räume," In: *Aisthesis. Wahrnehmung heute oder Perspektiven einer anderen Ästhetik* (Leipzig 1991) und Elisabeth Bronfen, "Noir Wagner," In: *Liebestod und Femme Fatale. Der Austausch sozialer Energien zwischen Oper, Literatur und Film* (Frankfurt a. Main 2001).

ist, hilflos zuzusehen. Nachdem die beiden Mörder den Tatort verlassen haben, wacht sie die Nacht bei der Leiche ihres Geliebten, bis ihre Mutter sie am nächsten Morgen nach Hause führt. Bis zum Schluss hält Kimberley Piece somit an der Erzähllogik eines schicksalhaften Liebesromans fest, um für die Antinomien des *transgendering* eine universal verständliche Filmsprache zu finden. Aber sie erzählt auch eine Geschichte der Emergenz, und auch darin erweist sie sich als Schülerin des *neo-noir*. Über Brandons Leiche gewinnt Lana ihre Befreiung. Nachdem sie von ihrem toten Geliebten Abschied genommen hat, verlässt sie den Ort dieses schiefgelaufenen Liebesromans, um sich dem Phantasieszenario nun gänzlich zu widmen, von dem ihre Liebe von Anfang an getragen war - dem Begehren, Falls City zu verlassen. Es hat eine merkwürdige Schliessung stattgefunden. Auch am Ende von *Boys Don't Cry* befinden wir uns in einem Auto. Diesmal jedoch sehen wir die Fahrerin nicht im Rückspiegel. Kimberly Pierce zeigt sie uns *face-on*, wenn auch überblendet von den an ihr im Zeitraffer vorbei ziehenden Markierungen auf der Strasse. Auch sie lächelt, doch im Gegensatz zu Brandon, wird sie nicht von der Polizei angehalten, und deshalb in ihrem Lächeln auch nicht unterbrochen.

Where was the law?

Brisant an einer Gegenüberstellung zwischen Kimberley Pierces *Boys Don't Cry* und dem Dokumentarfilm *The Brandon Teena Story* ist vornehmlich die Tatsache, dass der Dokumentarfilm ebenfalls aus den Antinomien, die Brandon Teenas Zurschaustellung des *transgendered subjects* sichtbar werden liessen, eine Erzählung entstehen lässt, die nachträglich einen "ground of communality" im Sinne der Formulierung Wlad Godzichs schafft; in diesem Fall die Nullsumme des feministischen Kampfs gegen eine gesellschaftliche Sanktion von männlicher Gewalt gegen Frauen und Homosexuelle. Für Muska und Olafdottir ist die Tatsache zentral, dass Teena Brandons Aneignung männlicher Kleider und Verhaltensweisen, sowie ihre radikale Ablehnung ihre Weiblichkeit zu verstehen ist als eine Verdrängung von Homosexualität, die genau jene kulturellen Gesetze widerspiegelt, die ihr zum Verhängnis wurden. Die Flucht nach Falls City wird von den beiden Dokumentarfilmerinnen begriffen als Versuch, jene pejorative Kategorisierung abweichenden sexueller Präferenzen dadurch auszuweichen, dass sie sich ausschliesslich mit den Kodes einer *middle-american masculinity* zu identifizieren suchte. Gleichzeitig wird in den Interviews mit den vom Fall Betroffenen aus Falls City hervorgehoben, wie sehr diese von sich nachträglich behaupten, Brandon hätte ihnen etwas vorgetäuscht, hätte sie manipuliert. Die Frage der Geschlechterdifferenz wird von den Überlebenden also als Frage der Redlichkeit und Ehrlichkeit verhandelt. Dabei betonen die Dokumentarfilmerinnen, dass die Einwohner dieser Stadt, in der niemand toleriert wird der nicht der weissen unteren Mittelschicht angehört, ihrerseits gar keine Sprache haben, um die Hybridität Teena Brandons zu benennen. Für sie steht die Differenz zwischen Männlichkeit und Weiblichkeit fest, und jede

Überschreitung der Grenze ist eindeutig als Lüge zu verstehen. Das am Anfang zitierte Verhör zwischen Sheriff Laux und Teena Brandon nach der Vergewaltigung wird demzufolge von ihnen als Beispiel für ein fundamentales Missverstehen eingesetzt. Dabei greifen sie deutlich Michel Foucaults Analyse des Verhörs als Machtdispositiv auf, denn es geht ihnen weniger darum, den Sheriff als Vertreter des Gesetzes zu desavouieren, als zu zeigen, wie sehr innerhalb des von ihm vertretenen Rechtsdiskurses für eine grenzenaufbrechende Figur wie Teena Brandon kein Platz gefunden werden kann.[169] Das Anliegen des Dokumentarfilms besteht darin aufzuzeigen, dass ein Gesetz, das nicht fähig ist, sexuelle Komplexität sprachlich zu fassen, auch nicht fähig ist, für *transgendered subjects* Gerechtigkeit zu schaffen. Dabei entwerfen die beiden Dokumentarfilmerinnen ihrerseits ein auf einem einfachen Gegensatz basierendes Bild des Opfers. Auch sie wollen oder können die Antinomie nicht hören, die Brandons Beharren innewohnt, sie sei kein *dyke*. Stattdessen wird ihr Wunsch, sich die Gesten der *middle-american masculinity* anzueignen, eindeutig als Verdrängung ihres lesbischen Begehren gedeutet. Was es hingegen bedeutet, sich mit genau der sexuellen Position zu identifizieren, die man verabscheut, wird als Antinomie im Herzen des lesbischen Begehrens nicht mitreflektiert.

Wiederholt machen sie hingegen das Vergehen der Polizei sichtbar, die auf die Anklage Brandons nicht ausführlich genug eingegangen ist. Eines der beeindruckendsten Interviews ist mit Teenas Freundin Joann, die eindringlich die Frage stellt: "Where was the law? What was the law doin? If she identified her rapists, why didn't they pick them up? Its not like nobody knew where Nissan and Lawder were." Dem fügt sie hinzu, "what hurts me is the rape and the non-action of the police, and that at Christmas time, when the whole world is talking about peace, love, fellowship - you have the murder, the rape. She was raped on Christmas Eve and murdered on New Years Eve." Die Stärke der *Teena Brandon Story* liegt darin, dass dieser Dokumentarfilm verschiedene Zeugenaussagen gegenüberstellt, um die Widersprüche, die sich dadurch ergeben, deutlich zu machen. So halten Muska und Olafdottir der durchaus berechtigten Entrüstung Teena Brandons Freundin die Aussage des Polizisten John Larsens entgegen, um zu verdeutlichen, dass seine Auffassung vom Recht mit der Vorstellung Joanns von Gerechtigkeit für Homosexuelle keinen "ground of communality" haben. Er beschreibt seine Auffassung davon, warum die Polizei sich so nachlässig verhalten hat folgendermassen: "You have a girl, you have a person, who first says she is a boy, then turns out to be a girl, who has done some forgeries with her friend's checkbooks and has been in trouble with the law, and all of a sudden comes up and says this guy and this guy raped me. Well if we did that in society, we'ld have a lot of men locked up."

Somit machen sie auch auf jene unheilvolle Blindheit gegenüber männlicher Gewalt aufmerksam, die in *Boys Don't Cry* mitschwingt; genauer dem Umstand, dass

---

[169] Siehe Michel Foucault, *History of Sexuality*.

die Bürger Falls Citys für die Einschränkung von männlicher Gewalt deshalb ungern Verantwortung übernehmen wollen, weil sie so unhinterfragt ein Teil der dominanten Vorstellung einer *middle american masculinity* ausmacht. Wieder zeigt eine listige Gegenüberstellung zweier Stimmen den obszönen Kern der von Brandon auf so fatale Weise angestrebten Männlichkeit, diesmal zwischen dem Mörder Tom Nissan und dem US Marshall Ron Shepherd. Tom Nissan erklärt den beiden Filmemacherinnen: "Well I believe, had I not met Brandon and Lawder, I would have been in no mess at all." Auf deren Fragen, wie es gewesen wäre, hätte er nur Brandon und nicht Lawder getroffen, lächelt er verschmitzt, verweigert aber die Antwort; Muska und Olafdottir lassen ihrerseits den Zuschauer durch diese Verweigerung unzweideutig erkennen, wie sehr seine Selbstverteidigung auf der Entmenschlichung des Andersartigen beruht. Der U.S. Marshall hingegen spricht offen die Vorurteile aus, die bei diesem Falle zutrage gekommen waren: "They are cowards. They prey on people. They use weapons against unarmed people...those are acts of cowardice, they are nothing, they are just punks... I think there are people in this world, they don't view homosexuals, they don't people that are different from them, they don't view them as being equal, they think its o.k. I can shoot her, she's a lesbian, she's cross-dressed, she's a dike, she's less than human, and they rationalize their actions like that. I've seen it before." Diese für den Mitwesten typische Homophobie findet dann eine Materialisierung in der politischen Haltung derjendigen, die in Erinnerung an die Ermordete Teena Brandon vor dem Gerichtsgebäude von Falls City demonstrieren, während dort ein zweites Gerichtsverfahren gegen John Lotter stattfindet. Denn als weiteres Indiz für das Morsche im Gesetz, das erst nach dem Vollzug eines dreifachen Mordes (im realen Fall war auch ein afro-amerikanischer Freund von Candice an jenem tragischen Abend am Tatort und wurde von Nissan und Lawder ebenfalls erschossen) jene Männer für schuldig befinden kann, die Teena Brandon wegen Vergewaltigung angezeigt hat, ist die Tatsache, dass der Staatsanwalt mit Tom Nisson einen *deal* eingegangen ist, um von ihm jene Aussage zu erhalten, die ihm erlaubt hat, John Lotter die Todesstrafe zu geben. Darin könnte man durchaus eine Geste der Entlastung erkennen. Indem nämlich der Staatsanwalt in seinem Schlussplädoyer den einen der beiden Männer als *evil* bezeichnet, und deshalb für ihn die Todesstrafe vorschlägt, werden nämlich weiterhin die Antinomien der sexuellen Identität, die in dem Fall der *transgendered* Teena Brandon sichtbar wurden, nicht angesprochen. Für das Gesetz muss natürlich eine klare Differenz zwischen schuldig oder unschuldig festgestellt werden. In einem Dokumentarfilm hingegen könnte die Inkommensurabilität, die dieser Fallgeschichte eingeschrieben war, durchaus medial umgesetzt werden, beispielsweise in der Überlagerung antinomischer Stimmen. Der Zusammenschnitt verschiedener Kommentare zur Demonstration vor dem Gerichtsgebäude läuft hingegen auf einfache Lösungen hinaus. So hören wir einerseits die homophoben Stimmen der Bewohner Falls Citys, die Homosexuellen keine Existenzberechtigung einräumen wollen. Diesen halten die Filmemacherinnen dann die Stimmen aus der *gay and lesbian community* entgegen, die nach Falls City gekommen sind, um für ihre Menschenrechte zu kämpfen, beispielsweise Kate

Bornstein: "Everyone who fucks with gender has some kind of brush with this kind of violence. Everyone has their war stories. I've been raped once and held at gun-point twice, and so I moved to San Francisco and then Seattle, and its a lot easier, and you forget about this stuff." So sehr sie damit den vernünftigen Ausweg aus der Homophobie benennt, so sehr scheint hier die brisante Antinomie wieder verdeckt zu werden, von der der Fall Teena Brandons seine Resonanz erhielt; der merkwürdige Umstand nämlich, dass es Brandon genau an jenen Ort zog und auch festhielt, an dem sie nie in ihrer Hybridität ankommen konnte, und zwar deshalb, weil sie sich mit genau der homophobischen Kultur identifizierte, die per Definition einen Menschen wie sie nicht zuzulassen bereit war. Unheimlich und unheilvoll an dem *transgendered subject* Teena Brandon war genau der Umstand, dass sie sich gerade nicht als Teil einer *gay community*, verstand, und deshalb auch im Gegensatz zur lesbischen Aktivistin Kate Bornstein nicht hätte einfach wegziehen können in einen toleranteren Teil der U.S.A.

Am Ende des Dokumentarfilms lassen die beiden Dokumentar-filmerinnen die weiblichen Angehörigen der Verstorbenen wie der Angeklagten über den Urteilsspruch ihre Meinung äussern; sie erlauben Teenas Mutter, ihre Freude über die Todesstrafe als späte Gerechtigkeit für ihre Tochter zu verkünden, und stellen ihr die Unfähigkeit John Lotters Mutter, an die Schuld ihres Sohnes zu glauben, entgegen. Doch das letzte Wort hat bezeichnenderweise der Polizist Jon Larsen: "You think back to the little house south of Humbolt and the three people that died in there that night, and think of the fear that was going on that night to those three people, when you're watching your friend being killed, and know you're next, what's that like, and you have a baby right there, and you're afraid the baby is going to die, what kind of fear is that, but yet, way down the road somewhere, there's always the chance that they can get off, on some judge's decision that we did something wrong. But in my opinion we did nothing wrong." Die Entscheidung der Dokumentarfilmerinnen, mit der Selbstverteidigung des Gesetzes zu enden, dass sich gleichzeitig selbst demontiert, ist doppeldeutig. Einerseits heben Muska und Olafdottir damit ein letztes Mal hervor, dass es ihnen mit der *Teena Brandon Story* nicht um eine Liebesgeschichte, sondern um eine Erzählung der Gerechtigkeit geht. Gleichzeitig aber wird das Problem dieser Gewichtung deutlich. "We did nothing wrong," verkündet John Larsen, und verteidigt somit sowohl die Todesstrafe, die zur nachträglichen Sanktion von Teena Brandons Recht auf Leben verkündet wurde, als auch das Rechtssystem, das ihren Tod auf dem Gewissen hat, weil es für die von ihr zur Schau gestellte Verunsicherung einer *middle american masculinity* keine Sprache und somit auch keine angemessene Verhaltensweise finden konnte. In dem Sinne bringen Muska und Olafdottir auf Umwegen doch auch ihrerseits die schillernde Antinomie zum Ausdruck, um die es bei dieser Fallgeschichte immer auch gehandelt hatte.

4. MASCULINITIES/MASKULINITÄTEN: LITERARISCHE REPRÄSENTATION

Sven LIMBECK
Geschlechter in Beziehung: Die „heterosexuelle" Konstruktion gleichgeschlechtlicher Beziehungen im Mittelalter

Philipp SCHWEIGHAUSER
Concepts of Masculinities in the *Wife's Lament* and its Critical Literature

Ladina BEZZOLA LAMBERT
The Consumed Image: Male Friendship in Montaigne and Bacon

Joachim PFEIFFER
'... in Eurem Bunde der Dritte.' Männerfreundschaften in der Literatur des 18. Jahrhunderts"

Julia RICHERS
John Keats's Odes and Masculinities

Ingrid THALER
Masculinity and Culture at War: Sexualized culture and culturalized sexuality in Philip Roth's *Portnoy's Complaint*

Sven LIMBECK

Geschlechter in Beziehung: Die „heterosexuelle" Konstruktion gleichgeschlechtlicher Beziehungen im Mittelalter

Die Vorstellung, daß es sexuelle Identitäten gibt, die der Person inhärent sind und sich zu einer binären Taxonomie homo- und heterosexueller Orientierung ordnen, ist ein zeitlich und räumlich vergleichsweise eng umgrenztes historisches Phänomen. Im Laufe des 19. Jahrhunderts wurde eine männlich-homosexuelle Identität erfunden, die lesbische und heterosexuelle Identitäten als analoge oder komplementäre Konstruktionen nach sich zieht, weil sie diese paradoxerweise zur Voraussetzung hat. Das Konzept der Homosexualität unterstellt, daß ein auf das gleiche Geschlecht gerichtetes Begehren eine qualitative Differenz zu einer majoritär beglaubigten Normalität begründet. Es gibt dem Begehren ein Zentrum im Inneren der Person und versieht es mit einem autonomen ontologischen Status. Dabei indiziert die erotisch-sexuelle Praxis eine bestimmte sexuelle Identität, hat aber keine Definitionsmacht über die Person, weil die sexuelle Identität unabhängig davon vorhanden ist, ob sie sich in erotischer Praxis, Verführung und sexueller Erfüllung artikuliert oder nicht. Die Konstruktion der homosexuellen Identität als normwidrige Identität läßt sich als Ordnungsstrategie begreifen, die eine spezielle historische Ausprägung der von Judith Butler beschriebenen Zwangsordnung von Geschlecht, Geschlechtsidentität und Begehren darstellt: „‚Intelligible' Geschlechtsidentitäten sind solche, die in bestimmtem Sinne Beziehungen der Kohärenz und Kontinuität zwischen dem anatomischen Geschlecht *(sex)*, der Geschlechtsidentität *(gender)*, der sexuellen Praxis und dem Begehren stiften und aufrechterhalten" (Butler: 1991, 38). Die heterosexuelle Matrix verlangt, daß das natürliche Geschlecht durch eine eindeutige Geschlechtsidentität zum Ausdruck gebracht wird, aus der wiederum das heterosexuelle Begehren folgt. Die Diskontinuität von männlichem Körper und unterstellter nicht-männlicher Geschlechtsidentität, die im mann-männlichen Begehren zum Vorschein kommt, wird in der homosexuellen Identität beschworen und gebannt. Kulturhistorisch und -geographisch überwiegen Zeiten und Räume, in denen sich die heterosexuelle Matrix reproduziert, ohne auf die Hilfskonstruktion der sexuellen Identitäten zurückzugreifen. Dies verbindet, von anderen diskursiven Kontinuitäten abgesehen, die Antike mit dem Früh- und Hochmittelalter. Für diese Epochen läßt sich das Begehren sinnvollerweise als ein Handeln in Beziehungen verstehen, das eng mit Sprache korreliert oder selbst Sprache ist. Das Begehren vollzieht sich exzentrisch, außerhalb der Körpergrenzen, und erzeugt Subjekte und Objekte des Begehrens. Dabei versieht eine Grammatik des Begehrens die Subjekte und Objekte mit geschlechtlichen Signaturen. Geschlecht ist also keine personale Eigenschaft, sondern Effekt einer sprachlichen Handlung. Charakteristisch für „patriarchale" oder phallogozentrische Kulturen ist die als Realität aufgefaßte Verknüpfung von Handeln und Sprechen mit Männlichkeit (vgl. Braun: 1988, 83-128). Das Begehren erzeugt ein handelndes Subjekt und schreibt auf seine Körperoberfläche die Signaturen der Männlichkeit, zugleich erzeugt es ein passives begehrtes Objekt und schreibt auf dessen Oberfläche die Signaturen der Weiblichkeit. Im binär strukturierten kulturellen Diskurs der Geschlechtsidentitäten scheint der eine Effekt ohne den komplementären Effekt nicht möglich zu sein: „Somit ist die zwanghafte Einschränkung gleichsam in das eingebaut, was von der Sprache als Vorstellungshorizont.

Bemerkenswerterweise drückt die heterosexuelle Zwangsordnung, die sich den Anschein des Natürlichen gibt, auch gleichgeschlechtlichen Beziehungen ihren Stempel auf: „Die Reproduktion heterosexueller Konstrukte in nicht-heterosexuellen Zusammenhängen hebt den durch und durch konstruierten Status des sogenannten heterosexuellen 'Originals' hervor" (Butler: 1991, 58). In der Konstruktion gleichgeschlechtlicher Beziehungen gelingt es indessen nicht, jenen kulturellen Diskurs, dessen Effekt in der Unterscheidung zweier geschlechtlich definierter Körperbilder besteht, die den Namen „natürliches" Geschlecht erhalten, mit der Hierarchie und Dichotomie der Geschlechtsidentitäten voll zur Deckung zu bringen. Im folgenden will ich die Bedeutung des heterosexuellen Geschlechterdiskurses für die sprachlich-ästhetische Repräsentation mann-männlichen Begehrens im europäischen Mittelalter zeigen. An ausgewählten Texten der mittellateinischen Literatur, deren Gemeinsamkeit in der Markierung von Subjektpositionen besteht (Briefliteratur, Lyrik und Mystik) untersuche ich die sprachlich-literarische Hervorbringung unterschiedener Geschlechter in gleichgeschlechtlichen Zusammenhängen. Zunächst gehe ich auf die antiken und biblischen Grundlagen der mittelalterlichen Diskursivierung des Begehrens ein.

Päderastie und Effemination: Antike Paradigmata gleichgeschlechtlichen Begehrens

Die römische Gesellschaft leitet aus dem männlichen Begehren, das sich auf Frauen oder auf junge Männer richtet, keinen kategorialen Unterschied der begehrenden Subjekte ab. Für einen römischen Mann ist beides gleich richtig und gut. Dem gleichgeschlechtlichen Begehren sind indessen Schranken gesetzt, die eine hierarchische Asymmetrie des Arrangements gewährleisten sollen. Diese Asymmetrie spiegelt gesellschaftliche Machtverhältnisse und verlangt eine Ungleichheit von Alter (Erwachsener/Jugendlicher), Sozialstatus (freier Bürger/Sklave) und sexueller Rolle (aktiv/passiv) in einem gleichgeschlechtlichen Arrangement (vgl. Veyne: 1984). Der römische Dichter Martial (1. Jh.) beschreibt in einem Epigramm (IV 42) seinem Gegenüber namens Flaccus den idealen Knaben (Martial: 1990, 129). Damit er als Mann ein männliches Gegenüber begehrenswert findet, müssen mehrere Bedingungen erfüllt sein: Es muß sich um einen Jungen handeln, ein erwachsener Mann käme nicht in Frage. Weitere Ansprüche betreffen im wesentlichen das äußere Erscheinungsbild des Jungen:

sit nive candidior: namque in Mareotide fusca
pulchrior est quanto rarior iste color.
lumina sideribus certent mollesque flagellent
colla comae: tortas non amo, Flacce, comas.
frons brevis atque modus leviter sit naribus uncis,
Paestanis rubeant aemula labra rosis (V. 5-10).

[Weißer als Schnee soll er sein, denn in der dunkelhäutigen Gegend von Marea
/ ist das um so schöner, als diese Farbe dort seltener ist. / Der Glanz seiner
Augen soll mit den Sternen wetteifern, und weiches Haar umspiele / sein
Haupt, gekräuseltes Haar aber, Flaccus, mag ich nicht. / Seine Stirn soll niedrig
sein und nur ganz leicht gekrümmt seine Nase, / das Rot seiner Lippen möge
den Rosen aus Paestum gleichkommen.][170]

Lediglich aus den einleitenden Versen – und die Übersetzung muß hier
vereindeutigen, was im Lateinischen grammatikalisch auch auf ein Mädchen passen
würde –, wird erkennbar, daß hier ein Junge (*puer*, V. 2) beschrieben wird. Helle Haut,
langes Haar, sanfte Gesichtszüge, rosenrote Lippen entrücken das Bild des potentiell
begehrten Gegenübers einer eindeutig männlichen Geschlechtszuschreibung. Zwar ist
der *puer* anatomisch männlich, aber kein Mann, da er sich nach römischer Vorstellung
sich in einem Entwicklungsstadium befindet, in dem die kulturellen und sozialen
Merkmale von Männlichkeit bei ihm noch nicht voll ausgebildet sind, er seine
gesellschaftliche Rolle als Mann noch nicht erfüllen darf und kann. Die feminine
Physiognomie erzeugt ein androgynes Bild geschlechtlicher Uneindeutigkeit. Diese
Androgynie zeigt sich auch in dem erwünschten Verhalten des Jungen gegenüber
dem Begehrenden und dem gesellschaftlichen Umfeld:

saepe et nolentem cogat nolitque volentem,
liberior domino saepe sit ille suo;
nec timeat pueros, excludat saepe puellas:
vir reliquis, uni sit puer mihi (V. 11-14).

[Oft bedrängen soll er mich, auch wenn ich nicht will, und sich verweigern,
wenn ich willig bin, / ungezwungener soll er oftmals sein als sein Herr; / die
Knaben soll er nicht fürchten, meistens sich fernhalten von Mädchen: Den
andern gegenüber sei er ein Mann, nur mir allein ein Knabe.]

Der Sprecher wünscht sich von dem idealen Knaben, daß er die Kunst der Verführung
beherrsche, die sich in einer Dialektik von Begehren und Verweigerung vollzieht: Zur
Rolle des Jungen gehört es, sich als Begehrter zu verweigern, um noch

---

[170] Die Übersetzungen sämtlicher lateinischen Zitate stammt von mir.

begehrenswerter zu werden. Andererseits muß er in der Lage sein, von sich aus die Initiative ergreifen, sollte sein Liebhaber nicht disponiert sein. Obwohl ein Unfreier – freigeborene Knaben *(liberi)* sind für den römischen Mann tabu – soll er beim Liebesspiel freier und freizügiger *(liberior)* sein als sein Herr *(dominus)*, eine Freiheit, die wohl darin besteht, sich hinzugeben, obwohl er männlich ist, und die somit einen Geschlechtsrollentausch darstellt, eine Diskontinuität von anatomischem Geschlecht und Geschlechtsidentität, die für seinen erwachsenen Herrn nicht mehr statthaft wäre.

Und schließlich muß er dem Begehrenden exklusiv zur Verfügung stehen: Gegen die Verführung durch Gleichaltrige, die ihn ihrerseits begehren könnten, muß er sich zur Wehr setzen können; von Mädchen, die für ihn ebenfalls eine Versuchung darstellen könnten, soll er sich möglichst fernhalten. Es wird von ihm erwartet, je nach Situation zwei unterschiedliche Geschlechter hervorzukehren, in denen die Differenz von *puer* und *vir* kenntlich wird: In der Beziehung zu seinem Herrn ist er ein Knabe und gewährleistet dadurch eine hierarchische Polarität von „männlicher" und „weiblicher" Rolle im Liebesspiel; in seiner Beziehung zur Umwelt aber ist er ein Mann, der sich als solcher dem Begehren anderer potentieller Sexualpartner nicht hingeben darf, ohne diese Männlichkeit zu gefährden. In Martials Gedicht erweist sich Geschlecht somit als situative Konstruktion, die wesentlich von der jeweiligen sozialen Relation des geschlechtlich agierenden Individuums abhängt.[171]

Die geschlechtlich bipolare Konstruktion gleichgeschlechtlicher Arrangements bei den Römern erlaubt es aber auch bestimmte Formen mann-männlicher Erotik und Sexualität zu problematisieren. Dies betrifft bestimmte Sexualpraktiken, die mit Passivität und Weiblichkeit konnotiert werden (insbesondere Fellatio). Von einem Knaben wird erwartet, daß er beim passiven Analverkehr zumindest keine Lust empfindet; für einen erwachsenen Mann ist diese Form der Hingabe gänzlich unstatthaft und eignet sich in der Satire als Mittel der Diffamierung. Wer sich als als männlicher, erwachsener und freier römischer Bürger von einem anderen Mann koitieren läßt, manövriert sich freiwillig in die gesellschaftliche Rolle der Frauen, Unfreien oder Nicht-Erwachsenen; ihm wird Verweiblichung *(effeminatio)* vorgeworfen, die für den Römer den gleichsam monströsen Widerspruch von natürlichem und kulturellem Geschlecht darstellt.

Seneca beschreibt einmal *(ep.* V 47, 7) einen *exoletus,* einen Sklaven, der das Knabenalter, in dem er sich seinem Besitzer hingeben darf, bereits überschritten hat. Wie in dem Gedicht Martials wird hier in der Differenzierung von *vir* und *puer* die situative, von Gesten und Körpertechniken begleitete Konstruktion von Geschlecht augenfällig:

---

[171] Zu dem Gedicht vgl. auch Obermayer: 1998, 57 f., dessen Paraphrasen m. E. jedoch hinter der Subtilität des Geschlechterspiels, das Martial inszeniert, weit zurückbleiben. So ist von dem Jungen als von einem „sexbesessene[n] ‚Superboy'" die Rede, und V. 14 gibt Obermayer folgendermaßen wieder: „Dieser Traum-*puer* soll für alle anderen Mann, nur für mich allein Lustknabe sein".

Alius vini minister in muliebrem modum ornatus cum aetate luctatur: non potest effugere pueritiam, retrahitur, iamque militari habitu glaber retritis pilis aut penitus evulsis tota nocte pervigilat, quam inter ebrietatem domini ac libidinem dividit et in cubiculo vir, in convivio puer est (Seneca: 1988, 26).

[Ein weiterer, der Weinschenke, ist nach Art der Frauen geputzt und kämpft mit seinem Alter: Er kann dem Knabenalter nicht entfliehen, denn er wird zurückgehalten; obgleich schon von soldatischer Gestalt, bleibt er, glatt durch Rasieren und gründliches Zupfen der Haare, die ganze Nacht wach, die er zwischen der Trunkenheit seines Herrn und dessen Lust aufteilt; im Schlafzimmer ist er ein Mann, beim Gastmahl ein Knabe.]

Päderastie und Effemination sind zwei Seiten der gleichen Münze, die verdeutlichen, daß gleichgeschlechtliche Verhältnisse im alten Rom, oder doch jedenfalls ihre literarische Repräsentation, einem Modus des Begehrens folgen, der von Asymmetrie, Hierarchie und Polarität geschlechtlicher Rollen definiert ist.[172] Beide Aspekte bilden eine wichtige Grundlage der Diskursivierung mann-männlicher Arrangements im Mittelalter.

Das Hohelied und die „Entdeckung der Liebe im Hochmittelalter"

Zu den wichtigsten Quellen mittelalterlicher Vorstellungen von Liebe wird eine Sammlung altjüdischer Liebeslieder, die die Überlieferung König Salomo zuschreibt und als „Lied der Lieder" in den Kanon der alttestamentarischen Schriften aufgenommen wurde. Es ist darin aber nicht von Gott die Rede, sondern zwei Verliebte, ein junge Frau und ein junger Mann, bedichten sich gegenseitig, rühmen ihre Schönheit, laden sich ein, miteinander zu schlafen:

ego dormio et cor meum vigilat; vox dilecti mei pulsantis:
aperi mihi, soror mea, amica mea, columba mea, immaculata mea,
quia caput meum plenum est rore et cincinni mei guttis noctium.
expoliavi me tunica mea, quomodo induar illa?
lavi pedes meos, quomodo inquinabo illos? (Ct 5, 2-4)

[Ich schlafe, aber mein Herz wacht. Die Stimme meines Geliebten, der klopft: Öffne mir, meine Schwester, meine Freundin, meine Taube, meine Makellose, denn mein Haupt ist voller Tau, in meinen Locken hängen die Tropfen der Nacht. Mein Gewand habe ich abgelegt, soll ich es vielleicht wieder anziehen?

---

[172] Zur Homosexualität im alten Rom vgl. Meyer-Zwiffelhoffer: 1995, bes. 64-108; Williams: 1999.

Meine Füße habe ich gewaschen, soll ich sie vielleicht wieder schmutzig machen?]

Schon die Juden haben diesen erotischen Text allegorisch auf das Verhältnis Gottes zu Israel gedeutet. Ebenso hatte sich die christliche Exegese dem Problem profan-erotischer Dichtung im Kontext der biblischen Offenbarungsschrift zu stellen und folgte dabei jüdischer Tradition. Die Kirchenväter und mittelalterlichen Theologen entwickeln eine Reihe allegorischer Deutungsmuster, nach denen im Hohenlied der Liebesbund zwischen Gott bzw. Christus und dem neuen Israel, der Kirche, zwischen Christus und der Muttergottes Maria, dem Urbild der Kirche, zwischen Christus als Bräutigam und der Seele als Braut bildhaft dargestellt wird (vgl. Gollwitzer: 1988, 12). Man unterscheidet demgemäß eine heilsgeschichtliche, eine mariologische und eine mystische Richtung der Hoheliedauslegung (vgl. Ohly: 1958). Gemeinsam ist all diesen Deutungen, daß sie den profan-erotischen Literalsinn der Dichtung mit einem theologischen oder spirituellen Sinn versehen: Das Weltlich-Materielle ist nur Abbild einer höheren, eigentlichen Wirklichkeit, der Transzendenz; Geistiges wird durch Sinnliches ausgedrückt. Das Christentum, das dem Körper und der Sexualität grundsätzlich mit Mißtrauen und Ablehnung begegnet, rettet auf dem Weg der Spiritualisierung einen Text über Liebe und Sexualität. Damit steht aber der lateinischen Literatur des Mittelalters neben der problematischen, weil paganen, römischen Tradition der Liebesdichtung eine göttlich offenbarte Sprache und Bildwelt der Liebe zur Verfügung.

Die mediävistische Mentalitätsgeschichte hat in den letzten Jahren zu einer radikalen Kritik älterer kulturgeschichtlicher Vorstellungen von der historischen und gesellschaftlichen Universalität der Liebe geführt: „Die herkömmliche Betrachtungsweise von Liebe als epochenunabhängige anthropologische Konstante entspringt einer quellenmäßig nicht abgedeckten Rückprojektion gegenwärtiger Gegebenheiten" (Dinzelbacher: 1991, 1965). Insbesondere Peter Dinzelbacher hat mit Vehemenz die These von der „Entdeckung der Liebe im Hochmittelalter" vertreten (Dinzelbacher: 1981). Demnach gibt es im frühen Mittelalter, d.h. zwischen dem 5. und 10. Jahrhundert, Liebe im Sinne einer personalen und emotionalen, Erotik miteinschließenden Zuordnung zweier Individuen zueinander nicht: „Die Beziehungen zwischen den Geschlechtern erscheinen auf Sexualität und habituelle Vertrautheit reduziert. Die Beziehung zu Gott ist geprägt von respekt- bis angstvoller Distanz" (Dinzelbacher: 1991, 1966; ausführlicher ders.: 1989). Die Historizität und Konzeptualität von Liebe, die Dinzelbachers Überlegungen verdeutlichen, können von einer diskursanalytischen Betrachtungsweise bestätigt werden. Ob nun beabsichtigt oder nicht, suggeriert indessen die Rede von der „Entdeckung der Liebe" im Kloster und am Hof an der Wende zum 12. Jahrhundert, daß es zwischen Hochmittelalter und Neuzeit keine vergleichbare Diskontinuität wie zwischen Antike und Frühmittelalter und zwischen Früh- und Hochmittelalter gibt. Dann muß man allerdings fragen, aus welchem Grunde die geistlichen Zeugnisse der Mystik oder die profanen Dichtungen der Minne im hohen Mittelalter weniger ein diskursives oder literarisches Ereignis sein, also mehr von der Erlebniswelt der Individuen verraten sollten, als dies in der frühmittelalterlichen Rede von *amor* und *dilectio* der Fall war. Warum sollten affektive Liebesbekundungen im frühen Mittelalter nur „zwischen Kunst und Künstlichkeit schwankende Phrasen" sein (Dinzelbacher: 1989, 27), denen keine Wirklichkeit entspricht?

Freundschaft und dilectio spiritualis: Der Liebesdiskurs im frühen Mittelalter

Bezieht man in eine diachrone Betrachtung der Liebesdiskurse die literarische Repräsentation gleichgeschlechtlicher Beziehungen im frühen Mittelalter mit ein, wie Samuel Singer dies bereits in den dreißiger Jahren des 20. Jahrhunderts tat, läßt sich ein anderes Bild zeichnen. Singer setzte an die Stelle einer im Frühmittelalter nicht vorhandenen heterosexuellen Liebesdichtung Lieder und Briefe der gleichgeschlechtlichen Freundschaft, an denen er eine Verwandtschaft mit späterer erotischer Dichtung erkannte (Singer: 1935, 121-124). Wie Singer haben Literarhistoriker immer wieder die erotische Tönung der Freundschaftsliteratur mehr oder weniger irritiert zur Kenntnis genommen. Venantius Fortunatus (vor 540-ca. 600) kommt in der Geschichte der mittellateinischen Poesie eine Brückenfunktion zu, indem er dem Mittelalter die Tradition römischer Dichtung vermittelt. Seine Freundschafts-beziehungen sowohl zu Männern als auch zu Frauen bilden den Hauptanlaß seiner dichterischen Produktion; seine literarhistorische Leistung besteht nicht zuletzt darin, die Sprache der römischen Liebeselegie für die poetische Gestaltung zwischenmenschlicher Beziehungen fruchtbar gemacht zu haben. Eine gefühlsmäßige Unterscheidung von Liebe und Freundschaft kennen seine Gedichte nicht; *amor* und *amicitia* werden synonym gebraucht (vgl. Epp: 1995). In dem Gedicht an seinen Freund Jovinus (VII 12) betont Venantius, daß Freundschaft auch bei räumlicher Trennung eine innere Nähe herstelle:[173]

Nam cui cara fides animum sociauit amici
quod minus est oculis flagrat amore magis (V. 75-76).

[Denn wem liebende Treue das Herz des Freundes verbunden hat, / der entbrennt, desto weniger er ihn vor Augen hat, um so mehr vor Liebe.]

Bemerkenswert ist der literarische Charakter dieser Freundschaft. Die innere, emotionale Nähe zum Freund stellt Venantius im Vorgang des Schreibens her, bei dem er die körperliche Präsenz des Freundes, seine gefällige Gestalt („forma placens", V. 78), in einer überaus erotischen Sprache imaginiert:

---

[173] Zu dem Gedicht an Jovinus vgl. auch George: 1992, 146-150.

scribimus et haec dum, non sine te loquimur.
Affectu, studio, uoto tua brachia cingo
atque per amplexum pectora, colla ligo.
Ingrederis mecum pariterque moueris amator
et quasi blanda loquens oscula libo labris (V. 88-92).

[Und während ich dies schreibe, spreche ich nicht etwa, ohne daß du anwesend bist. / Mit meiner Leidenschaft, meiner Liebe, meinem Verlangen nehme ich dich in die Arme / und in der Umarmung umschlinge ich deine Brust und dein Haupt. / Du gehst mit mir umher und begleitest mich als mein Liebhaber ständig, / und indem ich zärtlich zu dir rede, hauche ich Küsse auf deine Lippen.]

Von einem Nichtwissen um die Liebe im frühen Mittelalter kann meines Erachtens angesichts solcher Zeugnisse nicht die Rede sein. Als klassische Epoche der Freundschaft gilt gemeinhin die sogenannte „karolingische Renaissance". Unter Karl dem Großen wird die Hofschule des Frankenreiches zu einem intellektuellen Zentrum, an das er 781 den angelsächsischen Gelehrten Alkuin von York beruft. Das kulturelle und pädagogische Leben an Hof und Hofschule dürfte sich zutreffend als homosozialer Raum beschreiben lassen. Heinrich Fichtenau drückt es auf seine eigene Art und Weise aus, wenn er von einem „echten Männerbund" spricht: „Mehrfach wird in ihm auch eine erotische Komponente deutlich, ohne daß wir sie freilich in ihrer Bedeutung überschätzen wollen. [...] Die Zeit, die keine Liebeslyrik kannte, hat die poetische Freundschaft im Männerbund mit Leidenschaft gesucht, wohl im allgemeinen ohne die Grenzen des Erlaubten zu überschreiten" (Fichtenau: 1949, 103). Gleichgeschlechtliche Freundschaftsbünde also, die sich hochemotional, auch erotisch und körperlich, aber nicht sexuell artikulieren. Alkuin (um 730-804) ist ein Hauptvertreter dieser literarischen Produktion. Im September 798 teilt Alkuin seinem Freund Arn, dem Bischof von Salzburg, den er *aquila* zu nennen pflegt, brieflich mit, er werde zum Kloster St. Martin (Tours) aufbrechen, um möglichst den Winter dort zu verbringen:

Et utinam veniat volando aquila mea orare apud Sanctum Martinum; ut ibi amplecter alas illius suavissimas; *et teneam, quem diligit anima mea, nec dimittam eum, donec introducam illum in domum matris meae* [Ct 3, 4]; et *osculetur me osculo oris sui* [Ct 1, 1]; et gaudeamus *ordinata caritate invicem* [Rm 12, 10; cf. Ct 2, 4] (Dümmler: 1895, 255).

[Und würde doch mein Adler (Arn) zum Beten im Fluge nach St. Martin kommen, damit ich dort seine ach so süßen Schwingen umarme; und ihn hielte, den meine Seele liebt, und ihn nicht mehr losließe, bis ich ihn in das Haus meiner Mutter führte, und er mich küßte mit dem Kuß seines Mundes, und wir uns aneinander freuen würden in ordentlicher Liebe.]

Die kurze Passage stellt zu wesentlichen Teilen eine Collage von Zitaten aus dem Hohenlied dar. Die Liebessprache des Paares wird umstandslos auf die Freundschaft zwischen Alkuin und Arn übertragen. Alkuin sehnt sich danach, die räumliche Distanz zu überwinden, um seinem Freund in voller physischer Präsenz zu begegnen. Die seelische Liebesbindung an den Freund soll sich durchaus in körperlicher Intimität ausdrücken können, in Umarmung und Kuß. Wenn im Hohenlied das Mädchen ihren Geliebten in das Haus ihrer Mutter führt, näherhin in deren Schlafgemach, so stellt dies einen Vermählungsakt dar. Gewiß versteht Alkuin dies nicht wörtlich, aber vielleicht doch so konkret, daß die *domus matris* hier für Kirche und Kloster St. Martin steht, wo die beiden Freunde im Gebet eine Art geistlicher Ehe vollziehen sollen. Vor dem bereits erläuterten exegetischen Horizont bewirkt die Bildlichkeit des Hohenliedes, in dem die menschliche Beziehung kodiert ist, zweierlei: Erstens, wie immer Alkuin und Arn ihre Freundschaft praktisch erlebt haben, in der sprachlich-literarischen Repräsentation wird das gleichgeschlechtliche Arrangement erotisiert. Die gegengeschlechtliche Erotik und Sexualität der alttestamentarischen Liebesdichtung wird für die expressive Emotionalität und Intimität der beiden Männer fruchtbar gemacht. Zweitens wird zugleich in die intime Beziehung der Freunde die traditionelle allegorische Deutung des Hohenliedes eingespielt. Die menschliche Beziehung wird dabei spiritualisiert, also mit einer transzendenten Dimension versehen. In der erotischen Rhetorik, in der die frühmittelalterliche Freundschaft zum Ausdruck kommt, zeigt sich die Entfaltung von mindestens zwei Sinnebenen: das profan-private zwischenmenschliche Miteinander als liebende Zuordnung zweier Individuen zueinander und die Spiritualität der Freundschaft, die als innerweltlicher Ausdruck der Gottesliebe verstanden werden kann.[174]

So gesehen fügt sich die christliche Freundschaft in ein platonisches Weltbild. Das Mittelalter hat zwar kaum direkte Platon-Kenntnisse, und auch die karolingischen Dichter, Theologen und Pädagogen kommen größtenteils noch nicht in Berührung mit dem Neuplatonismus eines Pseudo-Dionysius Areopagita, dessen Schriften erst in den Jahren 860-62 von Johannes Scotus Eriugena ins Lateinische übersetzt und damit zu einer Grundlage der späteren Mystik werden. Die christliche Aneignung des Neuplatonismus wird aber bereits durch Clemens von Alexandrien, den Begründer einer christlichen Pädagogik, und Origenes, den Erfinder der allegorischen Schriftauslegung, vollzogen. Als bedeutendster und einflußreichster theologischer

---

[174] Zur geistlichen Freundschaft bei Alkuin vgl. auch Fiske: 1961; McGuire: 1988, 117-127. Als Ausdruck homosexuellen oder homoerotischen Begehrens wertet Boswell: 1980, 188-192 Alkuins Briefe und Gedichte.

Neuerer leistet dann Augustinus eine Synthese von Platonismus und Heiliger Schrift (autobiographisch dargestellt in den *Confessiones* VII 9-13).[175]

Stark platonische Züge trägt die Freundschaftsdichtung des Reichenauer Mönches und späteren Abtes Walahfrid Strabo (808/809-849). Wie Alkuin ist Walahfrid in erster Linie Pädagoge. Sein Verhältnis zu dem uns nicht näher bekannten Liutger ist das eines Älteren zu einem Jüngeren. In zwei Gedichten an Liutger erinnert Walahfrid an die Begegnung mit ihm, beschreibt ihm das geistig-emotionale Band der *memoria*, das trotz räumlicher Trennung ihre Freundschaft erhält und ersehnt eine Aktualisierung der gegenseitigen Liebe *(dilectio)* in einem Wiedersehen. Mit teils aus Ovid entlehnten Bildern schildert er in Carmen 31 seine Sehnsucht, das Antlitz des Jungen wiederzusehen:

Unicus ut matri, terris ut lumina Phoebi,
　　Ut ros graminibus, piscibus unda freti,
Aer uti oscinibus, rivorum ut murmura pratis,
　　Sic tua, pusiole, cara mihi facies.

[Wie der einzige Sohn seiner Mutter, Phoebus' Licht der Erde, / wie der Tau den Wiesen, das Wogen der See den Fischen, / wie die Luft den Vögeln, wie das Rauschen der Flüsse den Auen, / so lieb, mein Kleiner, ist mir dein Antlitz.]

Das ebenfalls an Liutger adressierte Carmen 32 greift das Motiv der räumlichen Trennung noch einmal auf.

Audio, non video, video tamen intus et intus
Amplector fugientem et corpore, non pietate.
Certus enim ut fueram, sum semper eroque foveri
Corde tuo me, corde meo te. […]

[Ich höre, sehe nicht, sehe dennoch im Innern und im Innern / umarme ich den, der flieht mit dem Leib, aber nicht mit der Liebe. Denn so gewiß, wie ich war, bin ich und werde es immer sein, daß du mir gut bist in deinem Herzen, ich dir in meinem Herzen.]

Die deutliche Opposition von sinnlicher Wahrnehmung und innerlicher Empfindung verdeutlicht, daß Liebe hier als seelisches Geschehen verstanden wird, das unabhängig vom Materiell-Leiblichen ist. Die Parallelstruktur des Verses „Corde tuo me, corde meo te" verbildlicht einen inneren Gleichklang der befreundeten Seelen. Im Sinne dieses christlichen Platonismus ist die Seele des Menschen, sein Innerstes, nicht auf die Körperwelt hin geordnet, sondern stellt ihn in den Zusammenhang mit der

---

[175] Zur Bedeutung des Augustinus für das Christentum des Mittelalters vgl. Küng 1999: 342-364.

Transzendenz. Nicht mit seinem vergänglichen, unvollkommenen Leib, sondern mit seiner immateriellen, unsterblichen Seele ist der Mensch an Gott gebunden. Augustinus hatte in den *Confessiones* Gott folgendermaßen apostrophiert: „Sed nec anima es, quae est vita corporum [...], sed tu vita es animarum, vita vitarum, vivens te ipsa et non mutaris, vita animae meae" [„Aber auch die Seele, die das Leben der Körper ist, bist du nicht, sondern das Leben der Seelen bist du, das Leben der Leben, lebst, ohne dich zu wandeln, durch dich selbst, Leben meiner Seele"] (III 6,10). Und kurz darauf: „Tu autem eras interior intimo meo et superior summo meo" [„Du aber warst innerer als mein Innerstes und höher als mein Höchstes"] (III 6,11). Was die Liebenden oder Freunde bei Autoren wie Alkuin und Walahfrid verbindet, ist eine *dilectio spiritualis*, die durch die seelische Anteilnahme des Menschen an der Transzendenz erst ermöglicht wird. Das zwischen-menschliche Verhältnis entspricht dem Verhältnis von Mensch und Gott. Der leibliche Ausdruck von Freundschaft ist ein innerweltlicher Spiegel des Immateriellen. Am schönsten kommt dies meines Erachtens in einem Gedicht zum Ausdruck, das aller Wahrscheinlichkeit nach ebenfalls von Walahfrid (Nr. 54) stammt (vgl. Önnerfors: 1972, 87-92):

Cum splendor lunae fulgescat ab aethere purae,
Tu sta sub divo cernens speculamine miro,
Qualiter ex luna splendescat lampade pura
Et splendore suo caros amplectitur uno
Corpore divisos, sed mentis amore ligatos.
Si facies faciem spectare nequivit amantem,
Hoc saltim nobis lumen sit pignus amoris (V. 1-7)

[Wenn der Glanz des hellen Mondes vom Himmel scheint, / stehe du unter freiem Himmel und betrachte mit bewunderndem Blick, / wie es vom Mond her glänzt in klarem Schimmer / und in seinem einen Glanz er die Liebenden umarmt, / die am Leib zwar getrennt sind, aber in geistiger Liebe verbunden. / Wenn das Antlitz das liebende Antlitz nicht zu erblicken vermochte, / So sei dies Licht uns doch Pfand der Liebe.]

Das Mondmotiv greift vermutlich den Anfang der 15. Epode von Horaz auf („Nox erat et caelo fulgebat Luna sereno"), wo der Mond als Zeuge für die Liebesschwüre der Geliebten Neaera genannt wird. *Pignus amoris*, Pfand, Beweis oder Zeichen der Liebe, kommt bei Ovid mindestens viermal vor (*Met.* III 283; VIII 92; *Ars. am.* II 248; *Her.* IV 100) und steht jeweils im erotischen Kontext mann-weiblicher Beziehungen. Neben diesen Referenzen auf die klassische Liebesdichtung spielt der Dichter im Vers 6 auch auf eine Bibelstelle an: „videmus nunc per speculum in enigmate, tunc autem facie ad faciem" [„Wir sehen jetzt durch einen Spiegel in einem Geheimnis, dann aber von Angesicht zu Angesicht"] (I Cor 13,12). Auch diese berühmte und schwer verständliche Stelle steht in einem Text über die Liebe, dem sogenannten „Hohenlied der Liebe" des Paulus, wo die *caritas* in poetischer Sprache als höchste Geistesgabe gepriesen wird. Walahfrid verknüpft profan-erotische mit spirituellen Motiven und schichtet so wiederum zwei Sinnebenen in seinem Gedicht.

Noch deutlicher als bei Walahfrid wird die Kodierung mann-männlicher Intimität in der Liebessprache der römischen Dichtung in einem poetischen Dialog zwischen Notker Balbulus (ca. 840-912) und seinem Schüler Hartmann. Notker war im Kloster St. Gallen als Erzieher tätig. Als solcher erkennt er in Hartmann eine poetische Begabung und fordert ihn in zwei Gedichten auf, gemeinsam mit ihm eine neue Version der Vita des Klostergründers Gallus zu dichten. In einem Antwortgedicht schreibt Hartmann, er fühle sich dieser Aufgabe nicht gewachsen, weil er seinen Lehrer an dichterischem Talent für weit überlegen halte: „Taurum cupis fortissimum / Buclae tenellae iungere" [Eine allzu starken Stier willst du / mit einer sehr zarten Färse zusammenspannen] (V. 13-14; Berschin: 1980, 95). Das Bild von Stier und Färse, das die ungleiche Beziehung zwischen Notker und Hartmann veranschaulichen soll, entstammt wiederum einer erotischen Ode des Horaz (Carmen II 5). Dort erscheint die Geliebte im Bild der Färse, die noch nicht reif ist, sich mit dem Stier zu paaren. Das Bild der sexuellen Begehrens wird umstandslos auf das Lehrer-Schüler-Verhältnis umgemünzt. Hartmann sieht sich selbst in der Rolle der allzu früh begehrten Jungkuh.

Mystik

Wie die persönliche Dichtung entstammt die geistliche Literatur, in der nach einem vergleichbaren Muster mann-männliches Begehren dargestellt wird, dem monastischen Milieu. Notker Balbulus hat eine Hymne auf den Apostel Johannes verfaßt. Der Evangelist ist nach traditioneller Auffassung als Jesu Lieblingsjünger aus der Zwölfergruppe herausgehoben und wird in dem Evangelium, das nach ihm benannt ist, durchweg als „discipulus quem diligebat Jesus", als Jünger, den Jesus liebte, bezeichnet (Io 13,23; 19,26; 20,2; 21,7.20). Zusammen mit seinem Vater und seinem Bruder Jakobus sitzt er in einem Boot und flickt Netze, als Jesus vorüberkommt und die beiden Brüder beruft. Johannes verläßt den Vater und folgt ihm; die Legende weiß überdies von einem aufgelösten Verlöbnis. Beim Abendmahl ruht er an Jesu Brust (Io 13,23), ein Bild, das in den zahlreichen spätmittelalterlichen Christus-Johannes-Gruppen als Andachtsfigur gestaltet wurde. Notker bringt diese Szenen in einen unmittelbaren Zusammenhang:

Johannes, Jesu Christo
multum dilecte virgo:

Tu eius amore carnalem
In navi parentem liquisti.

Tu leve coniugis pectus
respuisti Messiam secutus,

Ut eius pectoris sacra
meruisses fluenta potare (Steinen: 1948, II 16).

[Johannes, Jesu Christi / vielgeliebte Jungfrau: / Aus Liebe zu ihm verließt du
/ im Schiff den leiblichen Vater. / Den zarten Busen der Braut hast du /
verschmäht und folgtest dem Heiland, / daß dir vergönnt wäre zu trinken /
das Heilige, das von seinem Busen fließt.]

Die Hymne beginnt mit einer Invokation des Apostels, die wie das Evangelium Jesu
besondere Liebe für ihn betont und ihn außerdem als Jungfrau adressiert. Diese
Apostrophierung als *virgo* ist keine Erfindung Notkers, sondern findet sich bereits in
Evangelienprologen des 3. Jahrhunderts und dient dazu, die vorbildliche Keuschheit
des Johannes hervorzuheben (vgl. Steinen: 1948, I 362). Gleichwohl hat der Jünger
damit im Liebesverhältnis zum Heiland eine weibliche Rolle. Die direkte
Gegenüberstellung von Berufung und Abendmahl verdeutlicht, daß dieses Verhältnis
in Analogie zur Liebe zwischen Braut und Bräutigam konstruiert ist: Die eheliche,
fleischliche Gemeinschaft wird ersetzt durch jene der beiden Männer, die sich ebenso
durch Intimität und körperliche Nähe auszeichnet, allerdings durch die Gottesnatur
Christi einen neuen Sinn erhält. Noch vor einer Mystik im eigentlichen Sinne setzt
Notkers Hymne das liebende Verhältnis zwischen Gott und Mensch in das Bild des
Lieblingsjüngers der an Christi Brust ruht. Typologischer Schriftauslegung folgend
projiziert er die Liebenden des Hohenliedes auf die Abendmahlsszene, wobei sich der
Busen der Geliebten (Ct 1,1.3; 4,5.10 u.ö.) und die Brust Christi entsprechen (vgl.
Rahner: 1931). Notkers Gedicht markiert noch keine Ich-Position, beschreibt die
Beziehung nicht als eigenes Erleben. Von einer Mystik im eigentlichen Sinne spricht
man daher auch erst seit dem 12. Jahrhundert. Zu den erstaunlichsten Beispielen der
Darstellung eines mystischen Erlebnisses als mann-männliche Liebesbeziehung zählen
die Visionen des Rupert von Deutz (ca. 1075/80-1129/30). Der einflußreiche Theologe
hat in seinen Kommentar zum Matthäus-Evangelium eine spirituelle Auto-biographie
inseriert (Buch XII). Schwere Zweifel Ruperts, ob er bereit sei, die Priesterweihe zu
empfangen, lösen sich nach einer Traumvision. Er sieht sich vor einem Altar mit
einem Kruzifix, aber Jesus am Kreuz ist lebendig und wendet sich Rupert zu:

Non satis hoc mihi erat, nisi et manibus apprehenderem, amplexumque
deoscularer. Sed quid agerem? Altius erat altare ipsum, quam ut eum attingere
possem. Vt ergo uidit eiusmodi cogitationem seu uoluntatem meam, uoluit et
ipse. Sensi enim ego quia uoluit et nutu uoluntatis eius ipsum altare per
medium sese aperuit meque introrsus currentem suscepit. Quod cum festinus

introissem, apprehendi *quem diligit anima mea, tenui illum* [Ct 3,4], amplexatus sum eum, diutius exosculatus sum eum. Sensi quam gratanter hunc gestum dilectionis admitteret, cum inter osculandum suum ipse os aperiret, ut profundius oscularer (Rupertus: 1979, 382 f.).

[Das war mir nicht genug, denn ich wollte ihn unbedingt mit Händen anfassen und den so Umarmten küssen. Aber was sollte ich tun? Der Altar war zu hoch, als daß ich an ihn hätte heranreichen können. Wie er also meine Überlegung oder meinen Wunsch erkannte, wollte er selbst auch. Ich spürte nämlich, daß er wollte, und auf Geheiß seines Willens öffnete der Altar sich in der Mitte und nahm mich, als ich hineinging, in sich auf. Sobald ich rasch eingetreten war, ergriff ich den, den meine Seele liebt, hielt ihn fest, umarmte ihn und küßte ihn ausdauernd. Ich spürte, mit welcher Freude er diese Geste der Liebe zuließ, denn während des Küssens öffnete er seinen Mund, auf daß ich tiefer küsse.]

Im Augenblick, da Rupert mit Christus Zungenküsse tauscht, wird ihm die Bedeutung dessen klar, was die Geliebte im Hohenlied spricht und er zitiert *in extenso* Ct 8,1-2, einen Sehnsuchtsruf der Geliebten nach ihrem Freund. Auch Rupert, obwohl er in dieser Szene eher als der Handelnde erscheint, projiziert sich in die Rolle der Braut. Deutlicher wird das noch in einer Vision, die ihm rund einen Monat später zuteil wird. Wieder liegt er im Bett, als er sieht wie sich das Bild eines Mannes („similitudo uiri") auf ihn herabsenkt und sich ihm einprägt wie ein Siegel in weiches Wachs. Er schreckt aus dem Schlaf auf:

uigilans sensi dulce pondus, uigilans delectatus sum, et quid dicam? *Anima mea liquefacta est* [Ct 5,6]; anima mea, Domine, paene defecit, paene de corpore effusa est. O quam uera concionatoris nostri sententia: *Adolescentia enim,* inquit, *et uoluptas uana sunt* [Ecl 11,10]. Porro ibi non uanitas, sed ueritas, ibi uiua et uera uoluptas (Rupertus: 1979, 383).

[Als ich wach war, spürte ich eine süße Last, als ich wach war, war ich voller Freude, was soll ich sagen? Meine Seele zerschmolz; meine Seele, Herr, verging fast, floß beinahe aus meinem Leib. Wie wahr ist, was unser Prediger sagt: Jugend nämlich, sagt er, und Wollust sind eitel. Aber hierin lag keine Eitelkeit, sondern Wahrheit, hierin lag lebendige und wahre Wollust.]

In Ruperts Vision sind die späteren als Beilager beschriebenen Erlebnisse der *unio mystica* vorweggenommen. Es ist ein seelisches Erleben, das sich in körperlichem Empfinden artikuliert. Dabei wird wiederum mit Rekurs auf das Hohelied die sexuelle zu einer spirituellen Wollust umgedeutet. Nun hat Caroline Walker Bynum nachdrücklich und mit gutem Recht betont, daß man die Wahrnehmungen und Empfindungen mittelalterlicher Menschen nur unzureichend mit moderner

Begrifflichkeit der Sexualität beschreiben kann, und dabei u.a. auf das Beispiel des Rupert von Deutz hingewiesen: „Auch verstanden die Menschen damals körperliche Empfindungen, die wir als erotisch oder sexuell begreifen, nicht in dieser Weise" (Bynum: 1996, 67). Das Erlebnis der Gottesliebe sei vom sexuellen Erleben unterschieden. In der Tat steht es außer Zweifel, daß Rupert hier weder einen sexuellen Akt beschreibt oder auch nur meint; es trifft indessen nicht zu, daß die Erotik in dem, was Rupert an Körper und Seele empfindet, lediglich von modernen Lesern in den mittelalterlichen Text hineingelegt wird; die Erotik ist durch Sprache und Hohelied-Motivik eindeutig indiziert. Mittelalterliche Menschen sind offenbar in der Lage den gleichen Handlungen, Gesten oder Symbolen eine Vielzahl unterschiedener Bedeutungen beizulegen, wobei sich die aktuelle Bedeutung aus dem Kontext erschließt (vgl. Ohly: 1977, bes. 9 f.). Dies hat Klaus Schreiner in seiner Untersuchung des Kusses und seiner vielfältigen Funktionen im Mittelalter eindrücklich dargelegt. Dabei ist es interessant zu sehen, wie sich vom Kontext determinierte Bedeutungen gleichwohl mit Bedeutungen anderer Kontexte berühren oder überschneiden können. So erkennen mittelalterliche Theologen die Notwendigkeit, den liturgischen Friedenskuß als Ausdruck des Friedens und der Eintracht unter den Menschen zu reglementieren. Als Kuß auf den Mund bot er die Gefahr, daß sich in die fromme Geste *lascivia, libido* oder *luxuria*, allerlei Kitzel der Wollust einschlich (Schreiner: 1990, 101). Diese Vieldeutigkeit der Zeichen, also der Worte, Gesten und Symbole, ist im Mittelalter theoretisch fundiert, insbesondere in der Lehre vom mehrfachen Schriftsinn. Wie aber die Schrift nicht nur in ihrem wörtlichen Sinn, sondern in einer Mehrzahl weiterer theologischer, eschatologischer und moralischer Bedeutungen zu verstehen ist, so auch die Welt und ihre Phänomene, mit denen im Diesseits auf das Jenseits verwiesen wird, so auch der Mensch, der als leib-seelische Einheit Anteil an Welt und Transzendenz zugleich hat (zur Zeichenhaftigkeit der Welt vgl. Eco: 1993, 79-115). So ist der Kuß für Rupert von Deutz nicht im modernen Sinne eine Metapher, „um seine mystischen Erfahrungen angemessen zu beschreiben", wie Klaus Schreiner will (1990, 97), denn seine ganze Existenz und sein leib-seelisches Erleben in der Vision sind voll realistisch aufgefaßt und nur als solche realistischen Phänomene sind sie zugleich auch Metaphern, die noch etwas anderes ausdrücken. Es sind aber echte erotische Erlebnisse, die Rupert als solche beglaubigt, indem er gerade ihren Mehrwert an Bedeutung betont, die fleischliche in eine eine spirituelle Wollust umdeutet.

Im homosozialen Raum des Klosters wird ein Liebesdiskurs kultiviert, der sich durch eine bemerkenswerte Flexibilität geschlechtlicher Rollenzuschreibungen auszeichnet: „Daß sich ein Mann im Kern seiner selbst und bejahend als Frau sieht, geliebt und eingenommen vom überlegenen Bräutigam, das gibt es in der gleichzeitigen weltlichen Literatur nicht. [...] So entstand [...] ein Diskurs über geistliche Liebe, der dem weltlichen Liebesdiskurs, wie er an den Höfen in Liedern und Romanen gepflegt wurde, verblüffend ähnelte, der ihn thematisch ergänzte, nämlich um die gegengeschlechtliche Imagination des eigenen Selbst, um akzeptierte

Möglichkeiten für Männer, mit weiblichem Empfinden zu begehren" (Störmer-Caysa: 1998, 141). Die weibliche Seele, die sich mit Gott vereint, und der wollüstig empfindende Leib gehen im sprechenden Ich des Mystikers eine Einheit ein. Und so ist das Kloster nicht nur realer Lebensraum der Mönche, sondern kann, wie Bernhard von Clairvaux es in seinen *Hoheliedpredigten* ausdrückt, zugleich auch ein Brautbett sein (Sermo 46 zu „lectulus noster floridus", Ct 1,15; Bernhard: 1995, 126). In der gleichen Predigt fragt er seine Zuhörer: „de felicitate sponsae, quae hoc amoris carmine ab ipso Spiritu canitur, aliquid recognoscere in temetipso" [„Erkennst du etwas vom Glück der Braut, die in diesem Liebeslied vom Heiligen Geist besungen wird, in dir selbst wieder"] (ebd., 130). Bernhard, der so gut wie nie von eigenen mystischen Erfahrungen spricht, macht seinen seine Mitmönchen hier ein klares Identifikationsangebot.[176]

Die Aktualisierung der Päderastie im hohen Mittelalter

John Boswell überschreibt in seinem Buch über Homosexualität im Mittelalter ein Kapitel mit „The Triumph of Ganymede" und behandelt darin u.a. hochmittelalterliche Dichtungen, in denen mittels intertextueller Referenzen auf die klassische Dichtung und Mythologie die Päderastie des Altertums aktualisiert wird. Auf die fast ausschließlich aus Frankreich stammende und unstreitig homoerotische Dichtung, deren Hauptvertreter Baudri von Bourgueil, Marbod von Rennes, Hildebert von Lavardin und Hilarius von Orléans sind, hat bereits die ältere Forschung seit dem Ende des 19. Jahrhunderts mit unterschiedlichen moralischen Bewertungen hingewiesen.[177] War sie einer sittengeschichtlichen Betrachtungsweise Beleg für „die weite verbreitung des lasters der knabenliebe" im Mittelalter (Dümmler: 1878, 256), spricht Boswell unverblümt nicht nur von „gay poetry", sondern auch von „gay poets", deren Texte hinreichende Beweise für die Entstehung einer „gay subculture" böten (Boswell: 1980, 243 ff.). Wo und wann es im europäischen Mittelalter zur Ausbildung homosexueller, oder besser: sodomitischer Subkulturen und Identitäten kam, ist umstritten. Aber die genannten Dichter des Übergangs vom 11. zum 12. Jahrhundert kann man gewiß nicht dafür in Anspruch nehmen, denn die Umwertung der literarischen Tradition in der homoerotischen Lyrik des Hochmittelalters wie auch der soziale Kontext ihrer Entstehung legen eine andere Deutung nahe.[178]

---

[176] Dies widerspricht der Meinung von Brauns, es gebe für die „Sexualsymbolik" der Mystikerinnen „keine Entsprechung beim Mönch, der sein Leben Gott verschreibt" (Braun: 1988, 176). Vielmehr geht, historisch gesehen, die erotische Kodierung mystischer Erlebnisse von Männern der hochmittelalterlichen Frauenmystik voraus.

[177] Zur Bedeutung dieses Dichterkreises für die Liebesbriefdichtung vgl. Ruhe: 1975, 23-34.

[178] Zur homoerotischen Dichtung des lateinischen Mittelalters vgl. auch Stehling: 1983; Düchting: 1992.

An der Schwelle zwischen frühmittelalterlicher Freundschafts-dichtung und hochmittelalterlicher Liebesdichtung steht sehr vereinzelt ein anonymes, um das Jahr 1000 entstandenes Gedicht, das nach seinem ersten Vers *O admirabile Veneris idolum* heißt (Strecker: 1966, 105 ff.). Der Sprecher, der sich in Wortwahl und Motivik als gebildeter Mann ausweist, schickt es einem geliebten Knaben hinterher, der ihn verschmäht und sich ihm durch eine Seereise entzogen hat:

O admirabile   Veneris idolum,
cuius materie   nihil est frivolum,
archos te protegat,   qui stellas et polum
fecit et maria   condidit et solum (V. 1-4)

[Ach, wunderbares Bild der Venus, / an dessen Stoff sich kein Überfluß zeigt, / der Herr beschütze dich, der Sterne und Himmel / gemacht und Meere und Erde gegründet hat.]

Der Knabe wird als Ebenbild der römischen Liebesgöttin apostrophiert. Damit eröffnet der Dichter einen mythologischen Vergleichshorizont, der auf den erotischen Inhalt des Gedichts hindeutet, spielt aber zugleich mit der Erwartung des Lesers, der noch nicht weiß, ob tatsächlich von einer Venusstatue die Rede ist oder metonymisch von einem geliebten Mädchen. Erst der Beginn der zweiten Strophe („Salvato puerum", V. 7) macht deutlich, daß der Angesprochene männlichen Geschlechts ist. Eine Invokation des christlichen Schöpfergottes, deren Vokabular der Hymnik und religiösen Literatur entlehnt ist, erfleht Schutz für die Reise des Knaben. Für weitere Segenswünsche greift der Sprecher indessen wieder auf die antike Mythologie zurück: Sowohl die Schicksalsgöttinnen Klotho, Lachesis und Atropos als auch die Meeresgottheiten Neptun und Thetis werden angerufen (V. 6-11). Dann wird der flüchtende Knabe noch einmal direkt angesprochen:

Quo fugis, amabo,   cum te dilexerim?
Miser quid faciam,   cum te non viderim? (V. 12-13)

[Wohin fliehst du – ich flehe dich an –, da ich dich doch liebe? / Was werde ich Armer tun, wenn ich dich nicht mehr sehe?]

Die schlichten Verse, in denen Liebesbekenntnis und Verzweiflung über den Verlust des Jungen zusammenfallen, erweisen sich in der Analyse als höchst kunstvoll: Die Formel *quo fugis* dürfte Vergils *Aeneis* (X 649) entstammen, wo auf das Liebesverhältnis von Aeneas und Lavinia angespielt ist. Die Interjektion *amabo* ist eine für die römische Komödie typische Vokabel, ebenso zitiert V. 13 den *Eunuchus* des Terenz: „quid igitur faciam miser" (V. 966). Der Dichter simuliert auf gelehrte Weise Mündlichkeit und suggeriert die unmittelbare Umsetzung von Gefühl in Sprache.

Dabei wird in V. 13 die Trennung von Liebendem und Geliebtem metrisch nachvollzogen: Die starke Mittelzäsur trennt das Sprecher-Ich vom angesprochenen Du. Die verrätselte Kurzfassung eines antiken Mythos eröffnet die dritte Strophe. Die in zwei Versen zusammengefaßte Geschichte von Deukalion und Pyrrha, die als einzige Überlebende einer Flut die Menschheit neu erschaffen, indem sie Steine, die Gebeine ihrer Mutter, der Erde, hinter sich werfen (Ovid, *Met.* I 313 ff.), will das Verhalten des Knaben erklären. Seine emotionale Härte gegenüber dem Liebenden leitet sich her von der physikalischen Härte des Steins, aus dem er geschaffen ist. Am Ende bleibt der Liebende in seinem Schmerz alleine:

Dura materies   ex matris ossibus
creavit homines   iactis lapidibus,
ex quibus unus est   iste puerulus,
qui lacrimabiles   non curat gemitus.
Cum tristis fuero,   gaudebit emulus.
Ut cerva rugio,   cum fugit hinnulus. (V. 14-19)

[Harter Stoff aus dem Gebein der Mutter / schuf die Menschen beim Werfen von Steinen; / einer von ihnen ist dies Knäblein, / das sich nicht sorgt um meine tränenreichen Klagen. / Wenn ich traurig bin, freut sich mein Gegner. / Wie eine Hirschkuh schreie ich, wenn ihr der Hirsch entflieht.]

Wie immer *emulus* im vorletzten Vers zu deuten ist, ich plädiere dafür, daß es sich nicht um einen unbekannten Dritten, einen Nebenbuhler, handelt, sondern um den Knaben selbst, der zum schadenfrohen Gegenspieler wird, indem er sich entzieht. Der letzte Vers läßt deutliche Bibelanklänge erkennen, die die gleichgeschlechtliche Erotik des Gedichts einer spirituellen Deutung öffnen. Das Verb *rugio* erinnert an einen Klagevers des Psalters: „rugiebam a gemitu cordis mei" [„ich schrie auf ob des Kummers meines Herzens"] (Ps 37,9; vgl. auch *gemitus* in V. 17!). Hier wird der Psalmist David, der dem Herrn sein Ungemach klagt, zum Identifikationsmodell für den an unerwiderter Liebe leidenden Sprecher des Gedichts. Die Motivik von Hirschkuh und Hirsch entstammt ebenfalls alttestamentarischer Dichtung: Im Hohenlied bedichtet die Liebende ihren Geliebten mit dem Vers: „similis est dilectus meus capreae hinuloque cervorum" [„Mein Geliebter gleicht einer Gazelle und einem jungen Hirsch"] (Ct 2,9). *Hinnulus* ist das Bild eines erotisch attraktiven Mannes; Hirschkuh und Hirsch symbolisieren die mann-weibliche Paarbeziehung, die hier indessen auf ein gleichgeschlechtliches Arrangement angewendet wird. Von Anfang an herrscht in der Beziehung zwischen Sprecher und angesprochenem eine Ungleichgewicht und eine geschlechtlich definierte Differenz. Dabei ist der Junge durch seine androgyne Schönheit und Jugend zunächst in der weiblichen Rolle. Noch in V. 16, wo er im zärtlichen Diminutiv als *puerulus* bezeichnet wird, bleibt eine Hierachie erkennbar. Der Sprecher ist ihm an Alter und Bildung überlegen. Am Ende

163

haben sich die Positionen aber verschoben und das hierarchische Verhältnis kippt. Da all sein Werben erfolglos geblieben ist, unterliegt der Ältere schließlich und projiziert sich nun seinerseits in die Rolle der Liebenden des Hohenliedes. Die traditionelle Forschungsmeinung, bei *O admirabile Veneris idolum* handele es sich um ein Knabenlied, ist nicht unwidersprochen geblieben. Benedikt Konrad Vollmann hat vorgeschlagen, das Gedicht als Abschiedsdialog eines Liebespaars zu interpretieren. Die erste Strophe mit der Anrede *Veneris idolum* sei dabei von einem Mann an seine Geliebte gesprochen, mit der zweiten und dritten Strophe antworte das Mädchen, das sich am Ende mit der brüllenden Hindin vergleiche. Nur wenn diese Vergleiche mit dem natürlichen Geschlecht einer Angesprochenen oder einer Sprecherin übereinstimmten, sei das Gedicht stimmig (Vollmann: 1988). Nun bildet die Feminisierung des Gegenübers in einer mann-männlichen Konstellation, wie zu sehen war, seit der karolingischen Freundschaftsdichtung ihre eigene mittelalterliche Tradition. In *O admirabile Veneris idolum* wird die Rückbindung an diese Tradition insbesondere in der Hoheliedbildlichkeit des Schlußverses kenntlich. Somit läßt sich das Gedicht als Zeugnis der *dilectio spiritualis* lesen. Überdies kennzeichnet der Redegestus den Sprecher als gebildeten Menschen, der sowohl in der antiken Mythologie und Dichtung als auch in der schulmäßigen Grammatik und Rhetorik bewandert ist. Diese Art von Bildung läßt sich mit keinem frühmittelalterlichen Frauenbild vereinbaren (was wohlgemerkt nicht bedeutet, daß es keine gebildeten Frauen gab!). Vielmehr setzt dieser Redegestus einen männlichen Sprecher und ein ganz bestimmtes gesellschaftliches Milieu voraus. Die Versatzstücke antiken Bildungsgutes verorten das Gedicht in einen exklusiv männlich besetzten, homosozialen Raum, näherhin in eine Kloster- oder Domschule. Das Arrangement von Liebendem und Geliebtem ist als Lehrer-Schüler-Verhältnis gedacht. Die mythologische Kodierung der Rede erlaubt es dem liebenden Lehrer in besonders weithergeholten Denkfiguren seine dialektische Kompetenz zu demonstrieren, zugleich aber das Gemeinte zu verrätseln, damit der Sinn nicht jedermann offenkundig ist.[179]

Die Einspiegelung des sozialen Raums der Schule in die homoerotische Dichtung läßt sich auch an hochmittelalterlichen Beispielen demonstrieren. Marbods von Rennes dichterische Tätigkeit muß vorab im Kontext seiner Lehrtätigkeit an der Schule von Angers gesehen werden. Von ihm stammt ein Gedicht über einen *beau garçon sans merci*. Er greift dabei auf ein Knabenlied des Horaz (Carmen IV, 10) zurück, das ohne wörtliches Zitat in amplifizierender Paraphrase nachgedichtet wird. Diese Praxis, „die Vorlage in freiem Spiel abzuwandeln", kennt man auch sonst aus dem mittelalterlichen Schulunterricht (Stotz: 1981, 9). Marbods Gedicht könnte also ein Schaustück für diese Art der Poesieübung gewesen sein. Horaz wirbt in der Ode um den jungen und verführerischen Ligurinus mit dem Argument, daß seine Schönheit vergänglich ist. Der Spröde werde sich, sobald sein Bart sprosse und er

---

[179] Eine ausführliche Interpretation des Gedichts bei Limbeck: 2001.

damit als Objekt des Begehrens nicht mehr in Frage komme, danach sehnen geliebt zu werden und bereuen, der Werbung nicht stattgegeben zu haben (Horatius: 1992, 234). Der Sprecher von Marbods Gedicht greift die Motive der Horazischen Ode auf und bietet zunächst eine ausführliche Schönheitsbeschreibung, wohlgemerkt des Horazischen Knaben, ein Du tritt nicht in Erscheinung:

De puero quodam   conponit Oracius odam,
Qui facie bella   posset satis esse puella.
Undabant illi   per eburnea colla capilli,
Plus auro flavi,   quales ego semper amavi;
Candida frons ut nix,   et lumina nigra velut pix;
Inplumesque gene   grata dilcedine plene
Cum vi candoris   vernabant luce ruboris;
Nasus erat iustus,   labra flammea, densque venustus;
Effigies menti   modulo formata decenti (V. 1-9; Werner: 1905, 5 f.).

[Horaz dichtete eine Ode über einen Knaben, / der wegen seines hübschen Gesichts auch ein Mädchen hätte sein können. / Seinen elfenbeinernen Hals umspielten Haare blonder als Gold, so wie ich sie immer liebte; / seine Stirn weißer als Schnee, seine Augen schwarz wie Pech; / und seine flaumlosen Wangen waren voll Anmut und Süße, / wenn sie in kräftigem Weiß und schimmernder Röte erstrahlten. / Seine Nase war gerade, seine Lippen flammend rot, seine Zähne lieblich; / die Gestalt des Kinns war in anmutiger Weise gebildet.]

Die Beschreibung folgt einem Muster, das bereits bei Ovid vorhanden ist und den Blick des potentiellen Betrachters von oben nach unten lenkt: Haare, Stirn, Augen, Wangen, Nase, Mund und Kinn. Wie bereits Ovid dieses Schema sowohl auf weibliche wie auf männliche Personen anwendet, sind auch bei Marbod die Formeln der Schönheitsbeschreibung austauschbar. Winfried Offermanns, der die Beliebigkeit von Marbods Floskeln des Schönheitspreises in Gedichten über Mädchen und Jungen im einzelnen nachgewiesen hat, stellt fest: „Wie sich der Formelschatz unterschiedslos aus der Beschreibung männlicher und weiblicher Schönheit entwickelt hat, so wird er auch unterschiedslos für beide verwendbar" (Offermanns: 1970, 141). Diese Ansicht ist zu differenzieren: Matthäus von Vendôme, Verfasser einer *Ars versificatoria* des 12. Jahrhunderts, betont, daß bei der Beschreibung bestimmte Eigenschaften wie Stand, Alter und Geschlecht zu beachten sind (I 46), und führt aus: „in femineo sexu approbatio forme debet ampliari, in masculino vero parcius. Unde Ovidius: 'Forma viros neglecta decet' [Ov. ars am. I 509]" [„Beim weiblichen Geschlecht sollte der Preis der Schönheit ausführlicher, beim männlichen indessen knapper sein. Ovid sagt dazu: 'Männern steht eine Vernachlässigung des Äußeren wohl an'"] (I 67; Matheus: 1988, 92). Die mittelalterliche Poetik kennt also sehr wohl einen Unterschied zwischen weiblicher und männlicher Schönheit. Bereits Vers 2 von Marbods Gedicht stellt eine Rechtfertigung für die nachfolgende Schönheitsbeschreibung dar: Explizit wird die Physiognomie des männlichen Beschriebenen als weibliche Schönheit charakterisiert, die es gestattet, ihn als Objekt erotischen Begehrens zu sehen (vgl. Stehling: 1983, 153-158). Die Art der Schönheit steht in unmittelbarer Abhängigkeit zu der Beziehung zwischen Betrachter und Betrachtetem, anders ausgedrückt: Geschlecht ist das Produkt eines Beziehungskontextes. Nachdem Marbod betont hat, daß die Schönheit des Knaben nicht ohne erotische Rückwirkung auf den Betrachter bleibt (V. 12-13), vollzieht er gewissermaßen eine „moralische Wende": Das gefällige Äußere des Jungen entspricht keineswegs seinem Charakter. Er bleibt von Liebeswerbungen ungerührt, weidet sich geradezu an den Qualen derer, die er abweist und deren Liebestod er billigend in Kauf nimmt:

Sed puerum talem   pulcrum nimis et specialem
Irritamentum   quorumlibet aspicientum
Sic natura ferum   plasmaverat atque severum,
Vellet ut ante mori,   quam consentiret amori:
Asper et ingratus,   tamquam de tigride natus,
Ridebat tantum   mollissima verba precantum;
Ridebat curas   effectum non habituras;
Et suspirantis   lacrimas ridebat amantis;
Illos ridebat,   quos ipse mori faciebat.
Impius ille quidem,   crudelis et impius idem,
Qui vicio morum   corpus vetat esse decorum.
Bella bonam mentem   facies petit et pacientem
Et non inflatam   sed ad hec et ad illa paratam (V. 14-26).

[Doch diesen überaus hübschen und besonderen Knaben, / Verlockung für alle, die ihn erblickten, / hatte die Natur so grausam und hart erschaffen, / eher wollte er sterben, als der Liebe nachgeben: / Kalt und undankbar, als wäre er ein Tigerkind, / lachte er nur über die zärtlichsten Worte seiner Bewerber; / er lachte über die Aufmerksamkeiten, die keine Wirkung zeigen sollten; / und er lachte über die Tränen eines schmachtenden Liebhabers; / er lachte über die, die er selbst dem Tod überantwortete. / Ruchlos ist freilich der, grausam und ruchlos, / der mit einem Mangel an Sitten verhindert, daß sein Körper ihm zum Schmuck gereicht. / Ein hübsches Gesicht verlangt einen gütigen und willigen Sinn, / keinen aufgeblasenen, sondern einen der zu diesem und jenem bereit ist.]

Das Gedicht mündet in eine allgemeine moralische Betrachtung, die die Aufgeblasenheit und Arroganz des Jungen als Fehlverhalten brandmarkt. Von Jugendlichen wird verlangt, daß ihrem schönen Äußeren im Inneren eine charakterlich-moralische Integrität entspreche. Gemäß mittelalterlicher Anthropologie soll eine Harmonie zwischen *homo exterior* und *homo interior* bestehen. Der Schluß des Gedichts wiederholt Horazens Argument der Vergänglichkeit von Schönheit und Jugend. So wird die mittelalterliche Reinszenierung einer antiken Liebeswerbung in einen Kontext gestellt, der weniger darauf abzielt, den Jungen zum Nachgeben zu überreden, als seine Verhaltensformen zu tadeln und zu verbessern. Sie fügt sich in das pädagogische Ambiente der Entstehung des Gedichts, in dem tendentiell die *correctio morum* eines Schülers durch seinen Lehrer im Vordergrund steht. Die souveräne Aneignung der literarischen Tradition verleiht dieser Art „Schuldichtung" einen spielerischen Charakter, der sich in der Ambiguität erotischer und pädagogischer Rede offenbart, denn was *hec et illa* in Vers 26 bedeuten, bleibt offen.[180] Nicht zufällig ist auch der wohl bedeutendste mittellateinische Dichter von Knabenliedern ein Schulmann. Hilarius von Orléans, dessen Lebensdaten (ca. 1075- nach 1145) höchst unsicher sind, lehrte in Angers und Orléans und hinterließ u.a. vier Liebesbriefgedichte an Knaben, die zu den freimütigsten und poetisch versiertesten Schilderungen gleichgeschlechtlicher Liebe im lateinischen Mittelalter zählen. Hilarius' Gedicht an einen englischen Knaben, *Ad puerum anglicum* (Nr. 9, Häring: 1976, 940 f.), beginnt mit einem Lob der Schönheit und Tugend des Angesprochenen, der mit seiner Gestalt die Blicke der Betrachter auf sich zieht (V. 1-4). Anders als bei Marbods Knaben entsprechen sich Inneres und Äußeres. Die Schönheitsbeschreibung fällt knapper aus als bei Marbod, greift aber gängige Topoi auf:

Crinis flauus, os decorum ceruixque candidula,
Sermo blandus et suauis. Sed quid laudem singula?
Totus pulcher et decorus nec est in te macula.
Sed uacare castitati talis nequid formula (V. 5-8).

[Blondes Haar, wohlgestalter Mund, lieblich weißer Hals, / schmeichelnde und süße Rede. Doch was lobe ich die Einzelheiten? / Im ganzen bist du schön und wohlgestalt und kein Makel findet sich an dir. / Doch eine so schöne Gestalt vermag gar nicht frei von Keuschheit zu sein.]

Vers 7 bildet nicht nur eine inhaltliche Klimax und Zusammenfassung der Schönheitsformeln, sondern stellt ein leicht abgewandeltes Zitat aus dem Hohenlied dar. Dort sagt der Geliebte seiner Freundin: „tota pulchra es, amica mea, et macula non est in te" (Ct 4,7). Wiederum ist ein homoerotisches Verhältnis in der Sprache der gegengeschlechtlichen Liebe des Hohenliedes kodiert, indem der Dichter den Bibelvers lediglich grammatikalisch an sein Gegenüber anpaßt. Das intertextuelle Spiel mit der Mann-Weiblichkeit des Geliebten hat ein Pendant auf der inhaltlichen

---

[180] Vgl. mit ähnlicher Deutung zu diesem Gedicht auch McGuire: 1988, 247. Zusammen mit einem motivgleichen Gedicht Baudris von Bourgueil stellt Jaeger: 1994, 315 f. u. 474 (Anm. 59) Marbods Knabenlied in den schulischen Kontext der *correctio morum*. Zu Ambiguität und Spielcharakter des Homoerotischen in mittellateinischer Dichtung vgl. Bond: 1986.

Ebene. Die folgende Strophe bietet eine mythologische Ätiologie der androgynen Schönheit des Jungen:

Cum natura te creauit, dubitauit paululum,
Si proferret te puellam an proferret masculum.
Sed dum in hoc eligendo mentis figit oculum,
Ecce prodis in commune natus ad spectaculum (V. 9-12).

[Als die Natur dich erschuf, schwankte sie ein wenig, / ob sie dich zu einem Mädchen oder zu einem Jungen machen sollte. / Doch als sie ihr geistiges Auge auf diese Entscheidung heftete, / siehe da, da erschienst du, geboren zum Wohle aller, wie ein Wunder betrachtet zu werden.]

Die schaffende Natur, als Göttin personifiziert, ist ein Lieblingsthema des 12. Jahrhunderts, das einem neuen rationalistischen Naturverständnis Ausdruck verleiht. Das hier gebrauchte Motiv, daß die Natur bei der Erschaffung eines hübschen Jungen zwischen den Geschlechtern schwankt, läßt sich seit der Antike aber häufiger belegen. Wörtliche Anklänge zeigen, daß ein dem Ausonius zugeschriebenes Epigramm hier unmittelbares Vorbild gewesen sein dürfte: „Dum dubitat natura, marem faceretne puellam, / Natus es, o pulcher, paene puella, puer" [„Da die Natur schwankte, ob sie einen Jungen oder ein Mädchen erschaffen sollte, / wurdest du, schöner Knabe, beinahe als Mädchen geboren"] (Riese: 1869, 180). Die poetische Repräsentation der geschlechtlichen Uneindeutigkeit, die in der römischen Dichtung eine Voraussetzung des päderastischen Paradigmas darstellt, wird von Hilarius aktualisiert und in den Kontext der insbesondere in Frankreich kurrenten naturphilosophischen Diskussion gestellt. Nur in einem habe die Natur einen Fehler begangen, fährt der Dichter fort, sie habe den Jungen als Sterblichen erschaffen (V. 13-20). Würde die Antike wiederkehren, dann würde Jupiter statt des hübschen Ganymedes den Angesprochenen in den Himmel führen (V. 21-24). Das Gedicht endet mit einer nicht zu übersetzenden Pointe, die auf die englische Herkunft des Knaben anspielt und eine Anekdote um Papst Gregor den Großen aufgreift:

Errant quidem, inmo peccant qui te uocant anglicum:
E uocalem interponant et dicant angelicum (V. 27-28).

[Freilich irren diejenigen, die dich Engländer nennen: / Sie sollten den Vokal e dazwischenfügen und Engel sagen.]

Von Gregor heißt es in Bedas *Historia ecclesiastica* (II 1), er habe auf dem römischen Sklavenmarkt überaus hübsche Jungen gesehen, die aus Britannien stammten, wo damals das Heidentum herrschte. Man teilt ihm mit, es handele sich um Angeln *(Angli)*, und Gregor hält die Bezeichnung für angemessen, da sie das Antlitz von

Engeln *(angeli)* besäßen (Beda: 1969, 132 ff.). Die Anekdote will, daß diese Begegnung zum Anlaß für die Missionierung Britanniens wird. Die englische Knabe in Hilarius' Gedicht erweist sich als ebenso engelsgleich, wie seine Vorfahren, die schon den heiligen Papst charmierten. Man hat in Hilarius' homoerotischen Dichtungen Parodien auf im Schulmilieu und unter Klerikern naheliegende sodomitische Verfehlungen sehen wollen, die zugleich die Souveränität des Dichters im Umgang mit antiker Mythologie und seine dialektische Kompetenz unter Beweis stellen sollen: „Als Demonstration intellektueller Komik war die Ganymed-Dichtung demnach nichts anderes als anspruchsvolle l'art pour l'art einer sich als modern verstehenden Dichtergeneration, welche neben, oder besser, im beabsichtigten Gegensatz zu den damals zahlreich wuchernden ernervierenden Zeitanklagen [...] nur unterhalten wollte, aber unter dem Druck allgemeiner moralischer Abwertungen ihre eigentlichen Absichten immer wieder zu verteidigen und zu tarnen hatte" (Latzke: 1983, 132). In der Tat reizt Hilarius von Orléans in seinen Knabenliedern das literarische Spiel mit der antiken Päderastie bis an ungeahnte und erst im Humanismus des 15. Jahrhunderts überschrittene Grenzen aus. Gleichwohl darf man dem hier behandelten Gedicht im Grunde genommen die gleiche Intention unterstellen, die schon bei Marbod kenntlich wurde. Mag auch ein bedauernder Ton durchklingen, das Gedicht ist ein Lob der Keuschheit. Seine pädagogische Absicht liegt nicht zuletzt darin, die geforderte Übereinstimmung von *homo exterior* und *homo interior* zu demonstrieren. Die nonchalante antik-erotische Bildlichkeit wird auch bei Hilarius von spirituellen Motiven ergänzt und überlagert, so daß seine Gedichte durchaus in die Tradition der *dilectio spiritualis* eingeordnet werden dürfen (vgl. auch Ruhe: 1975, 41 f.). Man muß sich noch einmal verdeutlichen, daß die schulpoetischen Zeugnisse der geistlichen Liebe weniger Ausdruck eines in der Wirklichkeit verankerten Liebesromans sind, sondern daß sie diese Liebe im Gedicht erst hervorbringen. Walther Bulst bezeichnet dies einmal zutreffend als eine „Wirklichkeit im Wort". Die Knabenlieder des Hilarius nennt er „Bekenntnisse durchaus irdischer, von leiblicher Schönheit entzündeter Leidenschaft und ihres Verlangens", die indessen zu verstehen sind als „Erfüllungen im Wort" (Bulst: 1954, 93). Anders ausgedrückt: Die spirituelle Liebe ist der Effekt eines Diskurses; Animation zur Sodomie indessen bleibt im ganzen Mittelalter, so auch für Hilarius, undenkbar.

Geschlechtergrammatik und Problematisierung gleichgeschlechtlicher Arrangements

Die überwiegende Anzahl der mittelalterlichen Zeugnisse über mann-männliche Sexualität problematisiert diese unter im weitesten Sinne moraltheologischen Gesichtspunkten. Mit einer entsprechenden Äußerung des Paulus (Rm 1,26-27) gelten gleichgeschlechtliche Sexualbeziehungen als Sünde wider die Natur und gegen Gott, ihren Schöpfer. Da sie die Möglichkeit der Fortpflanzung ausschließen, verfehlen sie den Zweck der Sexualität, die ihren Ort einzig in der ehelichen Gemeinschaft von Frau und Mann hat. Im Zusammenhang dieser Überlegungen interessiert mich ein bestimmtes Argumentationsmuster, das die moralische Disqualifzierung homosexuellen Verhaltens bezweckt und das im gleichen Milieu und zur gleichen Zeit wie die behandelten Beispiele der Schuldichtung floriert, mithin von dieser selbst angewendet wird. Alanus von Lille (um 1125/30-1203), der in Chartres studiert hatte und in Montpellier die freien Künste lehrte, schildert in *De planctu Naturae* mit nachhaltigem Erfolg gleichgeschlechtliche Sexualbeziehungen mit der Terminologie der Grammatik. Diese auf den ersten Blick befremdliche Metaphorik, die sprachliches und geschlechtliches Handeln korreliert, fußt auf der realistischen Sprachtheorie des Mittelalters, wonach Sprache in einem logischen Verhältnis zur Wirklichkeit steht. Zugleich findet im 12. Jahrhundert, insbesondere im Umfeld der sogenannten Schule von Chartres, die Entwicklung eines rationalistischen Naturverständnisses statt (vgl. Flasch: 1986, 226-235). Gerade in der Naturphilosophie eines Bernardus Silvestris erhält die prokreative Sexualität als natürliche und schöpferische Handlung einen Eigenwert. Wenn die Grammatik das logische System der Sprache darstellt und die Natur ihrerseits einer logischen Regelhaftigkeit unterliegt, dann läßt sich die Grammatik als Instrument der Natur- und Wirklichkeitserkenntnis gebrauchen, und spezieller: Die Regeln einer natürlichen Sexualität müssen den Regeln der korrekten Grammatik entsprechen; widernatürliche Sexualität kommt einem Verstoß gegen Grammatikregeln gleich.[181]

Die Dichtung macht sich die Grammatikmetaphorik zunutze, wenn sie gleichgeschlechtliche Sexualität zur Sprache bringen will. Im Umfeld des Hilarius von Orléans ist das Carmen buranum 95 *Cur suspectum me tenet domina* entstanden. Es ist aus der Rolle eines Mannes gesprochen, der sich vor seiner Geliebten gegen den Verdacht der gleichgeschlechtlichen Sodomie verteidigt. Eines seiner Argumente lautet: „Naturali contentus uenere / non didici pati, sed agere" [„Da ich zufrieden bin mit der natürlichen Liebe, / habe ich nicht gelernt, passiv zu sein, sondern aktiv"] (Vollmann: 1987, 346). Als Mann nimmt der Sprecher die aktive sexuelle Rolle ein, und zwar der Natur gemäß gegenüber Frauen; einem Mann gegenüber wider die Natur die passive Rolle einzunehmen liegt ihm fern. Hier werden die sexuellen Geschlechterrollen mit den grammatikalischen Genera verbi Aktiv und Passiv korreliert: Das grammatikalische Genus spiegelt die Natur des Sexus.

Im intellektuellen poetischen Spiel, wie es in der Schuldichtung gepflegt wird, ist dies nicht immer zwingend der Fall, wie das ebenfalls aus dem 12. Jahrhundert stammende Streitgedicht *Altercatio Ganimedis et Helene* zeigt (Lenzen: 1972). Streitgedichte lassen als poetische Disputationen über Für und Wider eines oftmals beliebig anmutenden Gegenstandes (Sommer vs. Winter; Wein vs. Bier etc.) verstehen und dienen der Einübung in die Dialektik. Sie haben daher ihren sozialen Ort in den Schulen, näherhin im Ausbildungsgang des Triviums (vgl. Walther: 1920, 17-27). Das Streitgespräch zwischen Ganymed und Helena verhandelt einen nicht ganz

---

[181] Vgl. Alford: 1982; Ziolkowski: 1985.

alltäglichen Gegenstand, die Frage, ob die Liebe zu Knaben oder die Liebe zu Frauen vorzuziehen sei. Der Dichter schildert zunächst einen *locus amoenus*, wo die beiden mythologischen Figuren sich der Liebeständelei hingeben. Als die beiden miteinander schlafen wollen, stellt sich ein Hindernis ein: Ganymed, der phrygische Knabe, legt sich so hin, als solle er die passive Rolle einnehmen:

> Erant ambo viridem super herbam strati
> Et futuri fuerant copula beati.
> Sed ignorans Frigius vicem predicati
> Applicat se femine, tanquam vellet pati (Str. 8).

[Beide lagen nun auf der grünen Wiese / und waren kurz davor, sich selig zu vereinigen. / Aber der unwissende Phrygier kannte die Position des Prädikats nicht / und brachte sich in eine Stellung zu der Frau, als ob er passiv sein wollte.]

Der Vergleich von sexueller Rolle und Genus verbi wird hier noch erweitert durch die Analogie von Satzstellung und Koitusposition. Zugleich wird das Fehlverhalten Ganymeds explizit als eine Form der Unwissenheit bezeichnet: Richtiges Sexualverhalten muß man lernen wie Grammatikregeln. Darüber kommt es nun zum Streit zwischen den beiden, und vor einer Götterversammlung, in der Natura, begleitet von Ratio und Providentia, als Schiedsrichterin fungiert, tragen Ganymed und Helena nun abwechselnd ihre Argumente für die gleich- und gegengeschlechtliche Liebe vor. In Helenas Vorwurf, Ganymed sei offenbar neidisch auf das weibliche Geschlecht („Sexum mulieribus invides aperte", Str. 29,3), – denn er will sexuell wie eine Frau agieren –, wird noch einmal deutlich, daß gleichgeschlechtliche Sexualität mit Passivität und Verweiblichung konnotiert ist. Für die Heterosexualität argumentiert Helena wiederum grammatikalisch: „Contrahuntur hic et hec naturali flexu" [„In der natürlichen Beugung werden *hic* und *hec* – maskulines und feminines Demonstrativum – miteinander verbunden"] (Str. 33,3). Diese *hic et hec*-Formel, die des öfteren in mittellateinischer Dichtung vorkommt, rekurriert zwar auf das grammatikalische Phänomen der Unterscheidung von mindestens zwei Genera (wobei das Lateinische nun allerdings drei kennt), entspricht aber nicht direkt einer Regel der lateinischen Grammatik. Eher im Gegenteil, denn Ganymed kontert:

> Impar omne dissidet, recte par cum pari.
> Eleganti copula mas aptatur mari;
> Si nescis: articulos decet observari;
> Hic et hic gramatice debent copulari! (Str. 36)

[Alles Ungleiche paßt nicht zusammen, sondern Gleiches gehört zu Gleichem. / In einer eleganten Kopula wird das Männliche an das Männliche gefügt; / falls du es noch nicht weißt: Man sollte auf die Artikel achten; / nach der Grammatik müssen *hic* und *hic* – maskuline Demonstrativa – miteinander verbunden werden.]

Grammatikalisch gesehen hat Ganymed in diesem Falle das stärkere Argument, denn das Lateinische verlangt in der Tat bei der Kopula die Kongruenz von Kasus, Numerus und eben Genus. Am Ende muß sich der „puer sexus inmemor", der Knabe, der sich seines Geschlechtes nicht bewußt ist, dennoch dem Schiedsspruch der Natura beugen; Helena und die Heterosexualität obsiegen.

Was sollte diese argumentative Artistik, dieses Schaustück der Dialektik mittelalterlichen Schülern eigentlich vermitteln? Grammatik, Rhetorik oder Poetik ließen sich an unverfänglicheren Gegenständen üben, zumal das Publikum größerenteils ohnehin zu keuschem Lebenswandel, wenn nicht gar zum formalen Zölibat verpflichtet war. Idealerweise sollten die Schüler weder die Argumente für die gleich- noch jene für die gegengeschlechtliche Sexualität in die Tat umsetzen. Auch hier wird man als sekundäre Zielsetzung die *correctio morum* vermuten dürfen. Als Nebeneffekt der Sprachbeherrschung wird den Schülern die Beherrschung ihrer Triebe eingetrichtert.[182] Eine mittelalterliche Schulaufgabe kann z.B. im Verfassen misogyner Verse bestehen. Dies zielt auf einen zweifachen Effekt: Der Schüler übt sich im Dichten von Hexametern etc. und lernt gleichzeitig, warum er sich von Frauen möglichst fernhalten sollte. Auch die homoerotischen und homophoben Verse der mittellateinischen Literatur dienen solchen Zwecken. Indem man das Thema der gleichgeschlechtlichen Liebe zur Sprache bringt, ja die potentiell Betroffenen selbst dazu animiert, dies zu tun, packt man ein vom homosozialen Raum bedingtes Problem, die Gefahr homosexueller Verfehlungen, gleichsam bei den Hörnern. Zugleich spiegelt sich in der grammatikalischen Kodierung gleichgeschlechtlicher Beziehungen das Konzept der geschlechtlichen Dichotomie. Einer der bedeutendsten Grammatik- und Rhetoriklehrer des 13. Jahrhunderts, Johannes de Garlandia (um 1195-nach 1272), widmet in seinem *Epithalamium beate virginis Marie* (Giovanni di Garlandia: 1995) einen Abschnitt der Sünde wider die Natur, wo es u.a. heißt:

Semivir antivirum patitur: nec femina nec vir,
   neutropassivum nomen habere potest.
Hermaphroditat eum Veneris Venus hostis [...] (II, V. 395-97).

---

[182] Zu einem ähnlichen Ergebnis gelangt Epp: 1996 bei seiner Untersuchung der sexuellen Anspielungen in der *Ars versificatoria* des Matthäus von Vendôme.

[Ein Halbmann gibt sich dem Gegenteil eines Mannes hin: Er ist weder Frau noch Mann, und kann als Neutropassivum bezeichnet werden. Eine Venus, die die Feindin der Venus ist, macht ihn zum Hermaphroditen...]

Johannes de Garlandia thematisiert in seinen Versen den Widerstreit von anatomischem Geschlecht und geschlechtlichem Verhalten: Der passive Mann produziert eine inadäquate weibliche Geschlechterrolle, ist im Endeffekt aber weder Mann noch Frau, sondern eine moralische Monstrosität jenseits grammatikalischer Norm und natürlicher Ordnung.

Resümee

Die lateinische Literatur des Mittelalters hat eine Fülle literarischer Zeugnisse über mann-männliche Arrangements hervorgebracht, die sich als Liebesbeziehungen verstehen lassen. Diese Beziehungen werden mittels changierender intertextueller Referenzen in zwei Traditionen eingeschrieben: in die pagane Geschlechter- und Sexualkonzeption der römischen Dichtung und in die theologische Tradition der Hoheliedexegese. Das hat auf die Beziehungen den zweifachen Effekt sowohl der Erotisierung als auch der Spiritualisierung. Insbesondere Zitate aus der alttestamentarischen Liebesdichtung versehen die geschilderten Arrangements, mittelalterlicher Hermeneutik folgend, mit einer transzendenten Sinnebene, die sich innerweltlich widerspiegelt. Dadurch unterscheidet sich die Tradition der *dilectio spiritualis,* die sich in Liedern und Briefen der Freundschaft, in spirituellen und mystischen Texten und in der Liebesdichtung niederschlägt, von der gleichzeitigen moraltheologischen Diskursivierung gleichgeschlechtlicher Sexualität als Sodomie und Sünde wider die Natur – ebenso wie von einer Sexualität tendenziell eher einschließenden homoerotischen Dichtung der Neuzeit. Um eine Genealogie der modernen Homosexualität geht es hier gerade nicht. Wenn man also von der Erotik gleichgeschlechtlicher Beziehungen spricht, dann handelt es sich hierbei um ein mit literarischen Techniken erzeugtes diskursives Ereignis. Das ist übrigens keine Besonderheit gleichgeschlechtlicher Beziehungen, da ja bekanntlich auch der Liebesdiskurs der hohen Minne einen asexuellen Eros propagiert. Die gleichgeschlechtlichen erotischen Arrangements in den hier exemplarisch vorgestellten Texten werden – wie in der Antike – asymmetrisch konstruiert.[183] Demnach unterscheiden sich Begehrender und Begehrter wesentlich durch Alter *(vir/puer)* und Bildungsniveau *(magister/ discipulus).* Zugleich bringt das Begehren eine artifizielle Dichotomie der Geschlechter und Geschlechterrollen hervor. Im Rückgriff

---

[183] Damit will ich freilich nicht behaupten, daß im Mittelalter nicht auch andere Konstruktionen gleichgeschlechtlicher Arrangements denkbar sind. Dafür ließen sich auf Symmetrie und Gleichheit beruhende Darstellungen von Freundschaft anführen (z.B. die weitverbreitete Legende von Amicus und Amelius).

auf klassische Schönheitsbeschreibungen wird der männliche Körper des geliebten Knaben mit Signaturen der Weiblichkeit versehen. Andererseits findet sich in den mystischen Beschreibungen der liebenden Begegnung mit Gott der umgekehrte Fall: Das sprechende Subjekt des Mönchs vollzieht an sich selbst einen situativen Geschlechtswechsel und sieht sich etwa als Braut Christi. Die „heterosexuelle" Konstruktion gleichgeschlechtlicher Beziehungen gibt eine Kontinuität vom frühen zum hohen Mittelalter zu erkennen, die die These von der Neuheit der Liebe im 12. Jahrhundert fragwürdig erscheinen läßt. Die Liebe als diskursives Ereignis operiert schon im 9. Jahrhundert und früher mit der Geschlechterdichotomie, setzt aber gerade keine (wirklichen oder erdachten) Personen voraus, die anatomisch verschiedengeschlechtlich definiert sind. Die Kontinuität der Liebe gründet sich auf die institutionelle Kontinuität ihres Entstehungskontextes. Dabei handelt es sich, wie gezeigt wurde, um den homosozialen und homophoben Raum von Kloster und Schule, in dem der für den Liebesdiskurs konstitutive hermeneutische Denkstil tradiert wird. Unbestritten sei, daß sich im Laufe von Jahrhunderten die Artikulationsweisen und diskursiven Techniken der Liebe wandeln, doch will es scheinen, als werde die Macht der heterosexuellen Matrix dadurch nicht gebrochen. An den dargestellten mittellateinischen Texten war zu zeigen, daß das gleichgeschlechtliche Begehren eine geschlechtliche Dichotomie erzeugt. Männlichkeit und Weiblichkeit werden dadurch als eine von der Asymmetrie der Beziehung und vom sozialen Raum bedingte Konstruktion kenntlich. Jenseits von Relationen hat das Geschlecht keine Bedeutung, erst im Kontext der Beziehung wird es sinnfällig.

Quellennachweise

Alford, John A., "The Grammatical Metaphor", in: *Speculum* 57 (1982), S. 728-760.
Augustinus, *Bekenntnisse*, eingel., übers. u. erl. Joseph Bernhart, Frankfurt a. M. 1987.
Beda, *Ecclesiastical History of the English People*, hg. Bertram Colgrave u. R. A. B. Mynors, Oxford 1969.
Bernhard von Clairvaux, *Sämtliche Werke*, hg. Gerhard B. Winkler, Bd. 6, Innsbruck 1995.
Berschin, Walter, "Notkers Metrum de vita S. Galli", in: Otto P. Clavadetscher (u.a., Hg.), *Florilegium Sangallense*, St. Gallen, Sigmaringen 1980, S. 71-121.
Biblia sacra iuxta Vulgatam versionem, hg. Robert Weber, 4. Aufl., Stuttgart 1994.
Bond, Gerald, "Iocus Amoris", in: *Traditio* 42 (1986), S. 143-193.
Boswell, John, *Christianity, Social Tolerance, and Homosexuality*, Chicago, London 1980.
Braun, Christina von, *Nicht ich*, 2. Aufl., Frankfurt a. M. 1988.
Bulst, Walther, "Das Daniel-Spiel", in: ders. (Hg.), *Gegenwart im Geiste. Festschrift für Richard Benz*, Hamburg 1954, S. 82-94.
Butler, Judith, *Das Unbehagen der Geschlechter*, Frankfurt a. M. 1991.
Bynum, Caroline Walker, *Fragmentierung und Erlösung*, Frankfurt a. M. 1996.

Dinzelbacher, Peter, "Über die Entdeckung der Liebe im Hochmittelalter", in: *Saeculum* 32 (1981), S. 185-208.

Dinzelbacher, Peter, "Liebe im Frühmittelalter", in: *Zeitschrift für Literaturwissenschaft und Linguistik* 74 (1989), S. 12-38.

Dinzelbacher, Peter, "Liebe II", in: *Lexikon des Mittelalters* 5 (1991), Sp. 1965-68.

Düchting, Reinhard, "Sonderlicher denn Frauenliebe", in: Theo Stemmler (Hg.), *Homoerotische Lyrik*, Mannheim 1992, S. 89-101.

Dümmler, Ernst, "Zur Sittengeschichte des Mittelalters", in: *ZfdA* 22, 1878, S. 256 ff.

Dümmler, Ernst (Hg.), *Poetae Latini Aevi Carolini*, Bd. 2, MGH Poetae Latini 2, Berlin 1884.

Dümmler, Ernst (Hg.), *Epistolae Karolini Aevi*, Bd. 2, MGH Epistolae 4, Berlin 1895.

Eco, Umberto, *Kunst und Schönheit im Mittelalter*, München 1993.

Epp, Garrett P. J., "Learning to Write with Venus's Pen", in: Jacqueline Murray, Konrad Eisenbichler (Hg.), *Desire and Discipline*, Toronto 1996, S. 265-279.

Epp, Verena, "Männerfreundschaft und Frauendienst bei Venantius Fortunatus", in: Thomas Kornbichler, Wolfgang Maaz (Hg.), *Variationen der Liebe*, Tübingen 1995, S. 9-26.

Fichtenau, Heinrich, *Das karolingische Imperium*, Zürich 1949.

Fiske, Adele, „Alcuin and Mystical Friendship", in: *Studi medievali* 2 (1961), S. 551-575.

Flasch, Kurt, *Das philosophische Denken im Mittelalter*, Stuttgart 1986.

George, Judith W., *Venantius Fortunatus*, Oxford 1992.

Giovanni di Garlandia, *Epithalamium beate virginis Mariae*, hg. Antonio Saiani, Firenze 1995.

Gollwitzer, Helmut, *Das hohe Lied der Liebe*, 7. Aufl., München 1988.

Häring, Nikolaus M., "Die Gedichte und Mysterienspiele des Hilarius von Orléans", in: *Studi medievali* 17 (1976), S. 915-968.

Horatius Flaccus, Quintus, *Sämtliche Gedichte*, hg. Bernhard Kytzler, Stuttgart 1992.

Jaeger, C. Stephen, *The Envy of Angels*, Philadelphia 1994.

Küng, Hans, *Das Christentum. Die religiöse Situation der Zeit*, München, Zürich 1999.

Latzke, Therese, "Die Ganymed-Episteln des Hilarius", in: *Mlat. Jb.* 18 (1983), S. 131-159.

Lenzen, Rolf, "Altercatio Ganimedis et Helene", in: *Mlat. Jb.* 7 (1972), S. 161- 186.

Limbeck, Sven, "Welches Geschlecht hat das Ich?", in: Boris Körkel (u.a., Hg.), *Mentis amore ligati. Festschr. Reinhard Düchting*, Heidelberg 2001, S. 253-274.

Martialis, M. Valerius, *Epigrammata*, hg. Derek R. Shackleton Bailey, Stuttgart 1990.

Matheus Vindocinensis, *Opera*, vol. III: *Ars versificatoria*, hg. Franco Munari, Roma 1988.

McGuire, Brian Patrick, *Friendship and Community*, Kalamazoo (Mich.) 1988.

Meyer-Zwiffelhoffer, *Im Zeichen des Phallus*, Frankfurt a. M., New York 1995.

Obermayer, Hans Peter, *Martial und der Diskurs über die männliche "Homosexualität" in der Literatur der frühen Kaiserzeit*, Tübingen 1998.

Offermanns, Winfried, *Die Wirkung Ovids auf die literarische Sprache der lateinischen Liebesdichtung des 11. und 12. Jahrhunderts*, Wuppertal 1970.

Ohly, Friedrich, *Hohelied-Studien*, Wiesbaden 1958.

Ohly, Friedrich, "Vom geistigen Sinn des Wortes im Mittelalter", in: ders., *Schriften zur mittelalterlichen Bedeutungsforschung*, Darmstadt 1977, S. 1-31.

Önnerfors, Alf, "Philologisches zu Walahfrid Strabo", in: *Mlat. Jb.* 7 (1972), S. 41-92.

Ovidius Naso, P., *Metamorphosen*, hg. u. übers. von Michael von Albrecht, Stuttgart 1994.

Rahner, Hugo, "De Dominici pectoris fonte potavit", in: *Zeitschrift für katholische Theologie* 55 (1931), S. 103-108.

Riese, Alexander (Hg.), *Anthologia Latina*, Bd. 1, Leipzig 1869.

Ruhe, Ernstpeter, *De amasio ad amasiam*, München 1975.

Rupertus Tuitiensis, *De gloria et honore Filii Hominis super Mattheum*, hg. Hrabanus Haacke, Corpus Christianorum. Continuatio Mediaevalis 29, Turnhout 1979.

Schreiner, Klaus, "Er küsse mich mit dem Kuß seines Mundes", in: Hedda Ragotzky, Horst Wenzel (Hg.), *Höfische Repräsentation*, Tübingen 1990, S. 89-132.

Seneca, *Epistulae morales ad Lucilium. Liber V*, hg. u. übers. Franz Loretto, Stuttgart 1988.

Singer, Samuel, *Germanisch-romanisches Mittelalter*, Zürich, Leipzig 1935.

Stehling, Thomas, "To Love a Medieval Boy", in: *J. of Homosexuality* 8 (1983), S. 151-170.

Steinen, Wolfram von den, *Notker der Dichter und seine geistige Welt*, 2 Bde., Bern 1948.

Störmer-Caysa, Uta, *Entrückte Welten*, Leipzig 1998.

Stotz, Peter, "Dichten als Schulfach", in: *Mlat. Jb.* 16 (1981), S. 1-16.

Strecker, Karl (Hg.), *Die Cambridger Lieder*, 3. Aufl., Berlin, Zürich, Dublin 1966.

Venance Fortunat, *Poèmes*, hg. u. übers. Marc Reydellet, Bd. 2, Paris 1998.

Veyne, Paul, "Homosexualität im antiken Rom", in: Philippe Ariès (Hg.), *Die Masken des Begehrens und die Metamorphosen der Sinnlichkeit*, Frankfurt a. M. 1984, S. 40-50.

Vollmann, Benedikt Konrad (Hg.), *Carmina Burana*, Frankfurt a. M. 1987.

Vollmann, Benedikt Konrad, "O admirabile Veneris idolum – ein Mädchenlied?", in: Udo Kindermann (u.a., Hg.), *Festschrift für Paul Klopsch*, Göppingen 1988, S. 532-543.

Werner, Jakob, *Beiträge zur Kunde der lateinischen Literatur des Mittelalters*, Aarau 1905.

Williams, Craig A., *Roman Homosexuality*, New York, Oxford 1999.

Ziolkowski, Jan, *Alan of Lille's Grammar of Sex*, Cambridge, Mass. 1985.

Philipp SCHWEIGHAUSER

Concepts of Masculinity in *The Wife's Lament* and Its Critical Literature

One way of thinking about the new men's studies is to say that they are a reaction against unitary concepts of masculinity. As Ulf Reichhardt and Sabine Sielke (1998: 569) point out in their introduction to a special *Amerikastudien/American Studies* issue on masculinities, the new men's studies tend to focus on the differences within the category of 'man' rather than conceptualizing man as a unified agent of patriarchal oppression. What may sound like an antifeminist backlash is in this view much rather a concern with issues of power *within* the sexes that by no means denies the importance of interrogating power relations *between* the sexes. On the contrary, as various practitioners of men's studies (Brod 1987, Connell 1987) insist, the structures of subordination existing between different types of maculinities, for instance between 'straight' and gay men, not only reproduce structures of subordination between men and women, but are actually based on them.

This is where the notion of 'hegemonic masculinity,' as developed in Connell's *Gender and Power* (1987), comes in. Hegemonic masculinity is that form of masculinity which is widely accepted to constitute the norm for what it means to be a man. It can be defined positively as including traits such as heterosexuality, bodily strength or technical competence or negatively as excluding forms of masculinity such as those of gay men, young men, or so-called effeminate men. As the term 'hegemonic' already implies, the relation between hegemonic masculinity and other, subordinated forms of masculinity is not primarily based on violenceeven though, as in gay bashing, it may involve violencebut it is a form of "social ascendancy achieved in a play of social forces that extends beyond contests of brute power into the organization of private life and cultural processes" (Connell 1987: 184). Connell lists religious doctrine, the mass media and welfare/taxation policies among other areas of life that are crucially affected by the power differential between hegemonic and other types of masculinities (184).

A decisive move in Connell's argument is to link the structures of subordination existing between different types of masculinity to those existing between the sexes. Asking himself why the ideology of hegemonic masculinity exerts such a powerful influence over men even though few men actually correspond to that ideal, Connell comes up with an answer that relates the power differential between men directly to that between men and women: "the major reason is that most men benefit from the subordination of women, and hegemonic masculinity is the cultural expression of this ascendancy" (184f.). As Connell makes clear, hegemonic masculinity is therefore "always constructed in relation to various subordinated masculinities as well as in relation to women. The interplay between different forms of masculinity is an important part of how a patriarchal social order works" (183). What Connell describes here is probably most visible in discourses that link homosexuality with effeminacy.

In what follows, I would like to apply Connell's insights about the problematic nature of unitary and exclusionary concepts of masculinity to a re-consideration of some of the critical literature that has been built up around the Old English poem usually referred to as *The Wife's Lament*. More particularly, I want to focus on the debate surrounding the gender of the poem's narrator. I will attempt to show how critical moves that do not stop short of emending the text in an effort to exclude the possibility of a female narrator, are based on unitary concepts of masculinity that affect both men and women in similar ways. Interpretations of *The Wife's Lament* tend to disagree on some of the most basic issues, such as the number of characters in the poem, or whether the text as it is transmitted is a fragment or not.[184] A majority of critics, however, agrees that the poem reports the lament of a wife who is first left behind by her husband, who embarks on a sea-journey. She is then seized and commanded to stay in a grove dwelling under an oak tree.[185] From that unhappy abode, she curses those responsible for her present situation and laments her fate, comparing her lot to that of happy lovers and thinking back on the better days she had spent with her husband. The poem ends with the wife's gnomic statements about the sufferings of separated lovers. What can be called the standard reading of the poem is based on the assumption that the poetic speaker is identical with the woman confined to exile in the underground cave.[186] As proponents of the standard reading are ready to admit, this interpretation of the poem does not dissolve all uncertainties about the story told. For instance, it remains unclear precisely why the woman has been banished to her miserable abode. Some seek the solution to this problem in lines 42ff., where a "*geong mon*" (l. 42), a young man, is introduced, who might be the wife's lover and the reason for her being punished with solitary confinement. This lover could or could not be identical with the "*ful gemæcne monnan*" (l. 18), the fully suitable man, the wife has found after the departure of her husband.[187] As Anne L. Klink (1992: 50) has shown, such conjectures must, however, remain speculative.

A significant minority of critics has chosen not to try to compose a credible story around the wife's banishment and instead dispense with the assumption of a female protagonist and a female narrator altogether. The first to refute the possibility of a

---

[184] For a reviews of different interpretations of *The Wife's Lament*, see Renoir (1975: 236f.) and Klinck (1992: 49-54). For speculations on the number of characters involved in the poem, see Klinck (1992: 50) and Ahrens (1999).

[185] Wentersdorf (1994) argues convincingly that the mysterious "*eorðscræfe*" (l. 28) is in fact "an ancient pagan sanctuary that included a cave opening up into other caves, located at the foot or in the side of a cliff or hill, in a wooden area with a great oak on or near the top of the cliff or hill" (372).

[186] For a recent affirmation of the standard reading, see Wentersdorf (1994), who provides the following answer to the question concerning the gender of the narrator: "Detailed reexamination of the linguistic evidence regarding this question has confirmed the now traditional interpretation, that *The Wife's Lament* is indeed a woman's lamentation" (357).

[187] For interpretations along these lines, see Sieper (1915: 223) and Ahrens (1999).

female narrator was L.L. Schücking, who already in 1906 claimed in his "Das angelsächsische Gedicht von der 'Klage der Frau'" that "all difficulties [of interpretation] dissolve easily once we relinquish the idea of a female lament, which only produces a hodgepodge of contradictions" (446).[188] As all subsequent critics following in his footsteps, Schücking had to contend with the first two lines of the poem, which contain three forms with feminine endings, namely "*geomorre*" (sad), "*minre*" (my) and "*sylfre*" (self/own), that seem to suggest that the narrator is female. Schücking's solution to the problem was simply to explain away the first two lines of the poem as additions by a scribe who did not understand the meaning of the text (447). According to Schücking, the poem actually began in line three before being corrupted by a scribe:

> Hwæt! ic yrmþa gebad, siþþan ic up aweox,
> niwra oþþe ealdra, no ma þonne nu. (Schücking 1906: 447)

Furthermore, Schücking argues, all the terms of address that other critics take as referring to a husband or lover would suit better the voice of a male "*wineleas wræcca*" (l. 9), a friendless exile, commanded to stay behind while his chief went on a sea-journey. In Schücking's reading, the poetic speaker is not an wife longing for her husband, but a retainer lamenting the absence of his chief. The mysterious "*geong mon*" of line 42 is in this reading not a lover, but refers to all those young men who suffer from a fate similar to that of the narrator.

The main problem with Schücking's interpretation concerns the sheer implausibility of his attempts to attribute the feminine inflections of the first two lines to a misunderstanding on the part of a scribe. For if the presence of a female protagonist and narrator is indeed as unlikely as Schücking claims—he even calls such a reading "impossible" (440) then why should a scribe have added two lines that precisely suggest this very impossibility? Almost sixty years after Schücking's original contribution, Rudolph C. Bambas in an article entitled "Another View of the Old English 'The Wife's Lament'" (1963) tried to substantiate Schücking's thesis by asserting that a poem narrated from the point of view of a woman would be a highly unlikely oddity within the corpus of Old English poetry (308). Bambas further insisted on the unlikelihood of a (male) Anglo-Saxon minstrel impersonating a woman (304). Rather than trying to explain away the first two lines, as Schücking did, Bambas suggests scribal errors as the cause for the words with feminine inflections and proposes to emend them. His essay ends as follows:

> As much as possible, the copy of the Exeter Book should be allowed to stand, but the emendation of *geomorre* and *minre sylfre* to suit the masculine speaker intended by the poet is a necessity. The scholarly effort to sustain the concept of a feminine subject has been ingenious and learned but should yield to a simpler

---

[188] All translations from Schücking (1906) are mine.

and more probable interpretation of the poem. For another title perhaps "The Exile's Lament" would do. (309)

Apart from the apparent objection that any attempts at legitimating one's interpretation with recourse to an alleged authorial intention are at best dubious, it must also be said that Bambas's reading little more than replicates Schücking's and therefore suffers from similar limitations. The most ingenious case for a male narrator so far has been put forward by Martin Stevens in his article on "The Narrator of *The Wife's Lament*" (1968). In contrast to Schücking and Bambas, Stevens does not opt for textual surgery as a way of dealing with the ominous feminine endings, but instead proposes that "the feminine inflections may have nothing to do with the sex of the speaker" (74). Put briefly, Stevens argues that the feminine *-re* endings of the words in question do not signal natural but grammatical gender. His argument rests on the assumption that the grammatical gender of "*sið*" (lot/plight) is feminine. The inflection of *minre* is not feminine because the speaker is a woman, but because it agrees with the grammatical gender of sið. The same applies to *sylfre*, whose feminine inflection is due to grammatical agreement with *minre*. Finally, *geomorre* is not an adjective with a feminine ending, but an adverb (in Old English, most adverbs are formed by adding *-e* to an adjectival form), so that *ful geomorre* would have to be translated as 'very sadly.' Stevens's reading is far more sophisticated and grammatically accurate than either Bambas's or Schücking's. Nevertheless, it also has its problematic aspects, for it cannot entirely do without emendations - Stevens proposes to change *sið* to *siðe* - and also crucially depends on the assumption that "*sið*" is feminine, which is controversial (Mitchell 1972: 232).

But what I am interested in is less the question of whether those who suggest a male narrator are right or not - I tend to side with those favouring a female voice but find especially Martin Stevens's case for a male narrator compelling[189] - than the language the claims for a male narrator are made in. The very undecidability of the debate about the narrator's gender should prompt us to ask what exactly makes a critic opt for one position rather than the other. In other words, what desires beside the striving for scientific accuracy or at least plausibility condition a critic's preference for one theory over the other? In what follows, I will attempt to demonstrate that it is in the rhetoric of the proponents of a male narrator that we find traces of a desire that precedes and exceeds the critic's desire to come up with a plausible interpretation of the text.

---

[189] Stevens has been challenged by Bruce Mitchell (1972), who does not regard Stevens's reading as impossible but concludes that "he relies on too great a combination of improbabilities" (232), of which Mitchell lists five (grammatical agreement of *minre* and *sylfre* with *sið(e)*, emendation of *siðe* for *sið(e)*, existence of a feminine noun sið, semantic necessity of emendation, identification of *geomorre* as an adverb). Stevens has more recently been defended by Mandel (1987), whose final sentence and interpretation of the poem's final two lines fits in smoothly with my claims concerning the rhetoric of the male narrator thesis: "In a dark world, then as now, men must behave rightly regardless of the attendant sadness" (173).

Ironically enough, what has prompted me to investigate structures of desire in Schücking, Bambas and Stevens is a passage in Bambas which raises this question in relation to the other critics, i.e. the majority of critics who uphold the female narrator thesis. Towards the end of his essay, Bambas writes, "The attractions of this view are considerable. It adds some range to a body of poetry that in theme is limited and monotonous and enables the modern mind to respond sympathetically to a culture in which women and a tender love story had a place after all, if only in one poem" (308f.). If this constitutes the desire of the other critics, what, then, I was led to ask, constitutes the desires of Schücking, Bambas and Stevens? We may turn to the first paragraph of Bambas's article to begin this investigation.

It is a commonplace observation that Old English secular poetry reflects the limited attitudes and interests of a primitive warrior culture. In such a culture, the only matters worth celebrating in verse are the affairs of heroic war chiefs and the brisk young men who follow them for gold and glory. The constant themes are the worth and dignity, the fortitude, loyalty, and generosity of the fighters who defend the tribe. Peaceable churls and slaves are hardly mentioned, and women are referred to so seldom and so briefly that the prominence given to the Danish queen, Wealhþeow in *Beowulf* is considered remarkable. (303) If a line of argument is referred to in a scholarly article as "a commonplace observation," we tend to expect the article to contradict that observation. Bambas, however, does exactly the opposite. On the very next page, he evokes precisely that image of a male-dominated society as he rules out the possibility of female minstrels: "From what is known of the transmission of poetry among the early Teutons, poems were recited or chanted by male scops or minstrels at drinking festivities from which women had withdrawn in good time. Of entertainment by female minstrels nothing is known" (304). Reading Bambas, one cannot help feeling that what underlies his attempts to dispense with a female narrator is a desire to preserve an intact and unified vision of the Anglo-Saxon world as a strongly masculine culture in which women occupied only marginal spaces. A canonical version of that vision can be found in Chadwick and Chadwick's *The Growth of Literature* (1932), where the "Heroic Milieu" is characterized as revolving around the activities of warfare and drinking, with horses and armour as the most precious possessions and courage, loyalty, and strength as the primary virtues. It is a vision that has become challenged at least since Dorothy Whitelocks *Anglo-Saxon Wills* (1930) and Doris Mary Stenton's *The English Woman in History* (1957); and it is a vision that has more recently come under fierce attack by feminist scholars because of its exclusion of any kind of female experience beyond passivity, endurance and suffering. In fact, Helen Damico and Alexandra Hennessey Olsen in their introduction to *New Readings on Women in Old English Literature* (1990) single out Bambas's contribution as "the culmination of androcentricism progressing from nineteenth-century paternalism to twentieth-century misogyny" (1990: 14). That this vision of a unified masculine Anglo-Saxon culture does not only exclude women but also other forms of masculinity becomes apparent in Bambas's discussion of lines 21-23a:

Bliþe gebæro ful oft wit beotedan
þæt unc ne gedælde nemne deað ana,
owiht elles;

In blithe demeanor we two had very often vowed
that nothing but death alone would separate us two,
nothing else;

What sounds very much like a marriage vow is explained by Bambas as follows: "Lines 21-23a [...] suit the fierce loyalty that existed between a chief and his follower" (305). If we put aside for a moment the unlikelihood of *reciprocal* vows of loyalty unto death between a chief and his follower and accept that these lines are spoken by a man to man, we must still account for the affectionate tone of the passage, which expresses feelings that go beyond the loyalty a retainer owes his chief. To put it bluntly, what strikes me as peculiar about Bambas's reading of the passage is precisely that these lines do not strike him as somehow 'queer.' While I am not claiming that *The Wife's Lament* is in fact about homoerotic love, I propose that Bambas's exclusion of that very possibility in the face of this highly emotionally charged discourse between men is based on a model of hegemonic masculinity which does define itself against other forms of masculinity, such as gay men. In order to discount the possibility of a female narrator, Bambas seems to find it necessary to downplay the affectionate tone of the poem, so as to be able to read the speaker's emotions as based on his "fierce loyalty"and nothing else.

We can already see a similar mechanism at work in Schücking's article. Anticipating and trying to pre-empt objections to his arguments for a male narrator, Schücking writes, "What can certainly not be held against our view is that the tone is too sentimental for a man" (447). What seems at first sight a concession on Schücking's part that even Anglo-Saxon men were capable of emotions like sentimentality, turns into something different as we read what he has to say about proponents of the female narrator thesis. For Röder, who considers the speaker to be a wife who longs for her departed husband and eventually finds him only to be hidden away because he fears for her safety, Schücking has nothing but ridicule: "Röder's plot, however, first of all suffers from a sentimentality that is somewhat too strong even for Anglo-Saxon standards" (441). What are we to make of this? Does Schücking mean to say that Anglo-Saxons of the tenth century were a particularly sentimental people? Certainly not. When he refers to Anglo-Saxon standards, he means those of the critics whose construction of a sentimental love-story does violence to the text. That Schücking identifies this type of criticism with a specifically British type of criticism becomes clear when he pours scorn over Stopford A. Brooke's interpretation of *The Wife's Lament*. Schücking begins by quoting from Brooke's reading of lines 47ff. and then (beginning with "etc.") adds his own comments: 'Then[190] with a rapid change she thinks of her husband as exiled from her. She is not angry with himand the whole of this passage is subtly thoughtbut full of tender womanliness, full of pity that he is deprived of her. She knows, he loves her still...but he who thinks her guilty and yet loves her, o what sorrow must be his?' etc. This is not Desdemona anymore, but much rather the bad melodrama of suburban London theatre and in that sense truly most 'modern in feeling.' (445) What surfaces in Schücking's disparagement of Röder and Brooke is a profound dislike not only of British criticism, but also of British cultural production, which he both considers to be too sentimental andone may reasonably conjectureeffeminate. More specifically, Brooke and Röder become the object of Schücking's scorn because their reading of The Wife's Lament impinges on Schücking's construction of Anglo-Saxon England as a purely martial society with archaic values, and in which neither the female voice nor sentimentality had a legitimate place.[191] So when Schücking denies that the tone of the poem is too sentimental for a man, he does not mean to say that men can be sentimental, too, but on the contrary tries to explain away the sentimentality, which would not fit the unitary and exclusionary concept of Anglo-Saxon masculinity he cherishes.

Let us finally turn to Martin Stevens's case for a male narrator. As I have already pointed out, Stevens's reading is far more subtle than either Schücking's or Bambas's, and it is certainly no coincidence that the editors of New Readings on Women in Old English Literature have singled out Bambas rather than Stevens as a glaring example for twentieth-century misogyny. Nevertheless, we can detect in Stevens traces of the same desire for a unified vision of Anglo-Saxon masculinity and Anglo-Saxon culture. Stevens's remarks on what others perceive as the highly emotional tone of the poem, for instance, do not only share Schücking's rhetoric of ridiculealbeit in a much more restrained fashionbut also Bambas's unwillingness or inability to even contemplate the possibility of homosexual desire: An amusing sidelight is the point that this very same poem which according to some commentators is such a subtle expression of a woman's feelings (one critic even interprets the "dawn-care" passage as "ungratified sexual passion") can be read as a man's monologue without requiring the change of a single word. (84) Maybe the real 'amusing sidelight' is that Stevens doesn't even consider to make what appears to be the most obvious link between the suggestion of "ungratified sexual passion" and his own reading of the poem as a man's lament for the absence of another man. As in Bambas, this possibility is excluded along with the presence of the female voice. But Stevens goes further than that. In a move that should remind us of Bambas, Stevens uses the apparent absence of female worlds of

---

[190] The quote from Brooke is English in the original. Schücking's comment (starting with "etc.") is translated by the author of this article.

[191] See Helen Damico and Alexandra Hennessey Olsen's (ed.) New Readings on Women in Old English Literature for recent attempts to "temper the narrowly martial image" (15) of Anglo-Saxon England.

experience from Old English poetry[192] to support his arguments against the female narrator thesis: "The fact is that the Old English poetic vocabulary in general yields little insight into what can be called exclusively a "woman's thoughts or feelings." And "The Wife's Lament" yields none at all" (84). It is in such passages that the desire for unitary models of masculinity shared by Schücking, Bambas and Stevens merges most clearly with a desire for unitary models of femininity, i.e. for a demarcation of "what can be called exclusively a "woman's thoughts or feelings."" Such models are problematic because they are exclusionary and because they only very reluctantly allow for deviance from the norm. As Patricia A. Belanoff points out in her refutation of the argument that the vocabulary of *The Wife's Lament* does not suit a woman's voice: "Perhaps it *is* inappropriate for a woman to *folgað secan* [seek service], but perhaps the very inappropriateness creates meaning in the poem and for the speaker" (1990: 197). While I find Belanoff's reading of *The Wife's Lament* as an exercise in the Kristevan semiotic highly problematic, I share her unwillingness to accept as given the rigid and unitary models of both masculinity and femininity that inform some of the criticism of *The Wife's Lament*. Maybeand this is what I take to be an essential convergence between gender studies and the new men's studieswe need a little less insight into what makes a woman a woman and a man a man than Schücking, Bambas, and Stevens still possessed.

Sources

Ahrens, Henry, "The Wife's Lament." *The Wife's Lament: Old English and Translation,* 1999. http://ucaswww.mcm.uc.edu/english/oe/wife/lament.html (10 May 2000).

Bambas, Rudolph C., "Another View of the Old English *Wife's Lament*." *Journal of English and Germanic Philology*, 62:2 (1963), pp. 303-309.

Belanoff, Patricia A., "Women's Songs, Women's Language: *Wulf and Eadwacer* and *The Wife's Lament*." *New Readings on Women in Old English Literature*. Ed. Helen Damico and Alexandra Hennessey Olsen. Bloomington and Indianapolis Indiana University Press, 1990, pp. 193-203.

Brod, Harry, "Introduction: Themes and Theses of Men's Studies." *The Making of Masculinities: The New Men's Studies*. Ed. Harry Brod. London etc.: Allen & Unwin, 1987, pp. 1-17.

Brooke, Stopford A., *History of Early English Literature: Being the History of English Poetry from It Beginnings to the Accession of King Alfred*. Philadelphia : Richard-West, 1892.

---

[192] For a compelling attempt to reclaim a voice for Anglo-Saxon women, see Christine Fell's *Women in Anglo-Saxon England and the Impact of 1066* (1984). Fell's central claim builds on the work of Doris Stenton (1957) and states that Anglo-Saxon women enjoyed a fairly high status and independence, which deteriorated sharply only after the Norman Conquest.

Chadwick, H. Munro and K. Kershaw Chadwick, "The Heroic Milieu." *The Growth of Literature. Volume I: The Ancient Literatures of Europe*. Cambridge: Cambridge University Press, 1932, pp. 64-79.

Connell, R.W., *Gender and Power: Society, the Person and Sexual Politics*. Stanford: Stanford UP, 1987.

Damico, Helen and Alexandra Hennessey Olsen, Introduction. *New Readings on Women in Old English Literature*. Ed. Helen Damico and Alexandra Hennessey Olsen. Bloomington and Indianapolis: Indiana University Press, 1990, pp. 1-26.

Fell, Christine, *Women in Anglo-Saxon England and the Impact of 1066*. Cambridge: Colonnade, 1984.

Klink, Anne L., *The Old English Elegies: A Critical Edition and Genre Study*. Montreal etc.: McGill-Queen's University Press, 1992.

Mandel, Jerome, "The Wife's Lament." *Alternative Readings in Old English Poetry*. New York etc.: Peter Lang, 1987, pp. 149-173.

Mitchell, Bruce, "The Narrator of "The Wife's Lament.'" *Neuphilologische Mitteilungen*, 73 (1972), pp. 222-234.

Reichhardt, Ulf and Sabine Sielke, "What Does Man Want? The Recent Debates on Manhood and Masculinities." *Amerikastudien/American Studies*, 43:4 (1998), pp. 563-575.

Renoir, Alain, "A Reading Context for *The Wife's Lament*." *Anglo-Saxon Poetry: Essays in Appreciation*. Festschrift for John C. McGalliard. Ed. Lewis E. Nicholson and Dolores Warwick Frese. London: University of Notre Dame Press, 1975, pp. 224-241.

Röder, Fritz, *Die Familie bei den Angelsachsen: Eine Kultur- und Literarhistorische Studie auf Grund gleichzeitiger Quelle*. Halle 1899.

Schücking, L.L., "Das angelsächsische Gedicht von der 'Klage der Frau.'" *Zeitschrift für deutsches Altertum und deutsche Literatur*, 48 (1906), pp. 436-449.

Sieper, Ernst, *Die altenglische Elegie*. Strassburg: Trübner, 1915.

Stenton, Doris Mary, *The English Woman in History*. London: George Allen & Unwin, 1957.

Stevens, Martin. "The Narrator of 'The Wife's Lament.'" *Neuphilologische Mitteilungen*, 69 (1968), pp. 72-90.

Wentersdorf, Karl P., "The Situation of the Narrator in the Old English *Wife's Lament*." *Old English Shorter Poems: Basic Readings*. Ed. Katherine O'Brien O'Keefe. New York and London: Garland, 1994, pp. 357-392.

Whitelock, Dorothy, ed. *Anglo-Saxon Wills*. Cambridge: Cambridge University Press, 1930.

Ladina BEZZOLA LAMBERT

The Consumed Image: Male Friendship in Montaigne and Bacon

In their collections of essays, both Montaigne and Bacon devote one of their longer essays to the subject of friendship—specifically, *male* friendship. Bacon's essay followed the one by Montaigne within only a few decades,[193] but the pictures of male friendship which the two texts present differ radically from each other. Montaigne's account of his intimate friendship with the late Étienne de la Boétie faithfully follows the protocol of *amicitia perfecta* established in classical theories of friendship for what was believed to be the highest level human friendship could reach. According to these theories, perfect friendship has no purpose, or rather its purpose is claimed to lie solely in itself: the men participating in such a friendship were expected to become better and wiser men through the experience of their friendship. Bacon, by contrast, offers practical advice regarding the most profitable use a man can make of his friends. He discusses friendship in the strictly economic terms of return on investment.

Yet beside these differences there are also interesting correspondences. One of them is the importance attributed to the friend's image as well as metaphors relating to portraits and to painting more generally. By focusing on the use of the image and pictorial metaphors in the two essays, I would like to show how the presence of the friend in text or image defines the speaker's identity in as much as in the contemplation of his friend he finds himself. As we will see, the image of the friend is however ultimately consumed by the text or by the other's gaze to ensure the main protagonist's survival in history. The primary function of the friend, it turns out, is that of a foil against which the man establishes himself.

Before I try to substantiate this claim, it will be necessary to review some of the most prominent aspects of the classical texts on friendship familiar at the time, at least to the extent that they are relevant to our topic. This will show which of the ideas put forth by Montaigne and Bacon (yet especially by the former) were part of a canon of ideas on the subject.

---

[193] Montaigne's *Essais* were first published in 1580 and substantially expanded and revised in 1588. The first published version of Bacon's essay "On Friendship" appeared in 1612; (it was not part of the earliest edition of Bacon's *Essays* published in 1597, which only included ten very short essays). The last edition of the *Essays* that appeared in Bacon's life-time was published in 1625. Bacon added many new essays in this edition and revised and expanded most of the existing ones. As Michael Kiernan argues in the introduction to his edition of the *Essays*, Bacon probably knew the French version of the *Essais* by Montaigne at first hand, but he does not mention Montaigne until the 1625 edition, when he paraphrases him in "On Truth". While Bacon's essays clearly differ both in style and thought from those of his French predecessor, "Bacon is the first writer to use Montaigne's title in English to designate the brief prose piece" (xlviii).

The two most influential classical texts on friendship are Aristotle's *Nicomachean Ethics*, books 8 and 9, and Cicero's *Laelius: De amicitia*. Whereas Aristotle offers his ideas on friendship as general observations in a treatise, Cicero uses dialogue form. He assumes the voice of Laelius to relate the latter's personal experience of a "glorious friendship" that united him with the recently deceased Scipio Africanus. Next to the argument proper, Cicero's text had a great influence on later writers for the way it established a genre: the use of dialogue form set a major literary model for both medieval and Renaissance writers on friendship. Moreover, by focusing on a friendship that has been disrupted through the death of one participant, Cicero's text strikes an elegiac note and moves friendship into the realm of memory rather than referring to it as a living relationship (Weller: 1978, 504). When Montaigne evokes his friend La Boétie from the dead, he too refers to friendship in the memorial mode.

An important characteristic of the classical concept of *amicitia perfecta*, or friendship of the highest order, is its exclusivity: it is reserved for an elite of virtuous and socially privileged men and is limited to two or a small number of participants. Moreover, perfect friendship "is characterized by nearly equal degrees of reciprocal esteem and benevolence and nearly the same good character in both parties" (Hyatte: 1994, 17). It turns out that friendship between virtuous men is sought on account of the similarities—the near identity even—of the parties involved. According to Cicero, "friendship is nothing else than an accord in all things, human and divine, conjoined with goodwill and affection" (131). True friends become mirror images of each other: "he who looks upon a true friend, looks as it were upon a sort of image of himself" (*ibid.*, 133). Despite the frequently repeated argument that true friendship must radically resist interest,[194] such friendship has a clear goal: it aims at self-improvement. The path there leads over the contemplation of the friend's image which turns into an act of self-contemplation.

> The excellent friend sees in his nearly equal partner an alter ego, a mirror of his own virtue and a source of self-knowledge, but the image that he beholds is not static: as he watches his partner improve through his beneficent assistance, he sees the reflection of his own self-betterment, of his increased virtue. (Reginald Hyatte, 18)

This works reciprocally.—True friends are thus rivals in virtue. This is why perfect friendship is essentially defined by self-love: "the true friend loves himself, and he desires his own betterment through self-knowledge" (*ibid.*).

To close this list, I would like to draw attention to one more aspect of perfect friendship as it is defined in these theories, an aspect which, though not mentioned explicitly, is nonetheless incontestably present: the *textual* quality of *amicitia perfecta*. Pairs like Orestes and Pylades, Theseus and Pirithous, Damon and Phintias, which

---

[194] See for example Langer (1994), especially chapter 5 "Morose Nostalgia, Interest, and the End of Friendship".

appear time and again in classical texts, were stock examples of friendship to the point of being proverbial. Many instances of perfect friendship in fact owe their existence largely to repeated acts of retelling. A good example is the story of the friendship between Palamon and Arcite related in Boccaccio's *Teseida*, which is retold in Chaucer's "Knight's Tale" and later used as a source by Shakespeare for *The Two Noble Kinsmen*, to be rehashed yet again by Dryden into a poem in heroic couplets. Similarly, Cicero introduces his own account of the friendship between Laelius and Scipio with no less than two framing narratives.—All these friendships depend primarily, if not exclusively, on an endless chain of textual regurgitations. The association of friendship and text and, more specifically, textual monuments is thus fundamental to the concept of perfect friendship. Before we turn to Montaigne, whose idea of perfect friendship in many points directly imitates the classical model of *amicitia perfecta*, let me summarize the classical features of perfect friendship presented so far:

(1) exclusivity and masculinity
(2) the close resemblance or identity of friends
(3) self-contemplation
(4) rivalry in attaining excellence in virtue
(5) the textual nature of friendship

In "De l'amitié", Montaigne draws a clear distinction between a perfect friendship, like the one he experienced with Étienne de la Boétie, and various other close relationships connecting human beings, such as filial affection, fraternal love, love for women, and others. Perfect friendship, he argues, is a thing most rare. It can only include two participants and it only exists between men. Montaigne argues that women by nature lack the kind of commitment and spiritual strength perfect friendship requires, but suggests that if women were fit for the task, a perfect friendship between man and woman would be likely to be even more fulfilling than one between two men, because it could satisfy both mind and body. Yet such a relationship between the sexes remains a fantasy of Montaigne's rather than a hope, for, as his discussion of friendship shows, one of the most fundamental qualities in the kind of perfect friendship he dreams up is the near identity (both in physical and social terms) of the two friends. That this could occur between two members of different sex, was unthinkable at the time.

When he finally turns to his friendship with La Boétie, Montaigne does not have much to say about the actual quality of their friendship except for the observation that he and his friend were one. His relationship with La Boétie thus confirms Aristotle's definition of friendship as one soul in two bodies, a definition he quotes in his text. Indeed, the fusion of the two men is claimed to be so complete as to leave no "seam" (*couture*, 318). Montaigne calls his friend "celui qui n'est pas autre, c'est moi" (323). He is I.

And yet it has repeatedly been suggested that the whole of Montaigne's *Essais* is first and foremost an *hommage* to the "other", his friend La Boétie. The most obvious reverential gesture toward La Boétie is, however, also the most ambiguous: In his famous introduction to the essay, Montaigne compares his work to a mannerist painting where the artist reserves the central spot for the painting that displays the crown of his artistry. The empty space surrounding this spot is filled up with so-called *crotesques*, monstrous creations of fancy (*peintures fantasques*, 310), whose only charm lies in their strangeness and diversity. Montaigne's own *Essais*, so the author suggests, are nothing but such grotesque and fanciful creations. The realization of the center-piece itself exceeds his abilities. For this reason, he has decided to borrow a text from his revered friend, La Boétie, which will occupy this place with dignity. The text is called *Discours de la servitude volontaire* and it is written "like an essay" (*par manière d'essai*, 310). La Boétie's text was to be placed at the exact center of the first book of Montaigne's *Essais*, thus representing the work's core while Montaigne's own essays were to serve as its ornamental frame. Yet—notoriously—the *Discours* is suppressed. Toward the end of the essay, Montaigne returns to the subject of the *Discours* with the explanation that he has decided not to offer it in this place since he has found out that it has already been published by political radicals with evil designs on the state. Instead of the serious *Discours*, Montaigne decides to give the place of honor to a more carefree work by La Boétie: to twenty-nine of his sonnets. Ironically and, of course, also significantly, these sonnets too are suppressed in the 1588 and subsequent editions of the *Essais*.

Why then should Montaigne draw his readers' attention so emphatically to a text he finally chooses to omit? The answers to this question that critics have come up with range from Montaigne's alleged political prudence to the argument that he invokes La Boétie's texts in order to efface them (Conley: 1998, 68).—If we consider the explosive contents of the *Discours*, the argument that its omission in the *Essais* is to be attributed to Montaigne's political prudence appears convincing: La Boétie's *Discours* sets out to ask why men and women of his time allow themselves to be cheated and oppressed, why they meekly turn over the fruits of their labor to worthless overlords, why they are everywhere in subjection. "The young La Boétie has in effect conceived the idea of nonviolent resistance": "The people need only reclaim what is theirs and they will be free" (Greenblatt: 1989, 226). This has led critics to conclude that in the embittered climate of France's religious wars, La Boétie's work seems dangerous to Montaigne.

However, the motive of political prudence becomes questionable when in his essay on cannibals, which almost immediately follows the chapter of the sonnets and shows interesting connections to the essay on friendship, Montaigne includes a version of La Boétie's social critique without paying tribute to his friend. Instead of referring to La Boétie, Montaigne presents this critique as a critical observation made by a visitor from what his narrow-minded contemporaries are wont to call a "barbarous" country. Montaigne has thus appropriated his friend's arguments and turned it into his own fictitious creation.—Assuming, then, that Montaigne invokes his friend's writings only to efface their author, let us look more closely at how this *effacement* is brought about. As we shall see, it is offered in the form of a critique of inadequate portraiture and the claim to replace it with a genuine counterfeit.

We should note first of all that the effacement is not total, for Montaigne "does not efface the traces of his altered intention" (Greenblatt: 1989, 227). The essay retains a scar at the point where La Boétie's *Discours* was to have been inserted or, to return to Montaigne's own metaphor: it leaves that 'seam' (the *couture*) which the total fusion of the two friends has allegedly made invisible. With regard to the texts, which survive their authors, the *merger* of the two men (to speak in anachronistic terms) has thus not been completely accomplished. Indeed, both the essay on friendship and the introduction to the sonnets that follows it, constantly emphasize the juxtaposition of La Boétie's texts with Montaigne's own. At the same time, the superiority of La Boétie's work over that of his friend becomes increasingly uncertain.

Right after his enthusiastic praise of La Boétie's *Discours* in the introduction, Montaigne explains that, after all, the *Discours* is still the work of a very young man. He therefore concedes that it does not represent the best work his friend would have been capable of. Indeed, had La Boétie, at a riper age, taken upon himself the kind of task Montaigne himself performs in his *Essais*, that is, had he written down all the products of his fancy (*ses fantaisies*, 311), the result would have been worthy of the Ancients. Montaigne is thus suggesting that his friend's true potential could only have been realized in the kind of project in which he himself is involved. Interestingly enough, Montaigne here refers to the enterprise of recording one's thoughts in terms strikingly similar to his reference to the *crotesques* earlier on, which he defined as *peintures fantasques*. While there the term was used depreciatively, here the reference denotes the highest form of praise. As a result, the frame formed by Montaigne's *Essais* gradually moves into center focus while the work of his friend is pushed into the margins. The essay in praise of a friendship that, at least to its audiences, is largely textual, thus becomes the site of a competition between texts.

Toward the end of the essay, Montaigne suggests that we ought to consider the *Discours* simply as a juvenile 'exercise' (*par manière d'exercitation seulement*, 327) rather than a serious work. La Boétie's 'essay' (the genre attributed to his text earlier on) has now been downgraded to an 'exercise', a piece clearly not meant for publication. Montaigne dedicates La Boétie's twenty-nine sonnets to the *Comtesse de Guissen*. The dedication begins as follows: "Madam, I am not offering you here any of my own works, partly because you own them already, partly because I can't find anything among them that would be worthy of you. But I wanted that these verses, wherever they are seen, carry your name in their title ..."[195] or, literally, 'carry your name in their *head*': *portassent votre nom en tête*.—Not only does Montaigne here repeat his by now even less convincing gesture of modesty and at the same time bring his own texts into focus, he moreover replaces the friend's head/image with that of the Comtesse.

The fact that the *Discours* is replaced by the twenty-nine sonnets is significant. Whereas this *Discours*, written *en manière d'essai*, invited comparison with Montaigne's

---

[195] My own translation of the original: *"Madame, je ne vous offre rien du mien, ou parce qu'il est déja vôtre, ou pource que je n'y trouve rien digne de vous. Mais j'ai voulu que ces vers, en quelque lieu qu'ils se vissent, portassent votre nom en tête"* (329).

Essais even as it was said to surpass these by far, the sonnets belong to an entirely different genre. They are therefore not likely to enter into competition with the *Essais*. The sonnets, though no doubt fresh and beautiful, rather resemble an ornamental addition. Indeed, they resemble the kind of ornamental frame of *crotesques* with which Montaigne's painter used to adorn his masterpiece. Accordingly, the roles of the frame and the core are reversed and La Boétie's work, first introduced as the masterpiece to which the *Essais* can only serve as introduction, is turned into a nice, but negligible ornamental flourish. (Its negligibility has been proven by the fact that it is omitted in most publications of the *Essais*).—But what is in the central picture? Hardly the portrait of the Comtesse? Rather, what we find there is the subject of the *Essais* themselves, Montaigne *tout nu*—the portrait he wishes to be remembered by: The painting metaphor used in the essay on friendship links this essay to the Preface, where the same metaphor is used repeatedly. As Montaigne insists: "it is myself that I am painting [...] I am myself the subject matter of my book".[196] And as though weary of the restrictive conventions and formalities his cultural surroundings force on him, he muses: "Had I been among those nations which are said to live still in the sweet freedom of the first laws of nature, I assure thee, reader, I would have gladly painted myself whole and stark naked."[197]—Is it possible that he also means the conventions that force him to deck his work with another man's sonnets?

But let us turn to Bacon to see what use he suggests a man should make of his friends. We shall see that his essay on friendship effaces the friend's image in a way strikingly similar to the effacement of La Boétie we witness in Montaigne's text. John Miller has argued that in contrast to Bacon's writings concerned with his scientific project, a project that concerns a joint enterprise not subject to time constraints, "the *Essays* address the needs of a single concrete self, bounded by time and space, and ambitious to achieve concrete results within those bounds." The problem this self has to confront is the scarcity of time: life is short. As a consequence, "efficiency becomes a paramount concern" (Miller: 1995, 340-41).

In the essay on friendship, Bacon is primarily concerned with how a man may best organize the economy of the self and transcend his image beyond the limited time and space allotted to him. Loneliness, as Bacon points out at the beginning of the essay, is omnipresent even in the most crowded places. He puts this in a memorable and frequently quoted phrase with Biblical overtones: "For a Crowd is not Company; And Faces are but a Gallery of Pictures; And Talke but a *Tinckling Cymball*, where there is no *Love*" (81; italics in the original).—The phrase alludes to a passage in 1 Corinthians 13 which reads: "Though I speak with the tongues of men and of angels, and have not charity, I am become as sounding brass, or a tinkling cymbal." However, the biblical allusion is misleading. Bacon's idea of friendship has nothing to do with charity, or to put it cynically, it only concerns charity toward the self. As regards the gallery of

---

[196] *"c'est moi que je peins [...] je suis moi-même la matière de mon livre"* (45)

[197] *"Que si j'eusse été entre ces nations qu'on dit vivre encore sous la douce liberté des premières lois de nature, je t'assure que je m'y fusse très volontiers peint tout entier, et tout nu."* (ibid.).

pictures, we will see that it has quite a different significance from what one would expect.

Friendship for Bacon is wholly functional. He defines three principal "fruits" of friendship: The ideal friend is first of all "a confessor, an anonymous receptacle of potentially dangerous passions, into which the overflowings of the self are vented and in which they are contained in secrecy" (Miller: 1995, 358). Yet, more importantly for our context, a friend serves as a screen onto which the self may project his thoughts. In this second function of a friend, Bacon sees the saying of Themistocles confirmed which holds that *"speech [is] like Cloth of Arras, opened, and put abroad; Whereby the* imagery *doth appeare in Figure; whereas in Thoughts, they lie but as in Packs"* (84, emphasis and adaptation mine; italics in the original). According to Bacon, the friendless man has something beastly about him for he devours himself: "Those that want *Friends* to open themselves unto, are Canniballs of their owne *Hearts*" (83, italics in the original). It is in the friend that a man recognizes who he is. A friendless man equals men *"that looke sometimes into a Glasse, and presently forget their own Shape, and Favour"*—'favour' meaning 'features' (85). The Christian notion that the contemplation of God reveals to man, who has been created in God's image, both his origin and identity, is here transferred onto the friend. The image of the friend allows the self to recognize his humanity and his identity. Yet since the friend acts as a mirror, the contemplation of the friend turns into the contemplation of the self.

To return to the gallery of pictures mentioned at the beginning of Bacon's essay, it becomes clear that the aim of friendship in the Baconian mode would be to turn the anonymous picture gallery into a gallery representing the self. That the aim of friendship is to create at least one lasting portrait of the self, is suggested by the third fruit of friendship. Here the friend's function is that of the self's deputy, able to act in the interest of the self where the latter cannot do so himself: after his death or where modesty prevents it. A friend takes care of the self's unfinished business as well as his reputation. He carries his image into the world. To sum up, friendship as it is formulated in these texts is an art; and the artifact produced is the self.

Sources

Bacon, Francis, *The Essayes of Counsels, Civill and Morall*, Michael Kiernan (ed.), Oxford 1995.

Cicero, *De senectute, de amicitia, de divinatione*, William Armistead Falconer (ed.), London and Cambridge, MA 1959.

Conley, Tom, "Friendship in a Local Vein: Montaigne's Servitude to La Boétie", in: *South Atlantic Quarterly* 97:1 (1998), pp. 65-90.

Greenblatt, Stephen, "Anti-Dictator", in: Denis Hollier (ed.), *A New History of French Literature*, Cambridge, MA 1989, pp. 223-8.

Hyatte, Reginald, *The Arts of Friendship. The Idealization of Friendship in Medieval and Early Renaissance Literature*, Leiden 1994.

Langer, Ullrich, *Perfect Friendship. Studies in Literature and Moral Philosophy from Boccaccio to Corneille*, Geneva 1994.

Miller, John J., "'Pruning by Study': Self-Cultivation in Bacon's *Essays*", in: *Papers on Language and Literature* 31:4 (1995), pp. 340-61.

Montaigne, Michel de, *Essais de Michel de Montaigne*, 3 vols., André Tournon (ed.), Paris 1998, vol. 1.

Weller, Barry, "The Rhetoric of Friendship in Montaigne's *Essais*", in: *New Literary History* IX:3 (1978), pp. 503-23.

Joachim PFEIFFER

"... in eurem Bunde der Dritte". Männerfreundschaften in der Literatur des 18. Jahrhunderts

1. Einleitende Überlegungen

Das 18. Jahrhundert ist das Jahrhundert der Freundschaft - diese These ist in Literaturwissenschaft und Soziologie immer wieder vertreten worden.[198] So zutreffend diese Behauptung auch sein mag, so verlangt sie doch nach einer Differenzierung; denn Freundschaft ist in den schriftlichen Zeugnissen des 18. Jahrhunderts auf sehr unterschiedliche Weise codiert worden. Ich möchte in meinem Beitrag diesen unterschiedlichen Codierungen der Freundschaft nachgehen, aber auch den Brechungen und Verwerfungen, die dieser Begriff - oft unbeachtet von der Literaturgeschichte - erfahren hat. Nicht zuletzt soll auch die Frage gestellt werden, warum Freundschaft im 18. Jahrhundert als öffentlich wahrnehmbares und schriftlich fassbares Phänomen weitgehend eine Domäne der Männer geblieben ist.

2. Drei Beispiele der Freundschaft im 18. Jahrhundert

Ich beginne mit drei Beispielen, die für drei unterschiedliche Formen des Freundschaftskultes im 18. Jahrhundert stehen. Das *erste* Beispiel: Zwei befreundete Dichter verfassen in einem abgelegenen Landhaus satirische Gedichte, um sich gegen ihre zahlreichen Gegner zu wehren. Dieses "tolle Wagestück", wie sie es selbst nennen (Wild: 1999), wird zu einem Rundumschlag gegen alle und jeden - und schließlich zu einem Literaturskandal erster Klasse. Die gemeinsame Arbeit scheint den beiden außerordentliches Vergnügen zu bereiten, was aus einem zeitgenössischen Zeugnis hervorgeht. Zwei Damen, die mit den Dichtern befreundet sind, halten sich im Erdgeschoss des Landhauses auf und legen folgendes Zeugnis ab:

> [Sie] hörten über sich in der Dachkammer die Stimmen der dichtenden Freunde. In kürzeren oder längeren Pausen ertönte ein schallendes Gelächter, zuweilen von sehr vernehmlichem Fußstampfen begleitet. Wenn die Herren um 12 Uhr zum Mittagessen herunter kamen, waren sie äußerst aufgeräumt, und sagten mehr als einmal: Heute sind die Philister wieder tüchtig geärgert worden. (zit. nach Wild: 1999, 145 f.)

---

[198]. In literaturwissenschaftlicher Hinsicht findet sich die These vor allem bei Meyer-Krentler: 1984. Diesem Buch verdankt der vorliegende Beitrag wichtige Einsichten. In soziologischer Hinsicht ist besonders zu erwähnen Tenbruck: 1964.

Beim *zweiten* Beispiel handelt es sich um ein Gedicht. Ein Tyrannenmord schlägt fehl, der Attentäter wird auf frischer Tat ertappt und zum Tod verurteilt. Wegen einer dringenden Familienangelegenheit bekommt er einen Aufschub von drei Tagen, unter der Bedingung, dass sein Freund ihn vorübergehend vertritt und bereit ist, den Tod auf sich zu nehmen, falls der Verurteilte selbst nicht rechtzeitig zurückkehrt. Diese Rückkehr gelingt buchstäblich in letzter Sekunde, die Freunde fallen sich unter dem Kreuz gerührt in die Arme: "In den Armen liegen sich beide, / Und weinen für Schmerzen und Freude". Der Tyrann ist so beeindruckt von dem Exempel freundschaftlicher Treue, dass er den Attentäter begnadigt und sich dem Freundschaftsbund anschließt. Und noch ein *drittes* Beispiel: Um die Mitte des 18. Jahrhunderts schreibt ein Dichter an einen anderen, nachdem beide sich unter Schmerzen getrennt haben:

Alles hab' ich bey Ihrem Abschiede empfunden, was ein Liebhaber empfinden kann, selbst die kleinen Umstände nicht ausgenommen, die für ihn [den Liebhaber] so interessant sind. (Rasch: 1936, 208)

Wir erfahren leider nicht, was die "kleinen Umstände" sind, die sicher nicht nur für den Liebhaber, sondern auch für uns interessant gewesen wären. Dafür wird der Briefeschreiber nun ganz lyrisch und fährt mit folgendem Vergleich fort:

So steht die junge Braut,
Wenn, nach den ersten Küssen,
Ihr Schäfer sich von ihr entfernen müssen,
Vor einer Hütte still, die sie mit ihm erbaut. (Rasch: 1936, 208 f.)

Wohlgemerkt, es handelt sich hier um eine Männerfreundschaft. Diese Freundschaft wird - im Rückgriff auf literarische Traditionen - in die Sphäre des Erotischen hinübergeführt.

3. Die Autoren

Diese drei Beispiele illustrieren drei unterschiedliche Paradigmen des Freundschaftskultes im 18. Jahrhundert, und sie belegen seine differentiellen Codierungen: Hinter dem ersten Beispiel verbergen sich Goethe und Schiller, die stampfend und gleichsam schenkelklopfend ihre *Xenien* (1796) verfassen, um sich damit gegen ihre zahlreichen Feinde zu verbünden. Goethe und Schiller : eine der vielen Gelehrtenfreundschaften in der zweiten Jahrhunderthälfte. Bei dieser Freundschaft handelt es sich weitgehend - wenn auch nicht ausschließlich - um ein Zweckbündnis, das in den Briefen nur selten von emotionalen Ausbrüchen begleitet wird. Das zweite Beispiel stammt aus Schillers Ballade *Die Bürgschaft* (1798): ein Freund ist bereit, des Anderen Stelle auf dem Richtplatz einzunehmen; und der Andere ist so treu, dass er den Freund nicht im Stich lässt, sondern zum Ort der Hinrichtung zurückkehrt. Dieses Tugendmodell der Freundschaft ist von einer pädagogischen Absicht begleitet, und zugleich ist es in eine empfindsame Szenerie mit Tränen und Umarmungen eingebettet; insofern entspricht es der tugendempfindsamen Freundschaft, wie sie sich in der mittleren Aufklärung (zwischen 1740 und 1780) entwickelt hat. Im dritten Beispiel wird die Freundschaftdichtung zur Liebespoesie, sie wird erotisch besetzt: Dabei bedient sich die mann-männliche Liebe des Inventars der Schäferpoesie, der spielerisch-zärtlichen Liebe zwischen Mann und Frau. Der Brief, aus dem ich zitiert habe, stammt von Johann Georg Jacobi und ist an Johann Wilhelm Ludwig Gleim gerichtet (Näheres bei Rasch: 1936, 181 ff.). Schon im 18. Jahrhundert rief dieser erotisch aufgeladene Freundschaftsdiskurs Verunsicherung hervor, und selbst die gegenwärtige Literaturwissenschaft ignoriert diese erotische Spielart oder geht ihr aus dem Weg, selbst da, wo sie sich bei den Klassikern findet.

4. Paradigmen des Freundschaftskultes im 18. Jahrhundert

4.1 Freundschaft als Zweckbündnis

Schauen wir uns die drei Beispiele noch einmal genauer an. Zunächst die Freundschaft zwischen Goethe und Schiller: Die "Einübung" in diese Freundschaft erfolgte vor allem über den Briefverkehr - der Brief ermöglichte es, auch über Landesgrenzen hinweg Freundschaften zu begründen und zu erhalten, ja sogar, wie im Fall des Kreises um Gleim, ganze Netze von Freundschaften zu knüpfen. Dichter-Freundschaften waren oft Zweckbündnisse im literarischen Kampf - in diesem Sinn sind sie eher an der frühen Aufklärung orientiert (zum Teil auch an den ständischen Freundschaftsbeziehungen des Barock), weniger an dem tugendempfindsamen Programm der mittleren Aufklärung (die ab ca. 1740 einsetzte). Zwar enthält dieser frühe Freundschaftsdiskurs auch ethische Imperative (z.B. Verpflichtung zu gegenseitiger Hilfe und Treue), aber er ist noch nicht zum flächendeckenden Programm bürgerlicher Sozialität geworden. Jetzt überwiegt noch ganz der pragmatische Aspekt, die Zweckorientierung. So schreibt Crusius, ein Professor der Leipziger Universität, noch 1744 in seiner *Anweisung vernünftig zu leben*, Freundschaft sei "diejenige Vereinigung der Gemüther [...], welche eine genauere wechselweise Beförderung der Privatabsichten einzelner Personen zum Zwecke hat". (Meyer-Krentler: 1984, 29) Der *Politische Philosophus*, eine Schrift aus dem Jahr 1714, entwickelt eine Freundschafts-Programmatik, die sich fast wie eine bürgerliche Anleitung zum Erfolg liest. Wichtig sei, so heißt es darin, daß du in jeder von denen fünff Haupt-Facultäten einen rechten Hertzens-Freund haben mögest, nemlich (1) einen rechtschaffenen Theologum, theoreticum & practicum. Denn dieser kan dich so wohl in Religions-Streitigkeiten gründlich informiren, als auch zum thätigen Christenthum aufmuntern, und durch seinen Exemplarischen Wandel anfrischen. (2) Einen Juristen. Dieser kan dir in Contracten und in Processen guten Rath geben. (3) Einen Medicum. Dieser kan dich belehren, wie du deine Gesundheit erhalten, und denen Kranckheiten vorbauen, auch die verlohrne Gesundheit bald wieder erlangen könnest. (4) Einen Philosophum, theoreticum & practicum. Denn dieser kan dich wieder die abergläubische Furcht, welche die Unwissenheit der natürlichen Ursachen zur Mutter hat, bewaffnen: er kan dich auch in der Moral und Politic auf den rechten Grund führen. (5) Einen Oeconomum. Dieser kan dich anweisen, wie du etwas erwerben, und mit dem erworbenen recht umgehen sollest. (Meyer-Krentler: 1984, 28) Der Nutzen solcher Freundschafts-Kontakte leuchtet unmittelbar ein. Die utilitaristische Ausrichtung des Bürgertums wird darin sichtbar: der pragmatisch-vernünftige Aspekt dominiert alles Affektive. Aus diesem Zitat geht jedoch auch hervor, wie elitär der sich entwickelnde Freundschaftskult ist: Er ist eine Angelegenheit des gehobenen Bürgertums, der Akademiker, Dichter und Kritiker, nicht der breiteren Volksschichten.

4.2 Tugendempfindsame Freundschaft als sozialethisches Programm

Ab der Mitte des 18. Jahrhunderts wird der Freundschaftskult zum Katalysator sozialethischer Ideale. Über eine "wechselseitige Beförderung der Privatabsichten" geht Schillers Ballade *Die Bürgschaft* weit hinaus. Schiller lässt hier die Freundes-Tugend das erreichen, was die Revolution (d.h. die revolutionäre Tat des Tyrannenmords) nicht erreichen konnte: Freiheit, Gleichheit, Brüderlichkeit, die Demokratisierung des Tyrannen, der schließlich zum Freund und Genossen wird:

Und blicket sie lange verwundert an,
Drauf spricht er: Es ist euch gelungen,
Ihr habt das Herz mir bezwungen,
Und die Treue, sie ist doch kein leerer Wahn,
So nehmet auch mich zum Genossen an,
Ich sei, gewährt mir die Bitte,
In eurem Bunde der Dritte. (Schiller I, 356)

Ob dieser schnelle Gesinnungswandel eines Tyrannen überzeugt, ist eine andere Frage; immerhin war von ihm gerade noch als "Wütherich" die Rede, und für die Freundschaft hatte er nur Häme und Spott übrig. Auffällig aber ist etwas anderes: Aus dieser Ballade spricht die immense öffentliche Bedeutung, die der Freundschaft in der zweiten Hälfte des 18. Jahrhunderts zugemessen wurde. Freundschaft wird in Schillers Ballade fast zum politischen Programm, zum Verhaltensmodell für Herrscher und Politiker. Sie ist bei Schiller zum Träger eines sittlichen Ideals geworden: Die Freunde sind so sehr vom Sittengesetz durchdrungen, dass sie auch nicht einen Moment unsicher oder schwankend werden (vgl. Stenzel: 1984, 177). Innere Kämpfe finden nicht statt. Es gibt nur äußere Hindernisse, die den Verurteilten von der zügigen Rückkehr abhalten, keine inneren. Es ist bezeichnend, dass Schiller die *äußeren* Hindernisse gegenüber der historischen Vorlage (die Ballade geht auf eine Sammlung römischer Geschichten aus dem zweiten Jahrhundert nach Christus zurück) noch um zwei vermehrt hat; dadurch hat er die Spannung, aber auch die Entschiedenheit des Helden beträchtlich gesteigert: Neben dem Unwetter kommen dem Verurteilten nun auch noch eine Räuberbande und ein "glühender Brand" in die Quere. Jeder sollte verstehen: Die Idealität der Freundschaft siegt über die rohe Natur. Die Freundschaft versinnbildlicht hier die Idee der Humanität, und sie dient als pädagogisches Exempel. Entscheidender Katalysator für die pädagogische Wirkung ist die Rührung, in die die Freunde, das Volk, der König und wahrscheinlich auch der Leser versetzt werden. Der Wirkungsaspekt wird im Gedicht selbst thematisiert:

> Und Erstaunen ergreifet das Volk umher,
> In den Armen liegen sich beide,
> Und weinen für Schmerzen und Freude.
> Da sieht man kein Auge thränenleer,
> Und zum Könige bringt man die Wundermähr,
> Der fühlt ein menschliches Rühren,
> Läßt schnell vor den Thron sie führen. (Schiller I, 356)

Hier haben sich empfindsame Gefühlsintensität und aufklärerische Sozialethik im Programm der Freundschaft verbunden. Freundschaft ist in der mittleren Aufklärung zu einer bürgerlichen Sozialutopie geworden, deren Funktion darin besteht, den Individualisierungsschub der Aufklärung durch Sozialität auszubalancieren. Gegen den schrankenlosen Individualismus setzt der Freundschaftskult, jedenfalls in der Theorie, eine bündisch-föderative Utopie; erhofft wird die Geburt eines sozialen Individuums aus dem Geist der Freundschaftsgruppe, auch über ständische Schranken hinweg. Öffentliches und privates Verhalten soll zur Deckung gebracht werden, aufklärerisches Sozialethos und empfindsame Gefühlskultur sollen eine glückliche Verbindung eingehen. Die Strömung der Empfindsamkeit, die sich ab etwa 1740 unter dem Einfluss des Pietismus entwickelt, trägt wesentlich zur Emotionalisierung des aufklärerisch-vernünftigen Freundschaftsideals bei. Selbst Lessing scheint in der Sphäre der Freundschaft die Unmittelbarkeit der Empfindung der kalten Diskursivität der Sprache vorzuziehen. So heißt es in dem Gedicht *Abschied eines Freundes*:

> Erwarte nicht ein täuschend Wortgepränge,
> Für unsre Freundschaft viel zu klein.
> Empfindung haßt der Reime kalte Menge,
> Und wünscht unausposaunt zu sein.
>
> Ein feuchter Blick sind ihre Zaubertöne;

Ein schlagend Herz ihr rührend Lied.
Sie schweigt beredt, sie stockt, sie stammelt schöne,
Ums stärkre Wort umsonst bemüht. (Lessing I, 135)

Die Sprache des Körpers (der Blick, das schlagende Herz, die Tränen) scheint hier das symbolische Sprachzeichen ganz verdrängen zu wollen. Mit der empfindsamen Auffüllung des aufklärerischen Vernunft-Ideals sollte die Ganzheitlichkeit des Menschen wiederhergestellt werden. Doch genau hier liegen die Bruchstellen, durch die latent Bedrohliches sickert. Die Triebnatur, die durch die Vernunft gebändigt werden soll, findet in der Freisetzung der Emotionen ein neues Einfallstor. Wenn die Emotionalisierung zu sehr voranschreitet, werden Leidenschaften entbunden, die das prekäre Gleichgewicht erschüttern. Freundschaft hört dann auf, ein Garant bürgerlicher Sozialisation zu sein. Auf dieses Problem kommen die Theoretiker der Freundschaft, aber auch die zahlreichen Moralischen Wochenschriften unermüdlich zurück. Natürlichkeit und Sinnlichkeit dürfen sein, aber nur eng gepaart mit der Tugend. So schreibt Gellert, einer der wichtigsten Freundschaftsphilosophen, in seiner 24. *Moralischen Vorlesung*, die den Titel *Von den Pflichten der Verwandtschaft und Freundschaft* trägt: "wie reizend wird nicht die Freundschaft nicht, wenn sie sich zugleich auf Natur und auf Tugend gründet!" (Meyer-Krentler: 1984, 34) Ängstlich ist Gellert bedacht, der Leidenschaft keinerlei Platz in seinem Freundschaftskonzept einzuräumen. Im Grunde erhebt er sie weit über die Liebe zwischen den Geschlechtern, die durch den Trieb korrumpiert ist:

Die Liebe eines vernünftigen Freundes ist der untrüglichste Lobspruch für unser Herz [...]. Er stärkt durch sein Vertrauen meine Aufrichtigkeit, verschönert meine Absichten durch die seinigen [...], unterstützt mich in meinen Unternehmungen durch Rath und Beyfall, ruft mich güthig von Irrthume und Fehltritten zurück, [...] ist der Nächste bey mir in den Unfällen, wie er der Empfindlichste bey meinem Glücke war [...] Seiner edlen Seele darf ich mein Geheimnis, mein Vermögen, die Wohlfarth meines Kindes und meiner Gattin anvertrauen. (Meyer-Krentler: 1984, 35)

Die Freundschaft ist hier zuständig für all das, was wir heute eher der Partnerschaft zuordnen würden: Beistand in Glück und Unglück, Verantwortung für das Vermögen und die Kinder. Ein Misstrauen gegenüber der Geschlechterliebe wird hier spürbar, das mit der Rolle der Frau und mit einer Skepsis gegenüber ihrer Verführungskraft zu tun hat. Noch 1796 betont Johann Joseph Natter in seinem Traktat *Über die Freundschaft*, diese sei (im Unterschied zur Geschlechterliebe) vom Gefühl "zweideutiger sinnlicher Aufwallungen", von "gewaltsamer Leidenschaft" frei, da sie "der reinen, ruhigen Quelle der von besonnener Überlegung bewachten und geläuterten Empfindung" entströme (Meyer-Krentler: 1984, 51). Die Diskreditierung der Frauenfreundschaft hat hier ihren Ort.

4.3 Ausschluss der Frauen aus dem Freundschaftsdiskurs

Wenn in der Tugendempfindsamkeit die Freundschaft weitgehend als männliche Sozialisationsform beschrieben wird, so hat dies zunächst mit der Opposition von privater Rolle der Frau und öffentlicher Rolle des Mannes zu tun: Auch außerhalb des Hauses bleiben Frauen Privatpersonen, sie haben keinen Zugang zu öffentlichen Ämtern und stehen unter männlicher Vormundschaft. Frauen sind im 18. Jahrhundert nicht gesellschaftsfähig. Sie sind rechtlich unmündig; nur im Witwenstand wird ihnen rechtliche Verantwortung zugestanden. Freundschaft als universales gesellschaftliches Grundmodell ist insofern mit Frauenfreundschaft nicht vereinbar. Es gibt aber noch einen tieferen Grund für den Ausschluss der Frauen aus dem tugendempfindsamen Modell der Freundschaft. Parallel zur Entfaltung des Freundschaftskultes entwickelt sich in der zweiten Hälfte des 18. Jahrhunderts eine binäre Logik der Geschlechter, die es vorher in dieser Weise nicht gab. Die Frau wird nun dem Bereich der Natur zugeordnet, der Mann dem Bereich der Kultur (vgl. hierzu Schabert: 1995, 172 f. und Honegger: 1991). Von daher rührt die latente Abwertung der Geschlechterliebe gegenüber der Männerfreundschaft: Die Frau ist im Grunde ein nicht bezähmbares Naturwesen, das beständig unter sozialer Kontrolle gehalten werden muss (oder das man durch geschickte Verführung beherrschen kann). Schiller und Humboldt waren es, die diese Zweiteilung der Geschlechter besonders vertreten und in ihren Schriften popularisiert haben - im Unterschied zu Theodor Gottlieb von Hippel, der 1792 den Traktat *Über die bürgerliche Verbesserung der Weiber* schrieb, in dem er für die weibliche Emanzipation eintrat und die weibliche Befähigung zur Freundschaft verteidigte.

Humboldt veröffentlichte 1795 in Schillers *Horen* zwei Aufsätze, die die Dichotomie der Geschlechter zu beglaubigen versuchen: *Über den Geschlechtsunterschied und dessen Einfluß auf die organische Natur* und *Über die männliche und weibliche Form* (vgl. Meyer-Krentler: 1984, 53, Anm. 139) Bei Schiller sind es die Frauen, die unter den Bedingungen der Revolution ihre animalische Natur offenbaren:

> Da werden Weiber zu Hyänen
> und treiben mit Entsetzen Scherz,
> Noch zuckend, mit des Panthers Zähnen,
> Zerreißen sie des Feindes Herz.
> ("Das Lied von der Glocke", Schiller I, 440)

Das Bild der raubtierhaften Frau, das Schiller hier blutig ausmalt, wird in der weiteren Kulturgeschichte zum Erfolgsrezept. Es fügt zum gängigen Bild der reinen, keuschen Frau das Gegenklischee: die Verführerin, die Hure, die "femme fatale". Im günstigen Fall wird der Frau eine "fromme Natur" zugesprochen, aber Natur eben doch auch:

> In der Mutter bescheidener Hütte
> Sind sie geblieben mit schamhafter Sitte,
> Treue Töchter der frommen Natur. ("Würde der Frauen", Schiller I, 219)

Die Konsequenz aus dieser Fixierung des männlichen Blicks ist der Ausschluss der Frauen entweder konkret aus dem Kulturbetrieb oder abstrakt aus der symbolisch-kulturellen Ordnung. Hierzu noch einmal Schiller:

> Aber, zufrieden mit stillerem Ruhme,
> Brechen die Frauen des Augenblicks Blume,
> Nähren sie sorgsam mit liebendem Fleiß,
> Freier in ihrem gebundenen Wirken,
> Reicher als er in des Wissens Bezirken
> Und in der Dichtung unendlichem Kreis. (Schiller I, 219)

Die Frauen als vorkulturelle Wesen sind dem Augenblick verhaftet (sie brechen "des Augenblicks Blume"), sie sind aus "des Wissens Bezirken" und "der Dichtung unendlichem Kreis" ausgeschlossen.

Das heißt: die angestrebte Synthese von Natur und Kultur, von Gefühl und Tugend, von Privatheit und Öffentlichkeit ist, wenn überhaupt, nur in der Männerfreundschaft zu leisten. Mit dem anarchischen Einbruch der Triebnatur, den die Frauen repräsentieren, ist das tugendempfindsame Freundschaftskonzept nicht vermittelbar.

4.4 Freundschaft als Leidenschaft

Aus diesem Grund wird die Freundschaft der Liebe übergeordnet: denn die Liebe in ihrer erotischen Kontamination neigt zur Ausschweifung und ist im bürgerlichen Sinn schwer kontrollierbar. So wenig wie die andere Naturgewalt, die die Kultur nicht wirklich bezähmen kann: der Tod. Die Liebe als Passion wie der Tod werden als naturhaft-ungebändigter Einbruch in die kulturelle Ordnung empfunden, und deswegen stellen beide ein ernsthaftes Problem für die rationalitätsgeleitete Aufklärung dar. Heinrich Wolfgang Behrisch, ein Bruder des Goethe-Freundes, veröffentlichte 1776 eine Schrift mit dem Titel *Freundschaften*, in der er die folgende Bewertung vornahm: "Sie [die Freundschaft] ist erhabener als die Liebe, worzu die Freundschaft unter zwey Personen verschiedenen Geschlechts allezeit ausartet [...]" (Meyer-Krentler: 1984, 49). Die Freundschaft zwischen den Geschlechtern artet zu Liebe aus: diese verbale Ausartung verrät eine obsessive Angst vor der anarchischen Ungebändigtheit der Triebe. Der Durchbruch der Triebnatur kann auch die Freundschaft heimsuchen. Jede Übersteigerung des Gefühls ist deswegen zu vermeiden. Behrisch, der Verfasser dieses Freundschafts-Traktats, ahnt durchaus, dass gerade die Literatur in ihren bedeutsamen Produkten das bürgerliche Freundschaftskonzept permanent unterläuft und die Leiden-schaft in ihre Freundschaftsdarstellungen mit einbezieht:

Nahe an dieser [Liebe als Leidenschaft] gränzt übertriebene Freundschaft. Sie wohnt nur in dem Lande der Phantasie, in dem Gebiete der Romane, der Gedichte, der tragischen und komischen Bühne. (Meyer-Krentler: 1984, 49)

Liebe und Tod als Grenzgänger der kulturellen Ordnung sind bevorzugte Themen der Literatur, das weiß Behrisch, dessen Bruder mit dem Goethe des Sturm und Drang eng befreundet war. Gerade die Literatur des Sturm und Drang stellte sich immer wieder quer zu den Freundschaftstheorien, die die Moralischen Wochenschriften und die Popularphilosophen der Aufklärung verbreiteten. Werther verabschiedet sich gleich zu Beginn von dem tugendhaften und vernünftigen Wilhelm mit den Worten: "Wie froh bin ich, daß ich weg bin! Bester Freund, was ist das Herz des Menschen! Dich zu verlassen, den ich so liebe, von dem ich unzertrennlich war, und froh zu sein! Ich weiß, du verzeihst mir's." (Goethe VI, 7) Auf subtile Weise berührt hier das Frohsein auch den Abschied von dem Freund; von diesem Frohsein kündet schon die Vergangenheitsform: "Dich zu verlassen, [...] von dem ich unzertrennlich *war*". Werthers leidenschaftliche Emphase ist nicht vereinbar mit der vernünftigen Freundschaft Wilhelms.

Schiller hat in seinem *Don Carlos* den grundlegenden Konflikt zwischen der vernunftgesteuerten und der emphatischen, leidenschaftlichen Freundschaft dargestellt. Während Carlos an Posa hängt wie an der großen Liebe seines Lebens, geht es diesem um eine Idee, um die Rettung der Menschheit:

Für einen Knaben stirbt
Ein Posa nicht. Der Freundschaft arme Flamme
Füllt eines Posa Herz nicht aus. Das schlug
Der ganzen Menschheit. Seine Neigung war
Die Welt mit allen kommenden Geschlechtern.
(Vv. 5058 ff., Schiller II, 206 f.)

König Philipp räsonniert hier über Posas Freundschaftsverständnis, das auch den Infanten Carlos beunruhigt:

Doch sollen Millionen ihm, soll ihm
Das Vaterland nicht teurer sein als *einer*?
Sein Busen war für *einen* Freund zu groß,
Und Carlos' Glück zu klein für seine Liebe. (Vv. 3967 ff., Schiller II, 158)

Im Rückblick auf die gemeinsame Jugendzeit setzt Carlos die oppositionellen Freundschaftsmodelle ins Licht:

Da fing ich an, mit Zärtlichkeiten
Und inniger Bruderliebe dich zu quälen:
Du, stolzes Herz, gabst sie mir kalt zurück. (Vv. 215 ff., Schiller II, 16)

Freilich scheitert der geistreich gesponnene Plan Posas genauso wie das Glücksverlangen des leidenschaftlichen Carlos. Die empfindsame Freundschaft wird in der Literatur der Zeit immer wie der zu einem Grenzgang, der an den Rändern des Leidenschaftlichen und des Erotischen verläuft. Die schwärmerische Liebesfreundschaft des Kreises um Gleim und Klopstock gehört hierher (nicht umsonst lesen Werther und Lotte mit Begeisterung Klopstock), wobei die Erotik freilich durch literarische Codierungen, besonders der anakreontischen Schäferlyrik, gleichsam lizenziert wird. Wenn in Goethes Gedicht *An den Mond* von Freundschaft die Rede ist, dann verstößt der Text dezidiert gegen den sozialethischen Imperativ der bürgerlichen Freundschaftstheoretiker und greift auf das Inventar erotischer Zweisamkeit zurück:

Selig, wer sich vor der Welt
Ohne Haß verschließt,
Einen Freund am Busen hält
Und mit dem genießt,

Was, von Menschen nicht gewußt
Oder nicht bedacht,
Durch das Labyrinth der Brust
Wandelt in der Nacht. (Goethe I, 130)

Diese Anleihen am Liebesdiskurs kennzeichnen auch einige andere Gedichte Goethes, die er im Hinblick auf den abwesenden Schiller geschrieben hat - dies versuchte vor kurzem Katharina Mommsen nachzuweisen (Mommsen: 1992/93). Dies gilt vor allem für das Gedicht *Nähe des Geliebten*; die Abfassung fällt in eine Zeit wachsender Annäherung der beiden Dichter - in das Jahr 1795, in dem sich überraschende Wendungen in Goethes Briefen finden wie: "Lassen Sie mich auch abwesend nicht ferne sein." (25. Febr. 1795) oder: "fahren Sie fort, mich durch Ihre Liebe und Ihr Vertrauen zu erquicken und zu erheben." (10. Jan. 1795; Mommsen: 1992/93, 34) Wenn es stimmt, was Katharina Mommsen nachzuweisen versuchte, dann wäre *Nähe des Geliebten* ein Versuch Goethes, seine Freundschaft zu Schiller zum Ausdruck zu bringen und sie durch die Tradition der Liebespoesie zu beglaubigen. Schiller gab diesem Gedicht jedenfalls einen Ehrenplatz im Musen-Almanach des Jahres 1796; es erschien dort als erstes der abgedruckten Gedichte:

Ich denke dein, wenn mir der Sonne Schimmer
Vom Meere strahlt;
Ich denke dein, wenn sich des Mondes Flimmer
In Quellen malt.

Ich sehe dich, wenn auf dem fernen Wege
Der Staub sich hebt;

In tiefer Nacht, wenn auf dem schmalen Stege
Der Wandrer bebt.

Ich höre dich, wenn dort mit dumpfem Rauschen
Die Welle steigt.
Im stillen Haine geh' ich oft zu lauschen,
Wenn alles schweigt.

Ich bin bei dir, du seist auch noch so ferne,
Du bist mir nah!
Die Sonne sinkt, bald leuchten mir die Sterne.
O wärst du da! (Goethe I, 242 f.)

Im Zentrum steht das Motiv der geistigen Nähe trotz der leiblichen Ferne - ein Motiv, das im Jahr 1795 für die Freundschaft zwischen beiden Dichtern große Bedeutung hatte. In diesem Jahr erfährt Goethe von Schillers Erkrankung - der Austausch in Briefen erreicht in diesem Jahr seinen Höhepunkt. Die Forschung ging bisher immer davon aus, dass es sich bei dem Gedicht *Nähe des Geliebten* um ein Rollen-Gedicht mit einem weiblichen Sprecher-Ich handle. Die neue Deutung versteht es als Erlebnis-Gedicht des männlichen Autors Goethe, der den Adressatenbezug durch die Tradition lyrischer Liebes-Dialoge verschleierte. Aber selbst wenn man nicht so weit gehen will, es als Liebes-Gedicht von Mann zu Mann zu verstehen, so ist auf jeden Fall die thematische Nähe zu Goethes Lebensgefühl im Jahr 1795 vorhanden - dem Gefühl einer schmerzlichen Trennung von Schiller. Auf Goethes ungewohnt herzliche Briefe reagiert der erkrankte Schiller mit ungewöhnlicher Gefühlsintensität: "Herzlich verlangt mich nach einer freundlichen Spur von Ihnen. Damit etwas bei Ihnen sei, was mich Ihnen zuweilen vergegenwärtige, so gönnen Sie beifolgendem Bilde irgend einen Platz in Ihrem Hause." (16. Nov. 1795; Mommsen: 1992/93, 33) Beigelegt ist Schillers Portrait, das die Nähe des Abwesenden vermitteln soll - eine Praxis, die wir von Liebenden kennen. Im selben Jahr finden sich auch in Goethes Briefen ungewohnte Schlussformeln, wie z.B.: "Leben Sie wohl und lieben mich, es ist nicht einseitig." (18.3.1795) Die vielleicht schönste Stelle bezüglich seiner Freundschaft mit Schiller findet sich in Goethes Aufzeichnungen *Ferneres in bezug auf mein Verhältnis zu Schiller*:

Selten ist es aber, daß Personen gleichsam die Hälften von einander ausmachen, sich nicht abstoßen, sondern sich anschließen und einander ergänzen. (Goethe X, 543)

Goethe spielt hier auf den Mythos in Platons *Gastmahl* an: In der Rede des Aristophanes wird die gegenseitige Anziehung der Liebenden damit erklärt, dass sie irgendwann eine Einheit waren, dann in zwei Hälften geteilt wurden und von da an auf der Suche nach der anderen Hälfte sind, um wieder zur ursprünglichen Einheit zurückzufinden. Die Anwendung dieses Gleichnisses auf Schiller ist sicher das größte Kompliment, das Goethe seinem Freund machen konnte; der Freund wird hier als notwendige Ergänzung des eigenen Lebens angesehen. Wie dem auch immer sei - der Durchbruch leidenschaftlicher Affekte wurde dem tugendempfindsamen Freundschaftskult gerade da zum Problem, wo man am wenigsten damit rechnen konnte: in der Männerfreundschaft, die nach den Auffassungen der Zeit von weiblicher Naturhaftigkeit gerade frei sein sollte. Dass die Triebnatur in den mannmännlichen Freundschaftskult einbrach (jedenfalls in der Literatur), war einerseits irritierend, verlangte andererseits aber auch nach einer Korrektur des traditionellen Männlichkeitsbildes.

Dass Kleist diese Korrektur an der Schwelle zum 19. Jahrhundert ausgiebig vornahm, daß er verwirrende Geschlechtertausch-Geschichten erfand und den Freundschaftskult in seinen Briefen fast schamlos erotisierte, ist inzwischen selbst in der Literaturwissenschaft anerkannt. Kleist wirbelt die Geschlechterrollen gehörig durcheinander, wenn er Penthesilea den schutzlosen Achill besiegen lässt; wenn in der *Familie Schroffenstein* Agnes und Ottokar die Kleider und damit die Geschlechterrollen tauschen; wenn im *Schrecken im Bade* ein vermeintlicher Mann sagt, er wolle in das Bett des Großknechts steigen; wenn Kleist an einen Freund schreibt: "Ich habe Deinen schönen Leib oft, wenn Du in Thun vor meinen Augen in den See stiegst, mit wahrhaft *mädchenhaften* Gefühlen betrachtet. [...] Ich heirate niemals, sei Du die Frau mir, die Kinder, und die Enkel!" (7. Jan. 1805, Kleist II, 749 f.) Dass auch in Goethes *Wilhelm Meister* die Geschlechterrollen nicht der binären Unterscheidung des 18. Jahrhunderts entsprechen, ist inzwischen ebenfalls, nicht zuletzt durch die Geschlechterforschung, ins Bewusstsein getreten.

Doch dass selbst Schiller, der die oppositionelle Aufteilung der Geschlechter in bestimmten Schriften favorisiert und popularisiert hat, andernorts die Attribute der Männlichkeit mit weiblicher Erotik verbindet, ist in der Forschung geflissentlich übersehen worden. Dabei hat Schiller in den *Briefen über Don Carlos* ausdrücklich auf ein Projekt hingewiesen, das ihn in besonderer Weise und über lange Zeit hinweg beschäftigte. Im dritten Brief über Don Carlos heißt es:

"Sie wollten neulich im Don Carlos den Beweis gefunden haben, daß *leidenschaftliche Freundschaft* ein ebenso rührender Gegenstand für die Tragödie sein könne als *leidenschaftliche Liebe*, und meine Antwort, daß ich mir das Gemälde einer solchen Freundschaft für die Zukunft zurückgelegt hätte, befremdete Sie." (Schiller II, 230)

Das Projekt einer solchen "leidenschaftlichen Freundschaft", das sich Schiller für die Zukunft zurückgelegt hat, ist das Drama *Die Malteser*, das uns nur in Fragmenten überliefert ist. Aber das Erhaltene ist erstaunlich genug. Wichtig dabei ist, dass es sich keineswegs um ein beiläufiges Produkt handelt, vielmehr hat dieses Drama den Autor länger als jeder andere Stoff beschäftigt, nämlich über Jahre und Jahrzehnte hinweg, vom *Don Carlos* bis hin zum *Wilhelm Tell*. Bereits im *Carlos* ist der Stoff in Person des

Posa präsent, der nicht zufällig ein Malteser-Ritter ist. 1797 noch schreibt Schiller an Goethe:

> Doch gebe ich die Hoffnung nicht auf, den *Wallenstein* noch in dem nächsten Sommer in Weimar spielen zu sehen und im nächsten Herbst tief in meinen *Maltesern* zu sitzen. - Diese beschäftigen mich jetzt zuweilen, wenn ich von der Arbeit ausruhe. Es ist etwas sehr Anziehendes für mich in solchen Stoffen [...]. (Schiller II, 936)

Das Anziehende ist die leidenschaftliche Liebe zweier Ritter mit Namen Créqui und St. Priest, die bei der Verteidigung des strategisch wichtigen Forts San Elmo gegen die Türken ums Leben kommen - wobei Créqui sich für seinen Freund einsetzt und ihm in den Tod folgt. Die Skizzen Schillers verdeutlichen, wie sehr hier die Tabugrenzen des tugendempfindsamen Freundschaftskults durchbrochen sind und wie sehr Schiller den Naturtrieb, der weiblich attribuiert war, mit dem traditionellen Männlichkeitsbild verbindet:

> St. Priest heißt der schöne Ritter, und seine Schönheit gibt ihm gleichsam die Qualität eines Mädchens. Ihre Liebe ist von der reinsten Schönheit, aber doch ist es nötig, ihr den sinnlichen Charakter nicht zu nehmen, wodurch sie an der *Natur* befestigt wird. Es darf und muß gefühlt werden, daß es eine Übertragung der Geschlechtsliebe, ein Surrogat derselben und eine Wirkung des Naturtriebes ist. (Schiller II, 172 f.)

> (Die Freundschaft) muß vollkommen schön, dabei aber wirkliche Leidenschaft mit allen ihren Symptomen sein.Die Männerliebe ist in dem Stück das vollgültige Surrogat der Weiberliebe und ersetzt sie für den poetischen Zweck in allen Teilen, ja sie übersteigt noch die Wirkung. (Schiller II, 173, Anm. 1)

Es gibt wohl wenige Texte, in denen das alte Rollenklischee - der tapfere und heldische Mann - mit weiblicher Natur so ungeniert legiert wurde. Diese Art von Kultur-Natur-Synthese war für die damalige Zeit recht ungewöhnlich; Schiller schreibt hier dauernd vom Rande her, sozusagen im Kampf mit seinen eigenen Intentionen. Deswegen ist es kein Wunder, dass er über Jahre hinweg das Stück beiseite legt und immer wieder zu ihm zurückkehrt, in vergeblicher Bemühung, das "punctum saliens" der Handlung zu finden, wie er selbst schreibt (Schiller II, 937).

Erstaunlich ist, dass die wenigen Interpreten, die sich dem unvollendeten Stück zugewandt haben (Beyer: 1912; von Wiese: 1963, 421-427; Kraft: 1978; Derks: 1990, 370 ff.), die leidenschaftliche Beziehung zwischen den beiden Rittern außer Acht lassen, obwohl es doch schon im Figurenverzeichnis ostentativ heißt: "Créqui und St. Priest, Ritter, die sich lieben", und obwohl Schiller deutliche Hinweise darauf gibt, dass diese Beziehung der springende Punkt der Handlung werden soll..

Dass dieses Drama unvollendet geblieben ist, verwundert nicht. Es steht, abgesehen von der üppigen Briefkultur, vor Beginn des 19. Jahrhunderts fast einmalig da als Versuch, den männlichen Freundschaftskult in seiner bürgerlichen Ausrichtung um das Andere der Vernunft, um die Triebnatur zu erweitern, ohne in die Spaltung von Natur und Kultur, Trieb und Ordnung, Leidenschaft und Vernunft zu verfallen. Ein tapferer Ritter mit der "Qualität eines Mädchens": das wäre auch im kriegerischen 19. Jahrhundert noch Grund genug zur Empörung gewesen, und die Männerbünde des Nationalsozialismus wären schockiert gewesen über solch einen Gedanken. Die Rezeption Schillers im Dritten Reich übersah solche Texte geflissentlich, wie auch die Literaturwissenschaft nach 1945 sie geflissentlich übersehen hat. Erst das Ende des 20. Jahrhunderts hat mit Hilfe der Geschlechterforschung die Rollenzuschreibungen der Geschlechter neu reflektiert und der starren Festlegung der Geschlechtsidentitäten eine Absage erteilt. Ein *literarischer* Freundschaftskult, der die gesell- schaftlich-bürgerliche Instrumentalisierung der Freundschaft erst noch in Frage stellen müsste, ist in diesem Sinne nicht mehr nötig. Wohl aber die unermüdliche Arbeit an den Geschlechter-Mythen des Alltags, die auch das 20. Jahrhundert noch in großer Zahl hervorbringt.

Quellennachweise

Beyer, Adolf, *Schillers Malteser*, Diss. Phil. Tübingen 1912.

Derks, Paul, *Die Schande der heiligen Päderastie. Homosexualität und Öffentlichkeit in der deutschen Literatur 1750-1850*, Berlin 1990.

Dietrich, Hans [= Hans Dietrich Hellbach], *Die Freundesliebe in der deutschen Literatur*, Berlin 1996.

Goethe, Johann Wolfgang von, *Werke*, Hamburger Ausgabe, 14 Bde., hrsg. von Erich Trunz, München 1981.

Honegger, Claudia, *Die Ordnung der Geschlechter. Die Wissenschaft vom Menschen und das Weib. 1750-1850*, Frankfurt a.M. 1991.

Ingen, Ferdinand van; Juranek, Christian (Hrsg.), *Ars et amicitia. Beiträge zum Thema Freundschaft in Geschichte, Kunst und Literatur*. Festschrift für Martin Bircher zum 60. Geb. am 3. Juni 1998, Amsterdam 1998.

Kleist, Heinrich von, *Sämtliche Werke und Briefe*, hrsg. von Helmut Sembdner, 2 Bde., München 1983.

Kraft, Herbert, *Um Schiller betrogen*, Pfullingen 1978.

Lessing, Gotthold Ephraim, *Werke*, hrsg. von Herbert G. Göpfert, München 1970 ff.

Luhmann, Niklas, *Liebe als Passion. Zur Codierung von Intimität*, Frankfurt a. M. 1994.

Mauser, Wolfram; Becker-Cantarino, Barbara (Hrsg.), *Frauenfreundschaft - Männerfreundschaft. Literarische Diskurse im 18. Jahrhundert*, Tübingen 1991.

Meyer-Krentler, Eckhardt, *Der Bürger als Freund. Ein sozialethisches Programm und seine Kritik in der neueren deutschen Erzählliteratur*, München 1984.

Mommsen, Katharina, "Goethes Gedicht 'Nähe des Geliebten'. Ausdruck der Liebe für Schiller, Auftakt der Freundschaft mit Zelter", in: *Goethe-Jahrbuch* 104 (1992/93), S. 31-44.

Pfeiffer, Joachim, "Friendship and Gender. The Aesthetic Construction of Subjectivity in Kleist", in: Alice Kuzniar (Hrsg.), *Outing Goethe and His Age*, Stanford 1996, S. 215-227.

Rasch, Wolfdietrich, *Freundschaftskult und Freundschaftsdichtung im deutschen Schrifttum des 18. Jahrhunderts. Vom Ausgang des Barock bis zu Klopstock*, Halle 1936.

Schabert, Ina, "*Gender* als Kategorie einer neuen Literaturgeschichtsschreibung", in: Hadumod Bußmann u. Renate Hof (Hrsg.), *Genus. Zur Geschlechterdifferenz in den Kulturwissenschaften*, Stuttgart 1995, S. 162-204.

Schiller, Friedrich, *Sämtliche Werke*, hrsg. von Gerhard Fricke und Herbert G. Göpfert. 6 Bde. München 1980 ff.

Stenzel, Jürgen, "Über die ästhetische Erziehung eines Tyrannen. Zu Schillers Ballade *Die Bürgschaft*", in: Wolf Segebrecht (Hrsg.), *Gedichte und Interpretationen* Bd. 3, *Klassik und Romantik*, Stuttgart 1984, S. 173-180.

Tenbruck, Friedrich H., "Freundschaft. Ein Beitrag zu einer Soziologie der persönlichen Beziehungen", in: *Kölner Zeitschrift für Soziologie und Sozialpsychologie* 16 (1964), S. 432-456.

Wiese, Benno von, *Friedrich Schiller*, Stuttgart 1963.

Wild, Reiner, "Goethes und Schillers gemeinsamer Tagtraum", in: *Freiburger literaturpsychologische Gespräche* 18 (1999), S. 136-152.

Julia RICHERS

John Keats's Odes and Masculinities

Had I *a man's fair form*, then might my sighs
Be echoed swiftly through that ivory shell
Thine ear, and find thy gentle heart; so well
Would passion arm me for the enterprize:
But ah! *I am no knight* . . .

(*To* * * *, 1-5, emphases mine)

Women, lovers, muses, dryads, goddesses and other feminised figures abound in the poetry of John Keats. The merging of the poetic 'I' with a woman or the vanishing of the self into a utopian space of feminine beauty are two of the most central themes of his early poetry as well as of his later odes. Hence, he has been described as a poet who was excessively fascinated by the idea of representing "ecstatic or visionary experience as an erotic encounter with a female or feminized figure" (Wolfson: 1990, 325). Apart from representatives of New Criticism, there have probably been only few literary critics who have not commented on Keats's poetry in gendered terms. Not only Keats's contemporaries but also later generations have characterised him as 'feminine' or criticised him as 'effeminate'; as if he was challenging or diverging from an apparently 'masculine' style of writing. Rarely have studies pointed out that a concept such as 'manliness' was already at Keats's time a great issue that had to be heavily defended (an exceptional study is Fulford: 1999). Not only the non-literary world was occupied with fortifying the 'true' values of men but also the Romantic poets themselves have made 'masculinity' at times a core issue of their debates. There was, for example, a lengthy discussion among writers and poets whether or not the soul had a particular sex. In this controversy, most of the Romantics took a clear stand and concluded almost univocally that the soul had to be masculine. Even Coleridge who had become famous for his theory on androgyny stated: "Is it true what is so constantly affirmed, that there is no Sex in Souls? – I doubt it – I doubt it exceedingly" (quoted from Wolfson: 1998, 349).

Feelings and emotions – as they are well-known from the Romantic cult of sensitivity – were permissible as long as masculinity itself was not at stake. If poets showed qualities conventionally deemed feminine, it was always important to stress the overriding manly governance. For example, "there were islands of tolerance for manly tears" and also the "culture of mourning sometimes went to fetishistic extremes" (Wolfson: 1990, 332) but this kind of emotionalism was licensed only within a larger ideal of 'manliness'.

John Keats seems not to have fit into this kind of discourse. However, I would like to argue that his 'effeminate' poetry underwent a substantial change to a more 'masculine' style by the time he reached his famous odes. This paper will focus on three of his Great Odes and aims to investigate how masculinity is established and how the form of the ode, as a poem of praise, becomes a constituent part.

Keats's poetic discourse shall be put in relation to the gender practices within the particular cultural tradition of his time. What was considered masculine, what effeminate? Where can Keats be positioned in this gender discourses? To answer those questions, I will look at public as well as private events in Keats's life that are shown to have shaped the poems' creation and reception. It is important to note that the distinction between the poet and the poetic voice (or 'I') has been blurred by past and present critics whenever Keats's poetry was discussed in terms of its (un-) manliness. This paper will consciously do so as well. Since to historicise Keats's portrayal of the feminine and masculine is to draw nearer to both his notion of, as well as the contemporary discourse on, masculinity.

'Masculinity' (as much as 'femininity') is not in itself an isolated concept, but is always closely connected with ideas and concepts of the other sex. As binary oppositions, they eternally define each other. It is, thus, through the analysis of the female figures in Keats's odes that I will investigate his concept of masculinity. For this purpose, I have decided to focus on the following three odes: *Ode to Psyche*, *Ode to a Nightingale* and *Ode on Melancholy*. Other poems by Keats may be used for comparison, as well as extracts from his remarkable and often revealing *Letters*.[199]

On a superficial level, in each ode there is a female object of desire whom the love hymn is addressed to. On a deeper level, however, I would like to argue that each of those objects serve primarily and exclusively the (re-)constitution of the subject. The female characters in Keats's odes are simply a *topos*, detached from any sort of grounding in the 'real' world. They are a means to realise his masculine desire of self-possession and to reaffirm his identity. The encounter with these feminised figures serves as a journey into the *terra incognita* of the self and broadens its understanding – a process of submerging in the internal otherness. This approach to, and usage of, the feminine is, however, not a peculiar to Keats, on the contrary, "all the Romantic poets to a large extent explored in their poetry one of their culture's dominant ideological fantasies – that artistic power and creativity were possible for men only if they unified their masculine and feminine components" (Hoeveler: 1990, 2). Thus, it can be argued that women in Keats's poetry represent a symbolic quality within the masculine mind of the poet. Before analysing his odes, this paper will give a short introduction to the ode as a form of lyrical poetry as well as cover some of the key features of literary criticism on Keats. In addition, his own conceptions of women, whether real or ideal, will be gathered and reflected. Finally, I would like to thank Balz Engler for his valuable reading suggestions and Therese Steffen for sharing her extensive knowledge and her advice in the field of gender and masculinity.

---

[199] Extracts from the letters are taken from Hyder Edward Rollins (ed.), *The Letters of John Keats: 1814-1821*, 2 vols., Cambridge 1958, abbreviated as *Letters* in the text and followed by the appropriate volume and page numbers.

The ode as a classical form of lyrical poetry was rather slow to appear in England. Only in the Renaissance period were its two most distinct forms, Pindaric and Horatian,[200] revived and brought into the language. After some fruitless attempts by his predecessors, Ben Jonson was the first English poet to write an ode in the Pindaric tradition, namely his ode *To the Immortal Memory and Friendship of That Noble Pair, Sir Lucius Cary and Sir H. Morison* (1629). An example of a Horatian ode was Andrew Marvell's *Ode upon Cromwell's Return from Ireland* (1650). Later, Abraham Cowley was to publish his so-called *Pindaric Odes* (1656) which had much influence on the later poetry of John Dryden. However, G. S. Fraser noted that both Cowley and Dryden had not seen that the Pindaric ode was regular, and had created the English irregular ode, with lines and stanzas of varying lengths, which was to influence later generations of English poets (1971, 12). Whether classical or irregular, all of those odes had in common that they were poems of public or private *praise*. The public type of ode was often a praise of the great, written for a particular occasion and directed to a larger audience. Thus, those odes were referring to a context outside the 'inner reality' of the poet. An adequate example may be Tennyson's *Ode on the Death of the Duke of Wellington* (1852) as well as the majority of the odes mentioned above.

The Romantic poets made extensive use of the ode, examples are Wordsworth's *Ode: Intimations of Immortality* (1802-04), Coleridge's *Dejection: An Ode* (1802), Keats's *Ode on Indolence* (1819) and Shelley's *Ode to the West Wind* (1819). I would like to argue, however, that the Romantics broke with the tradition of public praise. None of their odes were addressed to a personage of fame or importance, nor were their odes meant for the public at large. They wrote odes that contained a private form of praise, referring to someone or something personally dear to them. At times even glorifying their own thoughts or emotions, they changed the original definition of the ode substantially.

---

[200] In general, the 'ode' meant a choric song, usually accompanied by a dance. Particularly known are the Pindaric and Horatian form of the ode. Originating from the Greek poet Pindar, who used to write odes for winners of the Olympic games, the Pindaric ode became known as a serious lyrical poem praising a particular public occasion or the great deeds of the person to whom it was addressed. The Pindaric ode followed a three-part scheme of strophe, antistrophe and epode. Later, the Roman poet Horace wrote poems that he considered to be *Carmina*, but which were afterwards universally acknowledged as *Odes*. In contrast to the heroic odes of Pindar, Horace's were more private and personal in style. They were written in stanzas of two or four lines, based on very regular metrical patterns that sometimes caused a certain loss of spontaneity. A discussion on the ode in general and on the English development in particular can be found in John A. Cuddon, *A Dictionary of Literary Terms*, London 1977, 451-454.

In his time, Keats was repeatedly mocked for his infantility and lack of masculinity.[201] Especially the *Blackwood's Edinburgh Magazine* did not miss a single chance to make its discomfort felt and publish mocking statements such as: "Mr Hunt is a small poet, but he is a clever man. Mr Keats is a still smaller poet, and he is only a boy of pretty abilities" (August 1818: 3, 522) A year later, after Keats had written his Great Odes, they patronisingly called him "a very amiable, silly, lisping, and pragmatical young gentleman" (December 1819: 6, 240). Posthumously William Hazlitt wrote in his famous essay *On Effeminacy of Character* about Keats's poetry: "I cannot help thinking that the fault of Mr Keats's poems was a deficiency in masculine energy of style. He had beauty, tenderness, delicacy, in an uncommon degree, but there was a want of strength and substance ... All is soft and fleshy, without bone and muscle" (quoted from Cox: 1996, 82). Hazlitt showed some appreciation and fascination for Keats's effeminate style, but at the same time he was also suggesting that Keats would have been (theoretically) capable of writing a more manly poetry "of strength and substance". A similar wording is found in the *Edinburgh Review* about thirty years later where Keats is characterised as a poet whose "passive part of intellect, the powers of susceptibility and appreciation" showed that "masculine energy ... in him either existed deficiently, or had not time for its full development" (October 1849: 90, 428).

Keats was grouped under second class 'feminine' poets which were seen as "separated from the first class of [masculine poets] by a distance as great as that which separates a truly manly man from a truly womanly woman" (quoted from Wolfson: 1990, 331). Even in the *Encyclopaedia Britannica* of 1857 Keats was criticised for having a "style of babyish effeminacy" characterised by a "nauseous sweetness". All those accounts and controversies about Keats's manhood suggest that the discourse on gender roles ran deep in the nineteenth century.

Recent feminist scholarship has hailed Keats as a poet who did not comply with male heroic poetry, but who was sensitive and emotional in style. Many treat him "as an exception to, or anomaly within, a monolithically conceived 'masculine' discourse" (Wolfson: 1990, 348). His poetical strategy of "no self" and "no identity" were set "against the strong ego boundaries and self-assertions taken to characterize 'masculine practices" (Wolfson: 1995, 2). Anne K. Mellor sees Keats "in the traditionally feminine pose of passivity, indolence and waiting" (1993, 182). Defining his poetry as non-masculine, she is even going as far as to make "an honorary woman" (Homans: 1990, 343) of him. An "ideological transvestite" who "self-consciously positioned [himself] within the realm of the feminine gender" (Mellor: 1993, 171, 174).

However, many commentators have failed to discern the 'masculine' undercurrent in Keats's poems. They have ignored the fact that Keats had very clear conceptions of

---

[201] For a collection of the contemporary reception of Romantic poets, *see* Theodore Redpath, *The Young Romantics and Critical Opinion 1807-1824*, London 1973.

what a man and a woman should be like. For new perspectives and a thorough revaluation of Keats, I am indebted to the numerous essays of Susan J. Wolfson who has conducted extensive research in the field of Keats and gender.

Keats and Women

> I am certain I have not a right feeling towards Women.
> (*Letters*, I, 341)

> It has been said that his poetry was affected and effeminate. I can only say that I never encountered a more manly and simple young man ...
> Barry Cornwall (Wolfson: 1990, 336)

In many of his letters, Keats bitterly complained about the power women held over literary taste: " The world, and especially our England, has within the last thirty year's been vexed and teased by a set of Devils, whom I detest so much [...]; These Devils are a set of Women, who having taken a snack or Luncheon of Literary scraps, set themselves up for towers of Babel in Languages, Sapphos in Poetry [...]. The thing has made a very uncomfortable impression on me. – I had longed for some real feminine Modesty in these things" (*Letters*, I, 163). Keats's harsh complaint was directed towards the growing number of women poets such as Anna Barbauld, Hannah More, Charlotte Smith and Mary Robinson. The poetic writings of these women were not only popular but also their publications sometimes outnumbered those of their male 'competitors' (Curran: 1988, 185-207). In their success, they undermined the solid-thought foundation of the exclusively male literary world.

Keats's angry complaint perfectly echoes the general (male) attitude towards women at the time: For many men, not only the revolutionary developments on the continent but also early 'feminist' women such as Mary Wollstonecraft posed a great threat to the old social order. Fearing upheaval and change, "Englishmen were more than ever determined that Englishwomen should stay in their familial places" (Fulford: 1999, 5). In this respect, Keats approved of a thinking which presupposed that activity and creativity, i.e. *Culture*, was masculine and the realm of passive *Nature* essentially feminine. Granting the female sex no real sense of responsibility, Keats dismissed women as "children to whom I would rather give a Sugar Plum than my time" (*Letters*, I, 404). For him, a woman was apparently not just a waste of time but also an annoying disturbance, "a cloying treacle to the wings of independence" (*Letters*, II, 144). In addition, he had a rather stereotyped conception of what women ought to be: meek, mild, modest and pretty. In a letter, he stated that he would not spend "any time with Ladies unless they are handsome" (*Letters*, II, 20). And also to Fanny Brawne, the one woman he loved excessively until the end of his short life, he wrote: "Why may I not speak of your Beauty, since without that I could never have lov'd you" (*Letters*, II, 127). It has often been stated that he did not only have severe problems with women but that he also had his difficulties with men. However, his letters reveal another stand: "When among Men I have no evil thoughts, no malice, no spleen – I feel free to speak or to be silent [...]. When I am among Women I have evil thoughts, malice spleen – I cannot speak or be silent – I am full of Suspicions and therefore listen to no thing – I am in a hurry to be gone" (*Letters*, I, 341). Keats went in his misogyny as far as to insist that "he does not want ladies to read his poetry: [...] he writes for men" (*Letters*, II, 163).

The "Maiden" in his Mind

Extreme sensitiveness is not an exclusive mark of femininity; it is found in men as often as in women. Henry van Dyke (Wolfson: 1990, 345)

The feminine figures in Keats's poetry had nothing in common with the "set of [She-]Devils" in the real world. Continuing the tradition cherished by generations of poets before him, women of Keats's thoughts and imagination served a particular literary and allegorical purpose. Hence, it is not surprising that he expressed man's maturing process in gendered terms. In the letter containing his famous description of the human life as "a large Mansion of Many Apartments" he writes: "The first we step into we call the infant or thoughtless Chamber, in which we remain as long as we do not think [..] we no sooner get into the second Chamber, which I shall call the Chamber of Maiden-Thought [...]. This Chamber of Maiden-Thought becomes gradually darken'd and at the same time on all sides of it many doors are set open" (*Letters*, I, 280-281). He described male maturation as a growth from an infant, through a maiden, and finally to a man.

Keats's description bears a striking similarity to William Wordsworth's idea of linking mental development with masculinity. For Wordsworth, the quest for poetical self-identity was inextricably bound up with the quest for manhood and masculine maturity. Similarly, Keats sought to write like a man, to pass beyond the feminine style, which he associated with the Chamber of Maiden-Thought. And thus, he saw himself proceeding from effeminate adolescence into manly adulthood by the time he reached his odes. A change of style in which also the 'women' of his poetry received a different purpose.

With the idea of the Chamber of Maiden-Thought, Keats was also claiming a certain wholeness and completeness for his poetic mind – a presumed claim to androgyny. In this sense, it could be argued that the 'effeminacy' Keats was always criticised for was for him part of a conscious poetic manifesto: a sign of poetic strength rather than a weakness. Closely linked with this idea were two other concepts he had developed. One was associated with the Chameleon Poet who was able to shift into someone else's body and take up his or her identity. In a letter, Keats explained that he wants to be "continually in for – and filling some other Body" (*Letters*, I, 387). The other concept Keats called Negative Capability which was the capacity to be "in uncertainties, Mysteries, doubts, without any irritable reaching after fact & reason" (*Letters*, I, 193). However, all of these poetic concepts were about to undergo substantial change in the odes.

The Odes

The Odes were written from March to September 1819. The *Letters* provide enough evidence for reconstructing their probable chronology. There is only one ode, the *Ode on Indolence*, where no precise date of composition can be given. Otherwise, the chronology of the Odes is as follows: *Ode to Psyche, Ode to a Nightingale, Ode to a Grecian Urn, Ode to Melancholy* and, finally, *To Autumn* which Keats did not call an ode but is still considered to belong to the ode cycle.

In the following, the Odes will be discussed in their original chronology. This choice allows not only to ask questions about continuation, development and change in Keats's poetic writing but enables an overall discussion on the ode cycle at the end of this section.

Ode to Psyche

> How to entangle, trammel up and snare
> Your soul in mine, and labyrinth you there
> Like the hid scent in an unbudded rose?
> (*Lamia*, II, 52-54)

The basic setting of the *Ode to Psyche* is a simple one: Wandering through a forest, the poet witnesses two lovers, Cupid and Psyche, lying in the grass and firmly embracing each other. He does not only like the idea of watching but he also dares to disturb them. Completely ignoring Cupid, he focuses his full attention exclusively on Psyche. He is fascinated by her fair appearance, in the same way as he was loving Fanny Brawne for her beauty. For him, Psyche is not only "Fairer than Phoebe's sapphire-region'd star" (26) but, in fact, the "brightest" goddess and "loveliest vision" (24) he has ever seen.

Reading the entire ode, it becomes increasingly apparent that he grants her no other quality than her breath-taking looks. By reducing Psyche to her outer appearance, he has managed to strip her of all her individuality and power. He makes her mute by claiming that she has "no voice" (32) and allows himself to take her most intimate "secrets" away ("pardon that thy secrets should be sung," 3): "The poet claims to be Psyche's champion, yet his benevolence is that of the despot. Psyche remains silently subservient, while the poet usurps the privilege of discourse" (Aske: 1985, 104). The female figure has become the silent and vanished object of male quest and representation, merely serving as a source for creating future songs.

215

Since he cannot *be* her (or be as beautiful as she is), he wants to *have* her – have her all for himself. To ensure that she will not suddenly disappear, he intends to build a prison-like temple to lock her up:

I will be thy priest, and build a fane
In some untrodden region of my mind,
Where branchèd thoughts, new grown with pleasant pain
Instead of pines shall murmur in the wind (50-53)

He intends to "labyrinth" her in a dark and unknown region of his mind where she will be kept under his authority – and unreachable for others. As in the passage from *Lamia* mentioned at the beginning of this section, and as in many another of Keats's poems, this impenetrable region is compared to a beautiful garden which he creates, plants and maintains:

A *rosy sanctuary* will I dress
With the wreath'd trellis of a working brain, [...]
With all the *gardener* Fancy e'er could feign,
Who breeding flowers, will never breed the same
(59-60; 62-63, emphasis mine)

This garden is not a representation of "real" nature, but a textual product. The poet "is to weave himself a private paradise, a pleasure garden or *hortus conclusus* in which he will be the omnipotent gardener" (Steyaert: 1996). In this sense, the poet has become the ultimate creator, the architect of a poetic realm in which Beauty is the ultimate source of inspiration whether it be in the shape of a woman or a garden.[202] Here, he will "breed" flowery thoughts that will never be the same. He procreates new compositions through the consummation of his love for Psyche. Ironically, by promising what he will do for her, the poem has already been written and come to an end. Similarly, he who wants to give her a voice ("let me be thy choir," 44; "[let me be] thy voice," 46) was the one to make her voiceless. Originally meant as a quest, his search for a Muse[203] has now become a conquest.

---

[202] Alan Bewell linked Keats's interest in gardening and his obsession with female figures in a very interesting and convincing way: "Looking at nature or flowers through Keats's eyes, we begin to see a woman; the desire for nature and to be a 'poet of nature' fuses with erotic desire and masculine authority: his bees 'wrestle' with flowers, his heroes sleep with nature, his eye ranges among flowers in a desire to possess them" (Bewell: 1992, 80).

[203] On the idea of the Muse in particular and women as allegory in general, *see* Simone de Beauvoir, *Le Deuxième Sexe*, 1st ed., Paris 1949. For a discussion of the dead beloved as muse, *see* Elisabeth Bronfen, *Over Her Dead Body: Death, Femininity and the Aestetic*, Manchester 1992, especially chapter 17.

Anne Mellor has argued that the poet has a self "that melts into the Other, that becomes the Other" (Mellor: 1993, 175) but it is more likely to argue that he does not so much seek unification with, as simply consume, the Other. In this sense, Margaret Homans has rightly pointed out that "Keats equates his imaginative project, then, not only with male sexual potency but also with the masculine appropriation of the feminine" (Homans: 1990, 344). It is, thus, not surprising that the *Ode to Psyche* ends with a highly sexual connotation when the goddess is expected to let her lover in:

> there shall be for thee all soft delight
> That shadowy thought can win,
> A bright torch, and a casement ope at night,
> To let the warm Love in! (64-67)

At that point one should note that "the male incorporation of the feminine" (Richardson: 1988, 19) can also be seen as a narcissistic act of self-love. Created in his mind, the woman exists but there.[204] She is not only the highly eroticised object of desire, but also the poet's very own imagination. Thus, catching sight of Psyche in the forest, he says: "I see, and sing, *by my own eyes* inspired" (43, emphasis mine). Being his own innermost psyche, Psyche becomes his ultimate auto-erotic Muse.

Ode to a Nightingale

> O let me melt into thee; let the sounds
> Of our close voices marry at their birth;
> Let us entwine hoveringly
> (*Endymion*, II, 815-817)

The ode begins with the poet's desperate wish to escape the pains and sorrows of the outer world. Slowly "a drowsy numbness pains" (1) his senses as if he had "emptied some dull opiate" (3) until he finally shifts into an apparently relieving dream world. There, he meets the Nightingale, a feminised figure described as a "light-wingèd Dryad of the trees" (7). Seeing her, he desires to

> leave the world unseen,
> and with thee fade away into the forest dim. (19-20)

---

[204] Karen Swann has linked this idea with the Lacanian theory of *la femme n'existe pas*, meaning that the woman does not exist "except as a fantasmatic construct, which, insofar as it occupies the place of the unattainable Other, figures the imaginary unity of identity 'itself'" (Swann: 1988, 90).

He wants to follow the Nightingale into her world – an enterprise which is depicted as a journey into a dark forest. It soon becomes clear that her 'habitat' has nothing in common with the 'real' world around him. Contrasting the desirable realm inhabited by the Nightingale, he describes the mundane "here" as a grievous

> Here, where men sit and hear each other groan; [...]
> Where youth grows pale, and spectre-thin, and dies;
> Where but to think is to be full of sorrow. (24, 26-27)

It is a "here" he wants to get quickly "Away! Away!" (31) from. At the same time, the Nightingale's place he is pining for is also described as "here" (38). It is a mysterious place that can only be entered through "charm'd magic casements" (69). If those windows have been found, they will be "opening on the foam / Of perilous seas, in faery lands" (69-70). Then, the journey into the 'other' world has been completed. Since Keats has decided to call both places "here", it can be argued that they should be understood as one and the same place, or more precisely, they should be viewed as two places in one and the same self. If the one world is the *conscious* outer world he experiences, the other world can be described as the *unconscious* within himself. Both exist "here" and both happen now, that is, at the same time.

In *Ode to Psyche*, the poet just wanted to possess the woman and keep her locked up in his mind. Here, he is tempted to go one step further and merge with her: Leave his "sole self" (72) and become one with the eternal Nightingale. However, he soon notices that to escape the world of self-conscious mortality and fade into the other, imaginary world is to die. On the one hand, longing for total de-composition, he says:

> many a time
> I have been half in love with easeful Death, [...]
> Now more than ever seems it rich to die,
> To cease upon the midnight with no pain
> (51-52, 55-56)

On the other hand, the empathy with the Nightingale and the escape into her "faery lands", that is, the pleasurable loss of identity will debar him from a return to an own, creative self. In her realm, he cannot be a gardener for there is no garden anymore – just "embalmèd darkness" (43). Here, where "there is no light" (38) he "cannot see what flowers are at my feet" (41). It is not a place where he can be active and create but, on the contrary, a place where he originates from, where he is being created.
Originally drawn towards the Nightingale's song, he ultimately rejects it for it has not only become femininely seductive ("the fancy cannot cheat so well / As she is fam'd to do, deceiving elf." 73-74) but also destructive of his masculine sense of self. Knowing that only *"Thou* wast not born for death, immortal Bird!" (61) he has to return to the mundane world before he will be forever "forlorn" (70):

Forlorn! The very word is like a bell
To toll me back from thee to *my sole self!*
(71-72, emphasis mine)

The poet recovers his sense of identity and, thus, puts an abrupt end to his project of Negative Capability. Having successfully travelled into his deeper (feminised) self, he can now start his "journey homeward to the habitual self!" (*Endymion*, II, 276). He knows that if he stayed in the feminine world for longer than a moment, he would not have been able to return to tell the tale. In a letter to Fanny Brawne he made an similar discovery. He wrote: "it seems to me that a few more moments thought of you would uncrystallize and dissolve me – I must not give way to it – but turn to my *writing* again – if I fail I shall die hard" (*Letters*, II, 142). His visit to Poesy's "faery lands" in the *Ode to a Nightingale* has given him the necessary inspiration to write. The feminised Nightingale of imagination has once again become a crucial aid to his literary production. It has also been pointed out that the nightingale is a symbol of the medieval troubadour, and thus, the poet himself. This assumption would correspond with the idea of the Nightingale's realm being the poet's own unconscious. Though the title implies that the ode is dedicated to a nightingale, it is more likely that the poem is about the poet himself and his voyage rather than about the bird. In this sense, it is not surprising that Andrew M. Cooper has called Keats's adventurous enterprise of the *Ode to a Nightingale* the "perilous seas of self-referentiality" (Cooper: 1988, 163).

Ode on Melancholy

Although all three poems selected for this paper have "Ode" in their titles, only *Psyche* and *Nightingale* were dedicated *to* somebody. The title of the Melancholy Ode implies, however, that this poem is meant to be *on* something. Hence, what is being praised is apparently not a person but a state of mind - namely melancholy. Whereas in the previous two odes, the poet was directly talking to the Nightingale and Psyche, respectively, here we know that he is not addressing his lines to Melancholy. It is not completely clear what kind of (male) person he is talking to but whoever it may be, the poet is trying to issue a warning to him. With a number of imperatives he seeks to convince someone suffering of depression that it is better to turn to Melancholy than to Death:

No, no, go *not* to Lethe, *neither* twist
Wolfs-bane, tight-rooted, for its poisonous wine; [...]
Make *not* your rosary of yew-berries,
Nor let the beetle, *nor* the death-moth be
Your mournful Psyche... (1-2, 5-7; emphasis mine)

He is urging the anonymous man, not to let Death be the "partner in your sorrow's mysteries" (8) for it will "drown the wakeful anguish of the soul" (10) forever. Instead, he should be well-prepared for the moment "when the melancholy fit shall fall / Sudden from heaven like a weeping cloud" (11-12). He should not retreat into nothingness, but should let Melancholy – who is now depicted as a woman – take him as a temporary playmate. The (conventional) idea of a woman taking a men into her power also fills Keats's numerous letters to Fanny Brawne. There, she is depicted as the one who is liable for his painful adoration of her. Though *he* is the one who is desperately in love with her, *she* is made responsible for having stolen his heart. Thus, he writes: "Ask yourself my love whether you are not very cruel to have so entrammelled me, so destroyed my freedom" (*Letters*, II, 123). Similarly, she is held responsible for his ever-growing fascination for her: "I wish *you* could invent some means to make me at all happy without you. Every hour I am more and more concentrated in you" (*Letters*, II, 311). The notion of entrapment is not only a dilemma but also a dominant theme in much of Keats's writing. The power of the feminine is seen as a pleasurable pain, or to use the wording of the *Ode*, an "aching Pleasure" (23). Pain and pleasure are for Keats as inextricably bound to each other as pain and writing. Idealising despair and suffering, he wrote in a letter to his brother George: "Do you not see how necessary a World of Pains and troubles is [...]? A Place where the heart must feel and suffer in a thousand diverse ways!" (*Letters*, II, 102). He believed that only through hardship and misadventure one would be able to be creative and productive. In the *Ode on Melancholy*, the suffering is caused by feminised Melancholy who has temporarily caught the masculine self in her "temple of Delight" (25). But like the poet's voyage to the Nightingale, he sooner or later has to find the strength to free himself from Melancholy's firm grip if he does not want to be desubstantialised. Feminine strength has to be brought under control:

> if thy mistress some rich anger shows,
> Emprison her hand, and let her rave,
> And feed deep, deep upon her peerless eyes. (18-20)

Then, restricting her subjectivity and expressiveness, her gloomy beauty can be enjoyed and used as a source of inspiration. But if someone fails to appropriate her, he will be taken by her, by the man-eater called Melancholy:

> save him whose strenuous tongue
> Can burst [her] grape against his palate fine;
> His soul shall taste the sadness of her might
> And be among her cloudy trophies hung. (27-30)

However, once again it should be pointed out that melancholy is not simply the monstrous creature depicted in those lines but actually a state of mind. And again we are confronted with a poet who managed to stage in the last couple of lines of *Ode on*

Melancholy "a drama in which the chief actor is the poet's 'complex mind', a mind whose consciousness of itself is always – self-estrangingly, creatively – a linguistic event" (O'Neill: 1997, 209).

Masculinity, Narcissism and the Ode as Form

"I know not why Poetry and I have been so distant lately I must make some advances soon or she will cut me entirely"
(*Letters*, II, 74)

"Upon whatever page of Keats's poetry there falls the shadow of a living woman, it falls calamitously like an eclipse."
H. W. Garrod (Wolfson: 1997, 169)

A list of similar quotes could be continued nearly *ad infinitum*, for Keats was indeed intensely fascinated by the idea of defining poetry as feminine - as a mistress he could desire and be in love with. In personifying his poetry as a woman, he was able to declare himself a male suitor courting Poetry. In Keats's thinking, an (ideal) woman meant beauty and thus belonged, as the object of men's gaze, under male ownership. He believed that looking at her would give him the necessary inspiration to write. She should be his food for thought, a feminine nurturer of masculine self-realisation. The Odes may be interpreted as the best examples for this abstract love affair and poetic courtship. In being a kind of sexualised act of writing, the Odes represent the intersection of Keats's two identities as Poet and as Lover. Whether he calls them Melancholy, Psyche, Nightingale, Imagination, Love, Ambition or Poesy, in his mind they are all women. In the *Ode on Indolence*, for example, we witness even three feminised figures at a time:

> The first was a fair maid, and Love her name;
> The second was Ambition, pale her cheek,
> And ever watchful with fatigued eye;
> The last, whom I love more, the more of blame
> Is heap'd upon her, maiden most unmeek, –
> I knew to be *my demon Poesy*.
> (*Ode on Indolence*, 25-30, emphasis mine)

The women he mentions are not just to look at, but are also assigned a certain function. His "demon Poesy," for example, is his favourite because all the "blame" for writing bad poetry can be "heap'd upon her" (29). She is not only responsible for the success of future poetic compositions, but also made liable for a failure of creativity. She is always both, the highest object of masculine desire and the victimiser of men. As his personal Muse, she is "the still object of his contemplation and the receiver of his anxieties, hope, desire and despair" (Watkins: 1990, 244). Or to use Keats's own wording: she is his "dearest Love / sweet home of all my fears / And hopes" (*To Fanny*, 9-10). In order not to give others the opportunity to speculate whether or not the women in his mind and poetry were meant to be he himself, Keats was cherishing the illusion that they had nothing in common with him. He had to keep them artificially very distinct from him, as objects of desire and vision – for if "his creative project is defined as courtship, the woman must remain resistant to him and intact or 'abstract'" (Homans: 1990, 345). Hence, Keats complied with a conventional pattern of male identity formation: instead of an *identification* with, he insisted on a fundamental *distinction* from the feminine.[205]

The (ideal) woman is both created by, and stimulating for, his thoughts like Psyche who had once become locked up in his Eden-like brain. Describing his mental admiration for the feminine he wrote in a letter: "When I was a Schoolboy I though[t] a fair Woman a pure Goddess, my mind was a soft nest in which some one of them slept" (*Letters*, I, 341). However, the odes discussed have shown that romantic admiration was soon superseded by the wish to possess or appropriate the woman praised. For the sake of the poet's personal self-realisation the woman's individuality had to be sacrificed. Thus, Psyche's beauty was transformed into beautiful thoughts and the encounter with the Nightingale was used to test the poet's sense of (him)self. Several researchers have elaborated on this point. For example, Diane Hoeveler has described the shift from admiration to consumption as a threefold process: First, "the Romantics cannibalistically consumed these female characters, [then] shaped them into ideal alter egos, and most of the time destroyed them by the conclusion of the poem" (Hoeveler: 1990, 9).

In this sense, the Romantic idea of self-loss was only a temporary means to find inspiration and deeper insight, and was finally repressed for self-positioning and self-comprehension. Marlon B. Ross (1988) has pointed out that almost every Romantic quest for an*other* sphere ends up in conquest, that is, in a world envisioned and claimed. The Other, the feminine, has to be conquered and incorporated if the poet is to reach a certain sense of wholeness. In order to become complete, he has to gain *full* possession of the goddess he desires. Referring originally to Fanny Brawne, Keats wrote:

O, let me have thee whole, all, all be mine!
That shape, that fairness, that sweet minor zest
Of love, your kiss, those hands, those eyes divine,
That warm, white, lucent, million-pleasured breast,
Yourself your soul in pity give me all,
Withhold no atom's atom or I die

---

[205] For a discussion on *identification* and *distinction* as important categories in the 'man-making' process, *see* Elisabeth Badinter, *Die Identität des Mannes: Seine Natur, seine Seele, seine Rolle*, München, Zürich 1997.

(*I Cry Your Mercy*, 5-10)

Down to the very last atom, Keats wanted to take complete possession of the woman he loved. Her individuality, her soul and her beauty shall devolve upon the poet. Then, he would presumably be able to "see the world *whole*, to assimilate both time and space into a vision that is both individual and collective" (Ross: 1988, 26). It was meant to be a Promethean victory of the poet's literary *Culture* over feminine *Nature*:

> Now I have tasted her sweet soul to the core
> All other depths are shallow: essences...
> (*Endymion*, II, 904-905)

Also Daniel P. Watkins has remarked that the feminine figure, in being conquered, is not only silenced but also transformed. She has not only been denied all human complexity but also made into a passive repository of the masculine desire for completion. Like an 'auxiliary tool' the feminine "is cherished because its subordination serves the masculine ego's carefully constructed sense of itself" (Watkins: 1990, 247). The masculine construction of self is one of the most important points found in the essays cited on Keats's 'consumption' of the feminine. For, I argue, it leads to the quintessence of his Odes. If these poems are not about the feminine figures called Psyche, Nightingale and Melancholy, the question arises what their exact purpose is. If they exist to literally portray and mirror the beauty of his thoughts, there is reason to believe that the odes are a kind of narcissistic self-praise.

The idea of women as mirrors is found in several of his poems. At one point, he is searching for his beauty in a woman and is "bending to her open eyes, where he was mirror'd small in paradise" (*Lamia*, II, 46-47). Also in the *Ode to Melancholy*, the woman functions as a mirror when he suggests to "feed deep, deep down upon her peerless eyes" (20). In supposedly looking into a 'real' woman, the poet is actually looking at her to see aspects of himself.[206] A direct reference to mirroring and Narcissus is made in one of Keats's early poems where he identifies himself with Narcissus who is "Drooping its beauty o'er the watery clearness, / To woo its own sad image into nearness" (*I stood tip-toe upon a little hill*, 173-174).

His constant preoccupation with the self as well as his enthusiastic striving for beauty can indeed be interpreted as a sign of Narcissism. He loves the woman in himself, for she is his own creativity. He comes to annihilate the distinction between himself and the desired object. This kind of annihilation has also been called "narcissistic similitude and involution" (Hagstrum: 1989, 78). Here, the ode is viewed as a poem without a concrete object of desire but with a subject at its centre of interest. There is an *objectless* desire that fulfils itself by yearning for itself. Or put differently, the mind is both subject and object, and full of desire for itself. Yet, on a superficial

---

[206] It should be mentioned that in her famous work *Speculum* (1974), Luce Irigaray has extensively elaborated on the idea of women mirroring the masculine self.

level, the subject is staged as part of the 'discourse of the other' but in doing so, the masculine subject is actually reading its own identity. Without pushing the feminine other in front, the ode would be addressed solely to himself. He needs the women and feminised figures to save himself from blatant Narcissism.

In this sense, each of Keats's odes can be described as "a true ode insofar as it becomes a celebration; it celebrates the authority of the poet's own voice" (Aske: 1985, 105). In his earlier writing, Keats had insisted on the distinction between "Men of Power" who "have a proper self" and "Men of Genius" who "have not any individuality, any determined Character" (*Letters*, I, 184). However, his later poetry in general and his Odes in particular seem to represent an end of his Negative Capability. He has come to realise that "the ability of the poet or genius to 'lose' personal identity, to expand and surrender the self, must depend at bottom on the exceptionally strong identity or self" (Schapiro: 1983, 36). Whereas his early poems disclosed a sense of 'effeminate' uncertainty and doubt, his Odes reveal a strong and masculine sense of self. The loss of selfhood is no longer something to strive for because it atomises the ability to name and represent.

Conclusion

My imagination is a Monastery and I am its Monk.
(*Letters*, II, 323)

In his earlier poetry, Keats might have called himself a chameleon in an infinite space of possible identifications – a poet wandering in an imaginary no man's land, shielded from any outer influence. However, his style changed substantially over time. Whether it was his personal choice as a consequence of a mental maturation process or whether the devastating criticism of his contemporaries forced him to change his 'chameleon' poetry is still not clear. Six months before his death, he had not only come to cement his imagination in a rigid Monastery, but made himself also its one and only Monk.

It seems as if in his later poetry he struggled to distance himself from his earlier 'effeminate' and 'feminine' writing. Whereas in earlier poems he was happy to merge with nymphs, dryads and fairies, in his "mature" poetry he saw himself "forced to contain and crystalize the feminine as a sign of his manhood, as evidence of his self-control" (Ross: 1989, 173). The shift to a more 'masculine' writing brought him, however, in a severe conflict with the given gender codes of his environment. Susan Wolfson has rightly remarked that "his overall syntax of gender is more zigzag than linear, and the total story more indeterminate than definitive" (Wolfson: 1995, 2).

On the one hand, Keats can be viewed as a poet who was challenging and enlarging the socially restricted definition of manhood. In so doing, he belonged to a group of poets and writers who did not at all feel comfortable with society's obsolete values and structures of authority that ruled Regency England. It also implies that there was not *one* homogenous, consistent 'masculinity' applying to all men, but that there were many, often competing forms of masculinities. On the other hand, Alan Richardson has argued that, in moving from an *Age of Reason* to an *Age of Feeling*, male writers did not so much change their sense of masculinity but, on the contrary, colonised the conventionally feminine domain of sensibility (Richardson: 1988).

Although Keats had to cope with an age which demanded that an author's gender be expressed in a specific style, Keats never coalesced with women of his age. It is, thus, a misconception to believe that fighting against conventional images of manliness, made him an 'honorary' woman. Though writing presumably 'feminine' poetry, by writing exclusively for men, he elected himself, after all, a member of the 'male club'. Tim Fulford has noted that Romantic poets found themselves in an uncomfortable and often paradox struggle for manliness. Though they were fighting against conventional norms, few doubted their own manliness. As a consequence, "their own identities – as authors and as men – were unstable [...], their Romantic masculinity a matter of anxiety, self-betrayal and weakness in the midst of apparent strength" (Fulford: 1999, 20).

Finally, Keats's letters give rise to a third, very personal aspect. It may be said that in all his writing on women, Keats was after all longing for emotional certainty. Most of his poems are accompanied by a spirit of loss or a painful farewell (as in *Nightingale*): "I eternally see her figure eternally vanishing" (*Letters*, II, 345). But perhaps he was longing for the moment when his fears of losing what he has just gained would come to an end. When he could be sure that his love will be heard and perhaps returned. Having become ultimately dissatisfied with a type of poetic writing solely composed of 'uncertainties' (as suggested in Negative Capability), he wished to gain full possession of his beloved one ("all be mine"). However, this drastic change may have been an expression of fearful hope and desire for a more stable existence. Hence, he wrote in one of his very last poems:

> Bright Star, would I were stedfast as thou art–
> Not in lone splendor hung aloft the night,
> And watching, with eternal lids apart [...]
> No–yet still stedfast, still unchangeable
> Pillow'd upon my fair love's ripening breast,
> To feel for ever its soft swell and fall,
> Awake for ever in a sweet unrest,
> Still, still to hear her tender-taken breath,
> And so live ever–
> (*Bright Star*, 1-3, 9-14)

Keats, John, *The Letters of John Keats 1814-1821*, Hyder Edward Rollins (ed.), 2 vols., Cambridge 1958.
Keats, John, *The Poems of John Keats*, Jack Stillinger (ed.), London 1978.

Aske, Martin, *Keats and Hellenism. An Essay*, Cambridge etc. 1985.
Badinter, Elisabeth, *Die Identität des Mannes. Seine Natur, seine Seele, seine Rolle*, München, Zürich, 1997.
Beauvoir, Simone de, *Le Deuxième Sexe*, 1st ed., Paris 1949.
Bewell, Alan, "Keats's 'Realm of Flora'", in: *Studies in Romanticism* 31 (Spring 1992), pp. 71-98.
Bronfen, Elisabeth, *Over Her Dead Body. Death, Femininity and the Aestetic*, Manchester 1992.
Cooper, Andrew M., *Doubt and Identity in Romantic Poetry*, New Haven 1988.
Cox, Philip, *Gender, Genre and the Romantic Poets, An Introduction*, Manchester 1996.
Cuddon, John Anthony, *A Dictionary of Literary Terms*, London 1977.
Curran, Stuart, "Romantic Poetry, The I Altered", in: Anne K. Mellor (ed.), *Romanticism and Feminism*, Bloomington 1988, pp. 185-207.
Fraser, G. S., *John Keats, Odes*, London 1971.
Fulford, Tim, *Romanticism and Masculinity, Gender, Politics and Poetics in the Writings of Burke, Coleridge, Cobbett, Wordsworth, DeQuincey and Hazlitt*, New York 1999.
Hagstrum, Jean H., *Eros and Vision: From Restoration to Romanticism*, Evaston 1989.
Hoeveler, Diane Long, *Romantic Androgyny, The Woman Within*, University Park, London 1990.
Homans, Margaret, "Keats Reading Women, Women Reading Keats", in: *Studies in Romanticism* 29 (Fall 1990), pp. 341-70.
Irigaray, Luce, *Speculum de l'autre femme*, 1st ed., Paris 1974.
Mellor, Anne K. (ed.), *Romanticism and Feminism*, Bloomington 1988.
Mellor, Anne K., *Romanticism & Gender*, New York 1993.
Mizukoshi, Ayumi, "The Cockney Politics of Gender. The Case of Hunt and Keats", in: *Romanticism on the Net* 14 (May 1999), http://users.ox.ac.uk/~scatt0385/cockneygender.html.
O'Neill, Michael, *Romanticism and the Self-Conscious Poem*, Oxford 1997.
Redpath, Theodore, *The Young Romantics and Critical Opinion 1807-1824*, London 1973.
Richardson, Alan, "Romanticism and the Colonization of the Feminine", in: Anne K. Mellor (ed.), *Romanticism and Feminism*, Bloomington 1988, pp. 13-25.
Ross, Marlon B., "Beyond the Fragmented Word, Keats and the Limits of Patrilineal Language", in: Laura Claridge, Elizabeth Langland (eds.), *Out of Bounds, Male Writers and Gender(ed) Criticism*, Amherst 1990, pp. 110-131.
Ross, Marlon B., "Romantic Quest and Conquest. Troping Masculine Power in the Crisis of Poetic Identity", in: Anne K. Mellor (ed.), *Romanticism and Feminism*, Bloomington 1988, pp. 26-51.

Ross, Marlon B., *The Contours of Masculine Desire. Romanticism and the Rise of Women's Poetry*, New York, Oxford 1989.

Schapiro, Barbara Ann, *The Romantic Mother, Narcissistic Patterns in Romantic Poetry*, Baltimore 1983.

Steyaert, Kris, "Poetry as Enforcement, Conquering the Muse in Keats's 'Ode to Psyche'", in: *Romanticism on the Net* 1 (February 1996), http://users.ox.ac.uk/~scatt0385/psyche.html.

Swann, Karen, "Harassing the Muse", in: Anne K. Mellor (ed.), *Romanticism and Feminism*, Bloomington 1988, pp. 81-92.

Vendler, Helen, *The Odes of John Keats*, Cambridge, London 1983.

Watkins, Daniel P., "Historical Amnesia and Patriarchal Morality in Keats's 'Ode on a Grecian Urn'", in: G. A. Rosso, Daniel P. Watkins (eds.), *Spirits of Fire, English Romantic Writers and Contemporary Historical Methods*, London, Toronto 1990, pp. 240-259.

Wolfson, Susan J., "A Lesson in Romanticism, Gendering the Soul", in: Thomas Pfau, Robert F. Gleckner (eds.), *Lessons of Romanticism, A Critical Companion*, Durham 1998, pp. 349-75.

Wolfson, Susan J., "Feminizing Keats", in: Hermione de Almeida (ed.), *Critical Essays on John Keats*, Boston 1990, pp. 317-356.

Wolfson, Susan J., *Formal Charges, The Shaping of Poetry in British Romanticism*, Stanford 1997.

Wolfson, Susan J., "Keats and the Manhood of the Poet", in: *European Romantic Review* 6 (Summer 1995), pp. 1-37.

Wolfson, Susan J., "Keats's 'Gordian Complication' of Women", in: Walter H. Evert, Jack W. Rhodes (eds.), *Approaches to Teaching Keats's Poetry*, New York 1991, pp. 77-85.

Ingrid THALER

Masculinity and Culture at War: Sexualized culture and culturalized sexuality in Philip Roth's *Portnoy's Complaint*

> My strongest interest is in the life of men. What is it—what does it *mean* to be a man in my time? If you put all my books together, you have a rather full portrait, no apologies given, what it is to be a man—a father, a son, a young son, an aging son, a lover, a psychotic maniac, etc. I've tried not to leave anything out. (*Mein Leben:* 1998)

This is how the American Jewish writer Philip Roth himself outlined the predominant theme of his work in 1998: masculinity. Critics agree with this account, although they are not always thoroughly pleased with the literary results of Roth's preoccupation: "With the possible exception of John Updike, Roth has plumbed the male psyche more thoroughly than any other American novelist of his generation. It can become tedious—he sometimes writes as if he is stuck in a bad marriage with his own legacy," Brian D. Johnson notes (1992, 254). Since the publication of his first book, *Goodbye, Columbus*, in 1959, which consists of a novella and five short stories, Roth has needed 24 books to excessively elaborate on the issue of being a Jewish heterosexual male in post-World War II America. His most recent literary product, *The Human Stain*, came out in April 2000.

In this essay, I would like to confine myself to a thorough analysis of Roth's fourth publication, *Portnoy's Complaint* (1969), that can be understood as exemplifying recurring assertions of masculinity in Roth's work. Except for two texts,[207] Roth always portrays a male protagonist who in various ways struggles to come to terms with his identity as a man. Roth's masculine self (and at the same time his Freudian *alter ego*) is the third-generation American Jew of his own age who observes changes in the social roles of the sexes.

In *Portnoy's Complaint* (1969), a late sixties' sexual liberation megaseller and until today Roth's most successful and most famous text, 33-year-old Alexander Portnoy delivers an uninterrupted monologue, structured on associative reflections, to his silent psychoanalyst, Dr. Spielvogel, on his couch. In 1969, the text challenged its contemporary readers in many respects and on many levels: It attacks assimilation into as well as separation from American mainstream culture on the grounds of ethnic distinctions,[208] and it attacks American perceptions of sexuality by exposing an American Jewish male's most intimate sexual longings and practices. The novel criticizes American Jewish and Gentile principles of constructing masculine roles,

---

[207] In *When She Was Good* (1967), Roth places Midwestern Gentile Lucy Nelson in the text's center; in *The Counterlife* (1987), he attempts to give Maria a voice of her own.

[208] For a discussion of its reception in the Jewish community, see Cooper: 1996, 108-124.

such as within the socially sanctified American nuclear family unit, and as a phenomenon distinctly shaped by the American experience. This American brand of masculinity, inscribed in *American* WASP history and literature, clashes with Alexander Portnoy's idea of representing *Jewishness* in America.

Portnoy refuses notions of a traditionally constituted masculinity as transmitted by his parents as well as American notions of what it means to be a man from outside mainstream society. He is unable to live up to any of these constructions. In the text, the construction of masculine gender identity is closely tied to a discourse on cultural identity. Being American as a male and reasserting one's masculinity takes place on the basis of cultural negotiations. Masculinity and culture are at war as Portnoy intermingles sexuality with culture and culture with sexuality and in that sense sexualizes culture and culturalizes sexuality. The most obvious impression that *Portnoy's Complaint* leaves in the general reader's mind after a first reading is the text's play with Freudian psychoanalysis. One cannot ignore the obvious ironic stance that drives the hyperbolic monologue, caricaturing its narrating "I" as another *grotesque* figure in the American literary imagination. The author's distance to the first-person narrator is established through this device. As Roth explains:

This is a man speaking out of an overwhelming obsession: he is obscene because he wants to be saved. An odd, maybe even mad way to go about seeking personal salvation; but, nonetheless, the investigation of this passion, and of the combat it precipitates with his conscience is what's at the center of the novel. Portnoy's pains raise out of his refusal to be bound any longer by taboos which, rightly or wrongly, *he* experiences as diminishing and unmanning. The joke on Portnoy is that for him breaking the taboo turns out to be as unmanning in the end as honoring it. Some joke. (*Reading Myself*: 1975, 19)

Portnoy wants to "save" his masculinity that is configured in very specific—and very odd—terms. Without ignoring this narrative distance, one can nevertheless analyze the cultural 'ingredients' of Portnoy's masculine desperation, 'ingredients' that reflect American and American Jewish assertions of masculinity.

The most obvious instance of Portnoy's struggle with sex and culture is his rejection of Jewishness. Portnoy argues that it generates a construction of masculinity he repudiates. According to the recounting of his childhood memories, the specifically American Jewishness he has experienced creates effeminate men, unmans them, and does not prepare American-born Jewish sons to grow into manhood. Portnoy's construction of masculinity, therefore, presumes an essentialist view of the sexes: There is an inherent, biologically grounded *manhood* (not masculinity) that is obviously clearly distinguishable from *womanhood* (not femininity). This means that, even though maleness is a specific innate state of a biologically male individual, it is nevertheless only a pre-condition every male has to work hard at to formulate into manhood. Portnoy claims that the Jewishness he has grown up with has not prepared him for growing into the idealized construction of masculinity he wants to delineate throughout his monologue, and has, therefore, left him confused, weak, and effeminate. His construction of masculinity is, though approached from an essentialist point of view, established as an evolutionary process that has been suppressed, misunderstood, and denied in his secular Jewish family. The idea of an essential masculinity that nevertheless needs to be achieved in order to run free causes Portnoy's masculine identity crisis since these two features inherent in the construction itself are incompatible. Portnoy does not only contradict himself in the very construction of his masculinity. The reader experiences Jewishness strictly from a phallocentric point of view as the novel is structurally designed as a monologue, thereby reducing perceptions to the singular realm of the male first-person narrator. Whether and in what sense Jewishness might be complicated to come to terms with as an American Jewish daughter is never discussed, not even mentioned. The text portrays being Jewish as a male presupposition American men of a Jewish background have to struggle with. Nevertheless, Portnoy insists that his Jewish background has made him effeminate. He generalizes his adolescent struggle as an archetypal experience all American Jewish males have to face. His struggle for masculinity is the Jewish male-as-a-son's inability to escape the females that perpetuate Jewish culture and morals in the US. This means that secular American Jewish culture is, in Portnoy's view, a culture that is clearly shaped and dominated by females, in particular, by mothers. Portnoy wants to reject his Jewish background because he experiences this culture as a matriarchy as opposed to the American mainstream patriarchy in which men excel. At the core of Portnoy's ethnic identity, therefore, lies another contradiction in which Portnoy feels trapped: Jewishness is an exclusively male condition; however, *male* Jewishness is shaped *by females*. The American Jewish male is caught, or so Portnoy claims, in perpetual son-ship. Being under too much Jewish female influence at home, particularly of his mother, he is unable 'to become a man.' Therefore, Portnoy experiences Jewish femininity as threatening to his masculine self.[209]

Portnoy's first encounter with Jewish femininity at home is frightening. His mother's menstruation is described as a bloody, undesirable experience Portnoy refuses to confront (42-44). His mother's body appears as a terrifying and painful entity. This childhood memory establishes the negative stereotype of the Jewish woman as undesirably feminine, as embodying a negative, painful experience of being a woman through the body. Portnoy not only fears but also despises this side of female bodily experience as alien to the human body he knows. He calls his reaction

---

[209] For a discussion of Jewish gender stereotypes see Prell: 1990. She observes that "[M]en and women [...] may be joined by ethnic ties but they often experience the consequences and meaning of their ethnicity differently" (249). She also examines the female stereotyping of the Jewish Mother and the Jewish-American Princess (JAP) and notes the striking absence of male stereotyping in American Jewish humor. This "suggests a fundamental incompatibility at the core of American Jewish culture. To be an American and a Jew necessitates relinquishing one or another of those identities. [...] The [...] stereotypical women represent the anxiety, anger, and pain of Jewish men as they negotiate an American Jewish identity" (252/53).

upon encountering these instances of female physicality "vulnerability" (43). This indicates that Portnoy is scared of and actually receptive to being 'taken over' by what he defines as a femininity that intimidates men. Portnoy describes these early encounters with the female body as disruptive and frighteningly alien to his fragile, boyish self. Yet, by admitting that his boyhood self is fragile, Portnoy undermines his own gender construction and establishes a self-conscious masculinity that is insecure even at the level of bodily experience. Portnoy refuses the femininity at home, which he relates to Jewish women, because it, as he claims, intrudes his masculine sphere and unmans him. The Jewish female embodies a femininity that undermines his sense of the gender constructions he tries to maintain, while it brings the distinctly female experience of this body as strikingly alien to the male body into perspective.

The Jewish women Portnoy encounters outside the house are not feminine in the way Portnoy wants them to be. These encounters take place in Israel and are tellingly entitled "In Exile" (241). The women embody the Jewish culture that despises American capitalist consumer society. They are aggressive, tough, self-assured, and overwhelmingly threatening to Portnoy's self-conscious masculinity. These women do not provide Portnoy with the assumption that their femininity is dependent on his masculinity socially and sexually, and, therefore, epitomize a femininity Portnoy is unable to deal with. Portnoy wants to conquer Jewish culture through the sexual conquest of Jewish women. In order to identify himself with a culture, Portnoy needs to feel attracted to this culture sexually and through women. "Yes, I would have (now that I was unaccountably here) what is called an educational experience. I would improve myself, which is my way, after all" (252), Portnoy describes his approach to Israel and being Jewish. This "improvement" turns out to be the "educational experience" of accepting Jewish women as desirable, as a non-threatening femininity by sexually "conquering" them. But Portnoy fails. Neither the Lieutnant of the Jewish army nor Naomi, who strikingly resembles his mother, fulfill Portnoy's demand for femininity (as he fails to fulfill their demands for masculinity). Portnoy's version of the Jewish romance does not end with the happily-ever-after male orgasm but with impotence: "*I couldn't get it up in the state of Israel!*" (257), Portnoy cries despaired. Portnoy refuses the femininity of strong and independent women and through this sexual refusal the Jewish culture of Israel. His homeland is the Jewish diaspora because he is as much a Jew as he is an American .

Portnoy desires "salvation," which means, he wants to acquire a sense of masculinity he feels comfortable with. He pits this ambition against his Jewish background that prevents him from achieving full masculinity, or, in the terms of the novel, 'real manhood.' Thus, masculinity, in Portnoy's sense, is clearly marked by the desire to be American, to assimilate into and to be accepted as part of mainstream culture. The construction of masculine identity is intermingled with the construction of cultural identity. Portnoy's refusal of his Jewish background seems to indicate that only the 'American man' embodies 'real' manhood. What Portnoy identifies as the 'American man,' though, is restricted to Gentiles. Gentiles are, according to Merriam-Webster's, all Christians (486). In Portnoy's and the popular understanding of

American Jewish culture, these Christians are white, preferably Protestant Americans of European descent, who, in Portnoy's view of America, form American population and shape its culture. Not only is Portnoy's notion of American-ness ignorant of the differential experiences of Jewish males and females and, therefore, sexist; his view on what constitutes America and being American is also deeply Eurocentric and enmeshed in imperialist WASP racism. America, in Portnoy's eyes, *is* Gentile. White Anglo-Saxon Protestant culture is the measure he uses for American-ness, dismissing any other ethnicities, ironically especially those underprivileged, uneducated ethnic minorities he represents in his public life as Assistant Commissioner for the City of New York Commission on Human Opportunity. But Portnoy does not want to behave like a Gentile *man* either. His masculine ideal, though aspiring to be called "American," refuses Gentile masculine behavior as well. The Gentile version of American masculinity "doesn't really appeal to him either " (Gottfried: 1988, 41):

[A] diet of abominable creatures well befits a breed of mankind so hopelessly shallow and empty-headed as to drink, to divorce, and to fight with their fists. All they know these imbecile eaters of the execrable, is to swagger, to insult, to sneer, and sooner or later to hit. Oh, also they know how to go out into the woods with a gun, these geniuses, and kill innocent wild deer, deer who themselves *nosh* quietly on berries and grasses and then go on their way, bothering no one. You stupid *goyim*! Reeking of beer and empty of ammunition, home you head, a dead animal (formerly alive) strapped to each fender, so that all the motorists along the way can see how strong and manly you are. (81) "This is, precisely, the attitude of many women (and some men) I know toward the pretensions of what passes for 'masculine' in American culture," Barbara Gottfried writes (41). Portnoy's description of American machismo does sound like a feminist stance toward American masculinity constructions. Nevertheless, Gottfried neglects to consider the context in which Portnoy presents this dismissal: He insists that it comprises all of Gentile culture and all of Gentile masculinity; he, therefore, excludes the female Gentile experience from the *human* experience and reduces Gentile masculinity to a monolithic entity. He adapts the negative stereotype of the Gentile male as the universal human experience, a well-known stance of patriarchal thinking and writing. Women are outside human society—outside the Jewish *and* the Gentile experience. His sense of the female is always presented in opposition to the human and destructive to the human (read male) identity. At best, Portnoy recognizes the establishment of stereotypical WASP male behavior as the norm not only for the constitution of masculinity but for all of society. Portnoy rejects machismo but still wants to be accepted in the Gentile patriarchal frame he defines as American culture. Even as he develops his own, Jewish-influenced construction of masculinity, he still desires acknowledgement from the WASP establishment and cannot withdraw from the standardization of this culture as the measure for American-ness. Portnoy's equation of the human with the male experience and his refusal of Gentile culture as a whole is, however, newly configured in his adoration of Gentile women. Even when he excludes them from Gentile culture defined as a celebration of macho rituals, they nevertheless embody and represent the desirable aspect of Gentile culture. He pejoratively refers to these Gentile women as *shikses*. Portnoy's adoration for them is *beyond* sexual arousal:

> But the *shikses*, ah, the *shikses*, are something else again [...] I am so awed that I am in a state of desire *beyond a hard-on*. My circumcised little dong is simply shriveled up with veneration. Maybe it's dread. How do they get so gorgeous, so healthy, so *blond*? My contempt for what they believe in is more than neutralized by my adoration of the way they look, the way they move and laugh and speak—the lives they must lead behind those *goyische* curtains! [...] O America! America! it may have been gold in the streets to my grandparents, it may have been a chicken in every pot to my father and mother, but to me, a child whose earliest movie memories are of Anne Rutherford and Alice Faye, America is a *shikse* under your arm whispering love love love love love love! (144-146)

Portnoy's sexual hunger for the feminine as embodied by the female is rooted in his desire for the cultural. In order to be integrated into American culture and, therefore, be acknowledged as masculine, Portnoy embarks on a sexual 'conquest' for Gentile acceptance of his masculinity. His desire for the feminine is a desire for the American mainstream culture he defines as Gentile. He establishes a role model of the feminine that serves to reaffirm his masculinity, a femininity that works as a complementary antipode to masculinity and is not threatening to his heterosexual masculine identity. His attraction to *shikses* as the embodiment of the complementary, desirable femininity works within this symbolical frame. His masculine self is able to accept this femininity as an alien cultural force outside his identity. That's why Portnoy seeks affirmation of his masculine self with non-Jewish women. Portnoy expects salvation from these women since he wants to establish his pre-formulated idea of the masculine through sexual encounters with *shikses* as the embodiment of femininity (see Forrey: 1982, 269). Portnoy's adoration of Gentile female attractiveness reads like a confession to a deeply rooted belief in the American idea. Portnoy does not need to behave like a Gentile man. He is convinced that the American promise realizes his individual freedom as a male Jew who can be as proud to be an American as any Gentile man. America offers a completely new situation for Jews in world history by recognizing their citizenship as Americans. [210] Portnoy's idea of being an American, though, is an integration into and acceptance by WASP culture and history. He envisions himself as being in one line with European imperialist conquerors and identifies himself as a child of the American idea:

---

[210] For historical qualifications of this remark, see the accounts of the American Jewish experience by Glazer (1988) and Sarna (1986). For an account of the Eastern-European Jewish immigration between 1880 and 1920, see especially Cowan/Cowan (1989). Further references can be researched at the American Jewish Historical Society's website at http://www.ajhs.org.

What I'm saying, Doctor, is that I don't seem to stick my dick up these girls, as much as I stick it up their backgrounds—as though through fucking I will discover America. *Conquer* America—maybe that's more like it. Columbus, Captain Smith, Governor Winthrop, General Washington –now Portnoy. As though my manifest destiny is to seduce a girl from each of the forty-eight states. [...] I am a child of the forties, of network radio and World War Two, of eight teams to a league and forty-eight to a country. I know all the words to "The Marine Hymn" and to "The Caissons Go Rolling Along" [...] Rooting my little Jewish heart for our American democracy! Well, we won, the enemy is dead in an alley back of the Wilhelmstrasse, and dead because I *prayed* him dead –and now I want what's coming to me. *My* G.I. bill—real American ass! The cunt in country-'tis-of-thee! I pledge allegiance to the twat of the United States of America—and to the republic for which it stands. (235/236)

Portnoy worships the Gentile woman as the epitome of femininity *and* repudiates the femininity transmitted as Jewishness, because it undermines his idea of the masculine. He experiences non-Jewish women, which he reduces to the gender construction of traditionally feminine, as protecting him against his feminized self. Similar to the construction of his masculine identity, Portnoy does not differentiate between gender and sex. Any experience with females is an encounter with the feminine, be it a bodily or a personal encounter with the female. Portnoy's rejection of Gentile conceptions of masculinity he does not try to imitate further complicates his sense of the American-ness he so desperately wants to acquire. In order to be attractive to *shikses*, Portnoy knows very well that he's better not trying to imitate being a *goy*, but instead refer to his (self-repudiated) Jewishness. Gentile women, Portnoy claims, are "lusting" for Jewish men exactly because they are *not* Gentiles:

Only what I don't know yet in these feverish years is that for every Eddie yearning for a Debbie, there is a Debbie yearning for an Eddie—a Marilyn Monroe yearning for her Arthur Miller—even an Alice Faye yearning for Phil Harris. [...] Who knew that the secrets to a *shikse*'s heart (and box) was not to pretend to be some hook-nosed variety of *goy*, as boring and vacuous as her own brother, but to be what one's uncle, what one's father was, to be whatever one was oneself, instead of doing some pathetic little Jewish imitation of one of those half-dead, ice-cold *shaygets* pricks, Jimmy or Johnny or Tod, who look, who think, who feel, who talk like fighter-bomber pilots! (152)

Sam B. Girgus reads the Gentile women's fascination with Jewish men as a reevaluation of Jewish intellect, most of all represented by Freud. Girgus' biased account of Portnoy as the archetypal Jewish man in America and his sexual attractiveness to women is a reaffirmation of Jewish masculinity as, in Portnoy's terms, an 'effeminate' masculinity:

Portnoy learns that because women also need to associate feelings with sexuality, they will be attracted to individuals who are not afraid of emotions and the so-called inner life. Thus, Portnoy's inner turmoil, which he perceives as signs of embarrassing weakness and immaturity, can appear to others as visible evidence of a vital emotional life. (1988, 138)

Girgus' euphemistic view on Portnoy as an *emotional* character misrepresents Portnoy's dismissal of females' emotions and his inability to view his antagonist in the sex-culture war, the stereotype of the *shiksa*, as *more* than the epitome of male heterosexual desire, or, in Portnoy's pornographic terms, as more than "tits and cunts and legs and lips and mouths and tongues and assholes" (104). Portnoy's adoration of non-Gentile women takes place exclusively on physical grounds and does not aim at emotional attachment. His desire for the Other is a compulsory obsession with female genitals, primarily the vagina, a desire that has not changed since adolescence:

While everybody else has been marrying nice Jewish girls, and having children, and buying houses, and (my father's phrase) *putting down roots*, [...] what he has been doing is—chasing cunt. And *shikse* cunt, to boot! Chasing it, sniffing it, lapping it, *shtupping* it, but above all, *thinking about it*. Day and night, at work and on the street—thirty-three years old and still he is roaming the streets with his eyes popping. [...] Where cunt is concerned he lives in a condition that has neither diminished nor in any significant way been refined from what it was when he was fifteen years old and could not get up from his seat in the classroom without hiding a hard-on beneath his three-ring notebook. (100-102).

The sexual desire Portnoy describes is a desire for a body the masculine self is not and does not know about. It, therefore, increases the sense of personal alienation on the grounds of sex. Femininity needs to be established as alien in order to maintain masculinity as a safe haven from becoming too soft and too weak, read becoming feminized. The Jewish femininity at home is too close to Portnoy's masculine identity, and therefore perceived as a threat. The stereotype of the *shikse*, as it is presented in the text, does *not* portray "love-goddesses" (Girgus: 1988, 128). Portnoy elevates the genitals of *shikses* above any other aspect exactly because that is his means of conquering Gentile culture, to feel superior: He "pursues non-Jewish [women] as status symbols out of a sense of inferiority that partly derives from his minority origins" (Nilsen: 1984, 501). The only "love-goddess" that Portnoy describes as a purely sexual object is also the most prominent *shikse*, Mary Jane Reed. Her given name appears late, in the last third of the text (on page 193). Instead, the reader knows her as "The Monkey" and as "the fulfillment of my [Portnoy's] most lascivious adolescent dreams" (106), "the sexual triumph of my [Portnoy's] life"(214). She is the only *shikse* in Portnoy's monologue who "approaches a rounded character with needs and capacity to love" (Cooper: 1996, 102). Exactly *because* Mary Jane fulfills Portnoy's sexual desires, she is also the most threatening (Cooper: 1996, 102) and, therefore,

Portnoy needs to degrade her intellectually and morally. Mary Jane Reed is, though highly physically attractive, uneducated and unsophisticated, or, as Portnoy phrases it, "not too very bright" (106). She is a model for underwear ads with a lower-class Midwestern past. Mary Jane cannot spell correctly and has been married to a millionaire who preferred extraordinary sexual practices, which, in Portnoy's eyes, morally degrades her. She also tells him that she once "did it *for money*" (199). Portnoy needs the figure (and the body) of Mary Jane in order to degrade her sexual willingness and her sexual pleasure as immoral. By degrading her, he lifts the burden of immorality off his back and elevates himself above her sexuality. Her sexually conscious femininity is defined as a gender Portnoy's masculinity feels superior to. Mary Jane is the fulfillment of Portnoy's innermost sexual desires, but because she embodies this sexuality as a lived reality, Portnoy cannot accept her.

Mary Jane Reed is only one example of the non-Jewish women Portnoy is attracted to, yet an overshadowing image, since she is the *shikse* who is referred to the most. The other two former Gentile girlfriends that are mentioned, Kay Campbell and Sarah Abbot Maulsby, are not sexualized in his masculine quest for cultural reassurance. Portnoy is enchanted by the social background they represent. Kay Campbell is "one of the great *shikses*. I might have learned something spending the rest of my life with such a person" (219). He is not attracted to her physical features but to the social class she represents. Portnoy does not even mention the sexual side of their relationship. He is fascinated by her because she is so different from the Jewish family ethnicity he knows. When he is invited to her family's Thanksgiving dinner, he explores the Gentile culture he comprehends as the embodiment of America: "Why, then, can't I believe I am eating my dinner in America, that America is where I am, instead of some other place to which I will one day travel" (227). Portnoy needs to degrade her and reduce her to her genitals too since she is another epitome of femininity. He refers to her as "The Pumpkin [...] in commemoration of her pigmentation and the size of her can" (216). When she refuses to convert to Judaism, however, Portnoy shows loyalty to his Jewish roots and leaves her. His attraction to her is gone: "[I]t would seem that I never forgave her. [...] I returned to New Jersey that June, [...] wondering how I could ever have been captivated by someone so ordinary and so fat" (231-232).

While Kay Campbell embodies the respectable Midwestern Middle Class, Sarah Abbot Maulsby, mockingly called "The Pilgrim," represents his conquest of WASP Brahmin society, his revenge for the discrimination of American Jews. Once again, his desire for her is not a result of mere sexual attraction. Portnoy is drawn to her because of what she represents. Sarah Abbott Maulsby is an "aristocratic Yankee beauty whose forebears arrived on these shores in the seventeenth century" (233). Portnoy intends to degrade her upper-class background by describing the sexual intercourse with her as ordinary and boring and by blackmailing her for oral sex. Her initial refusal makes him feel discriminated against as a Jew. In spite of that she is not as prejudiced as Portnoy imagines her to be and eventually gives in to his demands. Portnoy 'wins' the sex-culture battle. The *shikse* surrenders to the Jewish son:

[O]f course it couldn't have been clearer to me that despite all her many qualities and charms—her devotion, her beauty, her deerlike grace, *her place in American history*—there could never be any "love" in me for The Pilgrim. Intolerant of her frailties. Jealous of her accomplishments. Resentful of her family. No, not much room there for love. [...] No, Sally Maulsby was just *something nice a son once did for his dad. A little vengeance* on Mr. Lindabury for all those nights and Sundays Jack Portnoy spent collecting down in the colored district. *A little bonus* extracted from Boston & Northeastern, for all those years of service, and exploitation. (240/241; italics mine)

By dating these two women, Portnoy takes revenge on those Gentile males that discriminate against American Jews, as he knows from his father's stories about his workplace, a protestant insurance company. Feeling insufficient in the American realm of masculinity, Portnoy "tries to reconstruct his masculinity by lording it over those whom he can dominate, American women, or, if you will, *shikses*" (Gottfried: 1988, 41). Therefore, Portnoy claims to degrade the daughters of the social class of his father's boss. This is a step up the social scale for Portnoy. He "mixes romance with social climbing in Gatsby-fashion; in his flight from Jewishness he falls in love with the background of the Sarah Maulsbys and Kay Campbells" (Nilsen: 1984, 501). He "establishes an object relationship" to them (Nilsen: 1984, 501). Because Portnoy is unable to establish a personal relationship with any of the women he has been sexually involved with, they merely serve as objects of autoerotic sexual gratification: "what the penis sees, a one-eyed jack spying on the world, has no reality as a subject. The object of this third eye is a collection of signs foisted upon the libido by some malefic anti-superego" (Schehr: 1995, 228). Without commenting on the Freudian implications inherent in Schehr's argumentation, it can be stated that the subject-object relationship Portnoy establishes when in contact with Gentile women reduces them to mere objects of male heterosexual desire, objects of masturbatory fantasies. What Portnoy has been doing all along is to enhance his masculine self, to cherish his masculine ego. As with the Jewish woman he is unable to "conquer" sexually, all females are perceived as complementary means to reassert masculinity. Women are "cunts," whether they are Jewish or Gentile.

Despite his claim that being American will invest him with masculine identity, Portnoy clearly associates the desirable aspect of Gentile culture with the female and being American with being a Gentile woman. Portnoy's construction of American culture and American identity is contradictory and cannot be dissected into easy equations. Dating Gentile women means for Portnoy that he achieves what he longs for, that he proves his masculinity. Nevertheless, this 'victory' does not grant any sense of satisfaction or gratification. Girgus relates Portnoy's "unconscious desire" for the *shikse* to the "crucial aspect of American culture to perceive America in sexual and feminine terms" (128/129). There are many examples of early writings of the New World, in particular America, which perceive the untamed, "virgin" land as "a woman to be possessed," as "a feminine pastoral image": "While the land was female, men were hunters or yeoman farmers" (129). Girgus stresses the fact that the expansion into the West was described in similar terms and concludes that Portnoy is obsessed with Gentile women because they embody America. Unfortunate for the more valuable aspects of Girgus' analysis, he fails to take into account the obvious prejudiced gender perspective of these landscape and nature descriptions. It is not stated whether only male accounts have been analyzed or whether these descriptions can be found in men's *as well as women's* writings. Girgus' analysis fails, on the other hand, because he lightly sweeps over the easy equation of the antithetical concepts of nature and culture. Portnoy is not concerned about femininity as a metaphor of the American landscape. His sense of American-ness is firmly rooted in the negotiations of *cultural* identification. [211]

Even if Portnoy seemingly rejects his background, he nevertheless does not adapt non-Jewish concepts of masculine identity. The mixing of the cultural with the sexual realm is not dissolved into clear-cut antitheses. None of the two cultural realms is redeemed. Barbara Gottfried goes even further in her focus on the ethnicity of the male protagonist:

> [T]he crucial criterion in the test for manhood, the measure of all things, is *the successful negotiation of one's sexuality in a potentially hostile, impotence-inducing world*. Guilt isn't really the issue, partly because Portnoy's modus operandi is projective, rather than transformative, but finally because transgression, whether dietary or sexual, and its attendant guilt, doesn't get at the heart of Portnoy's complaint. What "unmanns" Portnoy is not guilt, but his inability to choose between the conflicting claims of Jewishness [...] and a more mainstream masculinity. (40; italics mine)

However, I cannot acknowledge the struggle for ethnicity as the focal point for Portnoy's search for masculine identity. The text goes beyond the simple reduction of ethnicity as the only grounds for personal conflicts. Portnoy insists on issues that exceed the boundaries of a specific ethnicity in conflict in the US. His discourse on culture as an experience of the American self cannot be easily divided into the nexus American vs. Jewish. Portnoy embraces neither. [212] The text portrays the development of a specifically American Jewishness that acknowledges and integrates American

---

[211] Girgus' thesis of the perception of the American landscape as feminine would rather fit Roth's nature descriptions in *American Pastoral* (1997). Gentile culture is unabashedly desirable in this text, and Roth's stress on the setting of this "assimilationist tale" (*Mein Leben*:1998), rural New England, does in fact identify nature as 'rightfully' belonging to the WASPs.

[212] In contrast to most Jewish criticism, Gross reads the text not as a repudiation of Jewish culture but as an affirmation of Jewish anti-Gentilism and, therefore, a "dangerous" book: "Portnoy's disgust and revulsion for gentiles are obvious to any objective reader. But the Jewish reader is not objective; he or she would rather denounce *Portnoy's Complaint* as unpleasant—sexist and anti-Semitic—than deal with it as dangerous" (1983, 177).

cultural and social identity as part of Jewish identity. This American Jewish identity is, although Americanized, nevertheless a Jewish version of being American. American Jewish culture is a specific, unique Jewish culture; it deviates from American mainstream culture. Because Portnoy associates certain values with his parents, he relates them to their and his Jewishness with its laws, rules and regulations, as, for example, the dietary kosher laws, and views his parents as representing a Jewish heritage that does not fit into his comprehension of American mainstream identity. On the other hand, Portnoy fails to acknowledge the Americanized family structure he grew up with: His father, Jack, is absent from home and working most of the time, and his mother, Sophie, stays at home to fulfill her traditional role as a housewife. Due to this mainstream generation gap, Portnoy's rejection of this traditional lifestyle as represented by his family cannot be called an exclusively Jewish trait; rather, his personal struggle as a son for acknowledgment from his parents appears as an archetypal experience of the individual male within the family unit he grew up with and has to solve as part of his identity conflict. Alan Cooper puts Portnoy's assertions about American culture into perspective:

> [M]any of his [Portnoy's] grievances are myopic: The Jews are not the only conscience- or custom-repressed group in America. The *goyim* are not one homogenous mass. Venturing outside's one's ethnic group for sexual adventure or proof of individuality marks a wider American conflict than just a Jewish one. Not only Jews value education and intellect. Self-mockery and invective are not exclusively Jewish arts [...]. (124)

Portnoy's cultural confusion is his sexual confusion—he infuses the realm of culture with the realm of sexuality. The American idea as a conglomeration of cultures is carried out as a sexual discourse. Portnoy believes he can redeem the cultural antitheses he experiences through his heterosexuality. He uses the terms of sexuality to describe his cultural understanding. The acceptance and repudiation of cultures occur as sexual attraction and repudiation. Culture, therefore, is identified if not replaced by sex. In Freudian terms, "Portnoy's pattern of relating sexuality, the unconscious, and America" (Girgus:1988, 131) is at the core of the text. Portnoy's sexual confusion as cultural confusion "demonstrates how the unconscious factors of guilt, ambivalence, and fear that are usually associated with sexuality, also play an important part in the acquisition of culture itself" (Girgus: 1988, 127). Portnoy's rejection of Jewish as well as Gentile culture is based on his identification of these cultures with gender, while constituting the human experience as male but also desiring access to American WASP mainstream culture through females. His attractiveness to Gentile women and his attraction to them are primarily based on cultural fascination for the Other, for what one is not. Portnoy's refusal of Jewish culture is a refusal of Jewish women as obstacles to acculturation.

Portnoy aspires to be masculine on the grounds of conquering America as a culture through sexuality. His gender confusion, expressed in cultural terms, reflects his ambivalent and inconsistent construction of masculinity as a self caught between the marginalized *abnormal* masculinity construction of Jewish culture and the *norm* of Gentile mainstream. In arguing this, however, I do not imply that Portnoy's understanding of Jewish masculinity is less sexist or less patriarchally defined than the mainstream norm. Masculinity is not only constructed through a sex-culture war, but it is seen and carried out through strictly and exclusively heterosexual lenses and does not lack its appropriate dose of homophobia as a reinforcement of the text's masculinity construction:

> Ma, Ma what was it you wanted to turn me into anyway, [...]? Where did you get the idea that the most wonderful thing I could be in life was *obedient*? A little *gentleman*? Of all the aspirations for a creature of lust and desires! [...] –how I made it into the world of pussy at all, *that's* the mystery. I close my eyes, and it's not so awfully hard—I see myself sharing a house at Ocean Beach with somebody in eye make-up named Sheldon. [...] There he is, Ma, your little gentleman, kissing someone named Sheldon on the lips! [...] There is worse even than that—there are people who fuck chickens! There are men who screw stiffs! You simply cannot imagine how some people will respond to having served fifteen- and twenty-year sentences as some crazy bastard's idea of "good"! (125)

Portnoy considers homosexuality as an instance of "obedien[ce]" to motherly demands and in that sense as being taken over by the threatening and castrating Jewish femininity. The exclusion of homosexual men in his definition of sexuality reflects his traditional view of sharp and exaggerated distinctions of feminine and masculine. Portnoy's construction of masculinity is the narcissism of the masculine self defined sexually through the phallus. Here, as in all other texts by Roth, monolithic, standardized masculinity is under cross-fire because the male protagonist himself realizes that the various identities that are assigned to him, are not identical with his own desires and wishes. The cleavage between the male individual's identity and the masculine fiction he is supposed to live up to makes the masculine self dissatisfied with his own identity and feel emasculated and unmanned. Since there is no other cultural or linguistic concept to name the phenomenon of non-standardized male behavior,[213] the masculine self himself as well as his environment consider him to be effeminate and feminized. Writing about this specifically masculine psychological dilemma in the postmodern world of the second half of the 20th century, Roth, however, knows no way out. He ironically distances himself from his characters and designs them as socially and sexually incompetent. The protagonist Portnoy believes that the exercise of male heterosexuality is a means of "salvation" for his identity conflicts as culture-sex war. As Roth himself points out, Portnoy is miserable in this search for salvation through sexual acculturation. He does not

---

[213] For an alternative concept of understanding masculinities, see Sedgwick (1995).

experience any gratification. His misery, though, is not taken seriously but appears ludicrous. His concept of masculinity is an object of ridicule, placed inside a joke; therefore, the author's distance to the main protagonist *and* his construction of masculinity is secured. The joke is on Portnoy. The hyperbolical frame questions its own construction.

This construction of masculine identity can be observed in all of Roth's texts. In 1969 Alexander Portnoy, in 1974 Peter Tarnopol, and from 1979 on Nathan Zuckerman with no end in sight. Unable to enact any masculinity construction sufficiently, neither their own nor those of their environment, the male protagonists are forced to accept their masculine 'misery.' Instead of leaving behind the standards of masculine gender construction, however, they resort to traditional notions of masculine identity with the hope that by adhering to conventional notions, they might be accepted in their very specific configurations between a non-standardized masculinity and a standardized Western patriarchal masculinity. Roth does not suggest a concept that at least softens the masculine struggle for identity in the fast-changing gender world. Instead, masculinity as constituted through the phallus works as a defense mechanism against the demands on the narcissist masculine self and against feminization. Male sexuality is mis- and abused as a weapon that degrades femininity and female sexuality. Portnoy's complaint is carried out as a psychoanalytically constituted war between masculinity and culture; however, no solution is offered to the drastic critique of patriarchal masculine identity underlying this text. Portnoy is impotent and the hyperbolic monologue ends with Portnoy's famous howl. Dr. Spielvogel's only line—the text's concluding words—indicates Portnoy's psychological condition: "Now vee may perhaps to begin. Yes?" (274). Yes, masculinity is deconstructed, but the cultural concept is only at the beginning of its reconfigurations when culture is sexualized and sexuality culturalized.

Sources

Roth, Philip, When She Was Good. 1967, New York,1985.
---. *Portnoy's Complaint,* 1969, New York 1994.
---. *My Life as a Man,* 1974, New York 1993.
---. *Reading Myself and Others.* New York 1975.
---. *The Counterlife.* New York 1986.
---. *American Pastoral.* 1997, New York 1998.

American Jewish Historical Society. <http://www.ajhs.org>
Berger, Maurice, Wallis, Brian, and Watson, Simon (eds.), *Constructing Masculinity,* New York 1995.
Bordo, Susan, *The Male Body, A New Look at Men in Public and in Private,* New York 1999.
Butler, Judith, *Gender Trouble, Feminism and the Subversion of Identity,* New York 1990.

Cowan, Neil and Ruth Schwarz Cowan, *Our Parents' Lives, The Americanization of Eastern European Jews*, New York 1989.

Cooper, Alan, *Philip Roth and the Jews*, Albany 1996.

Forrey, Robert, "Oedipal Politics in *Portnoy's Complaint*", in: Sanford Pinsker (ed.), *Critical Essays on Philip Roth*, Boston 1982, pp. 266-274.

Girgus, Sam B. "Portnoy's Prayer: Philip Roth and the American Unconscious", in: Asher Z. Milbauer and Donald G. Watson (eds.), *Reading Philip Roth*, New York 1988, pp. 126-143.

Glazer, Nathan, *American Judaism*, Chicago 1988.

Gottfried, Barbara, "What *Do* Men Want, Dr. Roth?", in: Harry Brod (ed.), *A Mensch Among Men, Explorations in Jewish Masculinity*. Freedom, CA 1988, pp. 37-52.

Gross, Barry, "Sophie Portnoy and 'The Opposum's Death:' American Sexism and Jewish Anti-Gentilism," in: Daniel Walden (ed.), *Studies in American Jewish Literature 3*, Albany 1983, pp. 166-178.

Harrison, Kathryn, "Connubial. Abyss, The mysterious narrative of marriage," in: *Harper's Magazine* 300 / 1797 (February 2000), pp. 83-88.

Johnson, Brian D, "Intimate Affairs," 1990, in: George Searles (ed.), *Conversations with Philip Roth*, Jackson 1992, pp. 254-258.

Jones, Judith Paterson, Nance, Guinevera A., *Philip Roth*, New York 1981.

Justad, Mark J., "A Transvaluation of Phallic Masculinity: Writing With and Through the Male Body", in: *The Journal of Men's Studies* 4/4 (May 1996), pp. 355-374.

Merriam-Webster's Collegiate Dictionary, 10th ed, 1997.

Mein Leben als Philip Roth, Bekenntnisse eines Schriftstellers, Dir. Christa Maerker, Südwestrundfunk, Stuttgart, S 3, 19 Oct. 1998.

Nilsen, Helge Normann, "Rebellion against Jewishness: *Portnoy's Complaint*," in: *English Studies* 65/6 (December 1984), pp. 495-503.

Prell, Riv-Ellen, "Rage and Representation. Jewish Gender Stereotypes in American Culture," in: Faye Ginsburg and Anna Loewenhaupt Tsing (eds.), *Uncertain Terms, Negotiating Gender in American Culture*, Boston 1990, pp. 248-266.

Reichardt, Ulf, Sielke, Sabine, "Masculinities – A New Phenomenon?", in: *Amerikastudien / American Studies* 3 / 4 (1998), pp. 561-575.

Rosen, David, *The Changing Fictions of Masculinity*, Urbana 1993.

Sarna, Jonathan, ed, *The American Jewish Experience*, New York 1986.

Schehr, Lawrence R., "Fragments of a Poetics: Bonnetain and Roth", in: Paula Bennett and Vernon A. Rosario (eds.), *Solitary Pleasures, The Historical, Literary, and Artistic Discourses of Autoeroticism*, New York 1995, pp. 215-230.

Schwenger, Peter, "The Masculine Mode" in: Elaine Showalter (ed.), *Speaking of Gender*, New York 1989, pp. 101-112.

Searles, George, ed., *Conversations with Philip Roth*, Jackson 1992.

Sedgwick, Eve Kosofsky, "Gosh, Boy George, You Must Be Awfully Secure in YourMasculinity!" in: Berger, Wallis, and Watson (eds.), *Constructing Masculinity*, New York 1995, pp.11-20.

Shostak, Debra, "Roth/CounterRoth: Postmodernism, the Masculine Subject and *Sabbath's Theater*," in: *The Arizona Quarterly* 54/2 (Summer 1998), pp. 119-142.

5. MASCULINITIES/MASKULINITÄTEN: ROLLENDRUCK

Martin LENGWILER
Männer und Autos in den 60er Jahren: Technische Artefakte als Gegenstand der Geschlechterforschung

Andreas THIELE
Männlicher Geschlechtsrollenstress über die Lebensspanne

Martin LENGWILER

Männer und Autos in den 60er Jahren: Technische Artefakte als Gegenstand der Geschlechterforschung

In jüngster Zeit wurden auch in der Schweiz die Ansätze historischer und soziologischer Männlichkeitsstudien verstärkt rezipiert, vor allem die angelsächsischen "studies on men and masculinities" (Brändli: 1999; Blattmann, Meier: 1998; Geschlecht: männlich: 1998). Dieser Beitrag versteht sich als kritische, methodisch-theoretische Zwischenbilanz dieser Diskussion. Ausgehend von zwei theoretischen Grundannahmen der jüngeren Männlichkeitsstudien soll im ersten Teil des Artikels versucht werden, einige weiterführende Forschungsperspektiven zu formulieren und insbesondere das Potential der aktuellen Wissenschafts- und Technikforschung für die Anliegen der Männlichkeitsstudien nutzbar zu machen.

Im zweiten Teil wird dieses methodisch-theoretische Anliegen an einem konkreten Beispiel diskutiert: am geschlechtsspezifischen Risikoverhalten von Männern im Strassenverkehr. Im Mittelpunkt dieses Abschnitts steht eine exemplarische Analyse der Beziehungsformen zwischen Automobilisten und ihren Fahrzeugen, wie sie in den 1960er Jahren, im Goldenen Zeitalter des Autos, in der Öffentlichkeit, etwa in Ausstellungen oder der Autowerbung, dargestellt wurden. Der abschliessende dritte Teil plädiert nochmals zusammenfassend für eine "technische Wende" der Geschlechterforschung, die nicht nur die sozialen Beziehungen zwischen den Geschlechtern, sondern auch die Bedeutung von technischen Artefakten für Geschlechterdifferenz und Geschlechterverhältnisse untersucht.

Männlichkeitsstudien und technische Artefakte

Wo steht die methodisch-theoretische Diskussion der Männlichkeits-studien heute? Zwei theoretische Grundpositionen seien hier angeführt, die die Männlichkeitsstudien der letzten Jahre geprägt haben. Davon ausgehend werde ich versuchen, einzelne weiterführende Forschungs-perspektiven aufzuzeigen.

Die erste Grundüberlegung der neueren Männlichkeitsforschung besagt, dass sich Männlichkeit nur relational begreifen lasse, das heisst nur im Zusammenhang anderer Männlichkeits- und Weiblichkeitsvorstellungen. Diese These wurde in den 90er Jahren in verschiedenen, soziologischen wie historischen Untersuchungen wiederholt geäussert. In der Soziologie vertritt diese These etwa *Robert Connell* (mit seinem Konzept der hegemonialen Männlichkeit), in der Geschichte unter anderen *John Tosh* und *Michael Roper* (Connell: 1999, 97-102; Roper, Tosh: 1991; Tosh 1994; Lengwiler: 1998). Männlichkeit als relationale Kategorie zu begreifen heisst einerseits, Men's

Studies zum integralen Teil der Gender Studies zu machen, und gleichzeitig nicht von einer einzigen sondern von einer Vielzahl von Masculinities ausgehen.

Die zweite Grundannahme betrifft die disziplinäre Verankerung der Männlichkeitsstudien und der Geschlechterforschung überhaupt. Wie die Gender Studies haben sich Männlichkeitsstudien nie als eigenständige Disziplin verstanden. "Masculinity" ist eine analytische Kategorie, die in verschiedene bestehende Disziplinen hineingetragen werden soll. Mit dieser Inter- oder Transdisziplinarität verbindet sich auch ein Methoden-pluralismus, der es manchmal schwierig macht, eine kontinuierliche methodisch-theoretische Debatte zu führen. Unbestritten hingegen ist, dass gerade die transdisziplinäre Verankerung der Gender Studies wiederholt methodische Innovationen auslöste. Die Men's Studies der 70er und 80er Jahre waren noch stark von der Geschlechtersoziologie geprägt, während sich in den 90er Jahren, im Zuge von linguistic turn und dem Aufschwung kulturwissenschaftlicher Ansätze das Interesse stärker auf narrative Quellen und Repräsentationsformen verlagert hat: dass man heute mehr von Masculinities statt von Men's Studies spricht, steht damit im Zusammenhang (Clatterbaugh: 1990, 1-14; Schissler: 1992; Lengwiler 1998).

Solche Ansätze der Männlichkeitsforschung sind auch in der Schweiz, vor allem in der historischen Forschung, rezipiert worden. In Basel boten zwei Ausstellungen Ende der 1980er Jahre Anlass für die ersten hiesigen "Men's Studies": 1988 eine Ausstellung über die Geschichte der "gay community" in Basel und 1989 die militärkritische Ausstellung "Réduit Schweiz" zum 50. Jahrestag des Ausbruchs des Zweiten Weltkriegs. Beide Ausstellungsbände publizierten Beiträge, die sich explizit als historische Männlichkeitsforschung verstanden (Trüeb, Miescher: 1988; Trüeb, Hagmann: 1989).[214]

Welches sind nun weiterführende Forschungsperspektiven der Männlichkeitsstudien? Ich werde zwei Anliegen skizzieren, auf die ich im zweiten Abschnitt genauer eingehen werde. Das erste Postulat auf der Forschungsagenda schliesst an den Einfluss von linguistic turn und kulturwissenschaftlichen Debatten an. In den letzten Jahren haben Männlichkeitsstudien sich vor allem auf die Ebene diskursiver Äusserungen und symbolischer Repräsentationen konzentriert (vgl. etwa die Beiträge von *Britta Herrmann* und *Walter Erhart*, sowie von *Elisabeth Bronfen* in diesem Band). Etwas in Vergessenheit gerieten dabei die Ebenen von Institutionen und sozialen Gruppen. Auch zum männlichen Alltagshandeln gibt es erst wenige Untersuchungen. Die kulturwissenschaftliche Debatte hat sich bisher noch zu wenig um sozialstrukturelle und handlungstheoretische Fragen gekümmert. Es fehlt vor allem

---

[214] Kuno Trüeb, bei beiden Ausstellungen mitbeteiligt, verfolgte diesen Ansatz weiter und schrieb im Rahmen des Projekts zu einer Basellandschaftlichen Geschichte eine umfangreiche Arbeit zum "Wandel des Männerbildes vom 1. Weltkrieg bis zur Gegenwart", eine Längsschnitt-Untersuchung von einigen ausgewählten Männerbiografien. Die Arbeit beruht auf einer qualitativen Auswertung von Interviews, orientiert an den methodischen Vorgaben der Oral History, blieb aber unveröffentlicht.

an der Vermittlung der verschiedenen Untersuchungsebenen - ein Problem, das auch mit der Interdisziplinarität des Forschungsfeldes zu tun hat. Es gibt also viel zu symbolischen Repräsentationen von Männlichkeit, da und dort auch etwas zu alltäglichen Männlichkeitserfahrungen, aber es fehlt noch an Kenntnissen wie diese Ebenen vermittelt werden (aus historischer Perspektive etwa die Beiträge in: Kühne: 1996; und: Hitchcock, Cohen: 1999). Die Vermittlung zwischen symbolischer Ebene, Handlungsebene und sozialstrukturellen Dimensionen ist eine der wichtigsten Forschungsanliegen für die nächste Zeit, und entsprechende theoretische Modelle wie etwa das Habitus- und das Mimesis-Konzept (vgl. den Beitrag von *Hermann* und *Erhart* in diesem Band), oder auch die Ansätze der Wissenschaftssoziologie, auf die unten genauer eingegangen wird, werden dabei von besonderer Bedeutung sein.

Die zweite Forschungsperspektive knüpft an die These der relationalen Männlichkeit an. Bis anhin wurden Männlichkeitsvorstellungen vor allem in einem sozialen Kontext interpretiert: als Ausdruck von Differenz oder Ungleichheit zwischen Gruppen von Männern und Frauen. Dabei blieben jedoch materielle Aspekte, etwa die Bedeutung artifizieller Gegenstände für Männlichkeitsvorstellungen, in der Regel ausser Betracht. In dieser Hinsicht könnten die Männlichkeitsstudien einiges von der Wissenschafts- und Technikforschung lernen. Weshalb soll gerade die Wissenschafts- und Technikforschung von besonderem Interesse für die Geschlechterforschung sein? Vor allem weil sich die beiden Forschungsbereiche in methodisch-theoretischer Hinsicht mit den gleichen Problemen auseinandersetzen. Hier wie dort geht es darum, scheinbar objektive oder natürliche Verhältnisse auf ihre soziale und kulturelle Bedingtheit zu hinterfragen. Sozialkonstruktivistische Ansätze waren nicht zufällig vor allem in diesen beiden Forschungsbereichen besonders erfolgreich (etwa: Hacking: 1999). Die Frage lautet also konkret: Was können die Männlichkeitsstudien von den aktuellen Ansätzen der Wissenschafts- und Technikforschung lernen?

Die Wissenschafts- und Technikforschung ist in jüngster Zeit von einem verstärkten Interesse für die materielle Dimension der Wissenschaften geprägt gewesen (Heintz: 1998, 76-84). Wissensproduktion, so die Argumentation, solle als sozial konstriert verstanden werden, doch nicht nur in einem ausschliesslich soziologischen Sinn, etwa vor dem Hintergrund konkurrenzierender wissenschaftlicher Kollektive. Wissensproduktion müsse vielmehr auch die materielle Ebene in Betracht ziehen, etwa die instrumentellen Verfahrensweisen, die Materialität der Untersuchungsgegenstände oder die synthetische oder hybride Erweiterung lebender Organismen durch technologische Artefakte (exemplarisch: Pickering: 1995). Zum Verständnis der Wechselwirkungen zwischen materieller und sozialer Ebene wurden dabei mehrere Modelle entwickelt, unter ihnen besonders einflussreich das Aktor-Netzwerk-Konzept von *Michel Callon* und *Bruno Latour*, sowie das Cyborg-Manifesto von *Donna Haraway* (klassisch: Latour: 1987; Callon: 1986; Haraway:

1988).[215] Auch in der Technikgeschichte wurde jüngst wiederholt auf das innovative Potential einer Verbindung von Geschlechterforschung und Technikforschung aufmerksam gemacht (Lerman, Mohun, Oldenziel: 1997; Wajcman: 2000). Im Mittelpunkt der folgenden Ausführungen steht ein möglicher Ausschnitt dieser Kombination: das Gendering von technischen Artefakten sowie deren Bedeutung für bestimmte Formen von Männlichkeit, dargestellt am Beispiel des Risikoverhaltens im Strassenverkehr.

Männliches Risikoverhalten im Strassenverkehr und das Modell der "risk personality"

Die Problematik, um die es geht, lässt sich an einer Illustration aus dem Nachruf auf den deutschen Chirurgen Gerhard Küntscher schildern (vgl. Abb. 1). Das Bild stammt aus dem aktuellen Handbuch zur Begutachtung von Arbeitsunfällen, privaten Unfällen und Berufskrankheiten in medizinischer und versicherungstechnischer Hinsicht (mit dem sprechenden Titel "Der Unfallmann", vgl.: Mollowitz: 1998, 582). Der Nachruf erschien zum Todestag des Chirurgen und ist im Anhang des Lehrbuchs abgedruckt. Küntscher war einer der bedeutendsten Unfallmediziner seiner Zeit und hatte sich vor allem mit seiner innovativen Frakturenbehandlung, der sogenannten Marknagelung, einen Namen gemacht. Küntscher ist 1972 gestorben, das Bild stammt etwa aus dem Jahr 1960. Sie zeigt den Chirurgen in Freizeitbekleidung am Steuer seines privaten Sportwagens. Die Abbildung, die auch an die persönliche Seite Küntschers erinnern wollte, trug die Legende: "Küntscher war ein Liebhaber von schnellen Autos, seinen BMW fuhr er grundsätzlich bei jedem Wetter ohne Verdeck."

Das Bild hat etwas paradoxes an sich. Küntscher wird als Liebhaber eines risikoreichen Fahrstils beschrieben, und gleichzeitig ist er ein Fachvertreter der Unfallmedizin. In der Nachkriegszeit hat sich der Strassenverkehr zur wichtigsten Ursache von Schwerverletzungen oder von Todesfällen entwickelt. In den 1950er und 1960er Jahren verdoppelt sich in der Schweiz die Anzahl der Verkehrstoten von rund 800 auf 1600 jährliche Opfer, mehrheitlich Männer (für die Schweiz z.B.: Ritzmann-Blickenstorfer: 1996: 334-335). Zweifellos arbeitete auch Küntscher als Chirurg nach 1945 vor allem mit Verkehrsopfern. Der Widerspruch zwischen seinem wissenschaftlichen Alltag als Unfallchirurg und seinem Freizeitverhalten ist offensichtlich. Dieses Paradox spiegelt sich, auf einer soziologischen Ebene, auch in den Präventionskampagnen der Unfallverhütung. Trotz Professionalisierung der

---

[215] Das Aktor-Netzwerk-Konzept versucht, menschliche wie nicht-menschliche Handlungsträger auf der gleichen Ebene zu stellen und die sozialen Netzwerke dieser "Aktanten" zu analysieren. Der Begriff des Cyborgs, für "cybernetic organisms", zielt dagegen auf die Verbindung lebender wie leblos-materieller oder synthetischer Elemente innerhalb desselben Organismus, wie etwa bei gentechnisch veränderten Organismen. Weiterführend vgl. etwa: Golinski: 1998.

Unfallverhütung ist der Effekt der Präventionskampagnen im Verkehrsbereich beschränkt. Die Unfallzahlen sind seit den 1930er Jahren fast kontinuierlich gestiegen, und nur die Einführung von Geschwindigkeitsbeschränkungen und des Sicherheitsgurtes hat zu einer vorübergehenden Dämpfung der Anzahl Verkehrstoter anfangs der 1970er Jahre geführt. Die Verhaltensänderungen, die mit den Kapagnen angestrebt wurden, bleiben bis heute schwer messbar und allem Anschein nach nur wenig signifikant (Huguenin, Scherer: 1982; Suva: 1979, 74-76).

Risikoverhalten im Strassenverkehr ist als ausgesprochen geschlechts-spezifische Erscheinung bekannt, was in jüngster Zeit zunehmend ins Blickfeld der sozialwissenschaftlichen Risikoforschung geriet. Ob im Verkehrsverhalten, am Arbeitsplatz oder im Investitionsbereich, die gängige These ist, dass Frauen sich grundsätzlich stärker risikobewusst - oder risikoavers - verhalten als Männer. Zur Erklärung dieses Phänomens werden häufig Modelle der Persönlichkeitspsychologie herangezogen. Männer verhielten sich risikofreudiger, so die These, weil sie eine stärker ausgeprägte Risikopersönlichkeit hätten (Lupton: 1999; Green: 1997, 136-138). Dieses Modell der "risk personality" oder der "risk proneness" (auch "accident proneness") hat eine lange und schillernde Gesichte, auf die ich hier nur kurz verweisen kann. "Risk proneness" war lange Zeit ein geschlechtsneutrales Konzept, und es ist aus heutiger Sicht ironisch, dass das Modell ursprünglich von britischen Epidemiologen zur Untersuchung der Unfälle in den Munitionsfabriken des Ersten Weltkriegs entwickelt wurde - ironisch deshalb, weil dort praktisch ausschliesslich Frauen arbeiteten (Froggatt, Smiley: 1964). Vor allem in der Zwischenkriegszeit hat sich das Konzept der "risk proneness" nachhaltig in Wissenschaft und Versicherungspraxis ausgebreitet, und obwohl es in der Nachkriegszeit wiederholt als ungenügend kritisiert wurde, wird es bis heute von verschiedenen Sozialwissenschaften, vor allem von der Ökonomie, häufig wiederaufgegriffen (Aronowitz: 1998, 110-144).

Nationalisierung, Technisierung und Gendering des Automobils

Die folgende Argumentation schlägt dagegen einen anderen Weg ein und versucht, männliches Risikoverhalten in kulturhistorischer Perspektive zu deuten. Die These ist, dass das Automobil in der Nachkriegszeit, vor allem in den 1960er Jahren, von einem elitären Luxusgut zu einem populären Massenartikel wurde, und dass dieser Verbreitungsprozess unter anderem angetrieben wird durch ein symbolisches Gendering des Autos. Als Folge dieses Prozesses wurden Autos, in erster Linie für die männliche Käuferschaft, zu einem emotional hoch besetzten Konsumobjekt. Im Rahmen dieses emotionalen Verhältnisses zwischen männlichen Automobilisten und ihren Fahrzeugen spielen risikobezogene Verhaltensweisen eine bedeutende Rolle. Diese These soll an Beispielen aus den öffentlichen Debatten ums Automobil sowie aus der Autowerbung der 1960er Jahre genauer dargelegt werden. Die Beispiele stammen alle aus der Schweiz, vor allem aus der "Schweizer Illustrierten Zeitung" sowie aus den Vereinszeitschriften "Automobil-Revue" und "Touring".

Seit den 1950er Jahren ist das Automobil zu einem der erfolgreichsten Massenartikel der modernen Konsumgesellschaft geworden. Die Zahl der im Verkehr stehenden Motorfahrzeuge betrug in der Schweiz unmittelbar nach Ende des Zweiten Weltkriegs 60'000 Fahrzeuge. Bis 1950 erhöhte sich diese Zahl bereits auf rund 150'000 Autos, 1960 waren es bereits knapp eine halbe Million, und 1970 eineinviertel Millionen Fahrzeuge. 1945 besass erst rund jeder fünfzehnte Haushalt ein Auto, 1960 bereits jeder zweite, und 1970 kommt ein Auto auf jeden Haushalt (Ritzmann-Blickenstorfer: 1996, 779). Die Automobilisierung der Schweiz fällt also in die 1950er und 60er Jahre.

Im Zuge dieser Entwicklung wird das Auto zu einem Objekt mit ausgesprochen geschlechtsspezifischem Symbolwert, was sich etwa an der Sprache der Autowerbung verfolgen lässt. Dabei sind die geschlechtsspezifischen Metaphern, die mit dem Auto in Verbindung gebracht werden, durchaus ambivalent. Das Auto wird nicht einfach mit ausschliesslich männlichen oder weiblichen Eigenschaften verbunden, es ist vielmehr ein androgynes Objekt. Weiblich assoziiert werden in der Werbung Qualitäten wie Sicherheit, Ästhetik, Komfort, indem diese Eigenschaften in den Inseraten meist durch Frauenfiguren verkörpert werden (Automobil-Revue: 1968/19, 13). Männlich konnotierte Eigenschaften betreffen vor allem technologische Aspekte wie Motoreneigenschaften, Steuer- und Bremssystem, oder Fahrleistung. Auch Geschwindigkeit ist in der Regel männlich besetzt (Schweizer Illustrierte Zeitung, 1960/11, 48).

Diese Ambivalenz von männlichen und weiblichen Eigenschaften richtet sich in erster Linie an ein männliches Lesepublikum. Nur in seltenen Fällen sind die Werbebotschaften auf eine weibliche Leserinnenschaft zugeschnitten, und dann vor allem in Abhängigkeit eines männlichen Käufers oder Besitzers (vgl. Abb. 2, Schweizer Illustrierte Zeitung: 1960/17, 54).

Ebenfalls bemerkenswert ist die reichhaltige Tiermetaphorik, mit der Autos oder einzelne Autoteile assoziiert sind. Dies beginnt bei den Bezeichnungen für einzelne Automarken und Modelle (VW Käfer, Jaguar, Ford Mustang etc.). Auch in der Werbung verkörpern Hunde, Katzen und andere Tiere Eigenschaften wie Bequemlichkeit, Zuverlässigkeit und Langlebigkeit (Automobil-Revue: 1960/25, 3; 1960/29, 3; 1960/43, 3).

Diese beiden Darstellungsstrategien, Gendering und Tiermetaphorik, sind miteinander verwandt. Es geht bei beiden darum, das technische Artefakt Automobil durch animistische und anthropomorphe Formeln zu beleben. Ein oberflächlicher Vergleich mit der Werbung für andere populäre Konsumgüter der Nachkriegszeit, etwa für Waschmaschine, Radio oder Fernsehen, lässt vermuten, dass das Auto einen ungewöhnlich starken geschlechtsspezifischen Symbolwert besitzt. Dieses Gendering wird insbesondere unterstützt durch zwei weitere grundlegende Assoziationstypen, die in öffentlichen Repräsentationen des Autos deutlich werden: der Nationalisierung und der Technisierung des Automobils.

Abb. 1:

- Quelle: Mollowitz: 1998, 582.
- Legende: Schnelle Autos - Hobby des deutschen Chirurgen und Unfallmediziners Gerhard Küntscher.

252

Ich hab jetzt einen Eigenen!

AMAG
Schinznach-Bad

Einen eigenen Zündungsschlüssel, vorläufig. Peter hat mir ihn gestern feierlich geschenkt — nach der Fahrprüfung. Die Fahrprüfung? Bestanden natürlich! Mit dem VW ist ja alles so einfach: das Schalten, das Lenken, das Wenden und Parkieren. Und Peter, der mir nie seine Füllfeder leihen würde, überlässt mir unsern VW ohne Bedenken... Er sei so robust und zuverlässig, dass «man ihn bei mir und mich bei ihm *sicher* wisse».

Geteilter VW ist doppelte Freude. Trotzdem haben wir ausgerechnet, dass *zwei* VW noch erfreulicher wären, dass zwei VW in Betrieb und Unterhalt weniger kosten würden als der frühere grosse Wagen. Vielleicht werde ich also bald einen Eigenen haben   meinen eigenen VW.

Abb. 2:

- Quelle: Schweizer Illustrierte Zeitung: 1960/17, 54.
- Legende: Das Auto als männliches Konsumgut - mit Ausnahme des Ersatzschlüssels.

Tatsächlich heisst Automobilist sein in den 1960er Jahren, verkürzt gesagt, an der nationalen Gemeinschaft teilzunehmen. Bezeichnenderweise sprechen die Behörden, nachdem 1958 der Bund per Verfassungsänderung mit dem Bau des Autobahnnetzes beauftragt wurde, vom Projekt der "Nationalstrassen". Und an der Schweizerischen Landesausstellung 1964, der Expo in Lausanne, wird der Ausbau des Autobahnnetzes in den 1950er und 60er Jahren geradezu zur nationalen Mission erhöht. Das erste vollständige Teilstück, die Autobahn zwischen Genf und Lausanne wird exakt auf den Zeitpunkt der "Expo 64" eröffnet, mit feierlichem Zeremoniell unter Teilnahme eines Bundesrates. Zudem kommt das Gelände der Expo buchstäblich unmittelbar an die Autobahn anstossend gelegen - und die Expo-Werbung fordert Besucherinnen und Besucher auf, den Besuch der Ausstellung mit dem neuartigen Erlebnis einer Autobahnreise zu verknüpfen (Touring: 1964/16, 1).

Die nationalstaatliche Symbolik prägt auch den Ausstellungsteil zum Thema Verkehr. Die Decke des Strassenverkehrspavillons beispielsweise ist von einem Meer von Fahrzeug-Schildern verhängt, die sich mittels Spiegeleffekten in einen "Himmel voller Nummernschilder" verwandeln. Dieser Himmel ist ein direktes Zitat der Landesausstellung 1939. Eine der zentralen Installationen der "Landi 39" war der Höhenweg der Gemeindefahnen: ein langer Saal, an der Decke die Fahnen aller Gemeinden der Schweiz (als Symbol der föderalistischen, direktdemokratischen Tradition) und im Fluchtpunkt des Saals die Fahne der Nation. Die Schweiz der Automobilisten an der Expo 64 zitiert dadurch unmittelbar die nationalistische Symbolsprache der "Geistigen Landesverteidigung" (vgl. Abb. 3 und 4).

Abb. 3:

- Quelle: Geschichte der Schweiz und der Schweizer, Basel 1986, p. 760.
- Legende: Das Original: Höhenweg der Gemeindefahnen an der Landesausstellung 1939.

Abb. 4

- Quelle: Touring: 1964/18, p. 12.
- Legende: Das Zitat: Himmel voller Nummernschilder im Verkehrspavillon der Expo 1964.

Vergleichbare Belege zur nationalen Symbolik des Verkehrs finden sich bereits in den 1950er Jahren. Die Jahresversammlung 1955 der "Vereinigung Schweizerischer Strassenfachleute" wurde beispielsweise an einem der Schlüsselorte des schweizerischen Gründungsmythos, der Rütliwiese in der Innerschweiz, abgehalten. Darüber hinaus erinnert auch das offizielle Foto der Jahresversammlung deutlich an die offizielle und weit verbreitete Abbildung des Rütli-Rapportes von 1940, bei dem der schweizerische General das höhere Offizierskorps zusammenrief, um die Weichen für die Verteidigungsstrategie der Schweiz im Zweiten Weltkrieg zu stellen - eine weitere Schlüsselszene der jüngeren Staatsgeschichte (VSS: 1988, 32).

Diese Assoziationen zwischen Militär, Staatswesen (vor Einführung des Frauenstimmrechts) und Autoverkehr machen deutlich, dass im Verlauf der 1950er und 1960er Jahre männliche Nation und automobilisierte Schweiz zunehmend gleichgesetzt werden, etwa nach dem Grundsatz: Liberté, Egalité, Automobilité.

Sozialhistorisch ist diese Entwicklung Teil der Konstitution der modernen Konsumgesellschaft (Tanner: 1998), was sich etwa in der Parallele zwischen geografischer Mobilität und sozialer Mobilität, von der viele Autoinserate geprägt sind, spiegelt. Noch bis in die 1950er Jahre besass das Auto den Status eines Luxusartikels, das der Kaufkraft gesellschaftlicher Eliten vorbehalten war. In den Anzeigespalten dominierten die gross gebauten amerikanischen Automobile von Produzenten wie Ford oder Chevrolet. Ende der 1950er Jahre setzt der unaufhaltsame Aufstieg des europäischen Kleinwagens ein, und Firmen wie VW, Morris, NSU, Simca oder Fiat richten sich mit ihren preisgünstigen Modellen an eine neue breitere Kundschaft. Auch die amerikanischen Hersteller stellen ihre Produkte schliesslich auf das europäische Kleinformat um. Der Autokauf ist in diesem Sinne eine symbolische Handlung, mit der die neuen Mittelschichten der Nachkriegszeit ihren Wohlstand signalisieren. Der Automarkt wird zum Standbein der modernen Konsumgesellschaft.
Der andere wichtige Begleitaspekt des Gendering ist die Technisierung des Autos. Es fällt auf, dass die technische Aussagegehalt der Autowerbung im Verlaufe der 1960er Jahre an Informationen und Details wesentlich zunimmt. Nicht nur dies: das Wissen wandelt sich zunehmend von einem Experten- zu einem Laienwissen. Symbolhaft wird dieser Prozess durch die Figur des "Experten" repräsentiert, der ursprünglich als Vermittler der technischen Informationen die Anzeigen bevölkert, aber im Verlaufe der 1960er Jahre zunehmend aus den Werbebotschaften verschwindet und durch eine unmittelbare Werbesprache, von Anzeige zu Leser, ersetzt wird (Schweizer Illustrierte Zeitung: 1960/17, 2; Automobil-Revue: 1968/17, 10). Auch hier ist wichtig, dass die Kommunikation zwischen Experten und Laien ausschliesslich von Mann zu Mann verläuft. Das Auto als Artefakt rückt mit Wegfallen des Experten in ein unmittelbareres, weniger expliziertes Verhältnis zum Automobilisten. Zudem bedeutet diese Entwicklung für den Fahrer einen Qualifikationsschritt bezüglich seines technischen Wissens.

Am Beispiel der Autowerbung in den 1960er Jahren lässt sich beobachten, wie ein technisches Artefakt, das Auto, zu einem Konsumobjekt mit hohem Symbolgehalt wurde. Geschlechtsspezifische Zuschreibungen sind in diesem Prozess eine entscheidende Strategie, die das soziale Verhältnis zwischen männlichen Autofahrern und ihrem Fahrzeug mitbegründen. Eine Autofahrt wird dabei für den Automobilisten zu einer mehrfach symbolischen Handlung: sie repräsentiert die Teilnahme an der nationalen Gemeinschaft, die soziale Mobilität der Nachkriegsgesellschaft, und einen technologischen Qualifikationsschritt - wobei jeder dieser drei Handlungen mit der Geschlechterdifferenz korrespondiert.

Dies kann zwar noch keine abschliessende Erklärung des Risikoverhaltens von männlichen Autofahrern sein, doch zeigt das Beispiel, dass das Verhältnis von Fahrer zu Fahrzeug weniger von rational-instrumentellen als vielmehr von emotionalen Elementen geprägt ist. Es scheint mir einleuchtend, dass die Unfallverhütung vor diesem Hintergrund Schwierigkeiten hat, mit rationalen Argumenten gegen diesen Symbolwert des Autos anzukommen.

Das Beispiel ist auch deshalb bemerkenswert, weil es illustriert, dass technische Artefakte ein gewinnbringender Untersuchungsgegenstand für die Geschlechterforschung sein können. Die Gender studies könnten viel von einer solchen "technischen Wende" profitieren. Die Geschichte der Autowerbung in den 1960er Jahren zeigt, auf welche Weise technische Gegenstände einen aktiven Anteil an der Ausprägung sozialer Geschlechterverhältnisse haben können. Das Auto ist nur eines von vielen technischen Gegenständen, die in einem dialogischen Prozess von geschlechtsspezifischen Aneignungen und Zuschreibungen schliesslich zu einem spezifisch männlichen Wissens- und Erfahrungsobjekt wurde. Solche Gendering-Prozesse können beispielsweise mithelfen zu erklären, weshalb die technische Berufswert bis heute gegenüber den Bestrebungen zur Geschlechtergleichstellung so erstaunlich resistent geblieben ist.[216] Gerade Männlichkeitsstudien sind ein besonders vielversprechender Ansatz einer solchen Geschlechterforschung, die am Beispiel der Technik eine Soziologie der belebten *und* unbelebten Welt mitbegründet.

Quellennachweis

Aronowitz, Robert A., *Making sense of illness: science, society, and disease*, Cambridge 1998.

Blattmann, Lynn, Meier, Irène (Hg.), *Männerbund & Bundesstaat. Über die politische Kultur der Schweiz*, Zürich 1998.

---

[216] Die amerikanische Technikhistorikerin Arwen Mohun hat kürzlich die Geschichte der Waschmaschine aus einer solchen Perspektive untersucht, insbesondere den gescheiterten Versuch, den Waschvorgang von der unbezahlten Frauenhausarbeit in den Bereich industrieller Fabrikarbeit zu verschieben (Mohun: 1999).

Brändli, Sabina, *"Der herrlich biedere Mann"*. *Vom Siegeszug des bürgerlichen Herrenanzuges im 19. Jahrhundert*, Zürich 1999.

Callon, Michel, "Some elements of a Sociology of Translation: Domestication of the Scallops and the Fishermen of St. Brieuc Bay", in: Law, John (Hg.), *Power, Action, and Belief: A New Sociology of Knowledge?*, London 1986, pp. 196-233.

Clatterbaugh, Kenneth, *Contemporary Perspectives on Masculinity. Men, Women, and Politics in Modern Society*, Boulder, Colorado 1990.

Connell, Robert, *Der gemachte Mann. Konstruktion und Krise von Männlichkeiten*, Opladen 1999.

Froggatt, Peter, Smiley, James A., "The concept of accident proneness: a review", in: *British Journal of industrial Medicine* 21 (1964), pp. 1-12.

"Geschlecht: Männlich", Sondernummer der *traverse. Zeitschrift für Geschichte. Revue d'histoire* 1998/1.

Golinski, Jan, *Making natural knowledge: constructivism and the history of science*, New York 1998.

Green, Judith, *Risk and Misfortune, A social consturction of accidents*, London 1997.

Hacking, Ian, *Was heisst "soziale Konstruktion"? Zur Konjunktur einer Kampfvokabel in den Wissenschaften*, Frankfurt a.M. 1999.

Haraway, Donna, *Simians, Cyborgs and Women: the Reinvention of Nature*, London 1988.

Heintz, Bettina, "Die soziale Welt der Wissenschaft. Entwicklungen, Ansätze und Ergebnisse der Wissenschaftsforschung, in: Heintz, Bettina, Nievergelt, Bernhard (Hg.), *Wissenschafts- und Technikforschung in der Schweiz. Sondierungen einer neuen Disziplin*, Zürich 1998, pp. 55-94.

Hitchcock, Tim, Cohen, Michele (Hg.), *English Masculinities, 1660-1800*, London 1999.

Huguenin, Raphael Denis, Scherer, Ch., *Möglichkeiten und Grenzen von Verkehrssicherheitskampagnen. Zur Theorie und Praxis von Unfallverhütungsaktionen*, Bern 1982 (BfU-Report 4).

Kühne, Thomas (Hg.), *Männergeschichte - Geschlechtergeschichte. Männlichkeit im Wandel der Moderne*, Frankfurt a.M. 1996.

Latour, Bruno, *Science in Action*, Cambridge 1987.

Lengwiler, Martin, "Aktuelle Perspektiven der historischen Männlichkeitsforschung im angelsächsischen Raum", in: *traverse* 1998/1, pp. 25-34.

Lerman, Nina, Mohun, Arwen, Oldenziel, Ruth, "Historiography and Directions for Research", in: *Technology and Culture* 38 (1997), pp. 16- 30.

Lupton, Deborah, *Risk*, London 1999.

Mohun, Arwen P., *Steam laundries : gender, technology, and work in the United States and Great Britain, 1880-1940*, Baltimore, Maryland 1999 (Johns Hopkins studies in the history of technology. New series 25).

Mollowitz, Günter G. (Hg.), *Der Unfallmann, Begutachtung der Folgen von Arbeitsunfällen, privaten Unfällen und Berufskrankheiten*, 12. Auflage, Berlin 1998.

Pickering, Andrew, *The mangle of practice: time, agency, and science*, Chicago 1995.

Ritzmann-Blickenstorfer, Heiner (Hg.), *Historische Statistik der Schweiz*, Zürich 1996.

257

Roper, Michael, Tosh, John, "Introduction", in: Dies. (Hg.), *Manful Assertions. Masculinities in Britain since 1800*, London 1991, pp. 1-24.

Schissler, Hanna, "Männerstudien in den USA", in: *Geschichte und Gesellschaft* 18 (1992), pp. 204-220.

Suva (Schweizerische Unfallversicherungsanstalt), *Ergebnisse der Unfallstatistik der zwölften fünfjährigen Beobachtungsperiode 1973- 1977*, Bern 1979.

Tanner, Jakob (Hg.), *Geschichte der Konsumgesellschaft. Märkte, Kultur, Identität*, Zürich 1998.

Tosh, John, "What Should Historians Do with Masculinity?", in: *History Workshop Journal* 38 (1994), pp. 179-202.

Trüeb, Kuno, Hagmann, Daniel, "Jetz brucht's e ganze Schwyzerma", in: Gut, Nadja und Bettina Hunger (Hg.), *Réduit Basel. 39/45*, Basel 1989, pp. 114-123

Trüeb, Kuno, Miescher, Stefan (Hg.), *Männergeschichten. Schwule in Basel seit 1930*, Basel 1988.

VSS Vereinigung Schweizerischer Strassenfachleute (Hg.), *VSS 1913 bis 1988. Eine Chronik über das Werden, Wachsen und Wirken der Vereinigung Schweizerischer Strassenfachleute*, Zürich 1988.

Wajcman, Judy, "Reflections on Gender and Technology Studies: In What State is the Art?", in: *Social Studies of Science* 30/3 (2000), pp. 447- 464.

Andreas THIELE

Männlicher Geschlechtsrollenstress über die Lebensspanne [217]

Männer und Gesundheit

Das Forschungsthema Mann interessiert in den letzten Jahren zunehmend auch die empirischen Sozial- und Gesundheitswissenschaften. Insbesondere die Forderung nach einer spezifischen Männergesundheitsforschung rückt dabei in den Vordergrund. Ein Grund für das verstärkte Interesse am Mann ist sicherlich, dass gerade im Kontrast zu den Befunden der Frauenforschung und der Frauengesundheitsforschung deutlich geworden ist, wie wenig fundiertes und empirisch abgesichertes Wissen über die sozialen, emotionalen und gesundheitlichen Problembereiche der männlichen Bevölkerung verfügbar ist. So findet z.B. in der Medizin der alternde Mann erst seit einigen Jahren besondere Beachtung. Das Interesse der Medizin am alternden Mann wird dabei häufig mit der demographischen Entwicklung der älteren männlichen Bevölkerung in den Industrienationen begründet (Schill, Köhn & Haidl, 1993). So hat der Anteil der Männer, die älter als 50 Jahre alt sind, in den letzten Jahren deutlich zugenommen und wird weiterhin ansteigen. Ein Vergleich der Lebenserwartung von Männern mit der von Frauen zeigt aber auch, dass Männer im Durchschnitt sehr viel früher sterben. Die durchschnittliche Lebenserwartung für einen Mann beträgt in den westlichen Industrienationen zur Zeit etwa 73 Jahre, die für eine Frau etwa 80 Jahre (Klotz, Hurrelmann & Eickenberg, 1998). Auch bezogen auf einzelne Todesursachen fällt der Geschlechtervergleich i.d.R. zuungunsten der Männer aus. So starben in den USA Anfang der 90ziger Jahre im Vergleich zu Frauen etwa doppelt so viele Männer an koronaren Herzerkrankungen, Herzinfarkten oder an Lungenkrebs und sogar viermal soviel Männer an Selbstmord oder Mord (Waldron, 1995).

Um die im Vergleich zu Frauen erhöhte Risikobelastung der Männer im Bereich von Gesundheit, Krankheit und Mortalität zu erklären, wird in den Sozialwissenschaften die Auffassung vertreten, dass die Gründe für die Differenzen in geschlechtstypischen Verhaltensweisen zu suchen sind. Für eindeutig verhaltensbasierte Ursachen einer erhöhten Mortalität bei Männern wie z. B. Risikoverhalten im Straßenverkehr, Mord oder Selbstmord mag diese Erklärung unstrittig sein, aber auch für geschlechtstypische Verteilungen der Morbiditätsraten im körperlichen und psychischen Bereich spricht - neben den zur Diskussion stehenden biologisch-medizinischen Einflüssen auf hormoneller oder genetischer Ebene (Daily & Wilson, 1999; Simon, 1999) - vieles dafür, dass auch maskuline Ideale

[217] Überarbeitetes Vortragsmanuskript basierend auf den Publikationen Thiele, 2000a und Thiele 2000b. Der Vortrag wurde gehalten auf der Tagung "Transdisciplinary Approaches toward Masculinities" am Englischen Seminar der Universität Basel am 24./25. Juni 2000.

und daraus abgeleitete Verhaltensweisen das Krankheitsrisiko erhöhen oder in spezifischen Lebenssituationen die Befindlichkeit beeinträchtigen können.

Aus psychologischer Sicht sind besonders jene Verhaltensweisen relevant, die stark mit den vorherrschenden maskulinen Rollenbildern verknüpft sind. So sind einschlägige gesundheitliche Risikoverhaltens- weisen, wie einseitige Ernährung, Rauchen und Alkoholkonsum, vermehrt bei Männern zu beobachten (Waldron, 1995), aber auch das als unabhängiger Risikofaktor für koronare Herzerkrankungen diskutierte Typ-A-Verhaltensmuster trägt eine eindeutig geschlechtstypische Färbung. So definieren Friedman und Rosenmann (1974) das Typ-A-Verhalten als einen"... action-emotion complex that can be observerd in any person who is aggressively involved in a chronic, incessant struggle to achieve more and more in less and less time, and if required to do so, against the opposing efforts of other things or other persons" (S.37, zitiert nach Schwenkmezger, 1994, S. 49). Letztendlich zeigt auch das Paradoxon zwischen Gesundheitserleben und Lebenserwartung bei Männern und Frauen, dass an den krankheitsbezogenen Mortalitätsdifferenzen in hohem Maße geschlechtstypische Verhaltensunterschiede beteiligt sind. So leben Frauen zwar länger, klagen aber zugleich über mehr subjektive Beschwerden oder gesundheitliche Belastungen und konsultieren daher häufiger ihren Arzt. Im Gegensatz hierzu fühlen sich Männer über einen langen Zeitraum in ihrem Leben gesund, klagen über weniger Beschwerden und nutzten sehr viel seltener medizinische Angebote und Maßnahmen der Gesundheitsvorsorge. Letzteres ist sicherlich eine wichtige Ursache für die Übersterblichkeit des männlichen Geschlechtes.

Auch im Kontext der Alternsbewältigung wird die Hypothese vertreten, dass eine einseitige Orientierung an maskulinen Werten im Übergang zum höheren Lebensalter zu Anpassungsschwierigkeiten führen kann. Ein besonders hohes Risiko liegt dann vor, wenn eine individuell sehr starre und wenig flexible Orientierung an männlichen Rollenidealen die Bewältigung von körperlichen und sozialen Altersveränderungen verhindert. So unterliegen z.B. die für "stark maskulin orientierte Männer" so zentralen Fähigkeiten, wie Kraft, Ausdauer, Potenz und Fitness, einer deutlichen Alterseinbuße (Thiele, 1998). Dabei bekommt die individuelle Orientierung an maskulinen Rollenidealen noch eine zusätzliche Brisanz im Alter, da Männlichkeitsideale in weiten Bereichen mit Jugendlichkeits-idealen übereinstimmen. So hat z.B. Hemingway die folgenden Zeilen an seinen Vater gerichtet (vgl. Lynn, 1987): "Um wie viel besser ist es, wenn man stirbt in der glücklichen Zeit noch nicht desillusionierter Jugend, man tritt ab im hellsten Glanze des Lichts und nicht mit einem verbrauchten alten Körper und zerbrochenen Illusionen. " Beide sowohl der Vater als auch der Sohn haben im Alter von 61 bzw. 57 Jahren Selbstmord begangen, ein trauriges Beispiel für die negative Konsequenzen maskuliner Ideale. Natürlich führen Anpassungsschwierigkeiten im Übergang zum höheren Lebensalter nicht immer zu einer solchen drastischen Konsequenz, wie der Freitod Hemingways in den sog. "besten Jahren". Wie Studien zum alternden Mann zeigen, gelingt es den meisten Männern im Übergang zum höheren Lebensalter durchaus, Wohlbefinden und Lebenszufriedenheit aufrecht zu erhalten (Thiele, 1998). Dies gilt aber insbesondere dann, wenn sie, trotz deutlicher körperlicher Verluste und Veränderungen, ihre Lebenspläne und das Bild, das sie von sich selbst haben, flexibel an die sich ändernden Bedingungen anpassen und sich mitunter von unangemessenen maskulinen Idealen lösen können.

Das Geschlechtsrollenstress - Paradigma

Ein Blick in die deutschsprachige psychologische Forschungslandschaft zeigt, dass eine psychologisch orientierte Männerforschung praktisch fehlt. So existieren nur wenige Arbeiten, welche die männliche Geschlechtsrolle und ihre Konsequenzen aus psychologischer Sicht erforschen oder explizit die Psychologie des Mannes thematisieren. Ganz anders dagegen in den USA. Dort hat sich seit Ende der 70er Jahre unter dem Label Men's Studies ein neues, interdisziplinär ausgerichtetes Forschungsprogramm in den Sozial- und Gesundheitswissenschaften etabliert, um die verschiedenen Bedingungen und Konsequenzen von Maskulinität sowohl theoretisch als auch empirisch zu analysieren. In der amerikanischen Psychologie hat dies vor wenigen Jahren auch zur Gründung einer eigenen Sektion (Division 51) im amerikanischen Psychologenverband (APA) mit der Bezeichnung "Society for the Psychological Study of Men and Masculinity (SPSMM)" geführt (Levant, 1992). Arbeiten aus dieser Gruppe zeigen beispielhaft, dass die Psychologie theoretische Konzepte und fundierte Forschungsinstrumente zur Erforschung von Männlichkeit bereit stellen kann (Levant & Pollack, 1995). Ein wesentliches Ziel der psychologischen Männerforschung ist es dabei, die von der Frauenforschung vorangetriebene Analyse der negativen Auswirkungen traditioneller Männerrollen und maskuliner Machtpositionen auf Frauen und Kinder - wie Benachteiligung, Sexismus und Gewalt - um die Analyse der negativen Konsequenzen zu erweitern, die Maskulinität auch für Männer selbst haben kann. Im besonderen werden dabei die Bedingungen erforscht, die sich auf gesellschaftlicher und auf individueller Ebene fördernd oder hemmend auf eine Veränderung der männlichen Rolle auswirken können. So gehört es zu den wesentlichen Grundannahmen der psychologischen Männerforschung, dass die männliche Rolle kein homogenes, unveränderliches und ausschließlich biologisch determiniertes Konstrukt ist. Viel mehr wird davon ausgegangen, dass sowohl gesellschaftliche Veränderungen, wie sie z.B. von der Frauenbewegung angestoßen wurden, aber auch Veränderungen der individuellen Lebenssituation und Lebensumwelt über die Lebensspanne hinweg, traditionelle bzw. gesellschaftlich dominante Rollenvorschriften in Frage stellen können. Wenn Männer aber trotz einer sich wandelnden Umwelt hartnäckig an maskulinen Rollenidealen festhalten, kann dies sowohl zu psychischen und interpersonellen Problemen (O'Neil, 1982, Solomon, 1982), wie auch zu gesundheitlichen Belastungen (Goldberg, 1977; Hollstein, 1992; Sabo & Gordon,1995) führen.

Um die dysfunktionalen und negativen Einflüsse der männlichen Geschlechtsrolle auf die psychische und körperliche Gesundheit von Männern theoretisch zu begründen und zu analysieren, hat Joseph Pleck (1981, 1995) das "Gender Role Strain" - Paradigma formuliert. Pleck betont in seinem Ansatz insbesondere den normativen Charakter von Maskulinität. Nicht die Übernahme geschlechtstypischer Eigenschaften im Sinne einer maskulinen Identitätsentwicklung und deren mögliches Scheitern stehen im Vordergrund seiner Theorie, sondern vielmehr die Effekte, die gesellschaftliche Annahmen und Vorschriften über Männlichkeit (cultural standards of masculinity) auf das Individuum haben können.

Pleck wendet sich bei der Formulierung seines Ansatzes explizit gegen psychologische Theorien, die er unter dem Gender Role Identity — Paradigma zusammenfasst. Bei diesen Theorien — z.B. der psychoanalytischen Theorie — wird eine gesunde männliche Entwicklung mit der Ausbildung einer stabilen männlichen Identität in Verbindung gebracht. Gewalt in der Schule oder Risikoverhalten und Drogenkonsum von männlichen Jugendlichen werden als Indikatoren einer gescheiterten Identitätsentwicklung gesehen und z.B. auch mit fehlenden maskulinen Rollenvorbildern begründet.

Nach Pleck dagegen entstehen negative Konsequenzen, Fehlanpassungen und psychische Beeinträchtigungen vielmehr aus dem inneren und äußerem Druck, sich an den Rollenvorgaben und den Maskulinitätsideologien (masculine ideology), wie Pleck die Rollenvorschriften für Männer bezeichnet, zu orientieren und sich dementsprechend zu verhalten. Der innere Druck zur Aufrechterhaltung von maskulinem Verhalten wird dabei durch irrationale Annahmen über Männlichkeit erzeugt. In der Literatur zur Männerforschung finden sich eine Reihe solcher irrationalen Annahmen, von den im folgenden nur zwei zusammengefasst aufgeführt werden sollen:

> Männlichkeit lässt sich am besten an der Macht, der Durchsetzungs- und Konkurrenzfähigkeit, der sexuellen Potenz und dem beruflichen Erfolg bemessen.

> Männlichkeit bedeutet, keine Schwächen zu zeigen, Gefühle zu vermeiden und emotionale oder soziale Unterstützung durch andere abzulehnen.

Der treibende bzw. stabilisierende Kern dieser Annahmen ist dabei eine irrationale Angst der Männer, bei abweichenden Verhaltensweisen als weiblich angesehen zu werden. Schon David und Brannon haben in ihrem 1976 erschienen Artikel "Our Culture's Blueprint of Manhood" einen Aspekt der normativen Maskulinität mit dem Label "No sissy stuff" belegt. Auch diese Autoren haben dabei die gelernte Angst des Mannes im Auge, durch vermeintlich "unmännliches" Verhalten als mädchenhaft und weiblich zu erscheinen. Bei entsprechenden Sanktionen und Gruppenreaktionen können dabei tatsächliche oder auch nur vorgestellte Verstöße gegen männliche Ideale und Gruppennormen die Angst vor der Weiblichkeit aktivieren und zu einer Überkonformität und exzessiven Anpassung an das maskuline Wertesystem führen. Dies ist z.b. häufig in Form von Mitläufer-Verhalten bei männlichen Jugend-Gangs zu beobachten. Dass der soziale Druck zur Übernahme geschlechtrollenkonformer Verhaltensweisen dabei schon in der Kindheit bei Jungen größer ist als bei Mädchen, wird durch eine Reihe von entwicklungspsychologischen Studien belegt, aber auch bei Erwachsen sind Männer einer wesentlich stärkeren sozialen Verurteilung unterworfen als Frauen, wenn sie rollendiskrepantes Verhalten zeigen und dem maskulinen Imperativ nicht entsprechen.

Pleck (1981) geht nun in den Grundannahmen zum "Gender Role Strain" - Paradigma davon aus, dass (a) die maskulinen Rollenvorschriften selbst heterogen sind und dass (b) der Anteil der Männer, die diese Vorschriften in ihrem aktuellen Verhalten verletzen, relativ hoch ist. Zugleich sei aber (c) der soziale Druck für Männer im Vergleich zu Frauen sehr viel höher, sich entsprechend der geschlechtstypischen Rollenvorgaben zu verhalten. Somit sind auch (d) die negativen Konsequenzen und sozialen Sanktionen für Männer sehr viel gravierender, wenn sie "unmännliches" Verhalten zeigen. Aufgrund dieser verschiedenen Formen des Rollendrucks bei Männern unterschiedet Pleck (1981, 1995) drei Quellen der Beeinträchtigung, die mit der normativen Kraft der maskulinen Rollenideale in Zusammenhang stehen: Trauma-, Dysfunktions- und Diskrepanzstress.

Trauma-Stress umfasst die psychischen Verletzungen, die aus einer an maskulinen Rollenidealen orientierten Sozialisation oder einer entsprechenden Erziehung von Jungen zu Männern resultieren. So ist es nicht unwahrscheinlich, dass z.B. die bei vielen Männer zu beobachtende geringere Offenheit im Umgang mit Gefühlen auf erzieherische Einflüsse (Jungen weinen nicht) oder auf Erfahrungen mit der peer-group (Hänseleien in der Schule) zurückgeführt werden können. Levant (1995) spricht in diesem Zusammenhang auch von einer männlichen Sozialisation zur Alexiethymie, der Unfähigkeit, Gefühle in Worte zu fassen, ein Syndrom, welches auch bei einigen schweren psychosomatischen Krankheitsbildern zu beobachten ist.

Dysfunktion-Stress umfasst die negativen Effekte, die mit männlichen Verhaltensweisen per se verknüpft sind. Die zentrale Annahme ist, dass die Orientierung an maskulinen Rollenidealen direkt negative Konsequenzen für die psychische und körperliche Gesundheit der Männer mit sich bringt, da die Verhaltensweisen, die von den maskulinen Standards nahegelegt werden, dysfunktional sind und sich negativ auf die Männer selbst oder auf andere auswirken können. In diesen Bereich gehören sowohl die Forschungsbemühungen, maskuline Eigenschaften zur Vorhersage der psychischen Gesundheit oder Adaptationsfähigkeit von Männern zu untersuchen, wie auch die Bemühungen, die Bedeutung von maskulinen Verhaltensweisen für Gesundheitsverhalten oder in extremeren Verhaltensbereichen wie Aggressivität und Kriminalität zu analysieren.

Diskrepanz-Stress ist im Kontext individueller Veränderungen über die Lebensspanne hinweg, aber auch im Kontext gesellschaftlicher, kultureller oder situativer Veränderungen, die wohl bedeutsamste Quelle für die Entstehung von aktuellem Rollenstress. Diskrepanz-Stress entsteht nach Pleck dann, wenn entweder das Selbstbild eines Mannes, seine individuelle Ausstattung mit z.B. kognitiven und körperlichen Ressourcen oder aber die situativen Anforderungen nicht mit den normativen Rollenbildern übereinstimmen. Die Diskrepanz zwischen den maskulinen Geschlechtsrollenstandards und den individuellen Charakteristika eines Mannes kann unter diesen Umständen zu einem niedrigen Selbstwertgefühl oder anderen negativen psychischen Konsequenzen führen.

Genau auf diese soeben beschriebene Diskrepanz zwischen internalisierten maskulinen Geschlechtsrollennormen und situativen Anforderungen bzw. persönlichen Ressourcen zielt auch die Definition des maskulinen Geschlechtsrollenstress ab, die Richard Eisler 1995 formuliert hat. Maskuliner Geschlechtsrollenstress tritt nach der Auffassung von Eisler dann auf, wenn ein Mann sich an der traditionellen Männerrolle orientiert, aber an seinen Fähigkeiten zweifelt, sich in einer Situation entsprechend dieser Rollenvorgabe zu verhalten oder wenn er sich aufgefordert fühlt, in einer Weise zu handeln, die in Widerspruch zur traditionellen Männerrolle steht. Dies wird um so wahrscheinlicher, je stärker ein Mann an vermeintlich unveränderbaren maskulinen Rollenidealen festhält. Eisler (1995, S. 212 - 213) fasst die Entstehung von Geschlechtsrollenstress in den folgenden fünf Grundannahmen zusammen:

1. The sociocultural contingencies that reward masculine attitudes and behaviors while punishing nonmasculine (i.e. feminine) attitudes result in the development of masculine gender role cognitive schema in the vast majority of individuals with XY chromosome patterns.
2. Masculine schema are then employed by men, in varying degrees, to appraise threats and challenges from the environment as well as to evaluate and guide their choice of coping strategies.
3. Based on their disparate experiences, there are important differences among men as to how committed they are to culturally accepted models of masculinity.
4. Masculine gender role stress may arise from excessive commitment to and reliance on certain culturally approved masculine schema that limit the range of coping strategies employable in any particular situation.
5. Masculine gender role stress may also arise from the belief that one is not living up to culturally sanctioned masculine gender role behavior.

In unseren Forschungsarbeiten am Institut für Psychologie der Universität Frankfurt betonen wir besonders zwei Aspekte, die bei der Entstehung von maskulinen Rollenstress eine Rolle spielen können:

— die sozialen und personalen Veränderungen über die Lebensspanne, sowie
— die Bedeutung der biologischen und psycho-physiologischen Ressourcen.

So sehen wir die Notwendigkeit, Effekte der maskulinen Geschlechtsrolle auf Erleben und Verhalten unter einer die Lebensspanne übergreifenden Perspektive zu analysieren. Maskuline Rollennormen und Verhaltens-vorschriften stehen in den verschiedenen Entwicklungsabschnitten mit denunterschiedlichsten Herausforderungen und Bedingungen in Wechsel-wirkung, seien es soziale Aufgaben und Anforderungen bei z.B. der Familiengrünung oder der Berufswahl oder seien es sich ändernde körperliche und psychische Ressourcen, welche bei unterschiedlichen Entwicklungsverläufen dem sozialen Konstrukt der maskulinen Rolle mehr oder weniger entsprechen.

Den biologischen, physiologischen und körperlichen Entwicklungs- und Veränderungsprozessen und deren Interaktion mit der erworbenen Rollen-orientierung gilt dabei unser besonderes Interesse in unseren Forschungsarbeiten. Wir gehen dabei von den Annahmen aus, dass
a) die persönliche Ausstattung mit körperlichen und psycho-physiologischen Merkmalen die individuelle Übernahme maskuliner Rollennormen und Rollen-orientierungen fördern kann, wenn diese Ausstattung dem in einer Gesellschaft vorherrschenden maskulinen Rollenbild entspricht, dass
b) maskuline Rollenorientierungen vermittelt über konkretes Verhalten wie z.B. Muskel- und Fitnesstraining oder die Einnahme von Androgenen, Einfluss auf körperliche und physiologische Aspekte eines Individuums nehmen kann und, dass
c) bei einer erlebten Diskrepanz von maskulinen Rollenidealen und eigener subjektiver Körperlichkeit maskuliner Geschlechtsrollenstress entstehen kann.

Um Missverständnisse zu vermeiden, ist bei der Analyse des Zusammenhangs von biologischen Merkmalen eines Individuums und seinen psychischen Orientierungen die Unterscheidungen von Verhaltensdeskription und sozialer Kategorisierung besonders zu beachten. So lassen sich im Sinne der *Verhaltensdeskription* Zusammenhänge zwischen physiologischen oder endokrinen Parametern und Verhalten beobachten. Dabbs, Strong und Milhun (1998) z.B. zeigen in einer Studie zum Einfluss von Testosteron auf Verhalten, dass Personen mit überdurchschnittlichen Testosteronskonzentrationen sich ruheloser Erleben, sich mehr Gedanken über Aktivitäten machen und dabei ihre Gedanken und Pläne sehr viel stärker auf die Gegenwart richten, stärkere Spannungen bei Inaktivität erleben und in den Tagebucheinträgen, die als Aufzeichnungsmethode in dieser Studie verwendet wurden, häufiger Aktivitäten mit Freunden erwähnen. Die Einordnung dieser Verhaltensweisen als typisch maskuline Verhaltensweisen - sei es durch einen Forscher, durch das soziale Umfeld oder durch die Personen selbst - erfolgt erst in einem zweiten Schritt durch *soziale Kategorisierung* in Gegenwart von in einer Gesellschaft dominanten maskulinen Rollennormen. Die Beziehung zwischen biologischen Faktoren und Verhaltensmerkmalen wird dabei als indirekt gedacht, d.h. sie ist durch zahlreiche Zwischenglieder vermittelt. Wenn z.B. ein hoher Androgenspiegel zu einem athletischen Körperbau führt, was wiederum sportliche Aktivitäten und physische Auseinandersetzung mit Gleichaltrigen anregt, so ist der in diesem Fall gegebene Zusammenhang zwischen Androgenspiegel und physischer Aktivität insofern indirekt, als dass er durch die mit einem athletischen Körperbau verbundenen Möglichkeiten und Konsequenzen vermittelt ist (Trautner, 1991). In diesem Sinne können die biologischen und konstitutionellen Bedingungen und ihre Passung zu den Geschlechts-rollennormen auf indirektem Wege über soziale Kategorisierungen die Rollenübernahme einer Person beeinflussen und rollenkonforme Verhaltensweisen verstärken.

Maskuliner Geschlechtsrollenstress kann dabei im Kontext der körperlichen Ausstattung entsprechend der Konzeption von Pleck (1995) in dreierlei Hinsicht entstehen. Erstens ist es denkbar, dass die durch die eigene Körperlichkeit forcierte Übernahme von Rollenorientierungen zu Verhaltensweisen führt, welche die Wahrscheinlichkeit zum Erleben von Dysfunktionsstress über die Lebensspanne hinweg erhöht. Zweitens ist zu erwarten, dass ein nicht unerheblicher Anteil von Männern hinsichtlich ihrer Körperlichkeit nicht den maskulinen Idealnormen entsprechen, so dass die Wahrscheinlichkeit Diskrepanzstress zu erleben besonders dann zunimmt, wenn diese Männer die dominanten Männlichkeitsvorstellungen dennoch selbst als wichtig und erstrebenswert bewerten. Drittens können körperliche Veränderung im Alter in Widerspruch zu den eigenen oder zu den von einer Gesellschaft an einen herangetragenen maskulinen Rollenidealen geraten und zum Erleben von Geschlechtsrollenstress beitragen.

Um die verschieden Hypothesen zum Zusammenhang von Körper, Rollenorientierung und Rollenstress zu analysieren, werden an unserem Institut zur Zeit zwei größere Projekte durchgeführt. Das erste Projekt befasst sich mit den Auswirkungen des körperlichen Alterns und deren Bewältigung bei Männer im mittleren und höheren Lebensalter. Die Ergebnisse aus einer ersten Studie dieses Projektes an 304 Männern im Alter von 35-64 Jahren legen nahe, dass maskuline Wertorientierungen im Alter eine erfolgreiche Adaptation an die körperlichen Veränderungen erschweren kann (Thiele, 1998, Thiele & Degenhardt, 1998). So erleben z.B. in dieser Studie besonders die älteren Männer mit hohen Testosteronwerten die stärksten Beeinträchtigungen im sexuellen Bereich. Dieser Befund führte zu der Hypothese, dass möglicherweise der Sexualhormonstatus die Geschlechtsrollenidentifikation insofern beeinflusst, als dass schon Jugendliche und junge Männer bei einem hohen Testosteronstatus und den damit Verbunden psycho-physiologischen Aktivierungen der Sexualität, der eigenen Potenz und damit zusammenhängend auch der körperlichen Attraktivität und Fitness eine vorrangige Stellung in ihrer Lebensführung einräumen. Die in diesem Kontext erworbenen Rollen- und Wert-orientierungen können im Alter mit den dann stattfindenden körperlichen Veränderungen in Konflikt geraten und die Wahrnehmung von Beschwerden verstärken. Die hier zugrundegelegte Annahme, dass schon im jungen Erwachsenenalter körperliche und psychoendokrinologische Prozesse die Orientierung an maskulinen Rollennormen forcieren kann, hat uns veranlasst, ein zweites Projekt zu initiieren, in welchem an jungen Männern der Einfluss von geschlechtsrollenbezogenen Wert- und Normorientierungen auf die psychischen Adaptation und den Geschlechtsrollenstress im Kontext körperlicher und endokriner Merkmale untersucht werden soll (Degenhardt & Thiele, 1998). Ergebnisse aus diesem Projekt sind Anfang 2001 zu erwarten, erste Analysen bestätigen jedoch zum einen den enormen Einfluss, den die Orientierung an maskulinen Rollenidealen auf das Erleben von Geschlechtsrollenstress hat, es gibt aber auch erste Hinweise, dass z.B. Körperkraft und Fitness mit der Orientierung an maskulinen Rollenidealen korreliert ist.

Quellennachweise

Dabbs, J.M., Strong, R. & Milhun, R., "Exploring the Mind of Testosterone: A Beeper Study", in: Journal of Research in Personaltity 31 (1997), S. 577-587.

Daily, M. & Wilson, M., "Darwinism and the roots of Machismo", in: Scientific American Presents 10/2 (1999), S. 8-14.

David, D.S. & Brannon, R.C., "The male sex role: Our culture's blueprint of manhood and what it's done for ua lately", in: D.S. David, R.C.   Brannon (eds.), The forty nine percent majority (pp.1-45), Reading, MA 1976, S. 1-45.

Degenhardt, A. & Thiele, A., Der Einfluss somatischer und endokriner Faktoren auf die geschlechtsrollenbezogene Wertorientierung und die psychische Adaptation bei jungen Männern, Unveröffentlicher Projektantrag an die Deutschen Forschungsgemeinschaft, 1998.

Eisler, R.M., "The relationship between masculine gender role stress and men's health risk: The validation of a construct", in: R.F. Levant, W.S. Pollack (eds.), A New Psychology of Men, New York 1995, S. 207-225.

Friedman, M. & Rosenmann, R.H. Type A behavior and your heart, New York 1974.

Goldberg, H. The Hazards of Being Male, New York 1977.

Hollstein, W., "Männlichkeit und Gesundheit" in: E. Brähler, H. Felder (eds.), Weiblichkeit, Männlichkeit und Gesundheit, Opladen 1992, S. 64-75.

Klotz, T., Hurrelmann, K. & Eickenberg, H.-U., "Männergesundheit und Lebenserwartung: Der frühe Tod des starken Geschlechts" in: Deutsches Ärzteblatt 95/9 (1998), S. A460-A464.

Levant, R. F., "The Society for the Psychological Study of Men and Masculinity" in: Journal of Men's Studies 1/1 (1992), S. 75-76.

Levant, R.F. & Pollack, W.S. (eds.), A New Psychology of Men, New York 1995.

Lynn, K.S. Hemingway, New York 1987.

O'Neil, J.M., "Gender role conflict and strain", in: K. Solomon, N.B. Levy (eds.), Men in Transition. Theory and Therapy, New York 1982, S. 5-40.

Pleck, J.H., The Myth of Masculinity. Cambridge 1981.

Pleck, J.H., "The gender role strain paradigm: An update", in: R.F. Levant, W.S. Pollack, (eds.), A new psychology of men, New York 1995), S. 11-32.

Sabo, D. & Gordon, D.F., "Rethinking men's health and illness", in: D. Sabo, D.F. Gordon (eds.), Men's health and illness. Gender, Power, and the Body, Thousand Oaks, CA 1995, S. 1-21.

Schill, W.-B.; Köhn, F.-M. & Haidl, G., "The aging male", in: G. Berg, M. Hammar (eds.), The modern management of the menopause, New York, London 1993, S. 545-565.

Schwenkmezger, P., "Gesundheitspsychologie. Die persönlichkeits-psychologische Perspektive" in: P. Schwenkmezger, L.R. Schmidt (eds.), Lehrbuch der Gesundheitspsychologie, Stuttgart 1994, S. 47-64.

Simon, H.B., "Longevity: The ultimative gender gap" in: Scientific American Presents 10/2 (1999), S. 108-112.

Solomon, K., "The masculine gender role: Description" in: K. Solomon, N.B. Levy (eds.), Men in transition. Theory and therapy, New York 1982, S. 45-76.

Thiele, A. & Degenhardt, A., "Does correlation between psychological findings and endocrine values justify substitution in aging men?", in: Rozenbaum, H., Birkhäuser, M.H. (eds.), Proceedings of the IV. European Congress on Menopause, Wien, 8.-12. Oktober 1997, Paris 1997, S. 491-499.

Thiele, A., "Männer, Maskulinität und psychische Adaptation im Kontext körperlicher Altersveränderungen", in: F. Höpflinger, P. Perrig-Chiello (eds.), Nach dem Zenit. Frauen und Männer in der zweiten Lebenshälfte. Bern 2000, S. 119-144.

Thiele, A., "Männlicher Geschlechtsrollenstress im frühen und mittleren Erwachsenenalter. Evaluation einer deutschsprachigen Version der masculine gender role stress scale". Zeitschrift für Politische Psychologie, 8/2+3 (2000b), S.138-159.

Thiele, A. Verlust körperlicher Leistungsfähigkeit. Bewältigung des Alterns bei Männern im mittleren Lebensalter, Idstein 1998.

Trautner, H.M., Lehrbuch der Entwicklungspsychologie, Band 2, Göttingen 1991.

Waldron, I., "Contributions of changing gender differences in behavior and social roles to changing gender differences in mortality", in: D. Sabo & D. F. Gordon (eds.), Men's health and illness: Gender, power and the body, Thousand Oaks, CA 1995, S. 22-45.

6. MASCULINITIES/MASKULINITÄTEN: FORSCHUNGSGEGENSTAND

Therese Frey STEFFEN
Masculinities/Maskulinitäten and its Mal(e)Contents

Therese Frey STEFFEN

Masculinities/Maskulinitäten: Gender Studies and its Mal(e)Contents

1. Maskulinität: zwischen Gewalt und Theoriedefizit

Zwei Tatsachen empfehlen einen kritischen Blick auf das Thema Masculinities/Maskulinititäten: Erstens war und ist es immer wieder die Alltagspraxis latenter oder manifester männlicher Gewalt gegen Individuen oder im kollektiven Auftritt, etwa in rassistisch-nationalistisch gefärbten Skinhead- oder Hooligan-Szenarien, Vorfälle, die Klaus Theweleit schon 1977 zur Frage "Männerkultur-Gewaltkultur?" bewegten und die auch den Untertitel dieser Überblicksstudie, "Mal(e)Contents," mitbestimmen.[218] Zweitens erstaunt das seit den 1970er Jahren vereinzelt, in den vergangenen fünfzehn Jahren jedoch im anglo-amerikanischen Raum exponentiell gewachsene Interesse an "Masculinities." Dieses Defizit hat sich im deutschen Sprachraum verspätet und erst zögerlich artikuliert, sei es, dass man(n) sich nicht (schon wieder) mit Gewalt auseinandersetzen oder als Prügelknabe dienen mochte, sei es, dass die Frauenforschung harterkämpften Boden ungern teilt, oder Europa US-amerikanischen Entwicklungen nicht folgen will, ihnen vielleicht ganz einfach nachhinkt.

2. Maskulinitätsforschung in den U.S.A.

Die Vielfalt an Zugängen und Reflexionsprozessen vor allem in den USA spiegelt sich in den Ansätzen einer Konzeptualisierung von "Masculinities/Maskulinitäten." Worum geht es in Studienangeboten wie *Men's Studies, [The] New Men's Studies, Studies on/of Men, The Critique of Men, Men and Feminism, The Men's Movement, Research on Men and Masculinities*, und Buchtiteln wie *The End of Masculinity, Masculinities at the Margin, Alternative Masculinities, Men in Feminism, Race Men*, oder in den Bereichen "Männerforschung," "Männlichkeitsforschung" und "Gender Studies"? Eine vorläufige Antwort lässt sich aus den genannten Büchern und Studienprogrammen sowie aus den Absichts- und Inhaltsangaben von zwei der drei einschlägigen US-

---

[218] Siehe dazu u.a. Klaus Theweleit, *Männerphantasien;* Lothar Böhnisch, Reinhard Winter, "Gewalt als Form männlicher Lebensbewältigung," *Männliche Sozialisation*, 195-210; Joachim Kersten, "Männergewalt und Frauenbewegung," *Gut und (Ge)schlecht*, 35-44.

amerikanischen Fachzeitschriften herausdestillieren. Einmal *Masculinities.*
Interdisciplinary Studies on Gender (1993-),[219] dann *Men and Masculinities* (1998-).

Masculinities. Interdisciplinary Studies on Gender versteht sich interdisziplinär und
sucht seit 1993, in den Worten des Hauptherausgebers, Michael S. Kimmel,

> to disaggregate singular, unitary, monolithic visions of masculinity,
> recognizing diversity among men's experiences. And we employ a lower case
> "m" to draw further attention to our efforts to contribute to that larger
> intellectual and political project of decentering masculinity from its position as
> the unexamined core around which social life has revolved. Through critical
> inquiry by women and men, *Masculinities* adds a new voice of men to that
> collective project—not as the disembodied authorial voice of objective reason,
> but men in their specificities, their embodiedness, their subjectivities.

Die hier von Frauen und Männern verfassten Beiträge stammen vornehmlich aus den
Gesellschaftswissenschaften ("social and behavioral sciences"). *Men and Masculinities*
jedoch, die jüngste der drei Zeitschriften, veröffentlicht seit 1998 sowohl empirische
wie theoretisch hermeneutische Beiträge,

> that use both interdisciplinary and multidisciplinary approaches, that employ
> diverse methods, and that are grounded in current theoretical perspectives
> within gender studies, including feminism, queer theory, and multiculturalism.
> It draws research from scholars specializing in men's studies, women's studies,
> ethnic studies, cultural studies, political science, communication, sociology,
> anthropology, management, and other social science disciplines.

Gemeinsam ist beiden Vierteljahresschriften ihr inter- und multidisziplinärer Ansatz
sowie die aus den Gender studies und *Women's studies* bekannten Fragestellungen zur
Konstruktionsmetapher,[220] zur kulturellen und sexuellen Identität wie zur
Repräsentation von Maskulinitäten. Während sich *Masculinities* noch explizit darum
bemüht, die männliche Vormachtstellung in Frage zu stellen, betont *Men and
Masculinities* die plurikulturelle Öffnung und Vielfalt ("alternative

---

[219] *Masculinities* ist aus Harry Brods *Men's Studies Review* hervorgegangen. Der Untertitel der
Zeitschrift lautete: "for the Men's Studies Task Group of the National Organization for
Changing Men," (1983-1993).

[220] Einerseits lässt sich Gender, verstanden als kulturelles Geschlecht, empirisch am Verhalten
von Menschen studieren. "Frauen" und "Männer" werden im Prozess des "doing gender"
"gemacht," d.h. sie sind selbst- und fremdbestimmte soziokulturelle Konstruktionen.
Anderseits versteht sich der sprachphilosophische und interpretationstheoretische
Konstruktivismus als kontingentes Spiel zwischen den Geschlechtergrenzen und -differenzen.
Beiden Konstruktionsvarianten ist daran gelegen, biologische Unterscheidungen zu relativieren
und zu betonen, dass Gender sich vor allem soziokulturell herstellt und tradiert.

271

masculinites/masculinities at the margin, diversity") im männlichen (Er)leben, eine Entwicklung, die wohl wesentlich Judith Butlers Aufbrechen und Erweitern der Dichotomie männlich-weiblich —in *Gender Trouble* (1990) und *Bodies That Matter* (1993)— zuzuschreiben ist und die in der "Gay and Lesbian Studies"-Bewegung und der "Queer Theory" fortlebt.

Die folgenden Kapitel erörtern sowohl das gewachsene wie gegenwärtige Verhältnis von *Masculinities*-Forschung und *Women's Studies,* als auch den Stand der *Men's Studies* im internationalen und deutschsprachigen Raum. Zur Sprache kommt dabei nicht nur ein problematisiertes Männerbild, sondern ebenso der geschlechtsspezifische männliche Rollendruck als Folge eines unbezwingbar autonomen "Körperpanzers" (Theweleit). Theoretische wie praktische Versuche zur Bewältigung männlicher Identitätskrisen, beispielsweise in sinnstiftenden Ritualen, runden das Bild.

3. Women's Studies und Masculinities-Forschung

Erst ein Blick zurück in die US-amerikanische Frauen- und Geschlechterforschung der 60er Jahre erklärt diesen Entwicklungsprozess der *Masculinities* und die daraus erwachsenen Forschungsansätze. Die Bedeutung, die "gender" damals als kulturell kodierte Bedeutung des Körpers erlangte, stand stets auch in engem Zusammenhang mit der afro-amerikanischen Rassenthematik und deren Rolle im amerikanischen Wissenschaftsdiskurs. So formierte sich die Frauenbewegung und die damit einsetzende feministische Literaturwissenschaft vor allem im Aufbruch der amerikanischen Bürgerrechtsbewegung ("Civil Rights Movement") wie auch in der Auseinandersetzung mit den Theoriedebatten des Poststrukturalismus, der Dekonstruktion um Jacques Derrida, (Yale School of Criticism),[221] und der Psychoanalyse um Jacques Lacan mit den Exponentinnen Shoshana Felman, Laura Mulvey oder Teresa de Lauretis. Dekonstruktion und Psychoanalyse nach Freud laufen in jenen Jahren unter dem gemeinsamen Nenner "French Theory."

Diese "zweite Welle" weiblicher Emanzipation nach der ersten, die 1920 zum Stimm- und Wahlrecht der Frauen in den USA führte, stellte traditionelle Frauenbilder und Weiblichkeitsstereotypen erneut radikal in Frage. Mit der Auflösung scheinbar natürlicher Geschlechterdifferenzen und -hierarchien, d.h. der Emanzipierung der Frau, ging jedoch eine vielbeschworene Krise des Mannes und der Männlichkeit einher, denn das herkömmliche, über Jahrhunderte zementierte Schema, nach dem der Mann als Mass für den Menschen und als Inbegriff der menschlichen Natur galt, musste aufgegeben werden. Dabei wurde vor allem die bisherige Abgrenzungs- und Bestimmungsgrösse "weisser, heterosexueller Mann" relativiert.

---

[221] Jane Gallop, Margaret Homans, Nancy Miller, Peggy Kamouf und Gayatri Spivak sind feministische Dekonstruktivistinnen. Vgl. auch Jacques Derrida, "Women in the Beehive: A Seminar with Jacques Derrida," *Men in Feminism,* eds. Alice Jardine, Paul Smith, 189-203.

Nachdem der Mann nicht länger als unteilbares und unanfechtbares Konzept, sondern als variables Bündel kultureller Normen begriffen werden musste, war die Zeit reif, Maskulinität auch wissenschaftlich zu thematisieren, nun als eine Vielzahl möglicher Maskulinitäten. Analog zu den *Women's Studies*, die sich in den 70er Jahren der Erforschung von Weiblichkeit in verschiedenen Kulturen und Disziplinen widmeten, etablierten sich rund zwanzig Jahre danach die *Men's Studies* als eigener Forschungszweig.

Wie in der frühen Phase der *Women's Studies* verfuhren die *Masculinities*-Untersuchungen dabei weitgehend in geschlechtsspezifischer Exklusivität. Zunächst waren es vornehmlich anglo-amerikanische Literaturwissenschafter und -wissenschafterinnen wie Jonathan Culler, Terry Eagleton,[222] Stephen Heath, Alice Jardine, David Morgan, Cary Nelson, Andrew Ross, Robert Scholes, Eve Kosofsky Sedgwick oder Paul Smith, welche danach fragten, wie literarische Texte Maskulinitäts-konzepte reflektieren, modifizieren und selbst wiederum neue Fiktionen von Männlichkeiten generieren (Jardine/ Smith1987/89: 55.) Es ging ihnen dabei um die Analyse von Männerbildern, genauer um die soziokulturelle stereotype Repräsentation von Maskulinitäten. Diskutiert wurde imfolgenden nicht nur die Demontage heroischer Männlichkeitsmythen, etwa des amerikanischen "Frontier-" und Westernhelden, sondern auch das geschlechtstypische "male bonding" (bzw. Männerbünden). Vielschichtigkeiten und Differenzen von Männlichkeit sowie die hierarchischen Machtverhältnisse innerhalb dieser Maskulinitäten wurden dabei sichtbar. Als kulturell produziertes und historisch variables Zeichenkonstrukt und Signifikat mutierte Männlichkeit nun ebenfalls zum kontingent diskutierten, kultur- und literaturwissenschaftlichen Forschungsobjekt. So unterschiedliche Autoren wie Nathaniel Hawthorne, Herman Melville, Walt Whitman, Rudyard Kipling, Mark Twain, Henry James, Joseph Conrad, E.M. Forster, Ernest Hemingway, aber auch Richard Wright, Ralph Ellison, James Baldwin, Amiri Baraka, John Updike, Joseph Roth, Robert Bly, Don de Lillo oder David Lodge lassen sich im kritischen Blick auf soziokulturelle und literarisch-fiktive Männermythen, Männlichkeitskonstrukte und Männerbande überraschend neu und kontrovers lesen.

Doch wurde, wie in den Gender Studies der USA üblich, zunehmend auch das Zusammenspiel von Männlichkeit mit anderen gesellschaftlich-kulturellen Kategorien wie Klasse, ethnische, politische und religiöse Zugehörigkeit oder sexuelle Ausrichtung ("Gay, Lesbian and Queer Theory") berücksichtigt. Und wie andere in dieser Zeit entstandenen neuen Fachbereiche—etwa Afro-American Studies, Asian-American Studies—richtete sich Frauen-, später Männerforschung bald interdisziplinär aus: Literaturtheorie orientierte sich an Geschichte, Ethnologie, Psychologie, Psychoanalyse oder Soziologie. Neue literatur- und kulturtheoretische Theoriediskurse wie "New Historicism," "Cultural Studies" und "Postcolonial Studies" entwickelten sich. Die Gesellschaftswissenschaften ihrerseits brauchten

---

[222] Vgl. Elaine Showalter, "Critical Cross-Dressing; Male Feminists and the Woman of the Year," *Men in Feminism*, eds. Alice Jardine, Paul Smith, 116-132.

literarische Textanalysen, um empirisch erhobene Daten zu reflektieren. Dennoch unterschieden und unterscheiden sich die Forschungsmethoden und -ergebnisse der Gesellschaftswissenschaften von denjenigen der Geistes- und Kulturwissenschaften. Die "social sciences"— auf quantitativen Erhebungen beruhend—konzentrieren sich auf soziale und klassenbedingte Unterschiede und Praktiken, setzen dabei Sprache und andere Formen der Repräsentation als transparent und gegeben voraus. Die Literatur- und Kulturwissenschaften wiederum analysieren genau diese sprachlichen und kulturhistorischen Bedingungen geschlechtstypischer Repräsentationen und unterschätzen dabei leicht den sozialen Kontext. Obwohl sich zahlreiche überschneidende, oft auch gegensätzliche Ansätze entwickelt haben, bleibt als gemeinsamer Nenner sowohl zwischen "social sciences" und "humanities"/"cultural studies" wie zwischen den *Women-* und *Men's Studies,* die poststrukturalistische Problematisierung aller Kategorien und Systeme, das Bewusstsein der Kontingenz aller Dinge und allen Denkens.

4. Inhalte und Institutionalisierungen von Masculinities

Die ersten *Masculinities*-Studien entstanden in den USA ab Mitte der 1970er Jahre, als der von Joseph H. Pleck und Jack Sawyer vorgelegte Sammelband
Men and Masculinity (1974) die geläufigen Vorstellungen einer eindimensionalen Männlichkeit radikal kritisierte. *Men and Masculinity* befreite den Mann sozusagen aus der biologisch vorgegebenen Rolle einer eindeutig definierten "gesunden" und "normativen" Geschlechterrolle. Nicht nur wurde das traditionelle Bild "Mann" von einer moderneren, soziohistorisch bedingten Vorstellung abgelöst, sondern die belastenden Seiten traditioneller heterosexueller Männlichkeit (popular boy code: "no sissy stuff;" "the sturdy oak;" "self reliance;" "control;" "give them hell") wurden als Geschlechtsrollendruck identifiziert. Nicht mehr die Abweichung von der Norm galt als krankhaft, sondern der Rollendruck wurde als krankmachend erkannt.

Von Mitte bis Ende der 80er Jahre versuchte eine neue Generation, analog zu den *Women's Studies, Masculinities* als eigenständiges Studiengebiet zu etablieren. Dies schien umso dringender, als in jenen Jahren die scheinbar objektive und wertfreie Wissenschaft als *Männerwissenschaft* entlarvt wurde: der Mann als Norm und Synonym für den Menschen, der Mann, der weibliche Erfahrung nicht wahrnimmt oder männlich klassiert, wurde entthront (Brod: 1987). Entscheidend und wegweisend waren in dieser Einsicht die drei folgenden, 1987 erschienenen einflussreichen Sammelbände: Harry Brod, ed., *The Making of Masculinities: The New Men's Studies,* Michael Kaufmann, ed. *Beyond Patriarchy: Essays by Men on Pleasure, Power, and Change,* Michael S. Kimmel, ed. *Changing Men. New Directions in Research on Men and Masculinity.* Alle drei Herausgeber engagierten sich mit Nachdruck in der antisexistischen, pro-feministischen *New Men* Männerbewegung (Walter 1996). Harry Brods erklärtes Ziel war, to eliminate the old hegemonic scholarship of 'man as male to man as generic human' and to establish 'the study of masculinity as a specific male experience, rather than a universal paradigm for for human experience' (Brod 1987; 1992: 40)

Obwohl schon länger vereinzelt *Men's Studies* Kurse angeboten wurden, entwickelten sich die *New Men's/Masculinities Studies* in den USA, gerade in der Nachwirkung von Brod, Kaufmann und Kimmel et al. um 1990 zur Disziplin (Clatterbaugh 1997). Noch ist das Angebot im Vergleich zu den *Women's Studies* verhältnismässig gering, doch registrierte Doyle (1995) ein Anwachsen des Angebots von 40 Kursen 1984 auf über 200 im Jahr der Erhebung. Seither hat sich die Zahl verdreifacht.

Doch nicht nur die bislang erwähnten liberalen heterosexuellen Gruppierungen fanden sich nicht mehr in den männlichen Rollenstereotypen zurecht, sondern auch das wachsende, im Zuge der AIDS-Bedrohung an die Öffentlichkeit drängende homoerotische Bewusstsein. Es wusste sich in der *Gay-, Lesbian-* und *Queer Theory* um Sedgwick, Butler, Fuss, Silverman, Dollimore, Sinfield seit Mitte der 1980er Jahre prominent zu artikulieren. *Gay-, Lesbian-* und *Queer Theory* haben sich seither ebenfalls zur eigenständigen Disziplin entwickelt.

Zwischen den beiden Feldern *Queer Theory* und *New Men's/ Masculinities Studies* bestehen sowohl Verbindungen wie Abgrenzungsschwierigkeiten. Nicht verwunderlich finden sich die *New Men's/ Masculinities Studies* auch in ständiger Auseinandersetzung mit den *Women's Studies* einerseits, mit konkurrierenden Vorstellungen von Männlichkeiten jenseits der *Queer Theory* anderseits. Um eine Konkurrenz mit den *Women's Studies* zu vermeiden, schlug Jeff Hearn schon 1990 die Bezeichnung *The Critique of Men* vor (Hearn/Morgan 1990). Diese "Kritische Männerforschung" nahm und nimmt, stets in Bezug auf die Resultate der *Women's Studies,* explizit und kritisch Männer in den Blick. Auch noch neun Jahre später räumte und räumt Jeff Hearn der Frauenforschung den steten politischen Vorrang ein: "control of Women's Studies and Gender Research, including Critical Studies on Men, needs to remain with women" (Hearn 1999: 5).

Dieser ausgesprochen anti-hegemonialen, pro-feministischen Ausrichtung der *New Men's Studies* oder "Kritischen Männerforschung" stellen sich jedoch die in den USA und international einflussreichen Arbeiten des australischen Männerforschers Robert C. (Bob) Connell entgegen. Sie sollen deshalb ausführlicher und kritisch besprochen werden.

Der Soziologe Connell oder sein französischer Kollege Bourdieu, die vor allem die Mechanismen der Aufrechterhaltung männlicher Macht betrachten, bringen nicht nur so diskutable Konzepte wie "hegemoniale Männlichkeit" (Connell) oder bestimmende "phallo-narzisstische Dispositionen" (Bourdieu) erneut auf den Tisch, sondern auch unterschiedlichste Anregungen für ein Praxisfeld, das von sozialpädagogischer Jungenarbeit bis hin zur sozialkonstruktivistischen männlichen Sozialisations-forschung reicht. Wiewohl die bewusste kritische Auseinandersetzung des Mannes mit seiner Erfahrung *qua* Mann auf verschiedenen Ebenen potentiell befreiend und erhellend sein mag, dürften doch vor allem Männer erheblich von einer erneuten Zentrierung und Zentralisierung des Mannes profitieren, wie sie diese beiden Forscher propagieren. Connell sucht zwar in seinem dynamischen Verständnis der Geschlechterverhältnisse, "gender" als soziale Praxis, die "kreativ und erfinderisch, aber nicht ursprünglich" (Connell 1999: 92) ist, zu bestimmen. "Gender" konstituiert und re-konstituiert sich *ontoformativ*, d.h. es erschafft sich seine Wirklichkeit prozesshaft selbst. Diese Auffassung von "gender" als "körperreflexive Praxis" ist wohl auf den Leib bezogen, aber nicht essentialistisch auf ihn reduziert. Doch wie offen und dynamisch Connells Konzept einer *hegemonial masculinity* (1995; 1999) auch angelegt ist, birgt es doch im Kern einen maskulinen Herrschaftsanspruch. Und wie eingeschränkt der Spielraum einer prozesshaften Geschlechterkonstruktion letztlich ist, offenbart sich an Connells Dreistufen-Modell, über das sich das soziale/kulturelle Geschlecht ("gender") im Sinne einer "hegemonialen Maskulinität" in der westlichen Welt konstituiert. Bestimmend sind die folgenden Beziehungsmuster:

1) Machtbeziehungen, vor allem auf männliche Dominanz bezogen;
2) Produktionsbeziehungen, die in der kapitalistischen Praxis zu geschlechtstypischen Arbeitsteilungen oder männlicher Vormacht führen;
3) Bindungsstrukturen emotionaler Art, die, nach Freud, in einem die Männerdominanz stützenden System der (Zwangs)heterosexualität formiert und reproduziert werden (Connell 1999: 92ff.; Walter 2000: 100).

Das so im ständigen Entstehen begriffene soziale/kulturelle Geschlecht (*gender*) verknüpft auch Connell mit den Kategorien "Rasse," "Klasse" oder "globale (Un)gleichheit." Auch er spricht nicht mehr von Männlichkeit, sondern von Männlichkeiten, oder eben von einer "offenen und dynamischen hegemonialen Männlichkeit." Mit Antonio Gramsci versteht Robert Connell dabei Hegemonie nicht nur prozesshaft, sondern vor allem als eine Kraft, die sich gegen jede Konkurrenz behauptet. Im Unterschied zur Tyrannei, setzt jedoch die *hegemonial masculinity* die Duldsamkeit der Beherrschten voraus. Dabei kann und darf die darwinistisch begründete Herrschaft herausgefordert werden. In diesem System aufgeklärter Dominanz sind, nach Connell, Hegemonieverhältnisse unterschiedlichster Art fassbar (Connell 1999, 97), denn Unterordnung, Komplizenschaft und Marginalisierung spielen nicht nur zwischen Männern und Frauen, sondern auch zwischen Männern. Nicht weiter verwunderlich rangiert in der Geschlechterhierarchie heterosexueller Hegemonie der homoerotische Mann zuunterst.

In seinen jüngsten Arbeiten interessiert sich Connell (1998, 96) sowohl für die Symbolisierung im Sinne der kulturellen symbolischen Repräsentanz der Geschlechter (Walter 100), wie auch für die Art und Weise, wie sich "hegemoniale Männlichkeit" im Globalisierungsprozess verändert. Er sieht dabei Kolonialisierungsprozesse nicht nur rassistisch, sondern vor allem auch sexistisch orientiert, denn die Geschlechterordnungen der eroberten Gesellschaften wurden nach den Prinzipien der

Verdrängung, Einordnung und Vermischung reorganisiert (1998, 94f.). Wiewohl Connell die ständige Regenerierung "hegemonialer Männlichkeit" in diesen Konzepten zu fassen und zu erklären versteht, beinhalten diese doch etliche Schwachstellen und Gefahren. Connell vermag sich nicht wirklich und konsequent von einer patriarchalischen Dualität Mann-Frau zu trennen. Die Frau bleibt bei ihm männlich dominiert. Zwar darf sie sich auflehnen und die männliche Hegemonie in Frage stellen; sie tut das jedoch stets aus der Rolle der gutmütig Duldsamen, emotional an den Mann Gebundenen. Halten wir fest: Robert Connells Geschlechterkonzept zementiert nicht nur geläufige Rollenmuster; es bietet auch keinen Ausweg aus der Sackgasse hegemonialen Vorrechts. Es ist an dieser Stelle zu fragen, inwieweit Antonio Gramscis Hegemoniekonzept in Connells Theoriegebäude nicht fruchtbar mit dem radikal kontingenten Hegemoniebegriff, wie er von Ernesto Laclau und Judith Butler in *Contingency, Hegemony, Universality: Contemporary Dialogues on the Left* (2000) vertreten wird, erweitert, gar ersetzt werden könnte.

5. Zum aktuellen Stand von Masculinities in den U.S.A.

Was sind sie nun, die *Men's Studies/Masculinites* im anglo-amerikanischen Bereich: kleiner Bruder oder benevolenter Patriarch von *Women's/Gender Studies* oder *Queer Theory*? Das Feld ist mitnichten bereinigt. Stellvertretend für andere Institutionen zieht Mark E. Kann in "Ongoing Tensions," (2000: 411-417) Bilanz aus der Sicht einer der ältestesten, 1971 gegründeten gemeinsamen Institutionen der USA: dem "Program for the Study of Women and Men in Society" an der University of Southern California (USC). Bloss aus politischen Gründen waren Männer im Titel des Programms eingeschlossen worden, schreibt er (Kann 411). Allmählich wuchs das Programm, und neben einer Mehrzahl weiblicher Dozierender unterrichteten Harry Brod und Mark E. Kann Kurse in *Masculinities*. In den 1980er Jahren gesellten sich zwei weitere *Men's Studies* Spezialisten zum Lehrkörper: der Anthropologe Walter Williams und der Soziologe Michael Messner. In den 1990er Jahren zum "Gender Studies Program" mutiert, gedieh das Programm weiterhin gut, bis 1999 der Vorsitz zu besetzen war. Ein Mann dafür kam nicht in Frage, "gender studies" wurden wieder zu "women's studies" umbenannt, als ob drei Dekaden männlicher Aufbauarbeit nicht existierten. Mark E. Kann benennt drei Gründe für die Spannungen:

Reason 1: Women's Studies is the foundation of gender studies and inspiration for men's studies. Accordingly, women's studies scholars claim a priviledged place in gender studies circles. Ultimately, men's studies scholars are second-class citizens and, in the foreseeable future, will retain second-class status.

Reason 2: Women's studies scholarship and men's studies scholarship tend to emphasize gender differences that deter academic cooperation. Today's scholarly focus on gender difference invites women's studies scholars to view much of men's studies, even profeminist men's studies, as a distraction from important gender issues, a devaluation of women's lives, and am apology for ongoing male domination.

Reason 3:The politics of Women's studies and the politics of men's studies often clash. In summary, many women's studie scholars do not trust the mixed, uncertain politics associated with men's studies. (Kann 2000: 412-414)

Diese Spannungen, Symptome für den blinden Fleck eines bislang unausgetragenen Machtdiskurses, sieht Kann auch in der Zukunft, betrachtet sie aber als grosse Chance. *Men's Studies* Forscher wie Tom Carrigan, Robert Connell und John Lee (Carrigan, Connell, Lee 1987: 80) räumen zwar ein, Gleichberechtigung der Geschlechter bedeute gleichzeitig auch Machteinbusse für Männer. Ausserdem bleibt den Männern noch viel Vertrauensarbeit zu leisten. Am erfolgversprechendsten scheint Kann die Tatsache, dass sich Frauen im "crossover" vermehrt selbst mit *Men's Studies* auseinandersetzen. Beispielhaft sind Studien wie diejenige von Laura McCall und Donald Yacovone, *A Shared Experience: Men, Women, and the History of Gender* (1998), weil darin sowohl die Interdependenz und Opposition der Geschlechter wie ihre je spezifischen Anliegen anerkannt und diskutiert werden. Dabei genügt es nicht, die sattsam bekannte Konstruiertheit des kulturellen Geschlechts auch für den Mann festzustellen. *Men's Studies* untersuchen im günstigen Fall die komplexen Prozesse des Mannseins und der Mannwerdung ("being and becoming gendered male: men, masculine, manly") nicht nur aus intellektueller Neugierde, sondern im Bewusstsein, dass ihr Forschen stets die Frau mitdenkt. Wachsen die *Men's Studies* wirklich zum brüderlichen Verbündeten der *Women's* und *Gender Studies* heran, pflegen sie ihre geschlechtsspezifischen Interessen, doch stets mit dem Ziel gerechter(er) Beziehungen zwischen den Geschlechtern.

6. Zum aktuellen Stand von Masculinities im deutschsprachigen Raum

Erst 1993, rund zwanzig Jahre nach Peck/Sawyer, *Men and Masculinity* (1974), diskutieren im deutschsprachigen Raum Walter Hollstein, Lothar Böhnisch und Reinhard Winter als erste ein problematisches Männerbild und den daraus resultierenden Geschlechtsrollendruck. *Männliche Sozialisation: Bewältigungsprobleme männlicher Geschlechtsidentität im Lebenslauf* versteht "Mannsein" als "emotionale Bewältigungskategorie." Als grundlegende Bewältigungs- und Erfolgsstrategien gelten nach Böhnisch/Lothar (in Walter: 2000) folgende geschlechstypische Charakteristika:

1) Externalisierung, Aussenorientierung (Aussenwelt wird wahrgenommen und thematisert; Innenwelt muss negiert, darf nicht thematisiert werden)
2) Gewalt (gegen Frauen, andere Männer, gegen sich selbst)
3) Benutzung (Funktionalisieren / Abwerten von Mensch und Umwelt)
4) Stummheit (fehlender reflexiver Selbstbezug; Männer reden über alles, nur nicht über sich selbst)
5) Alleinsein (Zwang zur Autonomie; mit allem allein fertig zu werden)
6) Körperferne (Nichtwahrnehmen der andern, des eigenen Körpers; Angst vor körperlicher Nähe / Intimität, Objektivierung von Frauen)
7) Rationalität (Abwertung und Verdrängung von Emotionalität)
8) Kontrolle (Selbstkontrolle, Kontrolle der Umwelt)

Die Bandbreite dieser spezifisch männlichen Verhaltensmuster erfordert einen interdisziplinären Zugriff. In der Tat hat sich seit den frühen Studien das Forschungsspektrum erweitert und differenziert und nutzt ein ganzes Spektrum an methodischen Zugängen moderner Geistes- und Sozialwissenschaft. Generell geht es um aktuelle wie zurückliegende Vorstellungen von "Männlichkeit" als auch deren Repräsentation in den Medien, im Film oder in der Literatur. "Männlichkeit" ist nichts Gottgegebenes, vielmehr ein komplexes Konstrukt der jeweiligen Gesellschaft. Ein zentrales Thema ist der Zusammenhang von männlichen (Selbst)-Bildern und Gewalt. Woher kommt diese Spannung, die sich plötzlich entlädt? Sowohl Machtbeziehungen, deren ökonomische Bedingtheit, wie emotionale Bindungsstrukturen sind zu untersuchende Parameter, die den maskulinen Rollendruck bestimmen.

An Fragestellungen und wissenschaftlichen Zugängen fehlt es also keineswegs: Aus historischer Sicht können etwa Aspekte von Technik und Naturwissenschaft im Verein mit institutionellen und strukturellen Bedingungen untersucht werden, etwa in der Thematik "Männer und Autos in den 60er Jahren." Aus psychologischer Sicht wäre das männliche Risikoverhalten allgemeiner anzugehen. Ausgehend von der niedrigeren Lebenserwartung der Männer kann beispielsweise der Einfluss von Rollenstress aufgezeigt werden, der nicht nur auf eine zunehmend kompetitive Arbeitswelt zurückzuführen ist, sondern speziell bei älteren Männern im Spannungsfeld von ideal viriler Jugendlichkeit und tatsächlicher (körperlicher) Verfassung auftreten kann. Ebenfalls einen präzisen Blick in die Alltagswelt, genauer in das schillernde Reich der Popkultur, wirft die Analyse von "Männlichkeit" als Performance, sei es in der Darstellung ambivalenter Rollenmuster bei Künstlern wie Madonna, Prince, Michael Jackson oder Marylin Manson, oder in Kinofilmen wie David Finchers *Fight Club* oder Kimberly Peirces *Boys Don't Cry*. Rollenmuster werden in diesen Performances durch die Verschiebung ins Uneigentliche, zwischen Parodie, Mimikry und Travestie zwar aufgebrochen und subtil hintergangen, anderseits nach aussen auch wieder verfestigt. Klaus Theweleit hat schon 1977 in seinem Buch *Männerphantasien* die faschistische Gewaltbereitschaft auf "Gender"-Bedingungen, d.h. auf spezielle männliche Rollenmuster zurückgeführt. In diesem Zusammenhang sieht jedoch Theweleit die Maskerade gerade nicht als Erfindung von Performance-

Künstlern, sondern als Schutzpanzer bedrohter, sogenannter "normaler Männlichkeit." Sein psychoanalytisch begründetes Konzept von dem stets durch Fragmentierung und Zerfall bedrohten Körper lasse den Mann einen "Körperpanzer" ausbilden. Jenseits aller Sterblichkeitsängste aber diesseits von Maskerade und Mimikry wehre sich dieser Körper gegen tradierte Bedrohungen. Die männliche Sozialisation und die spezifischen Männerdefizite, die sich vor allem unter der Perspektive 'Leiden unter der Männerrolle' artikulieren, thematisiert Theweleit in *Männerphantasien* wiederholt auch als männliches Abgrenzungs- und Kompensationsbedürfnis, das sich in Männerbünden das Wir-Gefühl zu stärken sucht. Wie nimmt sich dieses "male bonding" im US-amerikanischen Kulturraum aus?

7. Men's Movements in den U.S.A.

Seit Beginn der 90er Jahre formierten sich in den Vereinigten Staaten verschiedene Männerbewegungen ("Men's Movements"). Gemeinsam ist ihnen einerseits die Ablehnung feministischer Strömungen und Errungenschaften, anderseits die Suche nach "verlorener" Männlichkeit. Sie lassen sich in folgende Perspektiven fassen (Clatterbaugh 1997: 9-149).

1) *Die konservative Perspektive*. Die moralisch Konservativen um u.a. Phyllis Schlafly, verstehen die traditionelle Rollenverteilung als gerecht und soziobiologisch gegeben: Männer beschützen und unterhalten die Familie, Frauen kümmern sich um Haushalt und Kinder. Die konservative Gruppierung, der Frauen und Männer angehören, zählte zu den ersten Gegnerschaften der feministischen Bewegung in den 1970er Jahren und war massgeblich für das Scheitern des "Equal Rights Amendment" verantwortlich.

2) *Die männerechtliche Pespektive*. Sie sieht Rollenzwänge als gesundheitsschädigend und sozial einengend und versucht vor allem gegen Frauen die Rechte der Männer einzufordern. Die "Vaterrechts- und Männerrechtsbewegung" um Warren Farrell ruft direkt zum Angriff auf Feministinnen, Ex-Partnerinnen und den Staat.

3) *Die mythopoetische Perspektive*. In den späten 1980er und frühen 1990er Jahren formierten sich die "Mythopoeten" um den Lyriker Robert Bly. Seine 1990 veröffentlichte Parabel der Mannwerdung, *Iron John*, führte monatelang die Bestsellerlisten in den USA an. Tief in der Seele jedes Mannes lebe, so Bly, ein "primitiver, haariger Mann" — der Archetyp der Männlichkeit. Männer sollten in einer ritualisierten Gemeinschaft mit andern Männern wieder zu ihren "männlichen Ursprüngen" zurückfinden.

4) *Die sozialistische Perspektive*. Sexismus innerhalb der politischen Linken führte in den 1960er und 1970er Jahren zu einem Umdenken von männlichen und weiblichen

Rollenmustern. Maskulinitäten, so wird erkannt, gründen vorab in wirtschaftlich bedingten Strukturen, die verändert werden müssten.

5) *Die "Gay Male" Perspektive*. Die Homosexuellen erfahren und erleben sich als zunehmend diskriminiert und unterdrückt. Sie wenden sich sowohl gegen eine Zwangsheterosexualität wie einengende Männlichkeitsmuster. Homosexuelle Männer sind gegen eine explizite Homophobie unter heterosexuellen Männern.

6) *Die Afro-Amerikanische "Black Men" Perspektive*. Die Komponenten Ethnizität und Klasse bestimmen insbesondere den schwarzen Mann. Seine Identität ist seit der Sklaverei gefährdet, und auch danach immer wieder bedroht durch Migration, hohe Arbeitslosigkeit und, daraus resultierend, erhöhte Kriminalität. Einerseits erlebt der schwarze Mann seit der Bürgerrechtsbewegung einen ungewohnten soziokulturellen und wirtschaftlichen Aufschwung, anderseits sammeln sich arbeitslose Jugendliche in Ghettogangs.

7) *Die religiöse Perspektive*. Die "Promise Keepers" suchen nicht nur in der Nachfolge von Robert Bly, durch Initiationsriten in freier Natur den "Wilden Mann" zu erwecken. Sie führen als religiöse Männerorganisationen das patriarchalische Familienerbe weiter, berufen sich auf Jesus und wenden sich gegen Frauen, die sich unter dem Einfluss der Frauenbewegungen emanzipiert haben. Dezidiert fordern sie eine traditionelle Geschlechtsrollenteilung.

All diesen Männerbewegungen gemeinsam ist der Gestus der Abgrenzung und Ausgrenzung von Weiblichkeit als Formel zur Selbstdefinition, als einfachste Verteidigungsstrategie. Wiewohl diese populären Strömungen der "Men's Movements" nicht primär Gegenstand unserer Betrachtung sind, gehören sie dennoch in den Kontext von Maskulinitätsentwürfen.

8. Ausblick

Frauen wie Männer bewegen sich in Kulturen, in Ensembles von Sinndimensionen, die vielfach verknüpft sind. Bleibt der Körper die bestimmende Differenz? Zweifellos bestehen anatomische Unterschiede. Doch wir können diese Differenz weiterhin nur sprachlich und kulturell deuten. Über Sprache definiert sich, wer und was Objekt und Subjekt ist, was (männliche oder weibliche) Identität wird. Sprache hilft, diese zu formen, zu verändern, zu symbolisieren. Trotz und gerade auch angesichts der Mikrobiologisierung oder Femalisierung[223] des kleinen Unterschieds gehören Konfigurationen von Maskulinitäten als Gefüge sprachlicher und kultureller

---

[223] Femalismus ist gleichbedeutend mit Natalie Angiers und Mary Carlsons "liberation biology," welche den weiblichen Körper als dem männlichen überlegen darstellt. Vgl. dazu Natalie Angier, *Woman. An Intimate Geography*, 1999.

Bedingungen besonders untersucht. Gerade die kulturtheoretische Bewegung der Dekonstruktion wirkte einer stabilen monolithischen Bedeutung von Männlichkeit entgegen und ermöglichte weitreichende Implikationen und Begriffserweiterungen für die literatur- und kulturwissenschaftliche Forschung. Wie Judith Butler in Gender Trouble (1990) festhält, funktionieren Geschlechterrollen wie Gesetze. Sie erhalten ihre Macht erst aus dem nicht hinterfragten Glauben an deren Autorität. Diese Normen gilt es zu hinterfragen und aufzubrechen zu Gunsten beider Geschlechter.[224] Dann werden sich "Masculinities/Maskulinitäten" von ihren "malcontents" befreien und zu neuen "male contents" entwickeln dürfen.

Zitierte Werke/Auswahlbibliographie

ADAMS, Rachel, David SAVRAN (2001). *The Masculinity Studies Reader*. Forthcoming. New York: Columbia.

ANGIER, Natalie. *Woman. An Intimate Geography*. New York: Houghton Mifflin, 1999.

AUGUST, Eugene R. (1994). *The New Men's Studies. A Selected and Annotated Interdisciplinary Bibliography*. Englewood, Colorado: Libraries Unlimited.

BADINTER, Elisabeth (1993). *XY. Die Identität des Mannes*. München, Zürich.

BASOW, Susan (1986). *Gender Stereotypes: Traditions and Alternatives*. Monterey, CA: Brooks Cole.

BAU/STEINE/MÄNNER, ed. (1996). *Kritische Männerforschung: Neue Ansätze in der Geschlechtertheorie*. Berlin.

BARZ, Helmut (1991). *Männersache. For Men Too: a Grateful Critique of Feminism*. Trans. Katherine Ziegler. Wilmette: Chiron.

BEDERMAN, Gail (1995). *Manliness and Civilization: a Cultural History of Gender and Race in the United States: 1880-1917*. Chicago: University of Chicago Press.

BENEKE, Timothy (1997). *Proving Manhood: Reflections on Men and Sexism*. Berkeley: University of California Press.

BERGER, Maurice, Brian WALLIS, Simon WATSON (1995). *Constructing Masculinity*. New York, London: Routledge.

BLY, Robert (1990). *Iron John. A Book About Men*. Reading, MA: Addison-Wesley.

---. (1998). *The Maiden King*. New York: Henry Holt.

BÖHNISCH, Lothar, Reinhard WINTER (1993). *Männliche Sozialisation. Bewältigungsprobleme männlicher Geschlechtsidentitäten im Lebenslauf*. Weinheim.

---

[224] Zur Illustration diene das folgende Beispiel einer Doppelmoral: Über Jahrhunderte rechtfertigte die angeblich unkontrollierbare "Natur" der Frau die Vorherrschaft des kulturierten Mannes. Feste Zuordnungen wie "Mann-Kultur" und "Frau-Natur"—gleichbedeutend mit öffentlicher versus privater Sphäre— garantierten in der Folge die Vorherrschaft des Patriarchats in der Kontrolle über Frau und Natur. Wann immer jedoch Männer in Eros' Namen gegen Sitten und Gesetz verstossen, d.h. unkontrolliert und unkontrollierbar ihren sexuellen Neigungen nachgeben, betrachten sie sich weniger als kulturell verantwortliche Wesen, sondern ausgerechnet als Opfer ihrer hormonal gesteuerten "Natur."

BOONE, Joseph A., Michael CADDEN, eds. (1990). *Engendering Men. The Question of Male Feminist Criticism.* New York, London.

BORDO, Susan (1999). *The Male Body: a New Look at Men in Public and in Private.* New York: Farrar, Straus, Giroux.

BOURDIEU, Pierre (1996). *The State Nobility: Elite Schools in the Field of Power.* Cambridge: Polity Press.

BOWKER, Lee H. (1998). *Masculinities and Violence.* Thousand Oaks, CA, etc.: Sage.

BRANDT, Stefan Leonhard (1997). *Männerblicke. zur Konstruktion von Männlichkeit in der Literatur und Kultur der amerikanischen Jahrhundertwende.* Stuttgart: M&P Verlag.

BROD, Harry, Michael KAUFMANN (1994). *Theorizing Masculinities.* Thousand Oaks, CA, etc.: Sage.

BROD, Harry, ed. (1987). *The Making of Masculinities: the New Men's Studies.* Boston: Allen & Unwin.

--- (1992). *The Making of Masculinities: the New Men's Studies.* New York: Routledge.

BUCHBINDER, David (1994). *Masculinities and Identities.* Carlton, Vic.: Melbourne University Press.

BUTLER, Judith (1990). *Gender Trouble. Feminism and the Subversion of Identity.* New York, London: Routledge.

---. (1993), *Bodies That Matter.* New York, London: Routledge.

BUTLER, Judith, Ernesto LACLAU, Slavoj ZIZEK (2000). *Contingency, Hegemony, Universality. Contemporary Dialogues on the Left.* London: Verso.

CARBY, Hazel (1998). *Race Men.* Cambridge, MA: Harvard University Press.

CARRIGAN, Tim, Robert CONNELL, John LEE (1987). "Toward a new sociology of masculinity." *The Making of Masculinities: The New Men's Studies.* Ed. Harry Brod. 63-100.

CHINEN, Allan B. (1993). *Beyond the Hero: Classic Stories of Men in Search of Soul.* New York: G.B. Putman.

CLATTERBAUGH, Kenneth (1997). *Contemporary Perspectives on Masculinity: Men, Women, and Politics in Modern Society* (2nd ed.). Boulder, CO: Westview Press.

COHEN, Michèle (1996). *Fashioning Masculinity: National Identity and Language in the 18th Century.* New York: Routledge.

CONNELL, Robert W. (1987). *Gender and Power. Society, the Person and Sexual Politics.* Oxford.

--- (1987). "Männer in der Welt: Männlichkeiten und Globalisierung." *Widersprüche* 67: 91-105.

--- (1995). *Masculinities.* Berkeley: University of California Press.

--- (1999). *Der gemachte Mann Konstruktion und Krise von Männlichkeiten.* (Transl. *Masculinities).* Opladen.

CORNWALL, Andrea, Nancy LINDISFARNE, eds. (1994). *Dislocating Masculinity: Comparative Ethnographies.* London, New York: Routledge.

DIE PHILOSOPHIN. Forum für feministische Theorie und Philosophie. "Männerforschung/Männlichkeitsforschung." 22 (Oktober 2000): 5-144.

DOLLIMORE, Jonathan (1992). *Sexual Dissidence: Augustine to Wilde, Freud to Foucault.* Oxford, New York, etc.: Clarendon Press.

DOYLE, J.A. (1995). *The Male Experience.* 3rd ed. Boston: McGraw-Hill.

DUNCAN, Nancy, ed. (1996). *Body Space: Destabilising Geographies of Gender and Sexuality.* London, New York: Routledge.

EASTHOPE, Antony (1986). *What A Man's Gotta Do: the Masculine Myth in Popular Culture.* London: Paladin Grafton.

EDWARDS, Tim (1994). *Erotics and Politics: Gay Male Sexuality, Masculinity, and Feminism.* London, New York: Routledge.

---. *Men in the Mirror: Men's Fashion, Masculinity and Consumer Society.* London, Herndon, VA: Cassell.

ENGELFRIED, Constance (1997). *Männlichkeiten: die Öffnung des feministischen Blicks auf den Mann.* Weinheim, München: Juventa.

ERHART, Walter, Britta HERRMANN, eds. (1997). *Wann ist der Mann ein Mann? Zur Geschichte der Männlichkeit.* Stuttgart, Weimar: Metzler.

FALUDI, Susan (1992). *Backlash. The Undeclared War Against Women.* London: Vintage.

--- (1999). *Stiffed. The Betrayal of the American Man.* New York: William Morrow.

FEMINISTISCHE STUDIEN, "Männlichkeiten." 2 (November 2000): 3-172.

FIGURATIONEN. "Konstruktionen der Männlichkeit." Hg. Ines Kappert. 1 (2002).

FORD, David (1989). *Studying Men and Masculinity: a Sourcebook of Literature and Materials.* Bradford: University of Bradford Press.

FOXHALL, Lin, John SALMON, eds. (1998). *Thinking Men: Masculinity and its Self-representation in the Classical Tradition.* London, New York: Routledge.

GAVRAN, David (1998). *Taking it Like a Man: White Masculinity, and Contemporary American Culture.* Princeton, NJ: Princeton University Press.

GILMORE, David (1990). *Manhood in the Making: Cultural Concepts of Masculinity.* New Haven: Yale University Press.

GODENZI, Alberto (1989). *Bieder, Brutal—Frauen und Männer sprechen über sexuelle Gewalt.* Zürich.

GREGSON, Jan (1999). *The Male Image: Representations of Masculinity in Postwar Poetry.* Basingstoke: Macmillan; New York: St. Martin.

GURIAN, Michael (1997). *The Wonder of Boys.* New York: Putnam.

HADDAD, Tony, ed. (1993). *Men and Masculinities: a Critical Anthology.* Toronto: Canadian Scholars' Press.

HALBERSTAM, Judith (1998). *Female Masculinity.* Durham: Duke University Press.

HEARN, Jeff, David MORGAN, eds. (1990). *Men, Masculinities, and Social Theory.* London.

HEARN, Jeff (1999). "Getting Organised? The Politics and Organisation of Critical Studies on Men." *Kritische Männerforschung* 17 (1999): 4-6.

HINE, Darlene Clark, Earnestine JENKINS, eds. (1999). *A Reader in U.S. Black Men's History and Masculinity.* Bloomington: Indiana University Press.

HOLLSTEIN, Walter (1989). *Nicht Herrscher aber kräftig: die Zukunft der Männer.* Hamburg: Hoffmann & Campe.

--- (1990). *Die Männer-Vorwärts oder zurück?* Stuttgart: Deutsche Verlags-Anstalt.

--- (1992). *Machen Sie Platz, mein Herr! Teilen statt herrschen.* Reinbek bei Hamburg: Rowohlt.

--- (1999). *Männerdämmerung. Von Tätern, Opfern, Schurken und Helden.* Göttingen.

--- (2001). "Männlichkeit in der Revision. Noch kein Grund zum Optimismus." *Neue Zürcher Zeitung* 14./15. April, Nr. 87, 85.

--- (2001). *Potent werden. Das Handbuch für Männer. Liebe, Arbeit und der Sinn des Lebens.* Bern: Huber.

HOOKS, bell (2000). "Feminist Masculinity." *Feminism is for Everybody. Passionate Politics.* Boston: South End Press.

HURTON, Andrea (1995). *Kultobjekt Mann: Image, Typen, Medien, Bilder, Werbung, Styling, Symbole, Marketing.* Frankfurt a.M.: Eichborn.

HYDE, Sarah (1997). *Exhibitng Gender.* Manchester, New York: Manchester University Press.

JARDINE, Alice, Paul SMITH, eds. (1987). *Men in Feminism.* New York, London. Routledge.

JESSER, Clinton J. (1996). *Fierce and Tender Men: Sociological Aspects of the Men's Movement.* Westport, Conn.: Praeger.

KANN, Mark E. (2000). "Ongoing Tensions," *The Journal of Men's Studies* 8.3 (2000): 411-417.

KAUFMANN, Michael, ed. (1987). *Beyond Patriarchy. Essays by Men on Pleasure, Power, and Change.* Toronto, New York.

KERSTEN, Joachim (1997). *Gut und (Ge)schlecht. Männlichkeit, Kultur und Kriminalität.* Berlin, New York.

KIMBRELL, Andrew (1995). *The Masculine Mystique: the Politics of Masculinity.* New York: Ballantine.

KIMMEL, Michael S., ed. (1987). *Changing Men: New Directions in Research on Men and Masculinity.* Newbury Park.

KINLON, Dan, Micheal THOMPSON (1999). *Raising Cain. Protecting the Emotional Life of Boys.* New York: Ballantine.

--- (1996). *Manhood in America: a Cultural History.* New York: Free Press.

KNIGHTS, Ben (1999). *Writing Masculinities: Male Narratives in 20th Century Fiction.* Basingstoke: MacMillan. New York: St. Martin's Press.

KÜHNE, Thomas, ed. (1996). *Männergeschichte—Geschlechtergeschichte. Männlichkeit im Wandel der Moderne.* Frankfurt a.M./New York.

KUYPERS, Joseph A., ed. (1999). *Men and Power.* Amherst, NY: Prometheus.

MAC AN GHAILL, Máirtín (1996). *Understanding Masculinities: Social Relations and Cultural Arenas.* Buckingham, Philadelphia: Open University Press.

MAC INNES, John. *The End of Masculinity.* Buckingham, Philadelphia: Open University Press, 1998.

MAY, Larry (1998). *Masculinity and Morality.* Ithaca: Cornell University Press.

MCCALL, L., D. YACOVONE (1998). *A Shared Experience: Men, Women, and the History of Gender.* New York: New York University Press.

MANSFIELD, Nick. "Masculinity: Saving the poest-Oedipal world." *Subjectivity. Theories of the Self from Freud to Haraway*. New York. New York University Press. 92-104

MESSNER, Michael (1997). *Politics of Masculinities. Men in Movements*. Thousand Oaks: Sage Publications.

MIDDLETON, Peter (1992). *The Inward Gaze: Masculinity and Subjectivity in Modern Culture*.London, New York: Routledge.

MITCHELL, Lee Clark (1996). *Westerns: Making the Man in Fiction and Film*. Chicago: University of Chicago Press.

MORGAN, David H.J. (1992). *Discovering Men*. London, New York: Routledge.

MOSSE, George (1996). *The Image of Man. The Creation of Modern Masculinity*. New York, Oxford: Oxford University Press.

MURPHY, Cornelius F. (1995). *Beyond Feminism: towards a Dialogue of Difference*. Washington, DC: The Catholic University of America Press.

MURPHY, Peter F., ed. (1994). *Fictions of Masculinity: Crossing Cultures, Crossing Sexualities*.New York. New York University Press.

NAUMANN, Barbara, Ines KAPPERT, eds. (2002). "Konstruktionen von Männlichkeit." *Figurationen* 1.

NARDI, Peter M. ed. (2000). *Gay Masculinities*.Thousand Oaks, etc.: Sage.

NEWBURN, Tim, Elizabeth A STANKO (1994). *Just Boys Doing Business? Men, Masculinities, and Crime*. London, New York: Routledge.

ORTNER, Sherry B., Harriet WHITEHEAD, eds. (1981). *Sexual Meanings. The Cultural Construction of Gender and Sexuality*. Cambridge, New York: Cambridge University Press.

ORTNER, Sherry B. (1996). *Making Gender: the Politics and Erotics of Culture*. Boston: Beacon Press.

PENDERGAST, Tom (2000). *Creating the Modern Man: American Magazines and Consumer Culture 1900-1950*. Columbia: University of Missouri Press.

PETERSEN, Alan (1998). *Unmasking the Masculine. 'Men' and 'Identity' in a sceptical age*. London etc.: Sage.

PLECK, Joseph H. (1981). *The Myth of Masculinity*. London.

--- , Jack SAWYER, eds. (1974). *Men and Masculinity*. Englewood Cliffs: Prentice-Hall.

PLUMMER, David (1999). *One of the Boys: Masculinity, Homophobia, and Modern Manhood*. New York: Harrington Park Press.

ROSEN, David (1993). *The Changing Fictions of Masculinity*. Urbana: University of Illinois Press.

ROTUNDO, E. Anthony (1993). *American Manhood: Transformations in Masculinity from the Revolution to the Modern Era*. New York: Basic Books.

SCHACHT, Steven P., Doris W. EWING, eds. (1998). *Feminism and Men: Reconstructing Gender Relations*. New York: Routledge.

SCHINDLER, Thomas (1994). *Mythos Mann. Was ist noch dran? Ein Bericht zur Lage des Patriarchats*. Bergisch Gladbach: Bastei Lübbe.

SCHWALBE, Michael (1996). *Unlocking the Iron Cage: the Men's Movement, Gender Politics, and American Culture.* New York: Oxford University Press.

SCHWANITZ, Dietrich. *Männer. Eine Spezies wird besichtigt* Frankfurt a.M.: Eichborn, 2001.

SEDGWICK, Eve Kosovsky (1985). *Between Men. English Literature and Male Homosocial Desire.* New York.

SEGAL, Lynne (1990). *Slow Motion: Changing Masculinities, Changing Men.* London.

SEGELL, Michael (1999). *Standup Guy: the Second Coming of the Alpha Male.* New York: Villard Books.

SILVERMAN, Kaja (1992). *Male Subjectivity at the Margins.* New York, London: Routledge.

SIMPSON, Mark (1994). *Male Impersonators: Men Performing Masculinity.* London, New York: Cassell.

SMITH, Paul, ed. (1996). *Boys: Masculinities in Contemporary Culture.* Boulder, Colorado: Westview Press.

SINFIELD, Alan (1994). *Cultural Politics; Queer Reading.* London: Routledge.

STECOPOULOS, Harry, Michael NEBEL, eds. (1997). *Race and the Subject of Masculinities.* Durham: Duke University Press.

TAYLOR, Gary (2000). *Castration: an Abbreviated History of Western Manhood.* New York: Routledge.

THEWELEIT, Klaus (1983). *Männerphantasien.* 2 vols. Reinbek b. Hamburg. [Vol. 1 1977; Vol. 2, 1978]

VILAR, Esther (1977). *Das Ende der Dressur. Modell für eine neue Männlichkeit.* München, Zürich: Droemer-Knaur.

VÖLGER, Gisela, ed. (1997). *Sie und Er. Frauenmacht und Männerherrschaft im Kulturvergleich.* Ethnologica (Neue Folge, Bd. 22). Köln: Rautenstrauch-Joest Museum.

VÖLGER, Gisela, Karin von WELCK, eds. (1990). *Männerbande—Männerbünde. Zur Rolle des Mannes im Kulturvergleich.* Köln: Rautenstrauch-Joest-Museum, 1990.

VORLICKY, Robert (1995). *Act like a Man: Challenging Masculinities in American Drama.* Ann Arbor: University of Michigan Press.

WALTER, Willi (1996). "Männer entdecken ihr Geschlecht: Zu Inhalten,Zielen, Fragen und Motiven von Kritischer Männerforschung." *BauSteineMänner* ed. *Kritische Männerforschung.* Berlin 1996. 13-26

--- (2000). "Gender, Geschlecht und Männerforschung." *Genderstudien. Eine Einführung.* Eds. Christina von Braun, Inge Stephan. Stuttgart, Weimar: Metzler. 97-115.

WHITE, Kevin (1993). *The First Sexual Revolution: The Emergence of Male Heterosexuality in Modern America.* New York.

ZURSTIEGE, Guido (1998). *Mannsbilder—Männlichkeit in der Werbung. Eine Untersuchung zur Darstellung von Männern in der Anzeigenwerbung der 50er, 70er und 90er Jahre.* Opladen/Wiesbaden: Westdeutscher Verlag.

Beitragende

Ladina BEZZOLA LAMBERT erwarb ihr Lizentiat in Anglistik, italienischer Literatur und Komparatistik. Wissenschaftliche Assistentin am Englischen Seminar der Universität Zürich (1995 - 98) und in Basel seit 1999. Forschungsaufenthalte in den USA (Harvard University, New York). Dissertation zu "Imagining the Unimaginable" — interdisziplinäre Arbeit in den Gebieten Wissenschafts philosophie und Literatur.

Stefan BRANDT, Dr. phil., J.F. Kennedy-Institut, Freie Universität Berlin. MA 1992 zum Thema "Männlichkeitskonzeptionen in den Werken von Ernest Hemingway und John Steinbeck." Forschungsarbeiten an der Universität London. 1996 Promotion mit "Reading as a Man: Zur Konstruktion von 'Männlichkeit' in der Literatur und Kultur der amerikanischen Jahrhundertwende." 1999-2001: Habilitationsstipendiat der DFG; Gastwissenschaftler an der School of Cinema der University of Southern California (USC). Zahlreiche Publikationen zum Thema Maskulinität, u.a.: 1994 "Männerbünde und Massen. Zur Krise männlicher Identität in der Literatur der Moderne," in: *Das Argument*, 207,6, S. 992-994. 1998 *Männerblicke. Zur Konstruktion von 'Männlichkeit' in der Literatur und Kultur der amerikanischen Jahrhundertwende (1890-1914)*. Stuttgart: Metzler.

Elisabeth BRONFEN ist Ordinaria für Englische und Amerikanische Literatur- und Kulturwissenschaft an der Universität Zürich. Zahlreiche Aufsätze in den Bereichen Gender Studies, Kulturwissenschaften, Psychoanalyse und Film. Zu ihren wichtigsten Buchpublikationen gehören u.a. *Der literarische Raum* (1986), *Over Her Dead Body: Death, Femininity, and the Aesthetic/Nur über ihre Leiche*(1992; 1994), *Death and Representation* (mit Sarah Goodwin, 1993). Es folgen Ausgaben zu *Anne Sexton*(1995-1997), *Sylvia Plath* (1998), *The Knotted Subject: Hysteria and its discontents/Das verknotete Subjekt. Hysterie in der Moderne* (1998), *Dorothy Richardson's Art of Memory. Space, Identity, Text* (1999), *Heimweh: Illusionsspiele in Hollywood* (1999) sowie (mit Misha Kavka) *Consequences: Feminist Thinking in the 1990's* (2000).

Walter ERHART, Prof. Dr. phil. an der Universität Greifswald, ist mit Britta Herrmann Mitherausgeber des Bandes *Wann ist der Mann ein Mann? Zur Geschichte der Männlichkeit* (Stuttgart, Weimar: Metzler, 1997). Veröffentlichungen zur deutschen Literatur vom 18. bis zum 20. Jahrhundert. Habilitationsschrift über "Männlichkeit, Familie und Erzählen im modernen europäischen Roman."

Veronika GROB, lic.phil., studierte Literaturwissenschaften und Anglistik an der Universität Zürich. Ihre Magisterarbeit trägt den Titel "Home and Homicide, das Verbrechen als Erzählfigur." Sie ist Doktorandin und Lehrbeauftragte an der Universität Zürich und arbeitet in der Abteilung Spielfilm des Schweizer Fernsehens.

Britta HERRMANN, Dr. phil. (Universität Giessen) und Walter Erhart, Prof. Dr. phil. (Universität Greifswald) sind Co-Herausgebende des Bandes *Wann ist der Mann ein Mann? Zur Geschichte der Männlichkeit* (Stuttgart, Weimar: Metzler 1997). Britta Herrmann war Stipendiatin am Graduiertenkolleg "Geschlechterdifferenz und Literatur" der Universität München. Ihre Dissertation behandelt das Thema Väter und Töchter in der deutschsprachigen Literatur des 20. Jahrhunderts.

Martin LENGWILER, Dr. phil. ist Historiker mit besonderem Interesse im Bereich der Geschlechter- und Männerforschung. Promotion 1998: "Zwischen Klinik und Kaserne. Die Geschichte der Militärpsychiatrie in Deutschland und in der Schweiz, 1870 und 1914." Forschungsaufenthalt am Wellcome Institute for the History of Medicine, London: Habil. projekt zu "Insurance Sciences and the History of the Modern Welfare State." Zahlreiche Veröffentlichungen zu Maskulinität und Geschichte, u.a. in *Traverse* 1 (1998): Schwerpunkt: "Geschlecht männlich/Genre masculin." Aktuelle Perspektiven der historischen Männlichkeitsforschung im angelsächischen Raum.

Sven LIMBECK, Dr. phil., Studium der Fächer Germanistik, Anglistik, Romanistik und Mittellatein in Heidelberg und Freiburg i. Br.. Promotion mit einer Arbeit über "Theorie und Praxis des Übersetzens im deutschen Humanismus." Seit 1994 am Seminar für lateinische Philologie des Mittelalters in Freiburg i. Br.; seit 1999 wissenschaftlicher Mitarbeiter des Freiburger Sonderforschungsbereichs "Identitäten und Alteritäten." Zahlreiche Publikationen, insbesondere zu Homosexualität und Literatur im Mittelalter.

Alexander MARZAHN, Journalist, Feuilleton der BASLER ZEITUNG. Vgl. ebenda seinen Bericht zum Symposium unter dem Titel "Risikoverhalten, Gewalt und Schwangerschaftsphantasien", BASLER ZEITUNG, 27. Juni 2000, S. 42.

Joachim PFEIFFER ist Professor für Neuere Deutsche Literatur und Literaturdidaktik an der Pädagogischen Hochschule Freiburg i. Br. er publizierte u.a. "Friendship and Gender. The Aesthetic Construction of Subjectivity in Kleist." In: *Outing Goethe and His Age*. Ed. Alice Kuzniar. Stanford 1996, 215-227.

Julia RICHERS, lic. phil. I, studierte Osteuropäische Geschichte, Anglistik, Germanistik und Jüdische Studien an der Universität Basel und in Budapest. Sie ist wissenschaftliche Assistentin und Doktorandin am Historischen Seminar der Universität Basel.

Klaus RIESER ist Assistenzprofessor im Departement für American Studies, der Universität Graz. Lehre und Promotion an der Universität Innsbruck zu "Passagen zum Ende des Regenbogens: Ethno-Amerikanische Pidgin- und Interkulturen im Migrationsfilm" (Trier, 1996). Veröffentlichungen in den Bereichen Film, Gender

Studies, Multiethnizität. Forschungsaufenthalt 1997-1999 in Los Angeles zum Thema "Maskulinität und Film" mit dem Arbeitstitel *Borderlines and Passages: Difference and Transformation of Media Masculinities.*

Elisabeth SCHÄFER-WÜNSCHE lehrt gegenwärtig am Institut für Sozialwissenschaften der Heinrich-Heine-Universität Düsseldorf. Als Amerikanistin konzentrierte sie sich vor allem auf African American, Postcolonial, Cultural und Gender Studies. Zu ihren Publikationen gehören Arbeiten über John Edgar Wideman, Harriet A. Jacobs, Michelle Cliff und Chitra Divakaruni sowie Studien zur Populärkultur. Sie co-edierte (mit Patrick B. Miller und Therese Frey Steffen) *The Civil Rights Movement Revisited: Critical Perspectives on the Struggle for Racial Equality in the United States* (LIT Verlag, 2001) und verfasste Autoren- und Werkportraits für das *Metzler Lexikon amerikanischer Autoren* (Metzler, 2000). Ihre Dissertation, *Naming and Claiming: Afrikanisch-Amerikanische Ethnonyme für Weiße*, erscheint im Francke Verlag, 2001. Sie arbeitet an Projekten zu Autobiographie, Rasse und Ethnizität aus nationaler und globaler Sicht.

Philipp SCHWEIGHAUSER, lic. phil. 1 ist Doktorand und wissen-schaftlicher Assistent am Englischen Seminar der Universität Basel. Forschungsaufenthalt an der UC Irvine 2000-2001. Seine Dissertation trägt den Arbeitstitel "Toward a Literary Acoustics: The Noises of American Literature, 1860-1980." Das Projekt verbindet Fragen nach der sozialen Funktion von Literatur (Literatur als Rauschen in den Kanälen der Kultur) mit Analysen literarischer Repräsentationen von Geräusch, Lärm und Rauschen. Publikationen zu Nabokov und der Frage von Einheit und Pluralität in Henry Adams und Michel Serres.

Therese Frey STEFFEN ist Assistenzprofessorin für Englische und Amerikanische Literatur- und Kulturwissenschaft, sowie Gender Studies an der Universität Basel. Sie war Fellow (1995-96) und ist nun Associate des W.E.B. DuBois Institute for Afro-American Research an der Harvard University. Neben ihren Publikationen zu Shakespeare, Eudora Welty und Rita Dove, gab sie, zusammen mit Elisabeth Bronfen und Benjamin Marius Schmidt, *Hybride Kulturen. Beiträge zur anglo-amerikanischen Multikulturalismus-Debatte* (1997), heraus, gefolgt von *Crossover. Cultural Hybridity in Gender, Ethnicity, Ethics* (Tübingen: Stauffenburg Discussion, 2000). Jüngst erschien die erste Monographie zum Werk von Rita Dove, *Crossing Color. Transcultural Space and Place in Rita Dove's Poetry, Drama, Fiction* (Oxford University Press, 2001).

Barbara STRAUMANN, lic. phil., studierte Deutsche und Englische Sprachwissenschaft an der Universität Zürich und ist daselbst wissenschaftliche Assistentin. In ihrer Dissertation zum Thema "Hitchcock and Nabokov," untersucht sie die Interdependenz von Textualität und Referenz, Exil und Gedächtnis im Kontext der US amerikanischen Nachkriegskultur.

Ingrid THALER, M.A., lehrt gegenwärtig an der Philipps-Universität Marburg. Sie studierte Anglistik und Germanistik an den Universitäten Heidelberg, Leipzig und Freiburg i. Br. und war 1997-1998 Stipendiatin an der Brandeis University. Arbeit als Journalistin und Mitarbeiterin einer Bibliothek. Magisterarbeit im Bereich"Masculinities."

Klaus THEWELEIT, einer der "profiliertesten und eigenwilligsten Gelehrten ohne Amt," studierte Germanistik und Anglistik in Kiel und Freiburg i. Br.. Er lebt als freier Publizist daselbst und nimmt Lehraufträge und Vortragsverpflichtungen im In- und Ausland wahr. Berühmt wurde Theweleit durch das Werk *Männerphantasien* (1977), der bis heute unübertroffene Klassiker zum Zusammenhang von Männerphantasien und faschistischem Bewusstsein. Theweleit untersucht darin die Werte, Zeichen und Codes unserer modernen Gesellschaft, ergründet die sozialen, kulturellen, psychologischen und politischen Paradigmen und vermag auf überraschende und bestechende Weise ihre mehr oder weniger geheimen Querverbindungen aufzuspüren. Ausserdem wichtig und anregend sind unter vielen andern die Publikationen *Das Buch der Könige* (1988; 1994); *Objektwahl. All You Need Is Love* (1990); *Das Land, das Ausland heisst* (1995); *Ghosts* (1998), *Der Pocahontas-Komplex* (1999); *Männerphantasien* 1 + 2 (Neuausgabe 2000).

Andreas THIELE studierte von 1987-1993 Psychologie an der Universität Frankfurt a.M. und ist daselbst Wissenschaftlicher Mitarbeiter am Institut für Psychologie der Universität Frankfurt. 1998 Promotion über den alternden Mann, aktuelle Forschung zu biopsychosozialen Aspekten der Maskulinität bei jungen und alten Männern.

Dominique ZIMMERMANN, lic. phil. I. studierte von 1992-1999 Philosophie, deutsche Literaturwissenschaft und Neuere Geschichte an den Universitäten Basel und Wien mit den Schwerpunkten feministische Philosophie, Ethik und Aesthetik sowie Theorien zur Sexualität im Grenzbereich von Philosophie und Psychoanalyse. Abschluss bei Annemarie Pieper zum Thema "Geburt und Philosophie. Zusammenhänge und Parallelen der Kind- und Kopfgeburt in verschiedenen Philosophiekonzepten." 1999 Eröffnung einer Philosophischen Praxis in Basel.